A Life in a Poem

Selected previous publications by David Rosenberg

Poetry

Disappearing Horses
Night School
Paris & London
Leavin' America
Frontal Nudity
The Necessity of Poetry
The Lost Book of Paradise

Translation/Transformation/Restoration

Blues of the Sky
Chosen Days
The Book of J
A Poet's Bible
Dreams of Being Eaten Alive

Prose

See What You Think: Critical Essays for the Next Avant-Garde
Abraham: The First Historical Biography
An Educated Man: A Dual Biography of Moses and Jesus
A Literary Bible: An Original Translation

A Life in a Poem

Memoir of a Rebellious
Bible Translator

David Rosenberg

Shearsman Books

First published in the United Kingdom in 2019 by
Shearsman Books Ltd
50 Westons Hill Drive
Emersons Green
BRISTOL
BS16 7DF

Shearsman Books Ltd Registered Office
30–31 St. James Place, Mangotsfield, Bristol BS16 9JB
(this address not for correspondence)

www.shearsman.com

ISBN 978-1-84861-664-6

ACKNOWLEDGEMENTS
Except for an excerpt appearing in *Chicago Review* (thanks to Joshua Kotin)
this work was read exclusively and closely by Rhonda Rosenberg, my closest,
and Grace Schulman, Phillip Lopate, David Shapiro, Jonathan Rosen, Frank
Davey, Lawrence Joseph, Lewis Warsh, Gabriel Levin, and Anthony Rudolf.
Anthony's 2013 opus, *Silent Conversations: A Reader's Life*, was silent
encouragement. Many others, human and other, have kept me alert and are
embedded within the text. Thanks to Guggenheim Foundation for a grant.

:

cover photograph: 'Rosenberg, Texas,' by Rhonda Rosenberg

cover drawing: 'King David,' by Leonard Baskin
(copyright David Rosenberg, *Chosen Days*, Doubleday, 1980)

To Jed Sekoff

friend in need

Contents

Introduction: See Thyself

The Socratic demand "to know thyself" translates, in the biblical sense, "to see thyself." In my twenties, still on a career path as an academic poet, I focused on the postmodern necessity to see myself sitting at a table (mostly), a creature bent over a page (now a screen). The implied question was not just how this creature got created but what the act of creation might mean, beyond Aristotle's idea of imitating nature, *mimesis*. In one early poem, I compared myself as a writer to a cat diligently covering up its waste material. In another, a poem I reproduce in the chapter, 'The Poem of Authorship,' I see myself as a car at night, its headlights flashing across a billboard as if it's the page I'm writing. Within a few years, as I'd begun to translate the Bible, my focus sharpened: beyond seeing myself translating, I needed to see, imaginatively, the original biblical writer at his or her scene of writing, at a table within the palace archives, in ancient Jerusalem. To do that, and in addition to imagining myself into that ancient Hebrew writer, I became a historical researcher, in libraries here and in Israel— and in the streets of New York and Jerusalem, pitting the vocalization of English against Hebrew, modern and ancient. Did the ancient biblical writer also self-consciously see himself? We tend to think conventionally about biblical writing, that unlike our anxiety-ridden modernism it is not self-conscious; but I discovered how untrue that was, for the intense play of language, in endless ancient puns as well as the ironizing of historical scenes and narration, rendered the ancient writer self-aware. In the end, through many decades of working with the Bible, I can say that the gel seat upon which I now work, inserted into my Adirondack chair poolside, merges in my mind with a velvet pillow cushioning an ancient chair, one modeled in miniature after a throne.

Unlike a story, which usually has a beginning, middle, and end, a poem begins in the middle and ends in the middle. The Bible's Adam and Eve narrative is close to a poem because time in the Garden of Eden is collapsed into an image of human consciousness—which is also the thing that names with words. So our first parents have language before they have a historical life; time begins after losing the Garden. Even the word repeated in this narrative, "creature," holds the mystery of being in the middle of creation: objectively, as of the universe, and subjectively, of our uses of language to orient ourselves. The biblical writer explored the origin of the word creature like a poet-historian, digging into the soil of ancient myth. We began, as a creature in the Garden, in the middle of Creation. And when Adam and Eve are thrown out of the Garden, they find themselves in the middle of a natural world that preceded them.

Anyone's life is a story but life itself is a poem. Celebrity aside, if it's a life that holds together because of a persistent mission, like a poet's life—rather than some dramatic calamity or career that renders it a story—it's the arc of ideas met or discarded that we follow, rather than a tense plot. There better be tension, however, between life and thought, to hold us, and the voice of a memoirist may do this if, like Mark Twain in his classic monologues, a poignant struggle ensues between serious and comic reflection. It can also be more valuable to find the poetry of ideas that thread through a life than what holds it up with the suspenders of story and plot.

So it's attention to the process of thinking, the drama of it, that I'll hope to keep parallel with the drama in my life. Occasional smash-ups along the way—deaths and disagreements—might also resemble the incidental poetic mash-up. Like a poem, each chapter begins in the middle of my life in the present and weaves back and forth to the past. "Forth to the past?" Exactly, scientifically speaking. When we look straight up at any moment, all the light we can see is in the past, up to billions of years ago. If we look forward, we can expect that in another century from now we'll see even further back, and more closely.

The biblical prophets looked back at their present as if from years ahead, but they still provide our bedrock faith in history—back to David, back to Sinai, and even back to Eden. While I look at my personal history from a different angle in each chapter of this book, I always come back to the Bible and to a defense of poetry. Why poetry? Because it defends my need to be of two minds, and it first did so in my early teens when a crisis of faith in my parents' truths met a crisis of faith in society. Many of my peers conflated the two and either acted out a rebellion against them, as in rock 'n' roll and SDS, or did (and identified with) what they were told. Neither choice required full compliance; you could go along with them while harboring doubts. But poetry allowed me to go along with both. A poem spelled it out more clearly than any other art because words express knowledge (or a critique of knowledge) as in, "I don't know. I'm of two minds. My poem expresses that knowledge, a self-knowledge." My parents, for whom Jewishness best defined their lives, came straight out of the Hebrew Bible, even if I never saw them reading it (unlike granpa). They were full of character, argumentative, yet seemed to know when to hold their tongues in public. Society, on the other hand, while suspicious of shady rebels or criminals, tolerated the acting out of bohemians/beatniks, just as it did eccentric inventors/scientists. I understood that a poet could be both a biblical prophet in black turtleneck and a bohemian in a sports jacket, if he/she held both in mind, which tended to save one's art from cant. Yet I eventually found that the biblical mind was missing from poetry—that my parents' history, with its cultural treasure and political marginality, was missing. There were analogs—the Blues and the gypsy violin my father played—but nothing so deeply two-minded as the Hebrew Bible, pitting human history against unknowable Creation. Beyond Shakespeare or Charlie Parker, the Bible was cosmic: you lived in history and the present, like King Lear, but also in the afterlife of King David's psalms and promised land: a speaking back to creation.

The story I tell in these chapters weaves the culture of our moment with my unintended fate as a Bible translator. The late film critic Roger Ebert, in reviewing the biblically titled *A River Runs Through It*, said that "[Director] Robert Redford and his writer, Richard Friedenberg, understand that most of the events in any life are accidental or arbitrary, especially the crucial ones, and we can exercise little conscious control over our destinies." It was far from my thoughts to become a Bible translator; I was closer in sympathy to experimenting poets of my preceding generation, Reznikoff, O'Hara, Lowell, Plath. If you asked me what I wanted to be at age 6, it was the back alley scrap man (he had a horse and interesting junk); at 10, it was a Nancy Drew detective (she wore slacks?); at 14, it was Tony Curtis (I was understudy at Detroit's Vanguard Theatre). I assumed soul was merely what my Brady grade-school classmate, Aretha Franklin, would soon be identified with. Having soul meant having talent, or better yet, being especially *with it*. I didn't connect it to loss, to marginality—the opposite of intrepid Nancy Drew—until I began translating psalms in the early '70s. By then, I'd turned some of my own losses into poems, yet I still thought my destination was to be an academic, so that I could make a safe career out of exploring consciousness and binding together all that was "accidental and arbitrary" in my experience.

I had yet to encounter the precariousness of the soul. For that, I had to lose my professorship, my wife, my passport, and soon my father, until destiny fell off my social radar. Yet it was the soul-wrenching loss of what I thought modern writing should be—its adornment in personal experience and congenial fragments of the past—that pushed me past both the academic and the self-consciously experimental, past the poker face of postmodernism and the dossier of self-interrogation, and toward the restoration of the most deeply lost: the poets and prose writers of the Bible. Few ask where they came from, how they were educated, and what place the art of writing had in their culture. "Imaginative writers are compelled to swim in the medium of culture," wrote Cynthia Ozick of Jewish writers, yet shall we go on ignoring the swimming skills of the imaginative writers in ancient Hebraic culture? It doesn't have to matter if a writer serves a big C or small c creator-precursor, as long as the art created keeps open the path back to our original astonishment at creation—or, as poet Wallace Stevens called it, echoing Kant and somewhat reductive of the greatest biblical writers, a "felt reality," or "things as they are, but beyond us."

Looking back at the present as if it's the past, which is what establishes the poetry of biblical prophecy, is not quite what I can accomplish here, yet I want to suggest a weave of ideas, ranging from science and religion to poetry and the Bible, that reveals how evocative of ancient belief a writer can be in an age of disbelief. Why do we need ancient history and poetry? I keep coming back to this question in each chapter; whether yesterday or the last Ice Age, we need ever older origins to create poetry that can disarm our grandiosity about being more important than the dead (if only because we're alive). There's nothing better for a living person than to have more life, but we are more than persons of the present, we are things with origins and an inheritance in the past—and the past is what we most belong to, yesterday's and the world's. It's all ancient the minute we study the present, including what we take to be reality. Writing about Wallace Stevens, philosopher Simon Critchley says "reality retreats before the imagination that shapes and orders it. Poetry is therefore the experience of failure." That is, poetry, by acknowledging our failure to hold onto the present, holds onto our traces in the history of living things—and not merely our inscription into cultural memory. While the Bible lies at the origin of our culture, its poetic forms, including history, philosophy, and law, address this failure head on. How deep can we go into history, how far into origins, to experience the uniqueness of our failure and the hope for singing/hearing of it in the future?—these questions are a post-Holocaust poet's digging tools, if not toward the angels First Isaiah envisioned in infinite harmony on the *om* word, "holy", then toward a re-envisioning of the Hebrew poets behind that cosmic text and the rest of the book of Isaiah.

There's no putting the Holocaust behind us if we're going to face the murder in our hearts, the way The Ten Commandments did (I will elucidate it as a poem for its sublime concision). It will always be yesterday's history, like the slavery in Egypt was for Moses, who himself didn't experience it. Just as you can't bring back an innocent life you've murdered or been accomplice to—an enabler, a bystander, a forgetter—you can't bury your victim's once vital laugh and smile. You have to half-smile for them now, you have to embrace irony and deadpan, become aware there's no category for "what's me got to do with it," for an innocent irony or an unknowing smile. No rock music can forget its origins in the blues; no novel its genesis in Genesis, no art its origin in prehistoric caves. Rachel and Leah are like relatives to all deep readers of the Bible, no less than Muddy Waters, the Chauvet cave painters, and Zora Neal Thurston, Gertrude Stein, and Virginia Woolf are to me as a writer. But I feel even closer to Rachel and Leah's writers, who have been so deeply lost, like parts of my own life I still hope to face.

You can't read and pray at the same time, unless you know you are reading poetry. It's in the poetry of the Bible—"the greatest poetry in English is in the prose of the Bible," wrote Ted Hughes—that our crucial history is recorded, including the revelation that the present is the past, and that the future is a revelation of what's in our hearts. Not that my heart doesn't skip a beat when I dare to describe how poetry gets written. It's hard enough to explore how anything gets written, including the arc of a life, but to extend the inquiry into how the Bible was written is daunting even to state as a project. Perhaps it's enough to say I excluded prayer from my overt research, but not poetry.

Already by 1910, the Hungarian literary critic György Lukács, in *Soul and Form*, attempted to show how consciousness had replaced soul as a key concept of modernism. If the standard Judeo-Christian idea of soul is timeless, outside of conventional spacetime and dependent on its host in the physical world, then without such a soul we have no personal sense of the unknowable—of what may be unknowable to the human species. Do I want to read a contemporary writer who is soulless? Yes, of course, if he or she is really good, really chilling. But such a writer, like Lukács, will have no use for the Bible, Dante, Blake, or the soulful late Stevens or Celan. The latter two represent the soul in the form of a deep anxiety about the viability of the human species (in Stevens, the anxiety is mastered). It's an anxiety that we've lost our history, and with it our souls, so that only the possibility of a new poetry remains in its place.

In my experience, I had to fall, continue falling backward into a history that reached bedrock with the lost poets and writers of the Hebrew Bible. I had to trip and fall, for instance, through the soberly academic Kafka I had been teaching, to discover how uproarious were his textual ironies, his cockroaches and mousefolk. We had read his work in class in almost a hushed reverence, as if it was the Bible. Am I saying we should now read the Bible comically, since many writers have satirized it? No, but there's a close connection between elation and awe, as in the word dumbstruck, a condition I can imagine prevailed at the biblical scene of writing no less than when a poet like Shakespeare or Emily Dickinson put their pens down, reread their texts, and were gladly dumbfounded to see that the work could go no further, that it had reached its end. In my time, the Bible was read so heavily that it was an obvious task to somehow lighten it, and to bring the word to its apogee, as in enlighten, or as in the phrase, to see the light. In retrospect, then, the Hebrew Bible gave shape to my life as a North American poet after six youthful collections of avant-garde work dependent on lightening the academic reading of a Rimbaud or Mallarmé, when I translated them intertextually. That is, I envisioned them at their writing tables, elated by the lines that seemed to overtake them like the hare passing the tortoise. Eventually they would hone those lines in the slow work of pinning thought and feeling together on the page like a gorgeous specimen, with the writers akin in their creatureliness, like the tortoise focused on the finish line while the hare stayed too long at the bar. The biblical writers were also conscious of their physical presence above the papyrus, as if mediating the cosmic presence of a Creator—no less elated than Rimbaud, and then, like any great writer, falling to the hard work of refocusing, of getting the lines right with a rightness we can only sense by reestablishing the creative context and returning to the historical scene of writing.

"The dated look of the films is itself an image of time," wrote critic Leon Wieseltier on the power of old movies. The extent of inadvertent detail that a literary description provides is multiplied exponentially by movies. Poetry can't compete literally, but its images and resonances can be complimented by anti-images and anti-rhetoric, thanks to the full panoply of linguistic sound, imagery, and intellectual drama. The image or idea that is undermined in the poem's little theater is analogous to our unconscious, where, like any single word, it can reappear in different guise or meaning. Words have histories not only in cultures but in our minds, like the image of an industrious honeybee that becomes its opposite, an assassin, in a particular memory. (And any word is subject to an indeterminate number of puns, including when translated into another language.) So poetry, more than any other art, can provoke a wider access to history, both public and personal. In the Bible, there's an image of Abraham holding a knife over his bound son but also the anti-image of an angel hovering above, heard but unseen. I describe the nightmare of this scene, the Akedah (Sacrifice of Isaac), as a poem—one that can only be properly experienced if we consider the ancient author at his writing table. It's similarly helpful to know the director of a film, but there's so much greater detail of background and foreground, gesture and tone, in a film, that we can ask for less art. In the Bible, the art of the writing is bedrock, essential.

We take in movies of the present as if looking out the window, unmindful of our cultural situation. Older movies, however, are framed with the deeper resonance of historical and cultural context. They are time capsules, and unlike older books or paintings they provide an analogue for the unconscious: lost and inadvertent details, such as the grille on a '49 Mercury that has nothing to do with the story. And in films over time, we get to see the actors age completely apart from the characters they've played. Movie characters can also age and change over time, but the actors are real in another way: time works on them oblivious to their will or our own. The image of time we get is inexorable, something we know in our bones but is rarely so poignant. It may be there in old home movies or videos but never so stark, for although we might mug for the camera there we are not *artists* of character, especially at the level of the golden age of cinema.

What is more, the four minutes out of three hours during the annual night at the Oscars that represents the deaths of movie industry people of the last year is now so time-constrained that even a clip of the actors on screen has been erased, with only a kitschy air-brushed photo in its place, underlined not with silence but equally insipid music. Fortunately, it's mostly taboo to mess with the original films, just as it's been a taboo to change even a word of the Bible for thousands of years. Yet it took centuries for that ancient taboo to come on line, just as it takes time to realize the value of old films, many of which were discarded and are now lost. For that reason alone, I venerate the art of restoration, both of old movies and of the original scenes of writing the Bible. I want the writers and their cultural surround to give us back a sense of lost time reopened, so that their living flesh and blood can be transmuted in our minds into artists no less driven than our own today. That restorative transmuting I consider the next literary avant-garde. Of course, it's easier said in a critical essay than experienced in a poem. And it doesn't have to be portentous: the fish that swallowed Jonah doesn't have to be a real whale; it could even be a ridiculous project we took on and that consumes us.

After a youth editing and translating Baudelaire and surrealists like Desnos, honoring a droll covenant with the infinitude of consciousness, how was I to feel close to biblical writers? I had to face that they pushed past even further boundaries, toward a cosmic theater in which their countrymen are creatures bound into an existential covenant with their Creator. What does He—and life itself—want from them? To grasp the biblical writers working out the complications of the answer, in the form of our journey through human history, required that you sensed them alive and at play, however serious, with their language. Loss of those imaginative writers, for me as a writer, was the deepest loss; it pushed me beyond asking how the Bible was written, and in search of lost ancestors. "Why are you doing it?" my writing colleagues once asked. "Why throw your career as a poet away in order to become a rebellious translator, outside the game?" I didn't have an articulate answer. If I could put words in the mouth of the past, I might say: "It's the only way I know how to write the lost Jewish writers at the origin of Western culture into our lives now; they're the great cosmic players we no longer know how to be. By giving them their lives back, we make it possible to absorb their influence."

Let me set one recent scene before you that encapsulates my situation as a poet translated (or beamed up, if you're a Trekkie) into the biblical dimension. I'm holding an open box and Rhonda a broom, trying to corral a 3-foot-long young snake that our cat caught against the patio screen and was trying to kill, tiring it out with endless pawing vs. coiling/ hissing—play for the cat (she could choose to walk away) but life/death for the snake. Many tense minutes of staring into desperate snake's face and eyes, tongue flicking, body coiling backward, until we "convinced" it (anthropomorphically speaking) into our saving trap and set it free in the yard, "a narrow fellow in the grass," Emily Dickinson-wise.

"Several of nature's people
I know, and they know me"

It's that last line of Dickinson's that stuns again: it was seeing that the snake
saw me, *face to face*, that offered me a sense of my creaturehood. Unlike our
feline, it saw me not as predator—how could it know?—but as creature
(size not the issue, for it could spring to my height) full of mystery, anxiety-
provoking, dangerous only because it was there with me, not safely alone
in its lair. Our cat knows me as domesticated creature, careening slowly
about the house, staring into books and tablets, but for the snake I was
wild, unpredictable. How often am I aware of that, outside of imagination?
Even in the Everglades wilderness near our home, I'm on an official path—
boardwalk, gravel, earthen or watery, conscious I'm walking in civilization's
shoes. But with those minutes of snake consciousness, I was in the realm
of the supernatural soul, an unknowable essence of myself that I still can
feel naturally, like wind brushing by. It's but a brief imaginative step from
there, awakened to creatureliness, to the snake that speaks in Eden.

That gorgeous snake knows me, my innocence of its full knowledge, its
motives. Still, I sense its limitless canniness: I don't ask how it got there, yet
it asks of me that question, knowing I am blind to our mutual Creator. But
I will learn, when I leave it, what both of us in the garden are cut off from:
the Creator's uncanniness. As I read, even as I hear God talk and emote, the
words of the text echo the muffled words I heard beyond the womb. The
garden was there before me, as Sinai was, and Israel; but it was the Hebrew
writers in Jerusalem, rebelling against myth fixed in stone, who brought
expressive movement back to history.

Modern poets have sometimes done the same for classic myth. Writing
metaphorically about Orpheus, Cocteau says "the poet must undergo
many types of 'death' in order to achieve immortality through his art." For
myself, the central such decease was that of my career as a poet, when, at
age 29, after six published books of poetry, I turned into a Bible translator.
I've written unpublished volumes of poems since then, in addition to the
publication of a book-length poem, *The Lost Book of Paradise*, but the work
of my post-careerist life became a poetry of restoration. The scenes of writing
I labored to restore go back to the origins of written literature in Sumer,
reflecting the probable education of the biblical Abraham in ancient Ur. In
that book, *Abraham: The First Historical Biography*, it is the Bible's writers
in Jerusalem, many centuries later, whose education I primarily evoke—
yet for them too the literature of Sumer and Akkad were their classics, as
Greek and Latin were for Shakespeare and remain so for us. I would prefer
to have that literary trope change to "Greek, Latin, and Hebrew," so that
the Bible's hundreds of lost writers can take their imaginative place beside
Homer, Sophocles, Plato and Virgil. To do that, however, they must be

named, located in their Hebraic culture, and reimagined in their literary careers and educations. I'm satisfied that Roman letters are a start to taking on those names, so that J, E, S, and others are clearly biblical. It's not literally the names that are crucial, but rather the unique character of their lives as literary artists: poets and prose writers without whom the literature of the West, including today's, would be threadbare.

To return them from the dead, as it were, required that initial career-death I've noted, a type of Orpheus retrieving his wife from the netherworld. Such was the Greek myth that underwrote Cocteau's statement, and upon which he played throughout his career, including a cocking of the hat toward earlier musings on literary death by the likes of Lukács. To restore ancient Hebraic culture to the life of the imagination, I needed every contextual aid I could think of, high and low, that would throw light into the study rooms and archive libraries of biblical writers. Yet context was just what I had learned to disarm as an avant-garde poet, breaking down boundaries, or what Lukács called "the rift between speakers, listeners, and their surrounding world." Even so, Lukács was dismissive of experimental writing, and he would have accounted my project to restore Hebrew and English context as too experimental; though strangely enough, this most imposing of Marxist aestheticians would have been in sync with the most conventional of scholarly critics. So, with skeptics on left and right, bourgeois and bohemian, I was on my own, a Judaic Orpheus.

When I consider Moses's Ten Commandments and its sublime elaboration through forty years in the putative desert—as finally articulated centuries later, in the books of Exodus, Numbers, and Deuteronomy—I recognize the Bible's original writers in Jerusalem not for their personal independence but for their passion for independence *per se*, especially from worldly resentment. No Jewish writers since have come close to the honestly critical light they throw on Jews themselves. They are fearless, because they have a cosmic theater in which every word is scrutinized not for its sincerity ("all bad poetry is sincere," wrote Oscar Wilde) but for its resonance—historical, rhetorical, poetical and most of all, the depth of that resonance, as if listening down the well of human history toward the origin that is imagined our Creator is listening back from. Each word in the best writing of the Bible is measured against the irony of being a created creature. What is that irony but a grand unscrolling of how we got here, listening for direction in every scrap of history we can restore.

Jonathan Sacks, UK Chief Rabbi, writing in the *Times of Israel*, encodes rebellion into the imaginative life of Israel: "The great figures of Judaism—Abraham, Moses, the prophets—were distinguished precisely by their ability to stand apart from the herd; to be different, to challenge the idols of the age, to refuse to capitulate to the intellectual fashions of the moment.... Poetry, music, love, wonder [are] the things that have no survival value but which speak to our deepest sense of being." If I can elaborate, it is poetry that most gives voice to the Bible, not simply as a literary form but as the form to our lives (Torah is called *shirah*, which means both poetry and song in Hebrew). The Russian modernist Anna Akhmatova, in 1959's 'Prose About the Poem' (translated by Ronald Meyer) considered her life's work as a single poem: "The poem is a peculiar revolt of things.... It imperceptibly assumed events and feelings from different layers of time." I could take from Sacks and Akhmatova the rebellion that spun me past the adolescent and avant-garde ones, out into the ancient cosmic theater of biblical authorship, where human history consists of boundaries pushed, stretched and questioned but never detached from origins. In modern philosophical terms, Derrida refers to a "transcendental signified" (in 'Structure, Sign and Play') as a central point of origin to structure, including linguistic structure. He claims "the function of this center is to render meaning determinate," but he proceeds to deconstruct it in a manner similar to how the poetics of the Bible rebelled against a determined origin—whether in the unquestioned plurality of gods or Adam's rib—that can't be reinterpreted, seriously and playfully.

My wife Rhonda, upon reading that last sentence, worries that a reader has difficulty getting their mind around a biblical scene of writing. Whatever perspective a reader has picked up, from childhood onward, it is focused upon the Bible's text with its highly educated imaginative writers and historians hidden behind a curtain of forgetting. Why bother to reembody them now? The answer is central to my story because it also begs the question of why I, or anyone, would devote their life to writing. Just like a writer today, the ancient Hebraic author sat in a chair, drank his ancient tea or beer, and surveyed his sources in the form of papyrus scrolls spread across his table and shelves. That writer did not start from scratch or catch inspiration like lightning in a bottle. Like writers today (and long before the great rabbis) he or she felt the weight of history, worldly and literary, stretching back for two millenniums of written texts before the Bible, to the cradle of civilization in Sumer and beyond. When I began to write poetry in high school and university, I didn't think I'd need such a long education. You played with your imagination or memories; you read a modern poem by Yeats or Marianne Moore and tried a take-off on it. I lacked a sense of the strength of imaginative mind needed to write through an entire life and continue to grow. It was hardly a matter of instant access to dreams and emotions, experience and the unconscious—and yet a life would seem to stretch out that way, a series of serendipitous accidents and uncharted destiny.

Nevertheless, I write these chapters in a form of rebellion against the chronology of my accidental life. It's a loving rebellion, however; poetry's rebellion against beginning, middle, and end. The Hebrew Bible doesn't end, I discovered; it just stops, anticipating more history to come. That would be an anachronism, if it didn't resemble the end of a psychoanalysis. All those sessions, all those biblical chapters in the light of creation, are now internalized, so that the present—though already the past—opens up like a poem, never happy with an ending. What to do with that "ordinary unhappiness," as Freud calls it? It's a complicated poem with a complicated author, and needs further translation. So I found the most complex authors I could, the lost writers of the Hebrew Bible, and set out to acquire the scholarship I'd need to envision them. I wasn't seeking to become a visionary; I was hoping it would help me to envision my own life as a poet, born on one of the most horrendous days of the twentieth century.

The Poem of Explanation

I'm in one of the last great independent bookstores, Books&Books, late night 4th of July. Many samba-band listeners but not many book-buyers lured by the 20% holiday discount. I've collected a pile of books to check through three-legged stool-side, half of them found by Rhonda. She also finds owner Mitchell Kaplan, who, after an exchange of "You look greats," asks what I'm reading at that moment, which is a two-thousand-page $75 recent edition of Leopardi's *Zibaldone*, newly translated. You would not find this book in Barnes&Noble, but it's on Amazon as an e-book at less than half list price, plus it won't weigh heavy on your stomach as you read (unlikely you could hold it up in two hands). As an older guy, I can enlarge the e-book print, though I wouldn't mention this to Mitch, who I think still imagines us as young guys. He's more than a decade younger yet I'm surprised to learn he's already entered the age of existential awareness: after Rhonda tells him I'd had a heart bypass recently, he wants to know if I had a heart attack first (no) and how it all went down. In a heartbeat, I answered: I was riding my bike and noticed a pressure in my chest; called my doc, asking if I should take a Xanax for anxiety. "Have you been under heavy stress?" she asks. No, I answered, "but who knows?" Go to the emergency room and get checked out, she says, "you have nothing to lose." We go, we're night owls so we don't mind that it's midnight, plus less wait time. Actually, when there's suspect heart trouble, they take you instantly, we find, and within a few hours it's early AM and I'm looking at a 3D real-time image of the inside of my heart and arteries on a state-of-the-art machine. The blockages are clearly visible, though I still feel mostly normal, and the doc says you need an operation, which is backed up by his team of heart-pros. Serendipitously: "We can do it this morning," he says, "it's our surgery day." So no time to worry or think, we decide to get it over with, after a bit more medical encouragement.

I report all this to Mitch, who responds supportively that he was in Baltimore recently when a doc looked at a melanoma on his arm, saying it could be dangerous. "When you get back to Miami, I'd have it checked out immediately." No way was he going to live with that worry, says Mitch, and the doc dug it out right there and then. "I'd have done the same as you," he continues, "get on with your life like Philip Roth." We both knew Roth had a similar operation to mine two decades ago and went on to write more than half a dozen new novels, some of them his best. You can find the recent ones in Mitch's bookstore, but not much more of a literary backlist, which I've always been embarrassed to ask him about, knowing that literary history is his soft spot. For three decades he's been a national celebrity for hosting the

Miami International Book Fair, though his backstory includes being a high-school English teacher so frustrated by the younger generation's disinterest in dead authors that he left his job to risk opening a bookstore, one so avidly devoted to literary history that he named it "Books&Books" to spite the plague of stores at that time desperately named "Books&Things" or "Books&Birthday Cakes" or "Books&Dolls". Now the others have folded and Mitch's little chain of 7 stores, some of them pocket-size, are holding on, if barely. "But I can't even keep Singer in stock," he says. "The younger generation has no memory for literature and anyway the publishers won't reprint." There's an English teacher's pedagogical regret in his voice, so when Mitch says "younger generation," I think he's counting back from fifty-five, imagining his own onetime students.

Yet "no memory for literature" sticks in my mind. It seems to validate Harold Bloom's comment on the back of the *Zibaldone* book, that Leopardi had substituted his total consciousness for traditional ideas of "mind." Bloom's economy of literary history, however, fails to note the losses that a dedication to consciousness may entail, especially the loss of memory for literature. Today, that memory has been exchanged for a wider range of culture, from high to low, with new mediums stuffed into consciousness like photography and film; radio, video and TV; rock, comix and cyber forms such as blogs. That's not all bad, but Leopardi, writing almost two centuries ago, had far more room in his head for books, including the ancients and the Bible.

Perhaps when and if I reach eighty I'll be able to retire and prop up the 8 lb. vol of *Zibaldone* on my stomach as I read in bed. Can a writer, however, read without his or her deeper purpose of putting the wisdom acquired (if any) to work? That is, to add yet more exotic yeast to the next book he or she may write? Can one imagine Philip Roth reading now—reading even his own oeuvre—after publicly declaring that he will write no more? Of course not; to what purpose is reading to a writer if one can't write? It was a typical Rothian gambit, much like his ironic comment after I asked him to contribute to the journal I was editing in Israel in the early '80s, *Forthcoming: Jewish Imaginative Writing*: "I don't think I have anything Jewish to give you."

I reminded Roth of this when we met in the *Symphony Space* Green Room before 'An Evening with *The Book of J*,' when he accompanied his wife at the time, Claire Bloom, who would read from my translation, sandwiched in between expositions by Harold Bloom and myself. Roth smiled in recognition. "I still don't know if I have anything, but you could ask your friend Professor Bloom. Maybe I've missed something." Although Roth's books would not be found on Mitchell Kaplan's bookstore's "Jewish shelf" (I don't think it still exists) his books might certainly be found on such a shelf in any Christian bookstore.

When I reminded Mitch I was writing a creative memoir, he lamented that I'd need footnotes to explain who Isaac Bashevis Singer was. Mitch recalled how I first came to Miami in the '80s as Singer's editor, when the revival of Art Deco "South Beach" was just beginning, a couple miles downwind from Singer's '50s style condo—cinemascope apartment windows, 3D staircase from elevator to street—on Ocean Drive. One block over was Singer's main walking destination, a '30s-style imitation Manhattan drug store with long lunch counter and a few tables where he could work and nurse a glass of tea. "Sheldon's Drugs" was also our meeting place, source of the first "real" grilled cheese sandwich I'd eaten in half a century. It was barely thirty-five years ago that Singer won the Nobel Prize and not much more than twenty since he died, so when Roth mordantly claimed that nobody would be reading his own or any novels at all within a generation after he passed on, he should have proffered Singer for proof.

I can easily imagine Shakespeare and John Webster in their cups, in an Elizabethan pub, reflecting that few would remember their plays a generation after they were gone, the texts never published. It's taken more than four centuries, meanwhile, to get serious about the books influencing Shakespeare, as another book in my little pile at Mitch's bookstore seems to do. *Shakespeare's Montaigne* is a new paperback I can actually afford and will buy to not disappoint Mitch, who reads the title aloud when we saunter over to the cash register. "You're the last of the literati," he comments. "We need you to stay healthy." Rhonda chimes in: "Don't worry. The surgeon said he should have a good twenty-five years ahead of him, though David said: 'Is that all I can get?'"

"What egregious fools are we?" writes Montaigne. "'He hath passed his life in idleness,' say we. 'Alas, I have done nothing this day.' What, have you not lived? It is not only the fundamental but the noblest of your occupations." Just living, that is. But of course to really celebrate *that*, one could aspire to be a writer like Montaigne himself, or Shakespeare reading him in Florio's translation, which Greenblatt and Platt have just re-edited from the 1605 edition, for my shiny paperback. Like Montaigne, Shakespeare had a great mind—but no, we don't want to say that, it's the scope of their *consciousness* that keeps both of them alive to us—even if we're more obsessed today with testing the boundaries of consciousness, rather than the scope of what may live on either side. For Shakespeare, there's tragedy on this side and dreams on the other. A century ago, Freud was similarly occupied with dreams, but now we're fixated on neither dreams nor suffering but instead the erotic border town between them—a Tijuana, not Macbeth's Scotland. When our writers today probe the boundaries of consciousness, it usually leads to satire, and more dangerously, to the representation of psychosis for the individual and extinction for the species. For those circumstances we have the irony of "superheroes". The proof is all around us in the popular culture, which few writers can afford to ignore, anymore than Shakespeare could have avoided Montaigne, for whom "everything in a life is significant, and a preference for radishes has the same weight as the most exalted metaphysical reflection," states Greenblatt.

Someone may ask why I must bring in so much literature and contemporary culture. The Bible, they might say, is over the head of all that, and will still be read in the future after all this passes from view. Here is where I begin to rebel, for the issue is not that it's read but how it's read, how fertile it remains for writers yet to be born. It was so for me, but when I look around I find few poets or writers who are deeply engaged with both Bible and the secular culture, not to mention the literary avant-garde, which nourished my first few books of poems and the artists with whom I collaborated. I didn't start out that way; I came from an Ed Sullivan-watching immigrant family, one that I thought was too culturally deprived and against which I needed to rebel. At the time I began to write and envision my lifetime career, at age fourteen, I held the opinion that my Hebrew after-school education was a hindrance to immersing myself in literary history—nobody had pointed out to me the artistic depths of the Bible and its potential wellspring for postmodern writers, nor do I find writers today who are first grounded in contemporary literature before turning to the Bible as a source-text.

So how did it happen for me? Simply put, it came from my rebellion against the prevailing literary atmosphere and what I perceived as the backsliding of the avant-garde. I began to write my doctoral thesis in literature upon the fundamental American avant-gardist, Gertrude Stein, fueled by a righteous determination to expose how marginal her influence had become. It was 1969, I was in my mid-twenties, and Stein was still a few years away from having her oeuvre popularized once more by the onset of LGBTQ culture. My private agenda was entirely literary: to justify living and doing research in Paris.

The modern writers Ezra Pound and T.S. Eliot had stimulated me, but one day in grad school I came face to face with their resentment of the Hebrew Bible. That was a stain to be found on many modern writers, but in these two poets it was personal. If someone warned me not to read the Declaration of Independence, even if just because it's a nasty knock-off of the French Declaration of the Rights of Man, I'd probably fall to reading the U.S. Declaration the same day (where I might learn that the French Declaration came after, not before). The nastiness of Pound's indignation toward the whole Bible and Eliot's toward the O.T. Hebrew Bible sent me there, noting that the hundreds of Jewish writers behind it (those behind the N.T. are another story) were tarred with the same brush of primitivism—somewhat of a paradox, since the inhaling of primitive gestures had energized the avant-garde, even before Picasso and Apollinaire.

Anyway, they were dead wrong, as a study of the ancient Hebrew text uncovers a modernizing ambition to "make it new," in regard to both the worldly literary classics that preceded and the meaning of revelation. But that didn't come clear to me in a day, or even for several years.

When I began to penetrate below the surface of modern biblical scholarship I found myself rebelling against the stifling consensus of biblical critics, and not on religious or scholarly grounds but on the nature of interpretation itself. There wasn't a creative writer among them and thus no affinity for the ancient biblical poets; poetry and poetic narrative could be regarded from the outside in but not from the inside out. At best, the text was a skeletal jewel upon which critics applied a jeweler's eyepiece. What they disclosed was valuable, yet it served to further obscure the absence of any thought of the original writers and the vibrant Hebraic culture in which they wrote. Okay, so we don't have the bones of the writers, but that shouldn't preclude using comparative historical resources to imagine the authors as literary artists and not simply the art of a disembodied text (or, for the original anti-Semitic source criticism of the 19th century, a primitive authorship). What's the general excuse offered by biblical critics? That in "those days," writers were anonymous. Ha! Not only were certain names of Sumerian and Egyptian authors famous more than a millennium earlier, one can be fairly sure that Hebraic writers were honored in their time, no less than a religious writer in recent centuries, such as the Baal Shem Tov, even if he was not a modern "individualist". The way open for me to provide a writer's interpretation was to translate the text with a writer's sensibility. How I discovered that path will come clear in the chapters ahead; for the moment, my point is that the dismissal of the original authors by mainstream criticism paralleled the belittling of not only Gertrude Stein but contemporary culture and art in general. Without the contemporary, the sensibility in which high and low cross-fertilize is lost. (Tradition and popular culture is how biblical critics tend to represent it, deriding the latter as merely folkloric). A sensibility open to both, however, is crucial to the writer not only today, and not only for Shakespeare and Montaigne, but also for the writers of the Bible. The stories of Sodom and Gomorrah, Lot and his daughters, or of Judah and Tamar and a host of others running throughout the Hebrew Bible evoke an artistic sensibility open to the full range of literary history—and for the Bible's writers, that history stretched back thousands of years to the classical literatures of Sumer, Egypt, and other Mediterranean, Middle Eastern and Asian cultures. But I'm not purveying the well-known facts about how the provenance of Noah or the Golden Calf preceded the ancient Jewish text; instead, I'm focused on how the Hebraic writers turned their sources into a literary art comparable to Shakespeare's Cleopatra or Henry V. They did it with a bold imagination, just as "Shakespeare did not typically dream up new ideas for plays but rewrote, adapted and borrowed from the plots, characters and language of previous works," as a recent writer in *The New Yorker* informs us, as if it's news. In whatever way we denote the lost names of biblical authors, one would say the same for them, from the earliest J strand of Torah to the poets behind "Isaiah." And in the same way, Montaigne, as I will shortly show, borrowed the wind of Judgment Day in the *Book of Isaiah* (my translation), when pretense...

> ...on that clear day
> will melt away
> like dew on the ground
>
> men and women
> in the statues and masks
> of their pride
>
> will topple over
> like carved chess pieces
> in a gust of wind
>
> the little board
> on which they lived for power
> swept away with sand
>
> when only the Lord
> like a blue sky
> will be above us
>
> and the idols of dark thoughts
> like dreams
> passed away   utterly
>
> ...beyond the grasp of a man
> who reaches for power
> and cannot hold
>
> the breath in his nostrils
> who cannot grasp it
> whose sum total is less
>
> than that little wind
> blowing through him
> and the naked sail of his heart.
>   [from Chapter 2]

Of course, great writing is never "mere literature"; there is revelation in Shakespeare and Emily Dickinson, even if it is of a different order than in Isaiah or the Book of Exodus. The revelation of previously unremarked layers of human consciousness has been a specialty for contemporary poets, even though it is missing a cosmic dimension. But this, too, I hope to elaborate later. For now, I'll briefly illustrate the significance of a lower, or seemingly ordinary, popular art, for the Bible and for writers today.

Back in the 1990s, the film *Deep Impact* was a major Montaignean radish, an ordinary piece of pop culture, hard to avoid, like the giant comet it reveals to be on a path toward Earth. The issue was the extinction not only of the human species but "all life on the planet." Human ingenuity partly staves off the day, so that only the Atlantic and Mediterranean coastal cities are destroyed, namely "over a hundred million" people. We witness Manhattan submerged by a tsunami, the wave-top lopping off the head of the Statue of Liberty and sweeping the twin towers away while they still literally existed. So what's a hundred million anyway, since that many were killed in WWII alone. Life goes on; we rarely think of it. Nevertheless, there are biblical echoes in *Deep Impact* when the issue of total extinction is still in play. A kind of Noah's Ark for animals and plants is constructed under a mountain, etc. Meanwhile, even the black President, in a brilliant piece of foreshadowing in '97 (as acted by Morgan Freeman), laments that "our planet is in danger of extinction and our way of life wiped out." This scenario had not been faced before; even Cecil B. DeMille allowed for divine intervention. In *Deep Impact*, however, it's Darwin who's referenced in the expectation of an inevitable "extinction event" to rival the one that claimed the dinosaurs. We're face to face with the inevitability, in the form of families split apart and lovers lost, as in the last world war, and there's nothing to suggest we've learned anything as a species.

We're just as susceptible to mass psychosis as natural disaster, as suggested by another good, solid film, *The Dark Knight*, in which story-telling, human suffering, and the tenuous existence of our species are elements advanced in rivalry with contemporary fiction. Heath Ledger's psychotic character, The Joker, delivers wonderful variations on the "What do we have to lose?" theme, while Batman's main question is, "Must I sink to his level in order to defeat him?" One can think of Japanese and German mass psychoses in WWII or the current Iranian determination to "defeat Western values," towards which they're prepared for the long run, backed up with a potential nuclear threat. We have already sunk beneath their level, in their eyes, by having committed Hiroshima and Nagasaki, says their Supreme Leader— and The Joker indicts Batman in the same way, for the crime of killing our last best hope, in the person of Gotham's mayor. What threatens Batman, like all of us, is that he still holds onto a shred of the truth, while The Joker, like any psychotic or psychotic nation, is free to lie to heart's content.

I wouldn't have brought up these or any films in conversation with Mitchell Kaplan of Books&Books, for he's locked in an existential struggle with other media in order to keep his stores alive. I was tempted to buy the $75 *Zibaldone* as a gesture of support, even though I'd prefer the cheaper, lighter, and searchable e-book, so I could pick out passages that pertain to my thinking at a given moment. Even were I in my twenties, I wouldn't have the time in today's world to read through 2,000 pages concerning a literary history perchance very much still alive but long vanished from contemporary discourse. Yet I think Montaigne wouldn't hesitate to quote *The Dark Knight*. During his senior years, he locked himself away in his castle library crammed with books, though I'm sure today it would include cloud access to other media. "To think and write" was his intention, which turned out to be the writing of personal essays as memoir. Worrying me, Rhonda tells Mitch my memoir is not just about me but about species consciousness, a subject dear to "The Rosenberg Estate" (Rhonda, me, a domesticated animal, and the hundred wild species in our large subtropical yard and mini-forest). I'm a bit anxious; I don't want Mitch to think the memoir will be a New Age niche book rather than the jolt of literary history that he's already said he'll support to the hilt. "Since the human body is co-dependent with hundreds of microbe species it hosts, including species that evolved on our planet long before humans," continues Rhonda, "David's memoir shows how he's always made extinction the central issue. Since all species go extinct, he's kept a tragic open mind to how our species could become transhuman by co-evolving with computers and what that means for a writer. How many other writers besides David are imagining what it means to be read in the future not by humans but by machines?"

Now Mitch will really be depressed about his bookstores, I thought. Rhonda wasn't through, however. "David isn't thinking how his own writing will be read but about a most basic human text, the Bible. He gives that text an emotional interpretation to lay beside the usual translations, so that even a robot will be challenged by the necessity of human thinking and feeling." I interrupted Rhonda. "Dear, Mitch will think it's science fiction—" But Mitch too jumped in: "Science fiction is really starting to sell again." I didn't know if that was really true or Mitch was trying to soothe any friction between two of his best customers. It's a good thing, however, that I didn't blurt out: "It's really about how poetry is the essence of the human species." Mitch kept a well-stocked poetry section, but he certainly knew those shelves weren't going to save his bookstores.

We moved on to the in-store cafe and sat down. It was closed for the evening already, but with so little traffic in the store on a big-discount holiday—distant whistling of fireworks in evidence—we each wanted to find a mutually satisfactory note on which to part. Mitch told us about his last meeting with Singer, after the onset of his dementia, when he brought over a box of his books to be signed. "How do I know I wrote those books?" Singer protested. "Maybe they're forgeries and they'll take me to jail. I don't remember what I wrote anymore." I hesitated to now ask what happened to those books, though suggested they could be somehow denoted "the last unsigned books of I.B. Singer." Not even a snicker. But Mitch had a healthier ending: "Thank God he'd already written his memoirs!"

What is a memoir or a life, however, if it can't trace the trajectory toward dementia, or more generally, death? "You should have twenty-five good years," said the heart surgeon—as if prompting my memoir to devote the next ten to my childhood years and the following decade to post-adolescence through mid-life crisis. As for tracing the arc toward dementia, the mind works in tandem with feelings, not in contrast to them, so that the obvious drama is when the tandem breaks down, and mind or emotion runs rampant. To poeticize that, the story one could tell is of the past breakdown of society in world wars and the parallel threat to our species today by an appeasement of psychotic enemies/enablers. So let's say for now this poetry holds, and that I and my poetry are one in consciousness. That's where we seem to be today, where consciousness is everything we know; what's beyond, be it chaos or creator, is out of the picture. The poets of the Bible, on the other hand, faced the *chaos* of consciousness that wars brought home, and looked to the creation of the universe for signs of what lay behind it. If the universe is a poem, then imagining who wrote it girds us against the chaos of psychosis. We can imagine a psychopath well enough as Heath Ledger's The Joker, but the Biblical Prophets' constant awareness of psychotic nations at the gates—and acceptance of it as human limitations having to do with divine providence—is hard for us. And if our species is a poem, then its eventual extinction will still leave a poem behind—a more complex and influential one than the age of dinosaurs—if not a library of precarious texts.

Would boiling that down for Mitch relieve his anxiety? I don't think so; irony aside, extinction makes bookstores irrelevant. Our lives are all we have and they aren't fungible, as Montaigne would say, so he'd fit right in today, except his deeper sense of history and the classics would leave him less sanguine about our near-sighted preoccupation with human consciousness. Montaigne was more aware of our species limitations: "Myself, who brag so curiously to embrace and particularly to allow the commodities of life, whensoever I look precisely into it, I find nothing but wind. But what? We are nothing but wind. And the very wind also, more wisely than we, loveth to bluster and to be in agitation, and is pleased with his own offices, without desiring stability or solidity, qualities that be not his own."

Yet, to ask, What is a life? What is a poem? are species-conscious questions. Can we ask them properly without the Bible, which asks the framing questions: What is beyond life? What is a cosmic poem? Knowingly or not, Montaigne here is quoting from the biblical book of Ecclesiastes, more specifically than Isaiah, as when he refers "not to the matter but to the shape I give it." Shape, therefore, of the wind—given by his imagination. We are constantly startled by Montaigne's showing us how his selfhood is constructed. We're not used to such inner nudity; we still aren't today. It all speaks to our individual deaths, in which our consciousness will be lost but not what shapes we gave it—as in Montaigne's essays, Shakespeare's plays, Freud's theories, and the latest literary novel. I said something like that to Mitch, to encourage his commitment to "literary history" in his bookstores.

But what if all of that is wiped out (something I *didn't* say to Mitch) along with our species extinction. Yet we do get to the tip of that iceberg with the literary case of Isaac Bashevis Singer. In Singer's fiction, the consciousness of his protagonists tests the border of chaos or psychosis, making Singer as up-to-date as Batman. Beyond that, however, the tragicomedy in Singer's work is also up against the unavoidable question of his characters' extinction, whether in the Holocaust or in the damaged aftermath to it we are still living through. Today it ties in to species consciousness, reminding us again of human limitations. "But those limitations also drive the ingenuity to challenge them, to understand our flawed psyche, for instance. So I don't think you have to worry about lots of new literary books to sell," I say to Mitch, "because those flaws are what makes literature gripping. Neuroscience is never going to be as sexy, and the more that readers get bored with it, the more they'll want literary consciousness. You might even stock my *A Literary Bible* again…" Mitch ignored that last suggestion but countered optimistically, "We've been selling the new biography of Freud by Adam Phillips like mad. I haven't seen you since last summer when you were on a panel with him—how did that go?"

"Eye-opening. Adam's patter is sunny, even when it's about depression, but when he's there in person you see how depressed he really is, so the contrast is rich. Rhonda and I talked about it for a long time afterward. We decided that what was hidden in Adam's sensibility was a kind of Blues, or a sense of loss. He finds so much *there* in Freud that he has no time for what Freud might have lost in his life by pushing his father's Bible aside, along with the religion. Actually, our panel was about our recent translations—his of the Freudian oeuvre, though he only edited it, and mine of the Bible. I always feel a bit weird talking about the Bible with a Jew who hasn't bothered to learn a bit of Hebrew; it's probably how the Jewish vaudeville comics felt when they went mainstream and were telling a joke dependent on a Yiddish pun, which they then had to translate into English."

As I'm telling this, I realize that Mitch is in the same situation as Adam, feeling no regret for not having Hebrew or even more than a passing familiarity with the Bible, something essential to umpteen generations of their family histories. Freud offered an improvement on that, namely science and literature, so why should Adam consider the losses? Or Mitch, for that matter, which is why I didn't bring it up. Instead, I said of Adam's Freud bio, "I bet it's mostly women buying it, there's a lot in it about his absent mother and his trying subconsciously to make up for losing her through his women patients." I left it at that, though it was a superficial and unfair characterization. What Phillips was really getting at was how young Freud substituted culture for his mother. But I'd say his mother symbolized the loss of the Bible, the centuries of ancestral education in it that she was unable to pass on to him.

Uncannily, there's not a single mention of the Bible in Adam's book. One of his bio's reviews characterizes that loss without naming it. "Phillips speaks of his instant identification with other modern Jewish authors—Bellow, Roth, Mailer and Malamud. He eschews the 'Wailing Wall' mentality that permeates Jewish thought but completely embraces Jewish cultural identity." But what is that "Wailing Wall mentality" if not an active engagement with loss, in this case the loss of the Temple that the creator of the universe called home for a thousand years? For Phillips, like Freud, that wall remnant was the Hebrew Bible, a loss that he reactively mourned by substituting for it European culture. Yet sure enough, that lost Hebraic culture, like Freud's mother, haunted me as well, for my own mother also abandoned the Bible. I may have felt abandoned along with it, as Freud may have felt according to Phillips, and it drove me too into the arms of "literary history." That's a term Mitch used for what was being abandoned right in the midst of his bookstores, an abandonment looming ahead for the "literary history" that comprised the backlist that supported the sales ledger. Yet few will miss it, their consciousness stretched to the limit with internet access to *everything*. Nothing will ever be lost again, not even mother, because you can access her on the internet forever, through pics, sound clips, videos, posts and tweets. It will be culture completely absent the literary, as if puttering around the pristine extinct volcanoes of Mars can take its place.

2.

"Perhaps" muses Adam Phillips in his biography of Freud, "all a biographer can do, from a psychoanalytic point of view, is to keep repeating himself by describing the recurring preoccupations that make a life." In attempting the bios of J, S, and other biblical writers whose actual names are lost, I've repeatedly imagined their scenes of writing, the cultural context in which they wrote. It's part of my own lifelong project of getting ancient Jerusalem revealed—where hundreds of poets with their names long erased were behind the 40-odd books of the Hebrew Bible and plenty of others that are lost. It's still a struggle for readers to see ancient Jerusalem on an artistic par with Athens, Elizabethan London, and Paris.

And it's not hard to comprehend the difficulty. After all, assuming there were teaching institutions in ancient Jerusalem of some kind, today's academic would still be at loose ends without access to its authored texts. Athens provides Aristotle, Plato and so much more, while Shakespeare's texts go without saying for Elizabeth's London. So-called sacred texts, however, are considered solely the purview of religious studies these days. Apparently it was so even for Kant, who may have considered his concept of the transcendental as not enough self-aware to imagine the Hebrew Bible's writers, if indeed he even thought of them as writers in the cultural sense—that thought, however, had already occurred to Spinoza a century earlier. Certainly we know that the Jewish NT writers of koine Greek did not get college degrees, although the latest sociological evidence suggests that the disciples were in fact students of Rabbi Yeshua (Jesus of Nazareth), who himself had studied for more than a decade with Judaic scholars in Sepphoris. I explored this in a book, *An Educated Man*; nevertheless, the scholars and writers a millennium further back from the days of Jesus, in Solomonic Jerusalem when the early Bible was being written, predated the sacralizing of their texts by many centuries, right down to the book of *Ecclesiastes*, circa 4th Century BCE. Since religion departments in general don't concern themselves with cultural issues, and literature departments restrain themselves from interest in the Hebraic scenes of writing—or even bother to consider the human character and education of those hundreds of biblical poets & writers—how can I accredit Jerusalem with the intellectual ferment of early modern Paris (even if none of the latter's significant poets & writers graduated from the Sorbonne)?

So the question comes back to me: Why is it necessary to imaginatively re-create those scenes of writing? Lost is lost, one might answer; or, even now, interest in the psychological situation of a poet in Paris is submerged beneath a passion for mere texts—the disembodied texts, as it were—even when, in the case of Lacan, those texts can resemble a psychoanalytic session. While it's impossible to imagine the cafes of the Left Bank, no less than Elizabethan coffeehouses, empty of poets, we so take them for granted that one can't even think of Proust existing without them, even when he's locked away in his soundproofed rooms during the years of completing his masterwork—and even though Proust's text clearly required a cup of coffee (tea?) for its madeleine. Imagine my surprise, then, as I confronted the row of teahouses lining the lane leading from the palace archives to the main street of Solomonic Jerusalem with its scroll shops and ancient Levenger-type stores to "outfit our customers with high-quality products designed for reading, thinking, and creative expression". I found these streets not in a dream, but in a detailed diorama in the old David's Citadel Museum in modern Jerusalem. The biblical writers in those teahouses, redolent of the scents of India, whence originated the teas Solomon imported (along with scrolls of proto-Dravidian and Sanskrit) did not frequent synagogues, which were not yet in existence, but more likely spent much time in the Palace library, studying and translating not only scrolls but cuneiform-dense clay tablets.

Why must we know this? At the very least, to provide catnip to academics and camaraderie to the loneliness of contemporary writers; but in a larger sense, it goes beyond loneliness to what I'd call lostness, lost in time especially: Homo sapiens species time, the blur of civilization arising, and the contemporary fog in which the evil that an ideal society repels has become too difficult to make out. If we're blasé about interpreting history, no longer interested in the context for our lostness as the early Moderns had become, then that startling civilization at the origin and following millennium of the Bible remains enshrouded and more lost to us than a drowning man we've failed to save. We are the ones in danger of drowning, of course, so that the lost poets of Jerusalem, rediscovered, just might save us.

How? I could suggest how they saved me from being lost among contemporaries whose regard I was absorbed in winning while blind to my true peers: my inarticulate mother and father, whose educated ancestors in ancient Jerusalem walked the streets with the same but also a lighter tread, gaining inspiration from their deeply creative culture (my parents' lives more circumscribed, like all of us now, knowing and unknowing, by the Holocaust and its ongoing postscript). So I plan to tell that story of non-ironic and more uncanny lost generations in ancient Jerusalem, in contrast to Paris of the 1920s. What can be more ironic, one might ask, than the fact of historical absence for the Bible's writers and the thick culture supporting them? I'd say it's only ironic if you've failed to ask, as the dubious academic theories of ancient anonymity or modesty flunk at, like professional wrestling shows fudging the question of authenticity. If you formulate the question on your own, as I did while researching the pitch of irony when biblical authors make use of cliches or officialese, you can't help but realize that the scooting of the writers to the invisible margin becomes uncanny.

Nothing uncanny about where I had come from: I was a typical young doo-wop hot shot entering the 1960s, for whom Western culture was my straight man. I all but disowned my family and the seeming suburban vacuousness of the '50s for the bohemian intellectuality of the moment, with its intimations of madness, free love, and the unchained melody of ahistorical consciousness. I absented myself from belief in cultural bedrock, like Eliot's "these fragments I have shored against my ruins," although in place of Eliot's thunder in *The Waste Land* I acquired, eventually, the lightning of LSD. Feeling the psychedelic wind blow through that gripping absence of mind, I felt more lost than found, and so I rebelled again, turning against my cultural moment, to become a translator of lost origins. I explored that lostness by means of what I call the ICU, to which meaning has been consigned and in need of intensive care. ICU—interpretation, context, and the uncanny—the three necessary sisters for bringing alive a richness of meaning that can resemble a life: for me, it's the memory of an ancient writer's life closer to the origin of civilization. That may sound heavy, but think of it like animating a duck, giving it name and character: it was hard work but a joy to make Donald Duck strut. Instead of entertaining, however, the biblical writers, when acutely imagined, inform a world.

I wish my colleague Cynthia Ozick didn't feel the need to inform with this sentence in a recent book review she authored: "Lasting works hardly require us to be acquainted with the lives of the masters who bore them—they have pulsing hearts of their own". I fear it's a false truism, one that dismisses even the imagining of the Jewish writers of the Bible. Yes, we "know [next to] nothing of Homer," Ozick adds for emphasis. What we do know, however, is crucial: Homer had a culture in which he swam, along with the older Homeric Hymns, while the writers of the Hebrew Bible have had their cultural sea dried up, in part by the Christian doctrine that religion alone is the Jewish legacy, its writers anonymous monks and mythologized prophets whose inspiration was divinely delivered into their brains, sans a necessity for being steeped in the literary, historical, scholarly and anthropological arts. Jewish history is also complicit, conflicted between the divine and the human, which takes the form of privileging the scholarly to a fault (where's the *evidence* of writerly bones?). That, and the under-privileging of ancient Hebraic imagination, can make even an imaginative writer in Israel disinterested, if not intimidated by religious stricture or by deference to a strain of academic priestliness.

3.

Harold Schimmel, my Jerusalem poet colleague, writes

משורר זה מי שחי חיים של משורר, ושכל מה שהוא קורא ולומד הוא בסופו של דבר רק לצורך שירתו

which I translate as "a poet is someone who lives his life so that all he reads and learns is shaped by what his poems need." It's as if a life is an artifact of a poem, and yet I can't say life is a poem in the same manner as my chapter titles here suggest. You can speak to (in) a life, you can speak to (in) the universe, because we are, in Schimmel's sense, their poems—as creatures, creations. George Bowering, my Vancouver poet colleague (and first Poet

Laureate of Canada) writes to me in an email: "there are people who think that they are poets, who have an argument to make and make it as plainly as possible, with language that just has to be understood. Beware the poet who wants to be understood." So we need literary community to simply *acknowledge* our existence, and I had it in Canada, England, Israel, as well as New York, but now it's more amorphous and global on the internet. I exchanged emails with Canadian poet Frank Davey for years before I met him for a few days, as I portray in the chapter "The Poem of Authorship." What is poignant about the physical encounter is that his creaturely presence remains just as real as it was in email, and still is, so that it is of a piece with his "written" writing, when I read it in any form online. It's far from the old manner of letter-writing, partly because it's in the moment and it's ok to let posts slide—that unlike letters they can stay there in their moment and not beg for a reply. It's as if the boundaries of a life are indeterminate: In the past, I spoke to the dead writers on my shelves and on my devices, in the form of marginalia, but now it's as if their books are writing back to me, as if they are emails I simply acknowledge. I myself become an artifact of an indeterminate community, including readers/posters yet unborn, and I would be more lonely than ever in it—except that, like emails or posts not needing an answer, it's easier to be anywhere and still in instantaneous touch, within hailing distance. It's consciousness to consciousness, which is the edge that writing today brings itself to, namely consciousness, so that the body we live in, that very creation that is determinately born and dies, is poignant as an artifact of the past: we can look back at the present moment as if it was a history we hadn't written. A poem.

That's the looking back of the biblical writers that I take as Western bedrock. Nothing mythic about a poem; even the imagination is historical, needing a body and history to make metaphors. When the once-living authors of miracles and visions are contextualized, along with their creative cultures, history returns. Only a human imagination can write Genesis, Jeremiah, and the Gospel of Mark, whatever the unknowable quality of our creatureliness. It's our imagination up against the unknowable, dramatizing it. Not the modern commonplace about humans authoring sacred texts, however; creation authored us, big C or little.

Precisely because poems are our last vestige of cosmic drama, modern poetry is an endless reality-testing of it, as if we can't believe we were sensible in writing the Divine Comedy or Blake's epics, let alone the Bible. Our pop-scientific texts for the knowable cosmos are at the literary level of the Young Adult genre, though I wouldn't want to demean the artistry of the latter. Of course, it's easy to criticize; everyone's got an opinion online. I was once of the grandiose opinion that our latest antinomians, the Beats, would engage Sanskrit and the cosmic Vedas, or Olson would invade the Mayan, but when it was clear that consciousness required center-stage I

thought to resign from the poetry of self-proclamation and enrobe myself
in translation. It proved not entirely possible, however, even for the most
studious of Zen converts, if that's what Corman or Whalen once intended,
and translators themselves are the most zen-like in the language arts.

   "To decipher what Tolstoy wanted to say, the translator has to devise
an interpretation of Tolstoy's narrative voice in *Anna Karenina*," writes
the reviewer of Marion Schwartz's new translation. How was I to do that
for the poets behind Isaiah and Ecclesiastes, whose poetic voices required
imaginative re-embodiment? Only by falling back on my poetic education,
which required finding my own voice and then losing it, time after time.
That losing brought me closer to the lost cosmic theater where ancient
Hebraic poets looked back at themselves, as if they could find firm ground
in the past. It's a cosmic confidence in time whose complexity an Einstein
might recognize. For me, as a poet of consciousness, it's a lost confidence—
that may nevertheless be disarmed in a poem.

   Anything that has a beginning
   everything
   was a seed in the pot

   planted before existence
   and named by men
   as it flowed into the world

   man is also a kind of flower
   whose growth is defined
   and all that flows from his hands
   and with our own little names
   we can't argue with our creator
   a name that's boundless

   beyond identity
   like death which takes back our names
   and gives them to the living

   the more words we use
   the more bricks for the mausoleum
   building castles in the air

   that are ancient relics
   the moment we exhale
   passed on to ignorant children

when we die
they prefer sand castles
and when the tide comes in they will not cry

but watch   fascinated
no better or worse
than all preceding men

who knows
what the right thing to do is
with a life

that walks across a stage
of air
in a bathing costume of flesh

until night falls like a gown
over a beautiful woman
who sleeps alone

only our shadows remain
impotent watchmen
on the shore of the life

our blood flowed to
and suddenly they too are gone
as the sun again rises

piercing all wishes and dreams
and romances of the future
with the bones of light

we are stripped awake   leaving
a shadow on the shore
that had not seen its own body.

The consciousness of unknowable big C and knowable little c creator in this excerpt from Chapter 6 (6:10ff) of Ecclesiastes evokes a cosmic theater in which there is an imagined dialogue beyond or outside of limited human consciousness. It's as if the poet is seeing himself at the scene of writing, in almost a Vedic elaboration of the "consciousness of consciousness." I'd wish to have that ancient Indian poet also reimagined, and if there's a globally online influence my work could have, that would be it—though the restoration of the biblical writers has many more permutations to go through after I'm gone, not least in contemporary Hebrew.

4.

I am beginning to sift biography, cultural history, biblical studies, scientific encounters, and art and literary experience together, as if concocting a poem of explanation. If this essayistic poem shows a bit of how I came to write the chapters that follow, it doesn't finally explain it. There is no final explanation to a poem, only a disarming of misunderstandings, so that in the end we're more satisfied with the experience of being disarmed than the lay of life's battlefield. Nevertheless, these chapters will also delve into what makes a poem and how the Bible *in toto* can be comprehended as a poem that disarms cynicism about life's purposefulness. It portrays Israel's journey, no less than those of Homer's ancient Greek epics, as if nothing is more important than becoming conscious of life as a poem: not just one made up of innocence and experience, but one that requires a cosmic background, in which what is humanly unknowable of the heavens can still be kept in mind.

I'm inclined to disagree with A.O. Scott, film critic of the *New York Times*, who last week wrote: "Art is the domain of solved problems, even if the problems are formal and the solutions artificial." The great epics open out to an imaginable future—yet do not provide the ultimate solution to humanity's problems. even if centuries of interpretation insist upon finding it. It's the manner of the pursuit itself these bedrock works adumbrate, a pursuit that can also be understood in lyric and anti-lyric poems as a tiny journey. Finishing a poem, we learn to let go of needing a solution to the problem the poem itself might present. How to live, for example, is not solved in the Hebrew Bible, though the attempt to find the solution is refracted into several variant views, and these in turn entailed many centuries of study that composed the Talmud. Can't we say the same for other sacred texts? But that would be missing the point of reading the Bible as a literary and cultural library, of a specific Judaic culture, one that enlivened a cosmic theater whose visionary poetry we're still ambivalent about how to engage. Engage, if not re-live; resisting the cosmic drama, the foundational American poets Walt Whitman and Emily Dickinson still engaged with its poetic vision.

The dictionary defines explanation as "to make clear," but the poem of explanation is mainly pursuit, an arguing without a clear argument, so that a reader cannot judge it by the argument's merits. Instead, we'd best relax and appreciate the quality of the arguing, the engagement with life as a creation in which we are fundamentally unknowable creatures. Who, beyond yoga teachers, wants to hear this? The contemporary version of an explanation for existence is to ask whether consciousness is ultimately knowable, even as our poetry and art busily extend the experience of its boundaries. This, too, will not make science happy, by way of circumscribing its territory: the unknown, and not the unknowable.

But if we can make of science a poem, it will embrace Darwin and Freud, Marie Curie and James Watson, *in relation to* their pursuits: they too are creatures in relation to worms and nematodes, or to creations like atoms and molecules, or, for neuroscientists and evolutionary biologists, synapses and ecosystems. How will that poem of science, one that explores everything but resists explaining, expand our boundaries? Perhaps it will simply relax us from the furious desire to push into the future by lightening the load and jettisoning the "old science" in a poem such as the Bible, which was never shy about exploring our destiny in the universe. Is this simply another counter-intuitive proposition—like those made in the past in essays variously titled or subtitled "In Defense of Poesy"—that poetry can save us?

Wallace Stevens, whose every assay in prose can be boiled down to the question, "What is Poetry?", would not say but nevertheless suggests that a religion of the poem can take the place of conventional religion. It's neither a brief for religion nor a pumping up of poetry. It's a suggestion that poetry is necessary, but so too is water, though few feel that justifications for water or odes to its liquid state are in order. That poets are no longer tolerant of conventional religion and prefer the reality of water goes without saying; still, the loss of spiritual wine is regretted. As much as we'd let religion go, Stevens writes, "Yet we do not quite yield. We cannot. We do not feel free." Some readers of poetry might think they can disagree, thinking to themselves I'm a scientist, an atheist, a social activist, a realist—in short, I feel free to chuck the artifice. But really, how do we explain that of which we are merely moments, and how do we understand the human mind that, according to Stevens, "has added nothing to human nature." Religion, like poetry, does not have to change what is real; rather, it's an imaginative force that protects us from the violence of reality, a chaos we've looked into by means of Freud's definition of the unconscious or, in hard science terms, the physical chaos of a distant black hole. "It is a violence within that protects us from a violence without," writes Stevens, thinking of the imaginative struggle to create a poem or a religion. "It is the imagination pressing back against the pressure of reality." Taking the long evolutionary view, our being a social species afforded Homo sapiens a circling of the wagons and eventually producing a literary culture—which granted us, via the poem of the Bible for instance, a vision of a traversable world, inner and outer. Today, if you can't register the loss of such species-driven poetry, consider the loss if the poem of science were to lose access to the past, to fossils and to the historical origins of all things.

I don't see how I could have written the preceding paragraph until I could measure my own bumbling struggle for experience, coming up against Stevens, Freud, Wilson, Moses, the Bible's J writer, etc. In the chapters ahead, my underlying question that parallels Stevens's about poetry, might be cast as, "What is a Writer?" In asking it of the conventional biblical scribe, it begins a rebellion against "Anonymous," that totalitarian eraser of authorship. But I ask it here in the existential sense, of the Homo sapiens creature probing its mind: What does it know of the past it finds itself momently emerging from, and what can it portray of the unknowable— the larger, imagined world beyond the limits of its species-conscious knowing? Commonly, this would be the world of supernatural beings, a Supreme Being, or among certain Eastern religions, the absence of same. Among some modern poets, from Emily Dickinson to D.H. Lawrence, it's the splendid ruins, and among post-war writers, the absurd ruins. And for the postmodern, the stage is bare, yet still an inherited stage on which "to strut…", in the immortal (hence cosmic) imagination of our English Bard. I term this realm of the unknowable a "cosmic theater," posed in the mind at "the scene of writing"—whether it be the cultural history enveloping the biblical writer at his ancient but no less sturdy table, or that which surrounds and upholds the screen in front of me. So those are the terms I deploy to avoid the overwhelming desire of our age to attenuate the cosmic and domesticate the underworld of consciousness—to hold at bay the caricatures of our mad neuroscientists, fiendish cyber-techies, wizards of spiritual farming and witches of activist poetics, all of whom preach leaving the past behind. In my terms, such a leave-taking robs the scene of writing of its context and makes most memoirs about what happened to "me," rather than what can't happen, like my cat writing my memoir for me. Okay, that could be a neat trick, like Gertrude Stein's *The Autobiography of Alice B. Toklas*, but I mean *really* writing it. For the writer at the scene of writing, the unknowable and all that can be dramatized there *is* real, as real as the physical cosmos our soul confronts at midnight, according to Whitman:

> THIS is thy hour O Soul, thy free flight into the wordless,
> Away from books, away from art, the day erased, the lesson done,
> Thee fully forth emerging, silent, gazing, pondering the themes
>   thou lovest best.
> Night, sleep, death, and the stars.

But long before Whitman and the English language, there was the confrontation of the soul with itself in the mirror, in the poetry of Plato but more severely by the biblical poet behind Chapter 2 of Ecclesiastes. I had to rescue his scene of writing by superimposing my own, but that is key, to rescue. We have the texts, but the writers at their scene of writing need rescue. Translations too often bring back the text without the bodies. The majestic King James Version does that, its glorious narrative seeming to embody the Hebraic culture. Yet the bodies of the Jewish writers are rendered immaterial, and the brunt force of scholarly history suggests those writers wanted it so, wanted the anonymity of being "Anonymous." No poet, however, can be more humble than his words, which reach for immortality in the very sounds they make as they speak back to the universe. In that scene of writing, seated at his/her table, the poet is a creature with a name and an education, in need of rescue, along with the lost Hebraic culture that nurtured the art.

In the explicit equation of creator and Creator by the poet behind Ecclesiastes, I want his literal name but only so I can see him at the scene of writing, in perhaps the 4th Century BCE, a Jewish reconciler of body and soul: Was he as secular as Whitman or was he as religious as Kierkegaard? If I can imagine the answer, my reading is enriched with parallels that reach from earthbound transcendentalist poet, Thoreau, to Israeli poet Harold Schimmel. I know Harold, I've seen him at his desk, I understand the pressures brought to bear—worldly, political, literary, religious—and thus the context in which his poetry struggles for a way forward while sending down biblical roots. And so I tried to translate Ecclesiastes as if I was writing it (though the original writer was a bit of a translator himself). I was in my thirties then, an ephebe of wisdom at best. I was feeling my way through the Bible, in Manhattan's East Village, having recently returned from a summer in Jerusalem, spoken Hebrew in my ears.

Then I looked up
above my personal horizon
to see the sky

outstretching the sea
as wisdom
lightens a heavy body

a wise man's eyes
are in his head
while the absent-minded

professor or egoist
disdains to wipe his glasses
while he sinks to the bottom of the sea

but wisdom as quickly evaporates
the moment a body dies
shipwrecked beneath its headstone

the most penetrating realist
hits rock bottom
six feet under

and the farthest seer
on the beachhead of life
gets his mouthful of sand

so even wisdom is a pocket
turned inside out
when it's time to pay the body's burden

the blind will lead the wise
beyond the furthest suburb of memory
into total obscurity

reentering the city of the future
as dust to be swept away
from the pages of the present

so where will I go
with this wisdom   this breath
in the sail of a fool

and so I turned again
blind as a hurricane
against the sea of life

where all works sink
like jettisoned cargo
under the lidless eyeball of the sun

the whole cargo of civilization
was a weight on my shoulders
my life's work dead weight

all life depressingly empty
hollow as cardboard dumbbells
in a bad circus

a bad dream
in which my fame honor wealth
all the earnings disappeared in a thought

in a dream circus where a clown waited
cocky in his painted face
of identity

to inherit all my works
and I am not to know
if there's a mind and heart of depth

beneath the greasepaint
or it really is the face
of life's unrelenting sideshow

in which my successor my reader
discounts my lifework…

each night
our hearts lie wide awake
lashed to the body's ship

ferrying that load of heartache
from day to day
with the constant of breathing

to fill the sail
and ripple the pages
of an empty book

the best thing for a man
is to eat drink and be
just be

satisfaction in the flow
of works and days
as it is all the work

of a creator
making me
aware of my body

and by its satisfaction
my need to be here
a pen in the hand of the Lord—

who will feel the pressure
of his will
if not I?

and if what I do is pleasing
in his eyes
I will see through my own

a work graced with beauty
a world open
to a fresh page of understanding

on which I create
my own happiness
an articulate self-knowledge

and if I project
only my own vision
with my tiny primitive hand-driven will

I will be the ancestral hunter
and gatherer   a slave
to the stalking of wealth and power…

Here, this poet depicts his scene of writing as if a movie of self-criticism, whereas what we have in movies today is a lust for verisimilitude, replacing the golden age love of the narrative itself, the drama ironized by the sheer love of the telling. Yet now we have the pained focus on identity "issues" and our contemporary ironizing of kitsch, so that Donald Duck can speak to Mozart in a poem (the real Mozart, not a bird named Mozart; *vide* John Ashbery). We need that kitsch so bad, because it once carried the authority of a real duck of nature. Now that Donald Duck has truly become a cartoon, more real as such than as a duck, we need to rescue natural ducks by means of stretching our consciousness, as our poetry and art attempt to do—and yet, we remain alone within ourselves. The real duck has lost its natural place in the narrative of our lives, and I would suggest that that duck's speaking quacks are no less real—no less a creation of the cosmos— than the writers of the Bible at their various tables in ancient Jerusalem.

At the moment, I hear my cat's meow to be let from the house into the screened-in patio. She wants to check the outdoor story she reads every day, always the same but with minor variations (major to her) of wind, passing flora and fauna, machine sounds, sirens, squirrel cluckings and birdsong, human voicings, and of course, the cornucopia of smells. We all need narrative, hence the endless fulfillment of it in current video games, cable TV drama, online threads and mega-church sermons. But can we pull back from this picture I'm posing and see ourselves watching? In that seeing we resemble writers alone in our chairs, no different than the biblical poet behind Ecclesiastes, contemplating the difference between real ducks (for the "ancestral hunter") and narrative ducks like Donald ("stalking wealth" as a real writer must, if only to pay the rent). And in the seeing of ourselves watching or reading "our hand-driven will," we've stepped outside the narrative and into a poem.

5.

Some routes I took to the Hebrew Bible: synagogue liturgy, historical studies, comparative ancient cultures, biblical and literary criticism, Freud, Buber, and among those I came to know, Steinsaltz, Frye, Robert Gordis, Harry Orlinsky, Nahum Sarna, Jeffrey Tigay, Chaim Potok, T. Carmi, and contemporary Israeli readers and friends, Michal Govrin and Harold Schimmel. Anyone can read these too, but there's also a new generation of women scholars, who are as likely to refer to the Hebrew Bible non-ironically as the "Old Testament" as they are to relate any longer to World War I as the "Great War." Scholarship, however, can take you just so far—about as far as the ticket window. Then you have to put your life savings, as it were, where your mouth is, and enter empty-handed into reading with a whole-hearted suspension of disbelief. What you get is human history condensed into the drama of Israel—and in particular, the Hebraic Jewish culture in which the biblical writers found their creative legs. What you won't get are answers to your anxieties about belief, faith, and the afterlife—those questions must be left at the door.

As I read, I take in God the Creator, Israel's God, as factual, a character as real as the water that consumes Pharaoh's army, the fire that consumes Sodom and Gomorrah, the air that Adam takes his first breath in, and Earth's Mt. Sinai that Moses ascends. There is no other honest way to read it. If God and his children of Israel do not come alive in your reading, then perhaps the writers are lousy or you are a lousy reader. You owe it to yourself to find out which. It's my contention that, more than a story or history, your reading of the Bible requires you accept it as a poem, a world in which things are said and dramatized on many levels, and into which you enter without an exit strategy, for a poem requires that you experience it like life: you know it will end but its meaning, as much as it may reverberate, will not be pinned down.

When you put the book down, the religious and existential questions will be back, and there are libraries of commentary and philosophy awaiting your consultation. There are also the living authorities, religious and secular, of whom you might ask those questions. Yet they are not the main questions as I see it. The Bible is bedrock, you can't cover it over, and the questions it engenders are how to think about the ways in which culture, science and religion are interdependent. Where is science in the Bible? you might begin by asking. True, it's not modern science, though much of ancient science points metaphorically to our day: try counting the stars, we are told, but they are infinite in number (to us too). The science of the Bible lies in its attention to history and rhetoric; the mythological sources it uses are subject to contextual interpretation and dramatization, and the language employed belies a rigorous linguistic sensibility. Just as most translations are skewed to reading literally, we modern people find it hard to estimate the imaginative methods of biblical art and culture. We can find many things the Bible got wrong about natural history, yet it won't be long before present knowledge might seem laughable to a future generation.

When I was in secondary school, Pluto was still a planet and Ceres was unknown. What's much funnier is that our solar system was assumed to be unique, as was our hominid lineage, but today's advances haven't diminished in the least the ancient poems of Homer and the Bible's myriad writers. Years of writing and teaching the literary arts, however, still weren't enough for me to get a handle on culture. It took, in addition, writing on art, film and natural ecosystems to broaden my meager perspective, and then years of studying the Bible in its original Hebrew before it could open out into its cultural and religious contexts. And then, speaking Hebrew while living in modern Israel provided a back window onto the Judeo-Christian context of North American culture. A bit later, in 1992, as writer-in-residence at Miami's Fairchild Tropical Botanical Garden, I worked with botanists and biologists to translate knowledge of plant evolution into cultural terms, from the Edenic to the existential. How do wild plants read, for example?—since they read light, air, temperature and their own root systems for a sense of their well-being. They also read invaders, benign or dangerous, and read fellow species in their environment. They domesticate species of insects and birds to protect and help themselves reproduce, just as we've domesticated cows and dogs. All this at the macro level, leaving out the crucial world of microorganisms. Just as plant life learns to recognize differences, Adam in Genesis—or early man—named the animals. But plants, you may want to interrupt, have no choice but to have faith in their circumstances, while we humans can withhold belief. If that is a true proposition, the Bible offers the truth-testing of it—as your read. Again, when you leave off reading, you're stuck with your own devices, invaded as they are by the necessary ephemeral methods in politics and academe.

For a commencement speech, David Foster Wallace wrote, "the liberal arts mantra of 'teaching me how to think' is really supposed to mean: to be just a little less arrogant, to have some 'critical awareness' about myself and my certainties." Wallace describes religious certainties as no less culpable than atheist ones. If you wanted to interject that religion is an illusion, you'd still be ignoring many nuances to the word, including the one about killing off illusions. Poetry too is an illusion, although the best kind, and I'd agree that religion might be called the poetry of the masses—as so too might be atheism. We can't live without poetry, which is why a lot of atheists feel compelled to quote contemporary ones like Philip Larkin and the deliciously unquotable Ashbery. Excerpts from the all-enveloping poem of any religion, however, are quoted all the time; I can only speak with authority about Judaism and Christianity, where often it's not the Bible that is quoted by ordinary people but less imposing poetry, such as 'The Lord's Prayer' or 'Silent Night.' But what interests me is the whole poem that characterizes a religion, what I describe as its cosmic theater. In it, there is far more nuance to the unknowable than dark matter or a black hole. We can't imagine a black hole caring about us, but the father image of the Judeo-Christian Creator is true to what a child comprehends: so much of parental action is inscrutable, unknowable to us. Even though it can all be explained when we grow up, that's when parental authority falls apart and we recognize we need more help in confronting the existential questions. Confronting is not necessarily understanding, and that's what a poem allows, such as imagining ourselves sheep with an omniscient shepherd in Psalm 23. In real life, we know that there are bad or careless shepherds too; even a religious person knows that, as soon as they walk out of church or synagogue. But when we enter the poem, it not only accounts for good and evil and indeterminacy, it reminds us that we may never know the innards of a black hole, but that such lack of knowledge is also worth knowing, like the unknowable Creator.

It surprises me, however, that even today, long after Darwin and Freud, our *creatureliness*, beyond simply our human qualities, is too easily avoided in favor of "what it's like to be alive" *in society*. I'm stuck in that daily, as soon as I awake and reach for coffee and newspaper, or rather, reading device. Proust boiled down that social concern some time ago, revealing the skeletal trail back through time to the origin of civilization. But who needs origins when we've got hold of inexplicable consciousness, a writer today might say, though I'd counter that without deep history—natural, cultural, personal— we're missing our solid skeletons, a loss of the only compass we have. I first sensed that consciousness will get us nowhere a week after a trip on lysergic acid, c. 1967, when the steering wheel of the Peugeot I was driving out to campus, for my 9 a.m. lecture on contemporary poetry, seemed to come off in my hands. I might as well have been a raccoon driving, and somehow I pulled over, turned off "Hey Jude" on the radio, and closed my eyes for a moment. Opening them, I asked myself, "How did I get here?" Then I remembered the acid trip and the flashes of simultaneity, as if past, present and future—infant, poet, old man—were all there at once, so that I thought I had finally learned something. But no, consciousness is directionless, unless you step outside of it, speak to it like biblical poets spoke to the universe. It's only then you can properly ask, How did we get here? You had to get created, comes the answer, and from then it took me about five years to ask of the Hebrew Bible how it got written, my secular question.

Rhonda asked me what I'd have done if I hadn't been born Jewish with a proclivity to learn Hebrew. Well, Sidney and Shelley, in their famous essays in defense of poetry, refer often to the "divine" poetry of the Bible. "The poet he nothing affirms, and therefore never lieth," writes Philip Sidney in the 16th century, perfectly understanding that the Bible is a cosmic poem. "Poetry is a mirror which makes beautiful that which is distorted," wrote Shelley in the 19th century, meaning "true" for "beautiful," in the cosmic sense. But unlike Sidney and Shelley, John Dryden read deep into the classics in his 'An Essay of Dramatic Poesy,' in yet another century, the 17th, and his lengthier and more deeply argued defense, while deploying a complex range of classical poets, contains nary a mention of the Bible. The most apparent reason is the Greeks and Romans have names, the Bible's writers next to none. So I wanted to say, let's just invent a passel of names for them, but eventually I discovered there *are* names, lent by the Higher Biblical Criticism, in the form of letters, like J, E, and S, or numbers: Isaiah 1, 2, 3, and even 6, for example. I'm not sure this would have been enough for Dryden, and it certainly isn't for poets today, in the almost two centuries going back to Blake. Yet without a deep history of civilization, we can't get a read on our bones—not just the evolutionary skeleton but the psychic one. It's not enough for a poet to visit the ancient caves in Europe and interpret the wall paintings, because that poet still needs to see him- or herself as coming through human cultural history: that which put the book-writing on papyrus into paper form, on the table beside us, as well as set the keyboard in front of us.

Some writers I've known seem to act like little creators, even godlike in their renunciations. Don't see something, don't say something. They abandon all that is unknowable, God along with any other representation of how they came to be. Evolution doesn't quite answer it, and chance doesn't either, because they, like the microbes who ate up carbon dioxide and made our atmosphere breathable, also came from somewhere. But I love them for their fierce renunciations, the writers. They teach creative writing as a discipline in which the writer's self-creation is secondary to the text's creation. I went over the boundaries when I was teaching it; I tried to focus more on who my students thought they were or could become, until one accused me of acting too much like a psychotherapist. After that, I exposed myself as a Bible translator, provoking them to ask me questions about whatever they never could before, concerning God and death and the soul, or anything existential, but I didn't get takers. Even at Princeton, they didn't want to personally articulate the question.

A year after the Fairchild residency, Rhonda and I moved down from New York into the former director of Fairchild's house, where we still live. In '95, we adopted the Everglades ecosystem, studying its wild flora/fauna and evolutionary history, while teaching writing workshops for scientists, starting with their journal notes and then extending them imaginatively into the broader culture, such as movies. The journals of repeated visits to Madagascar and the Amazon were filled with the astonished despair of tropical botanists whose education, even the young ones, had not prepared them for the devastated ecosystems of their "field work." I asked them to view Lanzmann's *Shoah*, for instance, and compare the talking heads of Auschwitz survivors with themselves, with the point being "listening to what survives." One wrote how she envisioned a doc with talking botanists and destroyed habitat, so that I was able to suggest not leaving out her responses to *Shoah*, since more people were aware of that than any nature doc. You've got to refer to mainstream movies too, I added, and think about them as popular representations of your culture—the same culture that could not tell a male plant from a female one, or that there even were such unisexual species. A couple of paleobiologists brought up fear of fossils, in terms of '50s films that represent them as frozen monsters thawed out by thermonuclear tests (global warming not yet on the horizon). They questioned whether the wariness of fossils, especially the nervousness or embarrassment suggested by our simian ancestry, is connected to fears of immorality. I suggested looking up contemporaneous reviews, since the *New York Times* of half a century ago is also a fossil: it reports its present day without the prophet's art of seeing itself as already part of the past. In the considerably longer view of poetry, there's no difference between biblical Isaiah and Darwin; for each, the past is a gorgeous gift, a fossil as huge as a planet, to be approached in all diligence as an interstellar explorer.

No matter if it's three thousand years ago in Jerusalem or yesterday in New York, history is always a foreign planet we're driven to colonize, at least imaginatively—if we're going to rediscover ourselves or at least survive. That's what even a '50s film like *Sunday in New York*, which I watched last night, is about: how to enter anew into intimacy, how to read the situation. Since it was marketed and perceived as a light comedy, that's all most viewers wanted out of it (the eggheads stayed away). The circumstances may be different in the 21st century but the emotional and moral focus required is the same, if you're looking for it. Unlike a poem, the drama of this Broadway play-based movie sews it all up by making "true love" itself a character, one that wins the day. Still, we can contextualize the movie as a poem because the situation is always unfolding like one, in which the characters struggle to hold conventional meaning at bay. We can't expect the Times's critic back in the day to have caught this—he's tied up by his own conventional thinking about the sexual freedom war (as if that made the ancient war between the sexes irrelevant). Bosley Crowther writes, "Well, the extent of the film's disconcertion and delight for a viewer will depend upon how prone one may be to a juvenile quandary… The twists of the plot are downright hackneyed… But the actors are all attractive, and so long as one can go along with them in their valiant attempts at pretending this is hot stuff, one may have a good time."

What is that "juvenile quandary"? Crowther and other critics, perhaps misled by Hollywood's promo for the film, think it's about when to go to bed with either a "fiancé" or "a stranger." The contemporary person, he implies, goes to bed first—and only *then,* having gotten sex out of the way, needs to ask questions later. The implication is that "the sexual revolution" has taken intimacy off the table, so that now, instead of anxieties about sex we can have anxiety about personal fulfillment. Questions about true love, which figure prominently in the film, don't even come up in the reviews, as if the subject has become as quaint as Valentine's Day cards—and as nonexistent as what's found in Sixties' New Wave films from Europe. Deneuve in *Belle de Jour* has a personality disorder, however intriguing, and not a question about true love. Or more precisely, the director Buñuel has less interest in such a question than in laying bare consciousness and the social conventions of his day—an artistic convention already over a hundred years old, going back to Flaubert's *Madame Bovary*. An artist, at least, can possibly learn more from Flaubert today than his near-contemporary, Karl Marx. And try to imagine Marx viewing *Sunday in New York*—yikes! Watch out, Mrs. Marx, when he gets home. The bourgeoises are in for it.

Most movie critics in 1963 were too happily ironized to get *Sunday's* sugar-coated concern with the difficulty and uncanniness of intimacy— "nothing huge," says one review!—and Bosley wouldn't get the openness and unconventionality of Jane Fonda and Rod Taylor's attempt to maintain their unwieldy integrity. "It's a film 'about' sex before marriage, upholding virtue," etc.—no no no! It's about feeling the complex negotiation of convention and instinct that constitutes falling in love. It's beyond infatuation, beyond lust; there's a need to disarm necessary protective conventions, that are there precisely because of the danger in "falling". As for the somewhat later "cool" version of *Sunday in New York*, namely Woody Allen's *Manhattan*, true love has become a question that's expired of its own breathlessness—like the death of God. Puppy love has taken its place, in the character of Brooke Shields, while the movie's true adult, Allen himself, has read true love's expiration date and has offered the substitute of art, in which we may lose ourselves along with our pretentious questions. The questions remain, of course—or else we would not prize the director so highly—hidden behind Allen's anxiety. It's the questions themselves we're now in search of, and whether they're to be found in philosophy, psychoanalysis, neuroscience or religion, they seem no longer necessary for art. Instead we have art's probe of consciousness in all its fulsomeness, and it fits our time well: we can get lost in it and still feel we are getting somewhere new, like Columbus discovering the "New Indies." At least Columbus's new world helped us discover the old world "savages" within us, though it took five centuries and some scientists like Darwin, Weber and Freud for that to happen.

Pardon me for speaking of "we" too often, even as I intend the Homo sapiens species and not the conventional social category in which there's a "higher" we, a more open-minded we, or an ironic we. We as a species are doomed to go extinct, let's not nit-pick about it. What grand exploits we have on the way to that final date is beside the point; therefore, it's no use my getting creative with self-deprecation and how dumb, lunk-headed, or pretentious I can be. Not when it's no longer possible to pretend we (and our artistic personae) are going to survive *Homo sapiens sapiens* extinction. Once, we could imagine it, of course, and probably the biblical poets did it best: *thy rod and thy staff, they comfort me* made it not only possible to happily identify with sheep but to recognize that we've been *domesticated*, by a higher being, and thus might also become transmogrified. That doesn't mean we're not going to suffer; *they went like sheep to the slaughter*, when applied hardly half a century ago to Holocaust smoke, still implied our species might transcend that fate. Now that we know 99% of all known species on Earth are extinct, and that the average mammalian species lifespan is barely a million years, I should be able to identify "we" with my unable-to-forget-this-fact writing persona, without risking much grandiosity. That's why I insist upon the visionary quality of poetry, which allows us to see the present moment as long past, and why I laud the historical imagination as it reveals where we come from, whether the Book of Exodus or the golden age of film and television.

Yet historicizing the context of 1950's conventions is not enough, nor is unmasking the contemporary context of our own cultural prejudices and ideals (even if we could). What matters is what happens to our sense of the uncanny when uncanniness has been co-opted as a *style*, one that puts a retro granny dress on innocence. We are always superior, as I've said, because we can't see ourselves as characters of the past, as in the poetry of the biblical prophets most explicitly, but as in all great poetry. The rest of us don't want to see ourselves dead already, that would not be (ahem) progressive, since it would cut off our ongoing project to create the future in our image. And that is precisely why poetry is so marginalized in our culture, and why we can't properly appreciate *Sunday in New York*. To do that, we need to see ourselves every bit as constrained by our historical and cultural perception, and then to step outside of ourselves—not to become fashionably disembodied but to imagine another character, with a body just like ours, timeless, but uncanny in its resemblance. I say "timeless" the way great poems are timeless, so that to take their journeys allows us to be transported anywhere in time that they were written, whether ancient Jerusalem and Athens or Enheduanna's Akkad and Confucius's China. Or, *Sunday in New York*. When we look up from reading such poems or analects, we are capable for a moment of seeing ourselves as the past; and when we live in a time like ours when the avant-garde has become a historical canon, then the truest art we can create is a form of restoration, bringing the past back alive, in its timelessness. I mean a poet with a poem like "On Looking into *Sunday in New York*" as much as with a new interpretation of *As You Like It*. Let's say for argument's sake it's a poor interpretation of Norman Krasna's *Sunday* or Shakespeare's play, the question remains of whether we can imagine it "better," more intensely, more beyond our mundane selves—although needing to return to those mundane selves and thus forgiving of them, just as we forgive Jane Fonda's uncertainty in *Sunday* and Rosalind's outrageous plot in *As You Like It*. For we have no certainty, not even that of abstaining from certainty, in the manner boiled down by the early avant-garde novelist Robert Musil: "One dies for ideals, because they are not worth living for."

6.

Let me explain my rebellion against biblical interpretation as an impossibility. Every sentient being knows whatever it does by interpreting. There is one place, however, where the impossible is ambiguous, and that's in a poem, a kind of theater in which opposites (natural and supernatural, for instance) can meet on stage without killing each other. It's by making a poem of interpretation, then, that I rebel… Permit me, however, to slow down this intro to my memoir for a moment. "There is a quotation from the psychiatrist D.W. Winnicott," writes Adam Phillips, "the wisdom of which, at that point in my development as a psychiatrist, I had yet to appreciate. 'It appalls me to think how much deep change I have prevented or delayed,' Winnicott wrote, 'by my personal need to interpret.'"

I take that "delayed" more ironically than Winnicott, perhaps; I translate delayed as "slowed down." Slow-motion, so as to see and absorb the change, as of one thing into its opposite, as one can see in a poem. A poem resists providing its own interpretation, since that would prevent deep movement—being moved, and becoming aware of it. When I drew closer to a view of the biblical poet, I found the strength of his Hebraic poetics was in parallelism and that to present it today, in English, required slowing the language down, as if into slow-mo. The illusion of repetition that parallelism creates zeroes in on the kernel of the image—or when it's not an image but a concept, the core of it. It's as if the image or concept was set vibrating, and out of the reverberation spills its core, its necessity. Most translators unwittingly speed up the ancient poetry by skipping over the harmonics, ignoring the subtlety of reverberations, and in effect, biblical poetry turns into a kind of rhetorical prose. So it came as no surprise that my stanzas were sometimes criticized for seeming to move too slow, especially compared to the conventional modernisms of nonstop verbal intensity. The ferocious ear of my early teacher and second mentor, Robert Lowell, was followed by avant-garde influences, Pound and Williams, and I touch on these—along with those in the music of Blues, of Satie and Ravel, and the paintings of Picasso—within the chapters ahead. Within 'The Poem of Audience,' in particular, I respond to critics who fail to read this avant-garde slowing-down as a means of refocusing, of zeroing in—as alert to details as an electron microscope, one exploring the minute traumas of misunderstanding that are preserved below the surface of language and cultural convention.

We've all fled the scene of an accident, such as the one of our birth. If poems could turn us around, in the direction of origins, toward Eden, the best one I know by a writer of our day (alas, too soon dead) is *The Martyrology*, by bpNichol, an author still unknown in the US or UK because he lived and published his six-volumed epic in Canada. My acquaintance with bp and his poem, starting when I lived in Toronto, continues to grow in me. It's a poem almost biblically unwavering in its focus on history made personal. In our time, that focus has opened onto the scene of writing, so that Canadian critic Frank Davey describes Nichol's poem, which takes in the full range of human history, as if "all its elements... are happening on the day of the writing." Likewise, when the biblical author J, in ancient Jerusalem, is writing of Moses at Pharaoh's court, we are there with her, as well as aware she is seated in Jerusalem. (Or unaware; history has mythologized the writing of the Bible since barely a few generations after J's existence.) Why should we need to be so aware? Because it brings back to us the Hebraic culture into which a biblical writer like J is born— and at the same time, it pushes aside the didactic assumption that her "inspiration" was either mystical or semi-plagiarizing of an earlier source, painting ancient Jewish culture in gauzy primitive tones. In an interview with Davey, Nichol had further described the writerly scene as presenting "a sense of the human being as a construct of what he or she knows at a given point in time: the absolute present of the writing & the reading," i.e. the "reading" as also representing the writer's use of sources. Again, why do we want to know the biblical (or any) writer as a particular human being in a particular time and place? More than enriching the text, more than bringing alive the lost time in which it was written, it renders a vision of us, its readers, as also historical. We might think we need this less for a still-living writer like Philip Roth, and yet articles and interviews with Roth abound, in which he recasts didactic assumptions no less deadly to his text than consensus biblical criticism.

Roth says of *Portnoy's Complaint*, "I was looking not for my catharsis as a neurotic or as a son, as some suggested, but rather for emancipation from traditional approaches to storytelling. While the protagonist may be straining to escape his moral conscience, I was attempting to break free from a literary conscience that had been constructed by my reading, my schooling and my fastidiousness—from a habitual sense of prose decorum." You may want to interject that the biblical author J was not so subjective as Philip Roth, and yet here Roth is supremely objective about the scene of writing, so that we also can imagine J straining for "emancipation from traditional approaches to storytelling" and the "prose decorum" that was the convention in other cultures and in her older sources. It accounts for just what is so alive and exciting about biblical writing, so unlike the works of so many cultures that would have sat beside it in the ancient library at Alexandria (torched, to our loss, two millennia ago). And a re-imagining of the biblical scene of writing forces us to recall the creativity of those other Jewish writers in ancient Jerusalem, to envision them also as having been "constructed" by their reading and schooling.

I've written considerably more about the authorial scene of writing within this book, and of how mere biblical scribes must evolve in our understanding into creative writers, no more or less human than our own. Meanwhile, this morning brings disheartening evidence once again that the current trend in academic teaching of the Bible continues to dispose of the original writers. In Everett Fox's nearly 900 pages of *The Early Prophets*, it's distressing to find not a single imagining of a biblical writer. There are a few mentions of generic "the writers," but they are always blotted out of view by what their texts are "about." And when it comes to what the writers themselves were about in their writing, they are assigned a political or sociological "agenda," rather than having any literary motives. In his intro, Fox quotes a mentor for his excuse: "In Jacob L. Wright's words (2009), 'the inherent resistance of biblical literature to clear authorial identification is its hallmark.'" As if it's impossible to imagine that the author's names were forgotten or erased, and even if they were so self-deprecating as to not breathe their names or their patron's names (what, no one to thank for sustenance?), wouldn't we want to know how such inhibition and constraint could yield so much historical drama and imaginative license?

All that Fox has translated from the Hebrew is a text full of author-less "stories" that he has self-consciously made to sound ancient, and all that he offers is what the "stories" appear to "mean," rather than having any literary awareness that what they say and what they mean produces an irony. For historical context, Fox contends that "a starting time for the writing down of biblical texts...[is] when literacy became more widespread." Can we ignore the telltale nervousness?—not "writing" but "writing down," and the judicious guess that it must have happened when lots of people could read. Yet the history of writing at royal courts throughout the ancient Middle East and Asia shows that writers were not anxious about having too few readers, though they were also writing in the name of their people's culture, as if any one citizen might read it. What is more, Fox speculates that the biblical stories were "cast [again, an evasion of being written] in written form, probably by elites," and yet these elites have no education that our contemporary scholar cares to imagine. Instead, we are told they are fulfilling a "nationalist agenda," as if they were propagandists. Maybe one or two were, or maybe it was their *sources* that were propaganda, but the majority were conscious of their written art, especially the great writer known in biblical criticism as the "Court Historian" or "S", as well as his Solomonic colleagues and writerly progeny. The history of King David, which S inscribes, may have a political tint, but no more so than applies in Shakespeare's history plays. Yet when appraising Shakespeare's work, we hardly begin with his political agenda; it may be worthwhile to imagine he was thinking of Queen Elizabeth, just as S may have been thinking of King Solomon, but we'd be nonplussed at being told that Shakespeare's plays were written as propaganda.

I can say this in Professor Fox's favor: his work raises a suspicion about other translations that can lead the reader back to the Hebrew. On the other hand, my colleague Robert Alter's translation, melodious as it may sound when compared to translation-by-committee, saddens me with its forbidding ambition, for it can deaden one's inmost desire to break past the academic roadblock of textual complication. We need to get past it, even if only to imagine the Hebraic education of the Bible's authors, and the scenes of writing at which their art bore fruit. Why not leave it alone? Again, I think it's about loss: it's the great Hebraic culture we've lost, in which the Bible's writers learned their art—and the reason that loss needs a reimagining is to invigorate our pessimism about the future.

I don't think it's simply in my nature to be confrontational, but if some of my comments sound so, here's my colleague in creative writing, the Booker-winning British author Howard Jacobson, who writes that he may have been "amicably provocative from the start—picking a fight with those who make the world more sanctimonious, more foolish and, in every sense, more impoverished than it needs to be." Perhaps I might be criticized here for quoting a novelist rather than an academic scholar; I assert, however, that it's their own creative arts-deficiency that scholars tend to ignore when confronting writers in the distant past, especially when those writers have been rendered anonymous. And perhaps I can be criticized for not naming enough translators and critics I not only approve of but am inspired by. I do name several in this book, of course, though not as many as in the lists I've passed out in translation workshops. One student of mine at Princeton asked if he really had to read Lydia Davis's new translation of Flaubert, since he was translating poems from the Persian. It doesn't matter, I said, you can *imagine* that Flaubert was Persian if you like, it's the *art* of translation we're studying. Yet I was wrong to state it so broadly; it's too academic. Flaubert at the scene of writing was, in all likelihood, a French provocateur, at least in the literary sense of storytelling that Philip Roth cites. Lydia Davis sees that. A Persian provocateur is another story.

Among his pronouncements on creativity, a communications professor at University of California-Berkeley is quoted in the *New York Times* as saying most people are risk-averse. "He refers to them as satisfiers. 'As much as we celebrate independence in Western cultures, there is an awful lot of pressure to conform,' he says. 'Satisfiers avoid stirring things up, even if it means forsaking the truth or rejecting a good idea.'" When I started out translating the Bible forty years ago, I was self-righteously appalled by the modern translations. You could say I was provoked by them, though that was not their intention. Instead, they appeared risk-averse to me, for there is no risk in taking the text for granted. But what's wrong with that? After all, modern scholarship for centuries has labored to present the text with integrity. It's that concept of "text," however, that is worrisome, for unlike the creative ways in which a stable text is destabilized by Freud or Derrida, it is disingenuous to the biblical text itself to expunge its scenes of writing in ancient Jerusalem. By doing so, a new translation sweeps under the carpet a creative Hebraic culture of writers that may not so much be fulfilling an agenda as expressing independence of mind. Neither are the biblical writers cogs in a communal mindset, as is conventionally asserted; they all exhibit difference in their use of sources, some more ironic, some even deadpan, and some creatively intertextual. You have to dig a lot deeper into the Hebrew than a freeze-drying of the authorless text allows, right down to the scene of writing. It's there that the original writer's creative struggles with his text can be discerned, as when the S writer, whom I translated in *The Book of David*, can be found ironizing a phrase of officialese—or paralleling an archaic term, such as the equivalent of "once upon a time," with a contemporary one, such as "many times over" or "it so happened," as in "Uriah [Bathsheba's murdered husband] *happened* to die," when S has already made it clear that it was less a happening than a plot against him.

Since Hebrew Bible stories are mostly concerned with historical truth and truth-testing, if they were movies they'd be unlike Bible movies and more like *The Grapes of Wrath* or *Tokyo Story*, about the tragicomic difficulties of the good life for even the most ordinary people. The Bible is a comedy in this Greek sense: David is not simply a "complex character"— all biblical figures are—but a real historical man, requiring a real history and a real author's struggle to carve it out. That struggle is the biblical writer's work, for each of them are the most truly complex characters to imagine. One day, some great movies will depict it. My agent once asked me to do a "film treatment" of J and S writing portions of the Bible, and Rhonda and I labored over it for a few months, but there were no takers. That was twenty years ago, and this year we've seen the trailers for several blockbusters about Genesis (Noah, Goliath) and Exodus (two Moses films), none of them referencing the writers and their Hebraic culture. The same can be said for the NT Gospels, with movies coming on Mary and Pontius Pilate, yet with no concern for their Jewish authors.

7.

In his latest volume, *Ardor*, Roberto Calasso seconds my motion for uncovering the scene of writing behind even texts held sacred. He credits that ancient Vedic scene with "The first image of what will one day be the study [room], not just of St. Jerome [the biblical translator; for Dürer's version, see my *An Educated Man*] but of every writer: that room which is a witness to writing and protects it with 'the cloak of initiation and of ardor.'" Yet Calasso lets the Sanskrit Vedas and their writers off the hook, claiming we know nothing of their civilization. We may know far less of it than ancient Israel, yet one can still wish for a poet-translator who will reimagine the writers by immersing herself in comparative linguistic study, coming up with a compelling theory. For myself, I became enamored with theory way back at my Bar Mitzvah studies, as I note in a chapter ahead.

Not long after, with no stomach for killing frogs and dissecting cats in tenth-grade biology, I was looking forward to eleventh grade physics, impressed by what I'd picked up about Einstein, astrophysics, and the magic word, to me, of "theory," as in quantum theory. There hadn't been much attention to the theory of evolution in biology class, or perhaps it was still taboo back in the late '50s, even in somewhat enlightened Michigan. Yet physics turned out to be heavily weighed down with the basic mathematics of theory, thinned out of even the abstract beauty I found in eleventh-grade geometry. There was so much to get straight in one's head that there was no room for the turbulent feelings of adolescence that I had trouble suppressing, especially after my steady, Judy, dropped me.

In retrospect, she came from a Swedish Lutheran family that never even wanted to meet me, while I was from the first few Jewish families admitted into our until-then *Judenrein* suburban township high school. It may have been a walk on the wild side for Judy, though I was closer to the nerdy stereotype than the varsity halfback Christian boy to whom she migrated. And then, still in eleventh grade, poetry smacked me in the face. I mean, I could *feel* it—though I wasn't sure what feelings were addressed—at the same time as it required a complex study of forms and themes that went back to the ancient classics. It was a world away, I thought, from the messy feelings that spilled out of my parents' unsatisfactory (unhappy?—I hardly knew) marriage. In poetry, wild feelings were domesticated into a form of intelligence, like my cat Bootsie; she'd be out at night doing God knows what but in the morning she'd be waiting at the front door, ready to enter the big animals' ordered lair. In the first poems I wrote, sonnets and "Greek lyrics", I was excited how confused feelings of adolescent joy and despair bubbled up into forms that the adult world of Western Culture admired, transmuted into theories of the "ecstatic" and the "tragic".

I was still fifteen when I discovered a kind of poetry in rock 'n' roll and the Blues, which struck chords down to my childhood inner city street education, which I'm about to investigate. It was roughly the time I got hold of anthologies of contemporary poets, men and women in accompanying photos who looked like they'd figured out how to think about science and everything else without the need of blocking off the civilized workaday world from the wilderness of feelings. Earlier I'd thought of becoming an architect but I could no longer reconcile sitting at a drafting board all day when the despairing feelings of losing Judy climbed up my throat. I'd already read of how writers and artists would drink and smoke as they worked, but not even my father, without a college degree, could afford to be the least bit high around his industrial-grade popcorn popping machines, or when delivering to movie houses and persuading the concessionaires that his product was still superior to that coming out of the first oil-sputtering portable poppers. Not that I wanted to drink or smoke weed; I dreamt instead of becoming a very straight writer, a poet like Wallace Stevens or Robert Lowell (whose madness I was still innocent of, though later I'd become his student assistant). Moreover, the poets I read seemed to be above religion and ideology; this might have been a problem when you consider that Milton, Donne and Eliot were my high school favorites, but I was innocent of it, just as I was of difference (theoretically speaking, not Holocaust-speaking) as glamorized by '50s continental literary theorists. While the exoticism of difference, whether social, racial or religious, had crept into poetry long before, it was not yet the crumbling hierarchy that would lead to a post-racial Obama. But I had already assumed Milton and Donne were post-religious, using religious myth the same way as Dante and Ovid; and that they did not go to church or synagogue. That Donne served as a cleric and Milton as church historian had escaped my attention, which tended to push history aside.

And that would include personal history, such as my Hebrew School and synagogue education. As the junior congregation cantor prior to my voice changing, I chanted and sang the Biblical and Biblically-derived poetry of Prophets and prayers, but it was drummed into us diminutive worshippers that these texts were too exalted to be deemed poetry—just as many critics would still agree today, hesitant to imagine the original writers within their literary context. I did have inklings, however, that I was stuck within a huge poem, complete with voices from heaven, voices in dreams, and a voice from a burning bush. It was not the kind of poem, however, I could yet imagine that writers could compose, using their ancient cultural sources as paralleled by T.S. Eliot accessing Frazier's history of myth. It had nothing to do with belief, to my mind; already in junior congregation, my own belief did not hang in the balance, only my ability to act out my belief—just as I had acted the part of Brutus in a grade-school version of Julius Caesar.

Some say that a focus on the original writers of the Bible questions a reader's belief and destabilizes the need to hold the text sacred. There are many beliefs concerning the Bible, however, and the only one uniformly in question is divine authorship. Even here, Jewish tradition by itself subtilizes the issue: *how* that divinity is transmitted has many tributaries. When I chanted a portion of Isaiah at my Bar Mitzvah, at not quite 13, I understood that cultural tradition and not the Creator had stated a preference for chanting and for "becoming a man." As for how the words got there, I also learned in "Modern Hebrew School" that the original paleo-Hebrew alphabet was replaced by the Aramaic alphabet after the Babylonian exile, a fact that led me to my pre-teen wrongheaded theory that it was time for Torah scrolls to transliterate the Hebrew into English. I was already too giddy an absent-minded modernist. Yet I would not then or now argue for changing one jot or tittle of the Bible as it has come down to us. That sentiment is well-encapsulated in Leon Wieseltier's essay, "The Argumentative Jew," which, although it elucidates the Jewish tradition of disputation back to "the ancient rabbis," finds no reason to go further, back into the history of ancient Israel, and dispute the Aramaic alphabet of the Hebrew Bible. For all the genius and creativity of rabbinical interpretation, as displayed most anciently in the Talmud, the original Jewish poetry and prose of the Bible remains an unquestioned mystery—even as it is assumed to be a divine mystery. At least a Divine authorship or Mosaic authorship or Prophetic authorship—break it down as you will—recognizes that creators were at work. If the interpretive power of the rabbinic tradition honors that creativity, it also eclipses the poets and writers of the Hebraic cultures—and their artistic educations—that produced it. I can see how Talmudic disputation could influence and lead through the generations to a strong essayist like the living Wieseltier, but where is the connective tissue between the Hebraic Biblical writers and those of today? I submit it can't be found until a reimagining of ancient Israeli creative culture allows for a Biblical scene of writing. And for that, we need to explore the writers' educations: their artistic and worldly educations, and not merely their conjectured religious education.

As for the literary and worldly educations of the Vedic poets, even Calasso ventures little. Instead, he evokes quite daringly the scenes of their daily and ritual lives. It helps us dig deeper into the Sanskrit text but not into the mind of a poet, whatever his or her religious disposition. Many critics delve into Dante the Christian, as they do into Dante the poet, but sans bones or biographies of the actual Biblical or Vedic poets, why shirk the reimagining of their artistic resources? However ancient those great poets, their DNA was not one jot or tittle different from ours. And if they were not ardent arguers, their eyes and ears for literary art were opened that much more widely.

A new book climbing the bestseller list claims that, "In the early days it seems there was no such thing as a single Bible, no one fixed text, but this wild and variable tradition of the stories, with many different versions." Is that news to anyone, even if it's misbegotten? However, I changed a word in the quotation, from "Iliad" to "Bible," to indicate how deeply desired it is among historians and scholars to find a way around facing individual authorship. This critic, who seems to have little experience with imaginative literature, suggests that "Homer be thought of not as a person but as a tradition." Some Biblical scholars would gleefully pinch themselves to see that affirmed about the Bible, relieving them of responsibility to imagine how a writer works with sources, then or now. If you can fall for the notion that a "tradition" wrote the *Odyssey*, you might be willing to subscribe to the same about Shakespeare: there were many earlier versions of King Hamlet/Prince Hamlet stories, goes the argument set in the distant future, so the seemingly "fixed text" we have is merely the product of a Hamlet tradition. I'm afraid that's how I encountered "The Bible as Literature" as an undergrad, with a more nuanced fiction offered in grad school: it was an ancient pseudo-professor or two, dubbed "redactors," who are the worthy stand-ins for divine authorship. I rebelled against that diminution of Hebraic writers (further degraded by the contention they were oral, semi-literate poets) because it was just at this time, in the 1960s, that certain trendy critics seemed to suggest I could be an oral poet myself, given that I composed my poems in my head before the pen/device hit paper. Once documented on a page, texts were already a cultural production and I might as well have been anonymous. Even Allen Ginsberg played into this with the mantle of a bard, though anyone who'd encountered Allen in person, as I had, could not mistake his magnetic, individual personality. It was clear in his later years, as he burrowed deeper into Buddhism, that Allen was struggling to undress himself of that personality, and perhaps he consigned his royalties to a Buddhist school, but lost or Anonymous is unlikely to replace his name.

That current Homer exposé goes on: "Today we have an author obsession—we want to know biography all the time. But Homer has no biography." Since I and the Bible's writers are also targeted there, I recognize my rebellion anew; it's not against the Bible's poetry/prose but the covering up of it under a blanket anonymity. However much you venerate Anonymous, you can't fully confront its textual strength without envisioning a particular scene of writing. The "struck by lightning" approach to prophetic texts, which still works liturgically for those praying in church and synagogue, where only snatches of biblical text are encountered, won't do anymore for the literate reader, someone in solitude before their book or screen, for whom the distraction of consulting notes and commentary has been eased by a tap on any word or term for instant definition and layers of Google-accessible context. And with context comes a growing awareness of an ancient writer facing you across the ages—even though his work has been chopped and edited by redactors—whose name was known to at least his or her peers, if not her dog or cat.

I'm not making a blanket plea for poetry; most poetry hovers around the mediocre, and it's crucial to elucidate what is best. It's not always obvious, especially when ironic or deadpan. How do you teach people Deadpan? You can't, anymore than you can teach the Blues. It requires an uncanny focus of thought and feeling; too much of either, and the focus is lost. The same can hold true for religion. Like poetry, only some of it is strong and true, and that part is a truth-testing: a focus achieved by an uncanny alignment of thought and feeling. And just as religion is often bloated with sentimental feeling, science can be weighed down by aggrieved thought. In his latest book, biologist E.O. Wilson attacks religion as if there's no imaginative truth-testing in the Bible; science, however, is his knight-in-shining-armor of thought, where sentiment is repressed—as if the thinking mind didn't need the sensuous body with which to achieve a focus, an alignment of thought and feeling that has been worked out through evolutionary time. While Wilson is thinking of what for him amounts to the plague of religion, he also pushes art to the sideline—and with it, the art of the Bible. Does science have to be so literal-minded, more so than a strictly religious reading of the Bible itself? "Even the best-educated live on an *ad libitum* diet of novels, movies, concerts, sports events and gossip all designed to stir one or more of the relatively small range of emotions that diagnose Homo sapiens," he writes.

The sword of science, says Wilson, "cuts paths through the fever swamp of human existence." Science as iconoclast?

"I discovered that the affiliated Jew is the iconoclast of every age, and by the mid-1970s I realized that neither Leonard Cohen nor anyone else would be the sufficient truth-teller of my generation," writes Harvard critic Ruth Wisse. If we substitute "rebel" for "iconoclast," and apply it to my book's subtitle, then it might come out "Memoir of a Jewish Writer's Bible Translation." The popular culture, however, hasn't yet signed on to the term "Jewish" to connote iconoclast, though perhaps it can suggest an exotic or at least ambiguous minority. Not for anti-Semites, of course, for whom a rebellious Jew would equate with turning over their post-Jewish Messiah to the Romans. But in a chapter in this book, "The Poem of the Jewish Writer," I concur with Wisse that being a Jewish writer, especially today, requires an iconoclast—and it's even more true for a Bible translator. My early Jewish eidolon was the American Yiddish poet, Yehoash, who translated the Hebrew Bible into idiomatic Yiddish during the roaring twenties. Now that I'm some kind of an American postmodernist, my Jewish rebellion post-Holocaust, I return to biblical text with a sensibility of loss and an indeterminate poetics of possibility. If that last phrase sounds pompously vague, it's a mere stand-in for the lost self-confidence in which the artistic moderns, when they despaired, at least confidently despaired against the firm wall of literary history. Looking back, it may not have fully crumbled, poets today may seem to be in a repairing mode—yet we still have a ways to go, even to account for how quickly, in barely a score of years, Yehoash's supremely rich and self-possessed modernist Bible translation disappeared along with its audience, into the Holocaust and, locally, into the Jewishly-neutral English language.

A generous vein of ironic possibility is still open, building upon what can only be termed the deadpan. It allowed me to recognize the ancient irony deployed by the biblical Jewish writers, their faces (when we make the deep effort to imagine them) fixed not so much in a death mask or modern poker face but in a pose sometimes appearing grim, sometimes radiant, sometimes tragic or even comic (as in the deadpan prophet Jonah)—but always the same unflinching pose of truth-testing, the stern joy of it. As if to ask, What can the world throw at us now?

In this book I'm insisting that life is now more like a poem than a story with a beginning, middle, and end. The concluding lines of a Shakespearean sonnet or a Psalmist's psalm are an anti-conclusion, resonating back through the poem to its opening wish for more life, and informing us that our lives continually belie conclusion—as proof for which, his poem postpones the conclusion of Shakespeare's bodily death (and, as the bedrock of my creative endeavors, keeps alive the bodily existence of ancient Hebraic writers). A narrative is something we tell ourselves and is reflected in our social or public life, but a real estimation of the time we're now traveling through is never so clear. In a poem, the need for clarity, however, doesn't have to be as strong as the necessity of focus. Focussing feeling and thought together—this is the catharsis a poem offers, when that focus suddenly or uncannily appears, or as we say, "comes into focus." What is it we see then? As this book attempts to show, it all depends on caring about more than what we're looking at, because in a poem the scene of writing—the poet sitting at her desk or wherever—is included in the scene and helps to focus it. We are unaware of the poet, the writer, as we should be when we read, yet it's suddenly at the point of focus that we become aware of her, or should. Who is she? That is the question of my memoir: what am I, as I walk through the poem of my life? Part of an epic? As when Mark Greif, in *The Age of the Crisis of Man*, contends "the intellectual history of modernity may be written in part as the epic tale of a series of rebellions against humanism." I might say I rebelled against post-humanism: both the intellectual post-structuralist kind, which replaces the body with text, and the sentimental kind, with its sexless bodies, like those of scribes and scholars. For neither kind does the scene of writing figure as much more than the bodily need to leave it periodically for the rest room.

All season my cat has been making a philosophical investigation of our swimming pool, peering into it, contemplating me in it, perambulating it. Her question boils down to, Can I know it without jumping into it? She will jump at a small moving target in an instant, but with water she is as slow to reach a conclusion as Kant. I've always thought of myself as a slow starter, or at least affecting one. When I boxed out of the JCC in the Jr. Golden Gloves, my style was to appear overly cautious and perhaps fearful, drawing my opponent ever closer and more confident, until I could surprise him with a wicked left hook. This usually worked because I rarely faced the same opponent twice, or even competed in the same venue more than once. However, my career as a junior boxer came to a complete halt when I was knocked cold by a YMCA inner city opponent who ignored my strategy, slipped my hook, and countered with a punch I never saw. A mustache I grew early at 15 was intended to cover up the scar from the blow that ended my career in boxing. At the same time I was writing my first poems, so the mustache fit my poet's figure more accurately than a boxer's. And the underlying approach was similar: start out discursively, as if I was hardly conscious that i was writing a poem at all or that the reader was reading one, and then slowly but surely, creating a context in which the now somewhat inattentive readers could be stirred awake by discovering themselves in an unexpected context altogether. Who was this cat (in mid-century lingo) who knocked me out? I was hoping that question, addressed to the poet, would lead to an answer I might access. I think I was already willing to wait a lifetime.

Most of my early poems, like this one from my 20s, already asked this question, which contextualizes the scene of writing:

MAY 24

dear tom
aint writ to you in some quite time
no talk or wit

suffices
it's all timing
always easier to wait

see how audience feels
joke or moral spike
quick I'm tired of announcements

of poetry
foreign poetry
who's speaking

under the blanket
oh lady earth
untouchable adolescent

you do not like rock poetry
what is poetry?
you want rock

a hard mood strikes me
white brick wall
holes drilled in the asphalt

I lay my stogie down in Spoon Rest
look at rainbow
over Cocteau's bowtie

open your lips
white blind
we are bored with professionalism

held tight
all night
the window bursting.

A poem like this, elucidating a night of writing until dawn arrived through the Venetian blinds, followed my encounter with the classic French modernists Rimbaud and Mallarmé. I began to translate them intertextually, and from there to my improbable return to the Bible is the story I try to tell as if it were inside a poem. That is, by digging deeper into my past, scene overlapping scene, until a sudden focus can arise. It's a slow process, wary of critics/opponents who may take my style for myself. As my former coach, ex-Michigan middleweight champ Nate Coleman told me in his car as we drove back from my last fateful encounter, holding bloody compress to my lip: "I was worried about that guy," he said, "because he was watching you warm up, studying you, and saw that your left hook was your weapon." That vicious opponent was the first who took me seriously on my own terms. It wasn't a great leap from such self-knowledge to an understanding that such an opponent could now be internalized as the reader of my poem. And I myself would later inhabit the position of that reader as I focussed upon the original text of the Bible, trying to get behind it to the scene of writing.

8.

"One of my all-time favorite books is Pound's *Cathay*, and it seems to me if you can make over something from a distant time into a vivid and memorable modern poem, you're enlarging the current scope of poetry a bit." There's something missing in that formulation by poet Mark Ford. I wanted to make the issue more forceful, to *bring them back alive*—the historical writers as they were, paying them the respect of created characters, *creatures*. You need to care about their individuality to do that, as in a formative influence on me, John Berryman's *Homage to Mistress [poet Anne] Bradstreet* and in similar poet-to-poet evocations in prose, for instance Baudelaire's translations and commentary on Poe, Robert Duncan's *The H.D. Book* (and H.D.'s own *Tribute To Freud*), and Susan Howe's *My Emily Dickinson*.

When I now read the *Defense of Poesy* by Elizabethan poet Philip Sidney, I find his Creator was also a poet-to-poet evocation:

"Neither let it be deemed too bold a comparison to balance the highest point of man's wit with the efficacy of nature; but rather give right honor to the heavenly maker of that maker, who having made man to his own likeness, set him beyond and over all the work of that second nature, which in nothing he shows so much as in poetry, when with the force of a divine breath he brings things forth far surpassing her doings, with no small argument to the incredulous of that first accursed fall of Adam, since our erected wit makes us know what perfection is, but our infected will keeps us from reaching unto it."

Today, for lack of will to confront biblical authorship, the poem Sidney wishes to defend may more resemble a robot than Adam. Nothing against robots, but life will never transcend being a metaphor for them. Nor have we reached the point where society is taking robots or poems seriously again. Margaret Atwood has a long riff on robots in the *New York Times* this week, quoting various high-end to middling stories, literary and journalistic. It's all very cute, but to what end? Quasi-intellectual Entertainment. Shouldn't we at least be reading the science page? Meanwhile, a more serious poet than Atwood, Bernadette Mayer, has a new edition of a 25-year-old book described as "Mayer's ground-breaking works of writing consciousness." Is her ambition something more than the wish to entertain? Yet that is precisely the trouble with consciousness; it exists toward our species survival but most of the time that we are not working we need to be entertained, in this case by the appearance of learning something useful. The better we understand consciousness, the closer we get to—to poetry, Mayer might say. Neither here, however, nor in Atwood's survey of cliches about the future, are we challenged by the prophetic vision of the biblical poets, such as those behind Jeremiah, to look back upon ourselves from the future with great tenderness. Mayer's wild playfulness, like John Ashbery's, entertains us like an audience of childlike intellectual grownups, and that comes as close as literature does today in providing poignancy to our present. We learn, in other words, that our minds are like poetry, though that still falls short of the cosmic view, as in Jeremiah when, dizzy with grief, he sees the waves of exiled Jerusalemites staggering home—when he is actually seeing them leaving in the present. He sees that our very lives are poetry, created creatures on a journey unknowable to us. Yet if it's a journey on which we are at least like children, unsure of the final destination, then the possibility of a visionary future opens to us, from which we can see ourselves in the present, tenderly, little explorers creating robots.

There's not much in the latest literature that's more postmodern than Mayer. Looking back from the future, when our postmodern moment has become quaint, can we still feel tender toward it? Perhaps only as art, in which a visionary embrace could include the horrors of our age, when consciousness began to be defined by Auschwitz and Hiroshima. If it could offer, like Jeremiah, a vision of our staggering back to Jerusalem, toward a restoration of cosmic identity after destruction and slavery, then we would not only be exhilarated by our art's insight into our state of abandonment in the universe. We might imagine ourselves, beyond the highest entertainment of poetry and science, as able to mourn the loss of cosmic purpose and also rebuild it.

Look, the blind and the lame are returning
women heavy with child, and yes
even those already feeling birth pangs

a great congregation is coming
weeping openly, and among them little cries
of newborn infants—sweet and gracious tears

and I will lead them beside rushing waters
on fertile ground, on soil so smooth
not a foot will stumble on the way…

I will turn their sighing
into breaths of excitement
their sadness into blushes of joy…

their mourning changed into music
of birds alighting in trees, by windows
thrown open to new mornings…

returning home
from the lands of enemies
from beyond anguish to hope revived

vision is your reward…

mark your path well
plant guideposts and road marks
set your desire by the highway

your thoughts to the road leading home
turn back on it, my Maiden Israel
come back to these your cities.
    (from Chapter 31)

It's hard to imagine how you can read the Hebrew Bible deeply without its Jewish history and some feeling for the loss of its poets. Their narrative and poetry changes through the ancient centuries—the visionary poets behind Jeremiah are working with history in a way different from the Genesis writer who inscribed Joseph's prophetic dreams—so that you would be missing the poetry if you lacked the history of ancient Israel. In the same way, I find it hard to imagine how new readers of the New York School poets can read them without experience of New York School painters, who are their forebears and colleagues. Read Frank O'Hara but not be familiar with Pollack and Rivers? Schuyler without Mitchell and Porter? Ashbery without de Kooning and Motherwell? Koch without Johns and Freilicher? And yet these poets are now taught as if poetry was the only air they breathed, without cultural context. I was drawn to them in youth precisely because I was going to galleries to see the painters they engaged. And I had to do the same for Jeremiah and all of the Bible: to see through the characters and the cultural forms of history-telling—myth and legend, vision and dream—to how the writers behind them re-created those cultural forms to tell the history and psychology of Israel.

Among my parental poets in English, Ted Hughes (and Sylvia Plath expressing much the same but less explicitly) was the most biblically acute, after Charles Reznikoff. Referring to the Hebrew Bible—"the greatest poetry in English is in the prose of the Bible"—Hughes can be forgiven for having only the King James, where the preponderance of poetry is written out as prose. It looks that way in the Hebrew also, because the ancient precursors of paper were too precious to accommodate the white space of modern poetry. Anyway, poetry or prose, why not ask how it came to be written? Beyond textual matters, most answers would cite the beliefs of the writers, but beliefs do not account for poetry, let alone great poetry. The question itself, however, could not yet be articulated in Hughes's heyday because source criticism, a.k.a. the Documentary Hypothesis, was still under suspicion. Besides, the very term "documentary" belied the creativity of the original writers, and led to the still-prevailing notion that textual documentarians known as redactors are the ones who demand our attention. To get past that, one has to become conscious of not only the materiality of language but the divine aporia that poetry can contain. I don't know if the chemical languages of other sentient beings produce poetry, though flowers make a strong case for plant creativity, and the struggle toward the sun by rainforest flora suggests worship.

The avant-garde focus on the materiality of language strives for an intensity of alertness that may suggest extra-human poetry, as when early Homo sapiens explored new territory and gave rise to Orphic poetry. It lacks enough of a visionary psychology, however, for avant-garde poets to see themselves as mourners over modernism—which is how they may look from the future. Perhaps Gertrude Stein was the first of these, her deadpan mourning taking the form, first, of cubist experiment, and then of autobiography. She constantly explored the blending of the individual into the group as allowing for a visionary tension—and long before E.O. Wilson, in his *The Meaning of Human Existence*, highlights the biological origins and conflict between individual and group identification. Wilson laments the current lack of interest in evolutionary biology by poets, who he exiles to what I call the ICU of culture: in dire need of engendering an Eden mythos for science, a visionary poetics, and returning to the mainstream of life—sort of like Jeremiah's exiles coming back to Jerusalem as if resurrected.

One reason I refer to golden age cinema and TV, especially in the mainstream, is how they provide a way to think through not only my personal history but our cultural history. I see how I've outgrown the Fifties when I read contemporaneous reviews in the New York Times and The New Yorker that lambast movies of that day for their intellectual failures and seeming lack of art, exposing the intellectual critic's social prejudices. And yet in crucial respects nothing has changed, the same grandiosity is at work today. Watching *Home Before Dark* (1958) again, it's disconcerting to see how much more seriously the subject of mental illness was portrayed half a century ago than it is today. But the critical reception that awaited director Mervyn LeRoy was even more brutal than Jean Simmons got in the film, upon returning home after a year in the state mental hospital. Bosley Crowther of the Times writes, "This hapless [bi-polar] creature tears her poor self to tatters in a situation that is slightly absurd: she finds herself once more *confronted with the same circumstances* that impelled her into the asylum in the first place. If anything, they are worse…[and] for more than two hours Miss Simmons thrashes around in this unnatural situation." The italics are mine, to emphasize the critic's artistic disdain for a plot in which the situation of mental illness goes around in circles. But not only does it do so in natural situations, the plot's insistence on it faces up to how unnatural *it seems*—it's in the seeming that we should be shocked. Even the usually penetrating Pauline Kael of *The New Yorker* writes, back then, "Unfortunately, the script makes the heroine too sympathetic, and it has an edge of fashionable, self-congratulatory virtue—the 'one must be more understanding toward discharged mental patients' attitude." Perhaps I should be more sympathetic to Crowther and Kael; they're film critics, not psychoanalysts. Yet for God's sake, in Manhattan of the 1950s, couldn't they have been more psychologically literate? Half a century later, however, we're still thrashing around in denial about the need to address mental illness in its context, its family dimensions. Is there no social recourse for a family that can't handle it? No medical intervention, no financial help, no social awareness? Cops aren't taught how to tell a disturbed person from a criminal, and even today you best not tell your employer you're seeing a psychiatrist. So am I looney to suggest that poetry can help? Because it's in a poem that we enter the emergency room, the ICU, where we see that no person or idea is innocent, all our thoughts are relative, and the truthful resolution is that there is none, only the standing back that the poem pushes us toward, pushes us outside it, where we can forgive ourselves for not knowing everything. All that we "know" of why the sunset is beautiful or the run-over dog is sickening is that we're not as innocent of knowing as the unconscious sun. Yet like us, the sun has a life span, a character we ascribe to it, like the cultural name we're given in life; a poem, however, tells us there's something outside that life. Even when the poem presents the situation as absurd and there's nothing outside life but the absence of something, we're still instructed in how to step back from that absurdity and see ourselves mercifully in our unknowing.

> Lord, I'm just a worm
> don't point to me
> in frozen anger
>
> don't let me feel
> I more than deserve
> all your rage
>
> but mercy, Lord, let me feel mercy
> I'm weak, my spirit so dark
> even my bones shiver
>
> my shadow surrounds me—I'm shocked
> how long, Lord, how long
> till you return to shine your light
>
> return to me dear Lord
> bring back the light
> that I can know you by
>
> because those that are dead
> have no thought of you
> to make a song by…

Psalm 6 asks almost childlike why Creation treats us worse than a worm. Although they are shut up in the dark ground, worms do have a life and a song of working through the soil. The poet has no problem imagining the Lord's love for a worm, but can humans open their minds cosmically to imagine parental love toward a worm? Here, an ancient Hebrew poem can contemplate species consciousness, imagining a man who can literally be a worm—and not merely squirm wormlike out of responsibilities in a shallow metaphor. The poem deploys metaphor and idea like characters in the briefest of movies, yet instead of a final resolution there is revelation: we are speaking back to natural creation in the form of the Creator, intimate with the unknowable. It's as if we could speak to the sun (which poet Frank O'Hara did a few decades ago) in a revelation that it too—the sun, like us—has its limitations. A poem doesn't need the end to a story, other than making us conscious of ourselves at the scene of reading: we're able to step back from the poem and see ourselves as created creatures, just like a poem.

And like a poem, our minds create for us a state of mental balance; without it, we can't see ourselves, fail to be aware we are reading a poem. Take away poems from our lives, especially the absence of the Bible in secular culture, and although we may think we're normal, the balance we're hanging onto is mere social convention. Jean Simmons is not the most abnormal one in *Home Before Dark*, especially as she grows aware of her unconscious motives; it's her seemingly normal family that blindly tortures her who are seriously out of balance as they deny any awareness of their own unconscious selves. Recent generations have diminished species consciousness as well as the unconscious, trading them in for a concept of social authenticity, one similar to the old, post-noble savage cliché that only the rebel is authentic, rebelling against injustice. The ironic pretense of rebelling—such as on Twitter or at a Beyoncé concert—is self-conscious enough that it's also a form of rebellion. But senior rock critics like Greil Marcus think the Beyoncé patrons are demeaning former icons of socially conscious soul music like Aretha Franklin; perhaps instead, they are aware that a genre itself can become inauthentic if it's not open to Beyoncé's loving caricature. Such an ironic caricature admits that an age of innocence has passed, the brief golden age of soul music, and we are still lost. (For the next generations, Beyoncé may seem innocent, as Amy Winehouse already does).

Still lost—that's how I viewed the previous generation of scholarly Bible translators who rebelled against an increasing opacity to the biblical text (enforced, in English, by the King James translation). Their rebellion took the form of intense textuality, looking into the structural and rhetorical aspects of the Hebrew text. It proved liberating for a generation. Then it quickly turned into its own kind of opacity: suddenly it became clear to me that the original biblical writers were not merely avoided but more deeply buried beneath a scholarly lacquer over the text. So the time had come, it seemed to me, to dig past the text altogether and down toward the lost writers and their artistic culture of cosmic narrative and poetry. The freeing process had to be begin with translation, I thought, the kind of translation in which poets resuscitated poets, as Pound had done for ancient Chinese literature in his *Cathay* (1915) and Lowell had attempted for ancient Greek in his *Oresteia* (1978). (Likewise, Ted Hughes's *Oresteia* of '98, though too late to affect me). I had been a student of Lowell's, as I will describe, and my generation needed an even more rebellious approach to the ancient Hebrew text of the Bible, or so I persuaded myself (affected by the lifelong intertextual versions of New York City poet Charles Reznikoff). I thought I might invoke the cosmic wit and historical risk of the original Biblical writers: they were rebellious in their own way toward the literary history they inherited and its ironic conventions of presenting myth and legend as history. Still, they were not innocents, and like all great writers, they had to break through the hardened conventions they faced. They refined history and legend with an enlivening irony of *being there*—a drama of speaking straight into the face of the universe, as if it was engaged with us and not so indifferently playful as the conventional realm of cosmic beings that stood in for the unknowable.

So in '72 I began to translate a psalm as an ancient Hebraic poet might do, were he a contemporary American informed by my generation's intense focus on human consciousness, a consciousness that could hear an echo from infinity like a reverberating blues. The German visual artist and shot-down Luftwaffe flyer, Joseph Beuys, explained it for me, saying: "Auschwitz is a condition that outlasts Auschwitz into the world that surrounds us in ways we do not care to see. People must see that to prevent another Auschwitz, they must change themselves." Yet how? Leopardi, in the book I referred to when I began this chapter, concluded that "we possess no real knowledge of anything, because we ourselves are nothing, arising from and returning to nothingness, with nothing to hope for"—consciousness or no consciousness. And nevertheless, his book is so infused with the riches of literary interpretation that it comes to seem like a spiritual cloud—a poem of context—that surrounds human consciousness as a likeness of heaven. But it's all an interpretation of the past, of course, as if to suggest that the only way to change ourselves now is to creatively restore all that we can of what has been lost.

I don't argue that the Hebraic culture of the Biblical authors stood in place of religion, but I will insist that it went hand in hand with religion's cosmic theater, and was no nostalgia for the numinous—just as it wasn't for Homer. Before a reader begins to consider the authors, however, the Bible can seem like a piñata that splits open with a hundred cherished beliefs that no one could anticipate. I once edited two anthologies of almost a hundred memoirish essays by secular contemporary writers, *Congregation* ('87) and *Communion* ('96), about the Bible in their lives, and they were full of attempts to come to grips with the most outlandish misinformation (usually from childhood). How do we balance the eccentric and scandalously literal beliefs *about* the Hebrew Bible held by secularists with the extravagant renditions *of* the text by the religious? A colleague who read an early draft of the chapter 'The Poem of the Jewish Writer' tries to awaken me: "Geez, David, I've always thought since my days in my Anglican Sunday School that Adam & Eve must have been considered Jewish because they'd been created by the God of the Israelites. So afterward, their descendants—i.e. everyone—would have to be either Jews or lapsed Jews, like Cain, Anglicans, Caananites or Philistines."

"So I was thinking that if one was writing only 3,500 years or less after creation (not sure about my math, or about Biblical 'begat'-math) in a somewhat compact 'known world,' it would make sense to regard cuneiform texts as recording part of one's own history—one's own geographic history, and likely one's own people's history, since these would have to be written by descendants of Adam, no? Or am I missing something. Or perhaps by descendants of Noah (doesn't that story imply that Noah & his family were the only survivors of a planetary flood?).

"But does Judaism regard Adam & Eve as Jewish? (I suppose they aren't under the secular understanding of ethnicity as relational, but I doubt the relevancy of that here.) Or Noah as Jewish? Or does Jewishness begin only with Jacob & his 12 sons? So you see that your chapter has been making me confront imaginary puzzles that I've never faced objectively, though they're embedded in the Christian subconscious."

I answered: "See that's just what happens when you read the Hebrew Bible as literally as a fundamentalist. I guess we were all expected to be little fundamentalists in Sunday School, though even in college Bible courses the original writers are blended together with their sources, as if Shakespeare was a court historian when he wrote his history plays. The Bible is so culturally overdetermined that it's hard to imagine the intelligence of its writers—their Homo sapiens genes and intellectual capacity exactly the same as ours—as at an angle to their matter, just like any other writers, including their near-contemporaries in Greece and their forebears in Sumer. That is, the problems you refer to, concerning the time and space of various episodes, you assume are literal, when I would point out that the biblical writers take their history not simply as literal but as culture-bound. If the officious culture, religious or royal, says heaven's above hell's below, there's no reason a Hebraic writer would take that as incontrovertible fact, anymore than a writer today. Always there are a million other factoids, cultural and physical, that are constantly in doubt, such as the one about how a demon brought you your cold and that's why you say "God bless you" when you sneeze? Not to mention those eternal destabilizers, dreams and nightmares. Even a Neanderthal hunter would know not to trust absolutely that the cave bear is a spirit, whatever the official dogma of the day—perhaps promulgated by a Neanderthal proto-writer, weaving an oral web, who would nevertheless put his/her own spin on it.

"No doubt the Noahide history is fungible even to the biblical writers, who were quite aware their contemporaries in Egypt, Greece, Anatolia, India or Mesopotamia had competing genealogies. Jewish history begins with Abraham and Sarah conversing with Israel's God qua Creator, though as yet unnamed. He refused to speak anymore with them in Ur until they took literally his command to 'leave'. Anyway, it took me 400pp to straighten this out in my Abraham bio. As for what 'Judaism regards'—it depends on what faction or period you're considering, prior to the loss of ancient homeland. I would assume that most of the best writers then were in some sense unaffiliated, just as are Jewish writers now. The rabbinic Judaism we know today, however, beginning after the final Roman destruction, affiliates them all, as if the Christian Protestant schisms were folded back into Catholicism. But as a child of a Christian Sunday School I see your problem with getting history straight—and how it's compounded by my analogy, since the Christian schisms are millennia down the road from Yavneh, the Judean town in the first century A.D. where rabbinic Judaism was consecrated."

9.

The meaning of "rebellious" inheres in all authorship. To imagine any author, you have to move into a writer's context, his culture. So here is the problem for tradition and for academe: the culture leads in many directions away from the text, and in many instances, rebels against the text itself. Yet here I am, in the midst of Western culture, struggling to open a way for it *back* to the text. It's a double rebellion, going *behind* the text as well, as if we're on the trek from cosmopolitan ancient Egypt—but dragging a library of books behind instead of sheep and cattle. These books/scrolls/tablets are the sources the early writers of the Bible had, for they did not write in a vacuum. The conventional biblical critics try to pasteurize these sources, reducing awareness of the writer's struggle with them to one of "improving" on them. I'm sorry, but no writer improves on writers of the past; instead, his/her culture allows for a possibly fruitful engagement, resulting in the Hebrew Bible, just as my own American culture allows me to confront the ancient writers as if in a dialectic between poets. So that's one rebellion, against conventional scholarship and its head in the sand with regard to imagining the original writers and their aesthetic culture—not how the text works but how its writers worked. When academic critics give this a try, they get stuck in images of themselves—editors, redactors, canny committees of scholars—and at a loss to imagine how creative writers, behind each ancient strand of the Bible, work their sources uncannily into art.

So why should a talmudic dialectic with the authors, as I've described my angle into the text, seem rebellious as well to tradition, even in the broad Judeo-Christian sense? The Talmud has produced a huge quantity of commentary, some of it glorious—and much of it, as in the Gemara and the ensuing centuries of Midrash, in the form of self-consciously creative tales or "legends"—but its deep and endless arguments over biblical text are about meaning, the why but not the how of how the text came to be. In becoming an intertextual translator of the Bible, confronting ancient Hebrew with contemporary Western, or more specifically American culture, this dialectic appears to demote religious understanding in favor of cultural. And in doing so, it can seem to rebel against religious meaning, which in fact it does but not necessarily in an antithetical way. In place of meaning, my education in the avant-garde arts privileges process, the how we create over the why. Yet I am in rebellion too against my poetic education, as I describe in the Jewish Writer chapter, because it breathes no new life into meaning, especially the kind of cosmic meaning behind the Bible. And that is also the reason the Bible is so absent in contemporary literature; it's emphasis on the why of everything is a rebellion against the discrete poem; instead it asks for the poem of everything, raising meaning to poetry. The NYT obit this year for the American poet Alan Grossman, with whom I'd corresponded about modernist parallels to the Hebrew Book of Psalms, closed with an excerpt from a Grossman essay on poetics: "The poem is a trace of the will of all persons to be known and to make known and, therefore, to be at all." I imagine that this pathetic quotation out of context would make Alan laugh. You could substitute a hundred things for the word "poem" in that sentence, such as "epitaph" or "boxscore," so that it comes off as grandiose, a Grossman failing that he himself contended with in some of his poems. I, too, will do my best when characterizing poetry to backlight my own grandiosity, *to wit*:

> I am a half-narcissist. Part of me has always been able to see the world through others' eyes, so I had little trouble forming relationships. In retrospect, trouble in intimate relationships would eventually surface because I could not see *myself* through the other's eyes, only the rest of the world. I had to judge their opinion of me by their behavior but could not see through to their inner conflicts. I say "could not," but it was also "did not want to." That's the narcissist part of myself, which I turned into a poet in teenage years so as to justify myself to myself. An artist, I reasoned, as much as he delved into people's conflicts, could not afford to be distracted by them. Or, by the same reasoning, could an artist be distracted by analyzing his own conflicts, hence the general aversion to psychoanalysis (as opposed to symptoms therapy, whereby the therapist is generally referred to half-tenderly as a shrink). By resolving one's own unconscious conflicts, the narcissist-artist sees him- or herself with enough clarity to dispel the illusions of artistic grandiosity. However, that's more than enough to stymie many a creative writer. Who can write imaginatively without illusions?

Nevertheless, it opened up new territory for me in my early forties. Let me get in intellectual bio mode for a moment: it created more of a balance between thinking and feeling, and thereby widening my sources to include more fields, from literary theory and psychoanalysis itself to entering into the writing of biblical scholarship in creative nonfiction manner. Now, let me back up to note my earlier difficulty in maintaining intimate relationships when they intruded on the narcissism of my poetic vocation. You will understand how I could put that problem aside when you consider that of my university poetry-mentors—W.D. Snodgrass, Robert Lowell, Kenneth Koch, Donald Hall, Delmore Schwartz—three of them had spent time in mental institutions, thus reinforcing my early defenses against analytical introspection. Why would I want to gaze at the sun of buried feeling inside me? I knew it was there, and when I sat before my mentors I could see how they'd been burned by it.

Before there were filters for old telescopes, you didn't have to look at the noonday sun to believe its power was real. No one should look directly at the noonday sun to prove it exists, unless being blinded is proof. Instead, you judge its power indirectly, by reflected light on the moon, for instance. It's the same for the existence of the unconscious mind. You can't examine it by direct observation (neuroscientists measuring ecstasy to the contrary) but rather indirectly, beginning with the famous analytic techniques of Sigmund Freud. Before Freud, we already knew about unconscious processes in dreams, but after him we understood that these processes were ongoing 24/7, beyond our apprehension. As with the modern sciences of the macro and micro worlds our senses can't verify, the unconscious defies rational "proof" without an inventive prosthesis like psychoanalysis.

Religion is that prosthesis for encountering God—and even for describing his absence. That's why questions about God outside a religion's analytic culture are useless. Asking me if I "believe in God" is like asking me if I believe in the unconscious—belief is no more an issue than belief in the sun is, for a blind person. It's the nature of apprehension that counts: a telescope (for the sun as a typical star) or a text, one by Freud or one by the Hebraic biblical writers (which the NT Gospel writers, Jewish themselves, took for granted). What I can say as an article of faith is: I believe in the human writing of biblical texts as well as the quality of imagination called revelation or, in my terms, the aporia or irreducibility of great poetry. My way of looking at things, derived from a 20th century education, apprehends the universe as a poem, the unconscious as a poem, and the Creator as a poem. Some will say this reduces God to mere literature, but my experience of modern literature shows that a consciousness of the cosmic theater (required in which to conceive of the Creator) can actually infuse literature with greater dimension. Do we have such a poetry today that can compare to Dante's *The Divine Comedy* or the *Book of Isaiah*?

I think of Creator and creation as poems. I think of my own life as a poem, or a series of poems I'd call epic, as in "an epic of a life." It's a mistake, I think, to consider that "all you need is love." Love requires no text, but poetry does. I need a text because it tells me that there was also a creator of that text. When you abandon the creator of a poem, holding on to mere text, you've abandoned *me*—or so I felt when I found myself, as a freshman in an advanced creative writing class, comparing an ancient psalm unfavorably with a Robert Frost poem. The Frost was deadpan, and could be so because there was a Frost with whom we could identify, someone from our culture, but the psalm, separated from its Hebraic author, could not be deadpan—not aware that its creator, channeling whatever grief and joy, was an artist. Thus, the Psalm seemed naïve, and that was my point as I grandiosely favored Frost in my brief presentation to that class. Yet I was uneasy inside about it, I sensed I had abandoned the Hebraic poet, just as tradition had suppressed his authorship. That sense of abandonment has stayed with me, through decades of rebelling against it, struggling to reembody the lost writers and their artistic culture. First, however, I had to feel what it was like to be a disembodied avant-garde writer—a blind postmodernist. I went back to Mallarmé and his disembodied Orphism, re-translating him from French intertextually, with a New York School postmodern deadpan. It didn't quite reach into that sense of fundamental abandonment that went past my freshman year and was buried in my childhood. Somehow, when my father returned from the war as a disabled veteran, I felt (I was not quite four) he'd abandoned me—or the world had. Two years after my freshman writing class with poet W.D. Snodgrass, I rediscovered the Holocaust in Raul Hilberg's *The Destruction of the European Jews*. I had known it in childhood as well, via the album photographs of relatives, young and old, who had "died in the camps"—and through my surviving aunts and cousins with their tattooed numbers, who suggested the world had abandoned them. Yet I managed to contain this great maw of abandonment in poems I would write through my twenties, through abandoned jobs and lovers, in a transcendent high of poetic abandonment, freely translating Rimbaud, Mallarmé, Valéry ("Poems are never finished—just abandoned").

You could say my sense of abandonment translated into a rebelling against the lip-service to creativity I encountered when, at 29, I began to translate the Bible and found its authors abandoned by academe, by scholarship, and even by my literary colleagues. All preferred to look away from the deep well of creativity that lay behind its complex texts, though with wonderful exceptions like E.A. Speiser of Penn, who I encountered through his student, scholar Moshe Greenberg.

At my mother's graveside for the stone unveiling almost a decade ago, I sang four songs, three in Yiddish she had sung to me until I was not quite four years old and my father came home from France and the VA hospital, a disabled veteran. The songs had no father in them, except for the one in English, 'The Anniversary Waltz,' which doesn't get past the wedding night. So I held the infantile opinion that my father had abandoned me, which paralleled my mother's opinion that he'd been foolish to volunteer for the army when he was already too old to be drafted. It seemed no one considered my father a hero nor did he himself. I would later learn that he was of the opinion he'd abandoned his widowed mother in Hungary to come to America and, as he learned after the war, she'd been gassed in Auschwitz. Perhaps my own sense of abandonment resonated with my father's when I internalized the Jewish opinion that the world had abandoned us. Why? It was a mystery that went beyond anti-Semitism and included the beloved president FDR. Although it was a mystery that goes back to my early childhood, it remains one today. I can no more imagine finding the answer than I can pinpoint the source of my sense of abandonment in an unknowable universe.

"The brain is mysterious, and I want to spend my life in the presence of mystery," says a neuroscientist prodigy. Yet it's an ultimately knowable mystery: sooner or later, maybe in just a few centuries, its mystery will stand unmasked, like the moon's mystery has become. True mystery (in my book, so to speak) is unknowable, like the biblical Creator and "His" cosmic theater. Species consciousness reminds us of the limitations of our organs, but it still lacks a cosmic poetry beyond Darwin's trenchant prose.

Even the Creator of the Big Bang (which one might call a poem: it has both a "Who" and a "What" to it) has a backstory, evident as deGrasse Tyson of "Cosmos" fame holds in his hand a translucent ball the size of a squash ball. "This was the size of the entire universe in a fraction of a second after the Big Bang," he says. Tyson doesn't say it, perhaps doesn't even think it, but you look at that squash ball in his hand and you can't help thinking that a hand is holding it and so where did the hand come from? It's a dizzying thought, like looking high up into the dome of the Sistine Chapel in Rome to take in the hand of God, as represented by Michelangelo. Nevertheless, it's based on an understanding that the physical universe of spacetime is a text, and texts have writers, even imagined ones, or at least origins and sources.

As I write this in Miami, near midnight, seated outside by a secluded table at the all-night pizza joint, all is calm, a tropical winter night at room temperature. So what if the Earth is spinning at 70,000 miles per minute (sic) and also revolving around the sun at 100,000 miles per minute (sic), while the sun is revolving around the Milky Way center at 250,000 miles per minute (sic) and our galaxy is speeding into the universe at 500,000 miles per second (sic). Meanwhile, every second, trillions of neutrinos, many from other galaxies, pass through every person on earth. I know all this but my body doesn't; it's busy fighting myriad internal wars against enemy cell invaders. In addition, other microbe species are digesting "Power Pizza" ("Our Power is in the Dough").

So what is it I don't know? How do we know what it is that we can't know? I look at my cat Zorro (in memory; he died a few months ago; this is before we rescued the kitten Louise) and he doesn't know the figures mentioned above, yet he has a wise way of knowing what he can't know, the unknowable: his interpretive strength allows him to translate everything about me into his terms, so that, for instance, sitting for hours in front of a screen, computer, TV, or iPad, is "resting," just as reading a book in bed is. It doesn't matter what the device is or what's on it. When I'm clicking away on keypad, however, or talking on phone, that is "figuring"—figuring on when to eat, when to wash, when to go outside. The putting on clothes business is like rolling around in the dust, etc. etc. So why is it any different when we interpret what is unknowable to us, such as why we exist or what cats think of us (the best we can do is translate into our terms, i.e. we're surrogate parents etc.).

All of which is to say that while species consciousness is beginning to come back from its origins among the ancient European cave painters, it's still mostly bad news. What is the good news? Deep time, the realization that natural history is just as knowable as human history. Because the more we imagine the knowable, the clearer the contrast with the unknowable— and the more likely our poets are to dip their figurative pens into the wellsprings of the Bible's cosmic poetry.

In my mid-twenties I walked the figurative streets of ancient Babylon among St. Mark's Place hippiedom, drums pounding, incense wafting, used booksellers sitting on the sidewalks, their paperback wares spread before them like cheap talismans. Suddenly it dawned on me that I needed to return to Jerusalem, where, during a brief tour in '69, I'd witnessed a similar scene behind the Old City walls, only there the prospect was not new and echoed back a few thousand years. What kept me from making the connection before? It was the assumption that we were more sophisticated, more advanced than 3,000 years ago. I hadn't yet reread Darwin, to be reminded that, since our DNA and native intelligence is no different than a person who lived thousands of years ago, the crucial difference was simply that he or she would have different cultural resources, different modes of knowledge to work with and play off of. Three thousand years from now, when we'll have visual if not direct communication with extra-solar civilizations, our time might look knowledge-deficient, even primitive, to the newer humans. Yet even today, without the proper equipment, we still can deduce Earth-like exoplanets; we can't literally see them, but we deduce their existence with our relatively primitive telescopes. The same would hold true for a poet in ancient Jerusalem, who might deduce all sorts of historical facts from sources to which she had access, both oral and written, that are now lost. The history of the covenant-building at Sinai in the book of Exodus was inscribed by a poet who turned his or her sources into an overpowering tale of revelation, so that we're still affected by it today, no less than the history of King Oedipus. It's probably the greatest poem of revelation we have. What kind of a cultural Judeo-Christian does that make me? It's a question I address in the chapter, 'The Poem of the Jewish Writer.'

When I taught in Princeton's Creative Writing Dept., my colleague Colson Whitehead had just published a zombie novel (*Zone One*), more properly a deconstruction of apocalyptic zombiedom, playing on the existential dread of extinction. That dread corresponded to the frozen emotional life of some of my students, that feeling of being "dead inside." I had known it myself and refer to it as carrying a dead child within in my later psychoanalytic therapy. Post-therapy, the question for me became how to feel about *that*, about having been a kind of intellectual zombie-parent who finally gave birth to my inner child in the form of creative writings.

I had conceived of a buried child within cultural phenomena, finally reaching the bedrock of the Bible's original writers buried within the text. In the book of Deuteronomy, an ancient superego is speaking, as if the human conscience was trying to determine what is the upwelling of ego that threatens the group as a whole and thus longterm survival. But below the surface of seeming law code are striking layers of authorship: Moses the figurative writer rebelling against the older civilization and its concern with inherited lines of authority; Israel's encounter with older cultures' moral codes, depicted by Hebraic writers before, after, and within Babylonian exile as a critique of worldly consensus; the drama of community as vulnerable, in parallel to the individual, and in need of constant vigilance rather than obeisance. The deepest layer may come from tribal and oral proverbs, but these are sublimated, if not occulted, by the later writers (primarily D, the Deuteronomist, somewhat interestingly aligned with the writers who composed Jeremiah's poetic history-as-prophecy).

Even when a postmodernist rebels against Moses's rebellion and the Hebraic cosmic theater, she finds herself personifying creation and the mystery behind the Big Bang as an "it" with a purpose of "seeking us out." "'The questions in the world may be infinite, but perhaps the answers are few. And however we define that mystery, there's no escaping our essential obligation to it, for it may,' as Ehrenreich writes, 'be seeking us out.'" So writes a reviewer of Barbara Ehrenreich's memoir, *Living with a Wild God: A Nonbeliever's Search for the Truth about Everything*. But I think she has it backwards: there are not enough significant questions. There are plenty of superficial questions—and there are far too many answers, even serious answers, like those of philosophy and science. "There's no escaping our essential obligation to it," she writes—so that "It" is now in process of being personified. And then: "*It* may...' be seeking us out.'" Even here, in a book-length attempt at sublimation of the author's atheism, she can't avoid personifying the cosmic theater's "who"—and not the what—behind the Big Bang.

I wouldn't have noticed this in my youthful blind postmodernism; it took me several years and coincidental accidents to discover how hard it is to avoid Moses as he begins to pin down that cosmic theater on Earth. It's even harder, however, to keep Creation inanimate, as in: Natural selection is nature's engine that drives the evolution of species (even as an inanimate engine begs the question of who made it). A new species evolves when an accidental mutation occurs as DNA is being copied in the formation of a cell. But I would also call this "accidental" mutation a rebellious one—it rebels against expectation and consensus. We might say, therefore, that the human species exists thanks to a rebellion in which we evolved from a gorilla primate. Nothing against non-carnivorous gorillas—I'd call it a loving rebellion, in search of cosmic questions. You just can't jump, however, from gorilla language to a modern atheist or postmodern poet by jumping over the Hebrew Bible and its crucial rebelling against worldly consensus.

And rebellion, scientifically speaking, served to "create" us—to bring us here. Intellectually, a rebellion against consensus still drives scientific and creative thinking, though it's the poet's job to reinterpret and break free of the consensus in which he swims. The formative writers of the Hebrew Bible, J, E, and S (the "court historian") rebelled against the classical literary consensus of their day, which originated in Sumerian literature. J rewrote the Sumerian Flood story, among other Sumerian sources, to fit an Hebraic vision of history. In other words, this biblical writer did not "change" the story but rather updated it with the imaginative engine of a new Hebraic aesthetic genius. "Religion" would be the wrong word to describe the context for this reimagining; it was rather a cultural context in which a tradition of Hebraic writing had developed, first written down in cuneiform and proto-Hebrew, perhaps two centuries before J began the account that forms the basic strand of what were later called the books of Genesis, Exodus, and Numbers. Unfortunately, although the Hebraic genius for religion is attributed as founder of the complex monotheism we know today, what happened to the Hebraic genius for *writing*, along with its imaginative cultural resources? It's a question too rarely asked, even by writers. I first heard it as I was walking home from a party after a poetry reading, a bit high—but let me tell that story more fully within this book. It's more important for now that I sketch out what I had to know about the Bible in order to see it of a piece with my own postmodern drive to rebel.

The Hebrew Bible was not thoroughly translated, so far as we know, until the 2nd Century BCE, into ancient Greek. Many centuries before that, partial translations were made into Aramaic, so that other cultures, including the dominant ones of Babylon and Egypt, would have some knowledge of the Hebrew Bible—and thus at least some indication that it constituted a rebellion against dominant world culture, which was one of gods and paganism rather than a singular monotheistic God (one who could internalize within itself Creator, moral and ethical inspiration, and Israel's national God). However, the Bible's early writers, who rewrote human history in light of Hebraic monotheism, were not serving religion primarily but rather their Hebrew culture's need for historical and imaginative sources. Some critics like to ignore this need and instead substitute political or sociological necessities, so they interpret the Bible as a socio-political document—no differently than they might a modern novel—or even an ancient history, ascribing political motives to Herodotus, the Greek "father of history," for instance. But this is no way to read or interpret a complex literary text like the Bible (granted, it is other things too). Nor is it sufficient to read it solely as a religious text, whether supernaturally or humanly inspired. And since the Hebrew Bible is indispensable to Western culture (don't tell this to Wagnerians), we ought to encounter it as a cultural and literary artifact—at its nonconformist scenes of writing rather than how it was received.

10.

When I broke up with Judy at barely fifteen, too young to drive without a chaperone, the present I found myself in seemed so inferior to the past we shared during many months of going steady, that I thought I was lucky to find a way to dismiss that past as if it were a war that's finally over. In place of long phone calls in which we listened to each other breathe in silence, I spent hours locked in my bedroom writing prose poems about imagined out-of-body experiences. None of those quite approached my heart's perceived free-fall when I could not avoid passing Judy in the high school halls, holding hands with another guy. But at least I was trying to fixate on the aporia of the present.

Mostly when I think about the past now it's the twenty-plus years since I've been in love with Rhonda. When Rhonda reads a sentence like the last one in the preceding paragraph, she knows what aporia means but she worries that too many readers will be put off, thinking either that I was going over their heads or behind their backs in fear of waxing sentimental. Like true lovers anywhere, Rhonda and I sometimes finish each other's sentences (not always—hers can be long and wonderfully complex) so this one will end with a definition of aporia: a sentimental domestication of the unknowable, as if we only pretended it was unknowable. Jacques Derrida, the late French-Jewish philosopher and literary critic, resuscitated the term aporia in his work, but like a true poet he pretended both that aporias were something unknowable and yet at the same time knowable to him.

I would say the same for the great epic and biblical poems/narratives, in which gods or God are both unknowable and yet apprehended as anthropomorphic. Many of my poet-colleagues may roll their eyes, asserting like true scientists that it takes enough effort to dramatize things beyond our senses and common sense without resorting to put human-like faces on them. Most of them wouldn't be caught dead in Disney World, where ducks and mice and elephants speak like wise children. But Rhonda adds: be sure to make it clear that for a poet a real mouse's consciousness can both be unknown and at the same time speak a mammalian language. And be sure to point out, Rhonda adds, that you're not using the term unknowable here because it may be possible, in ten thousand years or so, to know a mouse's consciousness. The unknowable, on the other hand, will never be known by our species—never, as in Neverland.

The fashionable ultra-hip writer, George Saunders, says there's no more distinction between high and low in language—texture is all. That's a bit like saying no high and low in ideas: fresh is all. I go with that, though then the question becomes how do you measure fresh? Today, we seem to think, as Saunders says, texture is all, but that's because we give too much weight to consciousness, in which texture is apprehended. Even if consciousness appears to be a healthy challenge to omniscience, I don't think you can throw the baby out with the bathwater—conscience is the baby and the parent is the first god (or the breast, if you're a Kleinian/Freudian). So how do you keep omniscience around without it spawning superiority complexes? I think Hebraic culture had an answer for that as the Bible was beginning to be written: a contract, a cosmic Covenant. Against the Covenant, we the conscious ones could be disappointing, but the omniscient One could also be disappointing to us, were he to put his part of the bargain in jeopardy. Out of this tension, a literature grows. And within that art, the Most High and the rather low (us) becomes a more complex texture. And then, in every generation, it gets watered down and we require small c creators to heighten our consciousness. Still, even though Rimbaud was texturizing high and low over 150 years ago, the highest and lowest puns were also brought together in ancient Jerusalem, as in the Most High's self-identifying as "I am that I am," or in any number of names of people, places and things, like Yitzchak (Isaac): "you will laugh."

When I was a potential immigrant in Israel in the '80s, I was welcomed as a poet: "We need more poets here," said my employment counselor. However, my Israeli poet-colleagues were generally from an older generation, the kind that hanged, or hung out, in cafés. The café that I frequented in Jerusalem, "Ha-Tzrif" (The Shack), was now across the street from a building that housed computer start-ups. I was hooked on its patented cheap tomato-cucumber plate that I could pick at for hours, along with sips from a "cafe afuch." Suddenly an enhanced menu appeared, with fancy salads I could barely afford, and they were being consumed by guys younger than me in black t-shirts and retro sneakers. There were fewer women coming round and these preferred the new hipsters with a selection of credit cards in their wallets. Yet the guys were even less sexist than the poets had been and within a few years the women there were equally tech-savvy.

When asked what was the most important thing the Jews had contributed to civilization, President Shimon Peres might have been expected to say monotheism, or ethics, or independence, but instead he said: "Dissatisfaction—without a doubt." Pressed further in a late 2013 interview, Peres says, "Never satisfied; it's never good enough, always can be better." He's talking about improving the world, but tell that to the poets. Never be satisfied with the poem, and our best example of that in English-language literature is Shakespeare, who hardly bothered with preserving the texts of his great plays. Haven't seen a better example since Kafka tried to get his manuscripts burnt. What was he thinking, that the great stories weren't good enough? Adam Phillips likes to quote his mentor Winnicott's famous advice about being a "good enough" mother. Perfection not needed in mothering; worrying about it makes mother nervous; let nature carry some of the load. But does it follow to say nature "is not good enough," and extend President Peres's answer beyond humanity and ethics? We're always trying to improve her with domestication, with technology and other prostheses, physical and mental. At the same time, our improvements cause problems. We've learned in recent decades, for instance, that drying up wetlands to expand cities is courting ecological disaster. Atomic energy has led to—

—"To what end?" is the crucial and most dissatisfied question. It's often a sign of rebellion against society, which rushes forward with the latest kitchen aid, or conversely, demands holding on to retrograde social conventions. For instance, "'To what end?' should we educate women, it only leads to conflict." Of course, there's a good answer to that: "Conflict is good for us!" The ancient world—and probably the world today—doesn't quite buy into that, which is partly why the Jewish sensibility is often at odds with it. The Hebrew Bible and the later Talmud are rife with dissatisfaction and argument, questioning conventional wisdom.

The same holds true for translations. As soon as I found myself appalled by the imaginative quality of conventional translations of the Bible, I was consciously rebellious. In the late '60s, when intertextuality for avant-garde writers was commonplace, I might have been asked by a French scholar about my versions of Rimbaud and Valéry, "To what end?"—as if such creative translations could be mistaken for conventional ones, or misread as "improvements" on Rimbaud, and later the Bible. Homage would be my answer to a questioning of purpose, homage to the qualities of the original works, a contemporary art that might reflect something of their essence. A concert ad trumpets "modern reinterpretations of Baroque works." Nobody becomes anxious that this might be an experimental concert; in fact, it is advertised as a conventional one. Now imagine a book that consists of "modern reinterpretations of Biblical works." According to musical convention, you wouldn't expect "variations on a theme in Genesis" or "Psalm after losing a lover," for those are not interpretations of specific Biblical works but merely allusive. And yet, with certain exceptions that do not reference the original text, like MacLeish's *J.B.*, a play on the Book of Job, or Ridley Scott's recent movie, *Exodus,* where are the artistic reinterpretations? You could say we don't need them, we've got scholarly reinterpretations instead—but that's just it, for you've unconsciously demoted the *art* of the original beneath its putative meaning. And along with the art goes the original Hebraic culture in which it was created, as if only the religion mattered. Can we imagine that it's mainly the ancient Greek religion that matters in Homer's *Odyssey* or Sophocles' *Oedipus* trilogy? Unfortunately, scholars and literary critics address the art of biblical text while failing to reimagine the original artists and the Jewish culture in which they reinterpreted their sources and created their works.

In the complex *Book of Job*, whose source is a simple legend, Job's first words to God are, "Why did I have to be born?" We can relate; most of us have asked this question at some despairing point or other in our lives, even if we didn't articulate the words. Job is the epitome of suffering; everything has been taken from him, including his wife and children. Yet he is past caring about them. What—care for those already resting in peace? Well, yes, at least in memory; but Job is talking to God, after all, so it's also a cosmic question of caring for the souls of his family. Yet how can he, being tortured *in extremis*? How can he care even for his own soul, a question even Jesus posed on the cross? Finally, after he's acted out all that's humanly possible, God answers. Consider the crocodile, his maker says. Look at its exquisite armor, its body plated so that nothing could get through to harm it. Its jaws and teeth make yours (ours) minuscule by comparison. It's strength is legendary: the myth of Leviathan. So is this what you want, to be like a crocodile, armored against suffering? But the temptation to say yes is belied by the situation: Job is speaking to the Creator, who is speaking to him and to us, while the crocodile knows nothing of this. It's a situation of knowing, of caring.

"But is it possible God listens to prayers?" asks Rhonda. "No," I answer too glibly. "The Creator is outside spacetime, supernatural, and has no need to physically listen. Instead, he simply knows, knows everything. And that, too, is why he's unknowable to us. The way an accident is unknowable until it happens—if it was known or potentially discoverable, it wouldn't be an accident.

"What creationists and conspiracy theorists share is a deep disbelief in accidents like the ones that drive evolution" (George Johnson, NYT science writer). No, it's more than that, it's a bone-deep belief in our creaturehood and its unknowable purpose. George Johnson disbelieves in unknowability but rather upholds the belief that everything can, at least theoretically, be discovered by humans with the laws of nature—as our limited intelligence apprehends them.

Why not hold both in mind at the same time, knowable and unknowable. And when it comes to "a straight answer" about the existence of God—"Does he or doesn't he, according to you," I had answered Rhonda: Why not hold both in mind at the same time? Like consciousness that transcends meaning—like a poem, or at least a cosmic poem. Could we imagine that the best of the Hebraic poets weren't capable of that, of embodying a contradiction, when all good writing must? But the real question for them is the one Rhonda uses to cut short interminable arguments and beliefs: "To what end?"

Bill Nye, the PBS "Science Guy," writes that everything we have to learn in the future is from the evolutionary past, "the process by which we all came to be." Yes, that's pretty cosmic, it requires holding past and future in mind at the same time. But it vitiates the contradiction between the two, between past and future, living and dead. Only a poem can keep them in mind as a contradiction—toward the end of preserving the fundamental character of our consciousness.

The Poem of Lost Time

As York (Toronto) professor at 23, my students in "Contemporary Literature" were barely 2 or 3 years younger. I lectured 3 times a week on poetry while Dick Goldstein did the same for fiction. There were over a hundred students between us, only a handful of whom we knew personally: those with the gumption, unnecessary for their grades, to visit our office hours. This was still the European lecture-hall system, even though the experimental among my American authors were kicking out the jams—as one of them, guest Robert Creeley, who drove up from Buffalo, quoted the Detroit band leader of the MC5, the poet John Sinclair. One day, unannounced, my father drove up from Detroit to hear me lecture on Charles Olson, a poet he was unlikely to understand. What dad took in was my physical stance at the podium, the tone of my voice, and the puzzled attention of the students. Since I claimed preparatory seclusion before the lecture and then office hours after, Dad drove the long miles home without speaking to me. I only heard about it in a later telephone conversation: "you looked impressive." It may have been the first time since my Bar Mitzvah he saw me in a sports jacket, albeit Carnegie Street Edwardian wide-wale yellow corduroy. But I didn't like the compliment; my idea of "looks" had been to disarm authority and to perhaps disarm some of the students' fear of poetry. Even in the late '60s, of course, this was not fear of complexity but apprehension of a dead-end career path: the exemplary Olson essay I taught was 'In Cold Hell, In Thicket'.

One of my students went on to write a minor bestseller several decades later, the moving *My Cat Saved My Life*, in which he describes rescuing a kitten, Alice, who likewise rescued him from depression, forcing him to match her playfulness in writing. Many of the flower children I knew in the '60s were not so lucky; I visited one of them at Toronto's Queen Street Mental Health Centre, the poet Kati Hewko, when she could not pull out of an acid trip. Now she seemed fine and was about to be discharged after a week's residence, though I was shocked by the dozens of inmates wandering around her in various psychotic states, some of whom I recognized from the Toronto scene. Yet Kati sat and talked with me as if we were at a Starbucks (which of course hadn't existed then); her temporary psychosis had broken but she was still acclimated to the erratic behaviors of fellow patients. There wasn't a Starbucks either in Hitler's Berlin, and everyone seemed normal enough in the coffeehouses of the era, but the shadow of psychosis had fallen. You can trace it in this recent comment: "'The Nazi period will remain a thorn in Germany's side,' said Andreas Wirsching, director of the Institute of Contemporary History in

Munich. 'We will continually be confronted with the question of how it could be that such a highly civilized country plunged into such an abyss of transgression, into a regime of injustice and murder. That is a lasting question of humanity that can be nightmarishly relevant.'" But I think he's missing the real nightmare: killing the Jews could never have been enough, the blood-stains would need constant re-scrubbing and some had been turned into soap, as if memory of them could be washed away, the way a psychotic killer saws up the body of his victim (and in the Coen brothers' movie *Fargo* tries to stuff the limbs into a woodchipper). It is past murder and deep into the unique flaws within our species. It's assimilable, if it is, only as species shame, as being embarrassed to be human, like I was momentarily ashamed in my affectation of hippiedom while visiting the Toronto Asylum for the Insane, as it was originally known. But my shame was pedestrian, as if being improperly dressed for an occasion, as in the common dream of finding oneself walking down the street naked. It is a time in the dream that never existed, a lost time. To face it, and to guard your own embarrassment of being an ambitious survivor—someone lost *in* time and thereby imaginatively recoverable—you need to start deadpan.

Although the history of Hitler's Germany exists, is not lost, the Holocaust can't be accounted for by history, only by species consciousness and the deadpan look on the face of the first Homo sapiens—before we ourselves took credit for having evolved, idealizing our hands or the sounds coming out of our mouths. But only when our species has become extinct, says Rhonda, will we know if the present history we've all inherited, namely the drive to make the oldest ongoing writing civilization, the Jews, extinct in the 20th Century, was not repeated. Until then, why do we have to keep having this discussion, we ask ourselves by the pool, our cat perched on the ping-pong table. Only because Israel exists, says Rhonda, and the ongoing resentment against it, as to whether it's not perfect enough, forgiving enough, Socialist enough, or not like everyone else enough. No Israel and the discussion dies out—not for just the two of us but for the chance of Homo sapiens ever coming face to face with itself. Rhonda, in her skimpiest poolside attire, takes the Einstein position in this discussion: a responsibility for Jews is parallel to one for Homo sapiens. On the newest bio of Einstein, physicist Freeman Dyson asserts: "it presents Einstein's Jewish heritage as he saw it himself, not as the core of his being, but as a historical accident bringing inescapable responsibilities." If it's a secular accident how and where we are born into the world, then the Jewish accident that produced Einstein or any other Jew makes Bible-writing people like us responsible for more than Jewish history but for history itself, with the lost time of Creation at its origin—which resembles (perhaps) the origin of our galaxy and the supermassive black hole at its center that sustains it.

Got a haircut yesterday and see I have enough left to choose between neat swept back and distressed hair look, depending on how I feel. Does the distressed look suggest we still live within the Holocaust's shadow, or does it represent the opposite, a slavishness to style of the moment? Then we saw the Stratford *Antony and Cleopatra*, "live" in HD at our South of Miami cinema—Rhonda and I the only patrons, allowing us to discuss loudly, to comment and chomp popcorn like being at home. Mark Antony and Cleopatra vacillate between narcissism and diplomacy like most of us, revealing the unique trait of our species to imagine what another individual is thinking and to obsess over it. In other words, the direct opposite of the recent European killing machine, which rendered its civilian victims subhuman and thus beneath thought. The idea arises as I read today of poet-colleague Geza Rohrig at Cannes in cause célèbre new Holocaust film, *Son of Saul*. Geza thinks like us, as we discovered several years ago on his visit to Miami, after he'd translated me for a Hungarian Jewish literary journal. He reiterates in a Guardian interview today that humanity has been more gravely wounded by the Holocaust than we are ready to admit. "'I think it's fair to say,' says Géza Röhrig softly, 'that we haven't learned anything from Auschwitz.'" When it comes to the film's issue of slave labor survival, Geza says, "I see absolutely nothing I think is unethical. It was the only way for them to do their best to survive.". From what I know of him, he's saying survival, going on living, is a necessary virtue in its own right, even as it contradicts an EU consensus that survival, in the case of Israel, should be for the reason to do good, to care for others. "But what about that Dutch park last week, the one in the old Jewish neighborhood that was wiped out, that's been designated for a Holocaust monument?" asks Rhonda. "The new non-Jewish residents reject it. 'A park is carefree, for forgetting your cares,' they say."

That Dutch monument is to have the forty thousand names of the shipped-to-Auschwitz Dutch Amsterdam community written on it, including Anne Frank; the *New York Times* compared it to the DC Vietnam park monument. At least those names are no longer lost in time. The black hole that is lost time, however, is challenged by Israeli poet and novelist Michal Govrin, who convened a group in 2014 to investigate how memory of the Holocaust differs in each human mind, each one responsible for transmitting it, and to project such knowledge of uniqueness backward into a retrieving of the life bios of all six million Jewish victims to be engraved on a monument. NYC's Central Park couldn't hold it; they'll have to designate the entire city of Berlin (Vienna?) a park. Meanwhile, MacArthur grant installation artist Fred Wilson came through Miami for a talk on museum amnesia and his latest memory art project in Savannah. The new art museum abuts a former plantation where slaves made the bricks for old Savannah's buildings; many of those bricks are now part of the museum, which is a restoration of the old railway station. Wilson intends to research the lost names of slaves from the plantation so he can engrave one on each of the building's bricks. Later, Rhonda asks Fred—who noted that several of his conceptual projects in museum self-awareness are in Europe—if he's made any Jewish memory connections. "No," said Fred, "I'd have liked to, I made memory works in Polish museums, but they were interested in mainly their history of being surrounded by enemy countries. Nothing internal. I'd have liked to visit Auschwitz but nobody suggested it'd be useful to me."

I jumped in: "If the camps are like Jewish museums in Poland, couldn't the exhibits there be considered horrific conceptual art critiques of memory—huge piles of gassed persons' shoes and hair, for instance, and even a mound of eyeglasses torn from their faces?" Rhonda added: "We've hardly begun to know how to think about these exhibits." Fred: "Has anyone thought of it as art?" Rhonda: "You focus on how to think about such things, especially the absence they present; the absence, for instance, of the African slave laborers' names from the historical memory of Savannah." Fred thought a bit, then reiterated that he'd need to be invited and to be allowed access to everyone involved in operating Auschwitz like a museum. "I'd have to learn everything about it in order to find what's missing. Obviously the shoes and eyeglasses refer to the missing bodies, but they're just reminders. I don't think most people viewing those exhibits would ask themselves what they need to think about. They're reminders, period, of the horror show; no thinking necessary. It would be my job as an artist to make them something more, to present them in an art context where you have to ask, 'What do I have to think about here that hasn't been thought?' It's overwhelming that the dead are missing."

I shuffled a bit. We were standing in Miami's contemporary art museum courtyard, a few paces from where patrons were swinging in arty baskets, made for adults. But I couldn't imagine we'd even have this conversation if we were sitting; it required sensing you were an artifact yourself, in weight-bearing shoes. "What about us who are alive and how we think about what we see, in culture and history? Shouldn't that be a reason to visit Auschwitz as much as the Louvre?" asks Rhonda. I backed her up with my old art critic bona fides, having earlier offered them to Fred. "As in Savannah, your job is to make us aware of how we're looking at it, how the historical and cultural suppositions of the conservators of Auschwitz fail to place themselves there. In your terms, they're curators, but I'd call them bystanders as well, those who didn't or couldn't know how to think about their history as it was happening—and the same for the viewers. You would problematize their experience and deepen the mourning of death slavery, just as you do for American slavery." Fred held up his hand as if to stop a huffing train. "If it happens, I didn't intend it. I come to a site as a *tabula rasa*. My projects can take years. Being an artist at Auschwitz could take centuries. Just answering the first questions could make me an old man: 'Where would I live, who would support me, how much cooperation would I get?' And it'd be a hell of a project, to think what's missing in exhibiting hell itself, if there be exhibits in hell." Sensing some frustration in Fred, and as if to ameliorate it by putting an end to the conversation, Rhonda repeats and answers an earlier question. "'What can you think about in front of a mound of eyeglasses outside a gas chamber?' You can think, How am I going to live with that image for the rest of my life, to keep it vivid so that it's still there on my very last day—and on the last day of the human species?" At that point, we shuffled back toward the contemporary art museum's cafeteria, where a hostess held the door open for us. "We're closing in ten minutes," she offered kindly. "What can we eat in ten minutes?" asks Rhonda. "See that piece of cake that's shaped like a pair of dark sunglasses?" the hostess answered. "It's chocolate."

2.

Like many undergrads, I read the complete *Divine Comedy* by Dante in translation, though I doubt I could have weighed its value against other translations. As much as I grasped the visuals and even the ironies (with footnotes) of Hell, I did not connect with Dante's despair, often utter despair. That's partly because I couldn't yet express my own and partly because I confused his irony with comedy, about how short and fateful a life is. Dante's irony, as in the Bible, is protective, and I could not understand, at 19, its necessity: to allow the journey to proceed, through to the lost time, in the form of Edenic innocence, of re-encountering Beatrice; or, in the biblical journey, to arrive at Mt. Sinai, Jerusalem, and then through the lost time of losing the Creator's place on Earth, Jerusalem's Temple, and further through exile and back to Jerusalem. I was more likely to understand the hell of Rimbaud, in which poetry is a necessary protection against a visionary derangement of the senses, whether drug-induced or death-despairing, in either case a personal hell whose exit is aesthetic.

So I have to call upon poets and writers I read in youth who helped form my experience of—or more consciously, against—lost time. Not only books but other media, like movies, TV and art, that illustrate what "against" lost time might mean: a sort of pregnant amnesia that is an ironic analog for the Garden of Eden. And not a utopian Eden but its more complex vision of lost time as timelessness. I had hold of timelessness in the original modern poet, Rimbaud, who I began freely translating in '68, but it was only when I was translating the Hebrew Bible a few years later that I discovered in it a literary origin for pre-existence, for timelessness, that could interpret my early psychological experience (for it did not touch me first-hand) of—and not against—lost time: the as yet unnamed Holocaust, represented to me in prepubescence by the black photo-mounting paper in European family albums. Rimbaud's *A Season in Hell* (1873), in which the biblical Eden might be only the possibility of poetry itself, has no cosmic dimension, unless it's the disorientation of the soul. Bear with me as I tease this out. Confronting the Hebrew of the Bible in 1973, I said to my own disoriented soul that it should consider Adam and Eve's disorientation, and that of their descendants, after being forced out of Eden. *That* cosmic history underlay the biblical history of humanity, as it unfolded into the time of the original writers in Solomonic Jerusalem and later. They create a cosmic theater that can accommodate both the A movie of the patriarchs and Exodus, and the B movie of David and Goliath. There's a hell in both, from slavery to murderous war, but there's also the Creator, who knows more than we can ever know. By dramatizing His interest in human history, the Hebraic authors make room—in the Creator's opposing timelessness—for the lost time of our pre-existence. And I connected this pre-existence, in which we were created as creaturely individuals and as species, psychologically and post-Rimbaud, to the shame in all of us for having survived the Holocaust. Of course, like society in general I repressed the connection, though it was accessible to me when I translated. Mainly, I was living our common life, immersed in both A and B cultural pursuits or relationships that make life so interesting, as when they disarm, sometimes painfully, our pretensions to know everything. And at the level of art, there's the excitement in encountering a historical context to every moment that we'll never have enough time to unpack.

Not long ago, to be more specific, we watched *Top Gun* ('55) in which Sterling Hayden, a good but morally compromised man bound up in the hell of Wyoming—the frontier never presented more darkly—survives. Rhonda says what makes it a B-movie is Sterling (and his rejecting girl with a last-minute change of heart) gets a happy send-off from the surviving townspeople who just a few hours ago were ready to hang him. Even the "good people" of the town are morally bankrupt in their affections, as was the Roman background in Shakespeare's *Antony and Cleopatra* we saw just yesterday, but there the morally compromised lovers do not survive. That's what makes it an A drama, it doesn't evade the necessity of death, for the good and the bad equally. That was my comment, but Rhonda says the A movie, being more polished and slavish to the illusion of verisimilitude, is the bigger evader because it works on our ambivalence toward death: *we* are the survivors, in place of Antony and Cleopatra. More sophisticated, for sure, but that's the way civilization has it, going back to Aristotle on tragic poetry. So you're saying, I add, that what's deepest in Shakespeare is the unmasking of his Christian Humanist society, which is still ours today? We're pulled out of the audience, as it were; the whole theater (Shakespeare's "The Globe") is witness; we become Sterling Haydens and Karin Booths who, unlike them, are made aware of our impending deaths. Look, counters Rhonda, the fear and trembling that Aristotle ascribes to our witness of tragedy is civilization's cover story; it's a worked-up B-movie but we can't avoid that it's all, A and B, wish-fulfillment. And that's what we were talking about then, the wish to cover over the lost time at the origin of our evolution as a species, to displace it with the cover story of humanly invented civilization. It's such a poignant wish, especially in Aristotle, and never more greatly appreciated than in Shakespeare, who allows us to consider belonging to the fateful stars above our cities and fields.

"A time beyond boundaries" is what old colleague Harold Bloom, at age 85, calls lost time, allying it with my J translation of Eden, 25 years ago. Today, however, he disparages lost time as not worth knowing, as if it can only swallow us into a black hole. Unlike a poet, the critic in Harold didn't develop the complex deadpan with which to confront the lost time of Eden—where, as at the scene of Homo sapiens evolution, human flaw was conceived and became our moral inheritance. "Moral judgment is irrelevant to Moby-Dick and to Shakespeare," I find him saying today. Yet how to swallow it when, in *Antony & Cleopatra*, it is we on the Globe's benches who judge the pair's deaths by the moral standard of survival: morally, they deserved to survive, and not to have been sacrificed to whatever ideals. Same goes for Adam and Eve, who at least deserved their limited lifetimes, in which they putatively did not descend into evil. Like us, they didn't survive simply by accident: we'd like to think we deserve our survival.

But to survive lost time, to face Auschwitz, you need a dead pan. I first found it for myself in 19th century poets Baudelaire and Rimbaud, as I've said, whose deadpan selfhoods I responded to with my own deadpan translations of their French. I was in Paris for my doctoral thesis on Gertrude Stein, in my mid-twenties, and my first extended stay on the continent unnerved me. Walking past it, I was moved by Stein's old residence as I imagined it empty of her during the war, a nervous house with nervous modernist paintings, as she hid out the early '40s near a nondescript French village. But I was more seriously pulled toward Drancy, the Parisian suburb that served as concentration camp for masses of Jews in transit to the death camps. Max Jacob and Robert Desnos, two deadpan poets (mistakenly labeled surrealists) who I would attempt to translate, passed through there to their young awful deaths. But I took Baudelaire to be the father of deadpan. In the poem I translated that follows, he casually speaks to his soul without dread, deadpan—it's his soul itself that experiences the dread of Baudelaire's would-be worldly poem.

Anywhere Out of the World

In the hospital of life
the patients are all mad with desire
for a change of bed

this man wants to suffer next to radiator
this imagines getting better
under the window

wherever I don't happen to be
feels good to me
my soul and I have a running discussion on that

what do you think my pale shivering
of living in sunny Lisbon
warm and alive as a lizard

they say it's built with marble
people there hate plants so much
they uproot all the trees

and it's on the seacoast
made completely of light and mineral
and water to reflect them

but my soul is not responding

well since you're so glued to peace and quiet
as long as something is moving to watch
why don't we go live in Holland

a place you think of often in art galleries
stoned by the mast-forests of Rotterdam
great ships anchored beside the houses

total silence is all that comes from this soul
say how about Batavia
where the European spirit mates with a tropical beauty

nothing—could my soul be dead already?
so down you enjoy suffering?
then let's go to some really dead places!

we'll pack our trunks for Torneo
or even farther—extreme end of the Baltic
farther—we could set up house at lifeless North Pole!

where the sun barely skims through the world
and the bare-minimum strobe of light and dark
nicely frames the monotony

which is half of the picture itself.
And we can take long baths of darkness.
For entertainment the Aurora Borealis

sometimes will color our pages
like reflections of a fireworks display
in Hell—suddenly my soul is shrieking

in its wisdom: Anywhere!
I don't care—as long as it's out
of this world!

Turns out, Geza's film wins Grand Prize at Cannes this year. His role as a *Sonderkommando* doesn't win best actor, that would be asking a lot for two hours of deadpan, the less humorous kind, the kind where the multitude of faces, young and old, staring back at you every day, start out desperately alive and turn totally dead in less than an hour. And then you must bury them, or rather shovel them into the crematoria. But on the more common, everyday level, memory works that way, the persons you recall (called up from the dead past) generally fade out on the same day. You can recall them, however, again and again, and you can even make them do new things—assuming they are memories of living persons—and also change their tune or talk to you. If you're a poet, it's uncanny. If not, it's a step toward the danger of fantasy, not telling the difference between living and dead; a few steps more and you're living under the Third Reich.

Hi love,
You asked about the etiology of the autistic child or the schizophrenic one, and why others in the family ask what in the shared history could explain the psychosis of a family member. If the German Reich were that member of the family of nations, it would be just as misguided to ask why the psychosis of anti-Semitism. Yet neither bad genes or ideology, religion or propaganda can fully explain the oldest hatred—and it's the same with mental problems, the disinterest, as if it's been accounted for and must be lived with, old

news. Psychotic anti-Semitism, however, has always been beyond racism because the Jewish people are 1) most distinguishable by their long encounter with history, not by the typical trappings of skin color, physiognomy, geography, intelligence, values, *et. al.* The latter attributes are all filler for the fantasy of resentment. 2) The obsession with the Jewish people is so completely in the heads of the resentful that what they resent is projected onto and into the heads of the Jewish people—and what comes out of Jewish heads, i.e. cultural productions. And 3) the Nazi resentment was the consummation of anti-Semitism that's still unaccounted for, in which killing is never enough, and must be perverted at every turn to the point that it's antithetical to self-preservation, the most basic species drive. So, even self-destruction and extermination fantasy (at war's end they were still shipping people to the death camps when they needed the trains and fuel for their troops) remains a resentment of the Jewish encounter and ongoing persistence with history. Witnessing history, consciously, is what I think sets us apart as a species—as well as the resentment of that history. The *Volk*, however, is not historical encounter; it's myth, despite what German tradition thought then or the bystander nations now ask, What historical psychosis? By the time of the Third Reich it is unable to distinguish between real and imagined versions of itself, so if you ask how did it become psychotic I have only one answer: it was separated from reality by the willing ingestion of anti-Semitism—completely unlike a schizophrenic child. It is of another order, we're still learning how to diagnose it, and while we can do wonders for the individual schizophrenic or autistic person, we're still willing to look away from the anti-Semitism that manifests in whole societies today as "a world without Zionism," according to Wistrich, even in distant Malaysia. Families used to hide their autistic members, as if it bespoke family guilt. But there's little shame and much fantasy among the family of nations, where one in particular, the Jewish homeland, is singled out as being responsible for the disease.

Hope this helps, love.

Perhaps Abraham was responsible for anti-Semitism, the first rebellious Jew, leaving his Mesopotamian culture and his parents behind. When I wrote a book about him to square myself with the European culture my parents left behind—as if classic Greece and Rome equalled classic Sumer and Akkad—Abraham laid the foundation for ancient Israel the way modern pioneers escaping Russian pogroms did, in the 19th century. Nobody was intending to displace anyone, as in the way Abraham argued with God about saving Sodom and Gommorah: "Abram drew close. 'Will you wipe away the innocent beside those with contempt? What if there are fifty sincere men inside the city, will you also wipe the place away? Can you not hold back for the fifty innocent within it? Heaven forbid you bring this thing to light, to erase the innocent with the contemptuous—as if sincerity and contempt were the same thing. Can it be—heaven forbid—you, judge of all the earth, will not bring justice?'"

As a moral reimagining of trauma, with Sodom and Gomorrah (at bottom, an earthquake) a reprise of the Flood story, the Sodomites represent the anti-Semitic contempt of Abraham and Israel's God; they were the original anti-Semites. It's beyond racism, since there is nothing denoted of Abraham's skin color, his culture, his education and religion. He represents not a race but a position of resistance: against idol or mankind-worship, against the hallucination that we are self-created (as opposed to a self in society). And Abraham's anxiety about Sodom's total absence of tolerance may anticipate how others could blame his family for Sodom and Gomorrah's fate, resenting him and his God.

But in the poetry of Psalm 90, for instance, a poem of Creation, it's become clear that all of the human species and the entire universe are the referents, not simply Abraham's progeny or Israel. Already in the ancient Jewish state, questions of one's just place on the earth could be measured by the universe. Before that, however, Abraham is faced with the lost time—the black hole—of Sodom: "Abram arose that morning, hurried to the place he had last faced Yahweh, had stood there with him. Looking out over the upturned faces of Sodom and Gomorrah, over the whole face of the valley, he saw—so it was—a black incense over the earth climbing like smoke from a kiln." To acknowledge lost time is to plumb the deepest fantasy of anti-Semitism: the wish to wipe out the memory of Creation (or evolutionary history), along with its God. Species consciousness, including the awareness that each of our bodies is made up of millions of communities, isn't easy, and it's more common to lose the dialogue with Creation, like a poet who sits down to his writing table unconscious that language itself originates in lost time, along with the archaic bacteria still within us.

A new history of the non-death-camp German "concentration camps" is widely reviewed (including appositely by Adam Kirsch in *The New Yorker*, where it's still a pale echo of the capacious space allowed for Hannah Arendt on Eichmann a half-century ago). It all sounds dutiful, with typical praise for the author, as in *Tablet*: "He mostly avoids philosophical and ethical controversy, sticking to the facts of history." Not a mention here or anywhere, however, of the *psychological* controversy. Instead, the Germans are driven to their acceptance of bestiality by extreme ideological conditions. The mental disease of anti-Semitism is barely to be surmised, with only curt mention of it as a "cause" for the singularity of demonizing the Jews. Indeed, that singularity itself is vitiated by the emphatic comparisons to concentration camps of other nations, including the imperial British ones. Yes, the difference is stressed, even between German and Soviet *Gulags*, yet even there this book in 2015, *KL: A History of the Nazi Concentration Camps*, universally described as an extensive work, is but thin gruel compared with Solzhenitsyn's truly massive *The Gulag Archipelago*, first published in English more than forty years earlier. Even there, the Soviet psychosis is not adequately approached as a disease, while the German and pan-European psychosis of anti-Semitism is still a long way from being faced as a descent into lost time. It's easy enough to say our species is a flawed one and therefore requires vigilance; the hard work is to determine where the flaw originates, both in evolutionary and cultural terms. As a psychosis, a demented fantasy, it is just as real as my early childhood fantasy that I was being abandoned forever by my mother when she went out dancing with a strange man (my war-wounded father was still in the VA hospital). Mom was there next morning, my fear subsided, but in adulthood I was still in the shadow of fantasy that wives and lovers would abandon me *without an explanation*. Fortunately, I got my self-explanations in psychoanalytic therapy while in my forties, and I can say this without stepping on the toes of those who are anti-psychological: If you fantasize that someone in himself (or a people) could kidnap or is an implicit criticism of your belief system, perhaps by affecting to appear smarter, craftier, more ingenious, or more authentic, then your sense of well-being could become as destabilized as if that person had kidnapped your child—except that you would be insane, which is worse. I would amend that to "temporarily insane," a condition we are all familiar with—I felt like smashing something when the Marlins' closer blew the game, but fortunately it did not take over the city of Miami and cause it to literally murder the entire New York Mets team. And if it had, I would not be looking for social and ideological explanations; I would need to explore a mass psychosis. So that's how misguided such books as *KL* can appear; there is nothing wrong with its sober history of "the facts," in fact it's painfully necessary, but it's still just scratching the surface. Underneath lies a lost time that can never be retrieved, not even with the half a billion lives *in toto* lost in WWII having each name etched across a new global Appian Way of a monument. But I got ahead of myself—those total lives are lost in time, not *lost time* itself. The majority of those lives lost in time can be recalled in the context of families and communities that survive, yet when the families and communities are also exterminated, as they largely were in the Holocaust (we could mention Hiroshima and Dresden, except that those cities are rebuilt, unlike the myriad Jewish towns, villages, and neighborhoods, vanished forever) there is no going back.

A poet at her writing table is constantly feeling for a path that connects to the main road going back to Creation, by which I mean a semblance of Eden where things make so much sense that no explanation could ever be made or needed. She may recreate that Edenic lost time by offering up her own consciousness as a momentary placeholder for it, so that everything imaginable is contained therein, from the most gorgeous tree to its shadow, foreshadowing the vacuum of empty space. It's only a placeholder, however, for a time-bound author who, if she is a great one (Dickinson: "Come slowly—Eden!"), will reveal our Homo sapiens' loss of the dialogue with Creation. In its stead, sans the Bible's cosmic theater, we can fashion sublime soliloquies and avant-garde ironies of absence, but to whom are we speaking? Prospero's spirits, perhaps, or Dickinson's bees lost in flowers (her foreknowledge of species consciousness), but consider the Hebrew psalmist's main road to the universe:

PSALM 90

Lord, you are our home
in all time
from before the mountains rose

or even the sun
from before the universe
to after the universe

you are Lord forever
and we are home
in your flowing

you turn men into dust
and you ask them to return
children of men

for a thousand years
in your eyes
are a single day

yesterday
already passed
into today

a ship in the night
while we were present
in a human dream

submerged
in the flood of sleep
appearing in the morning

like new grass
growing into afternoon
cut down by evening

we are swept off our feet
in an unconscious wind
of war or nature

or eaten away
with anxiety
worried to death

worn-out swimmers
all dressed up
in the social whirl

you see our little disasters
secret lusts
broken open in the light

of your eyes
in the openness
penetrating our lives

every day melts away
before you
our years run away

into a sigh
at the end
of a story

over in another breath
seventy years
eighty—gone in a flash

and what was it?
a tinderbox of vanity
a show of pride

and we fly apart
in the empty mirror
in the spaces between stars

in the total explosion of galaxies
how can we know ourselves
in this human universe

without expanding
to the wonder that you are
infinite lightness

piercing my body
this door of fear
to open my heart

our minds are little stars
brief flares
darkness strips naked

move us to see your present
as we're moved to name each star
lighten our hearts with wonder

return
and forgive us
locking our unconscious

behind the door
and as if it isn't there
as if we forget we're there

we walk into space unawed
unknown to ourselves
years lost in thought

a thousand blind moments
teach us when morning comes
to be moved

to see ourselves rise
returning witnesses
from the deep unconscious

and for every day lost
we find a new day
revealing where we are

in the future and in the past
together again
this moment with you

made human for us
to see your work
in the open-eyed grace of children

the whole vision unlocked
from darkness
to the thrill of light

where our hands reach for another's
opening to life
in our heart's flow

the work of this hand
flowing open
to you and from you.

When I recreated this psalm in the '70s, I was in the immediate shadow
of my father's sudden heart-attack and death, and as I contemplated my
father becoming lost in time I wished for a universe in which the burst
of its origin was a statement, one whose translation and interpretation
was ongoing, and could conceivably be retrieved like an image sent into
space, its outwardly traveling lightwaves catchable-up-to somewhere, such
as my father's image. If that sounds too comix-like, it's really the old wish
for pushing the boundaries of time. I faced it head-on when translating a
portion of the major text of Kabbalah, the 13th century *Zohar*, in the '90s,
and I'll get to that in my chapter on translation. But it was in the late '60s,
in a free process of translating Rimbaud, that the poems of *Leavin America*
(in my imagination) took up the physical universe, as in:

New Moon

Those who sit
peppered with pock-marks
eyes ringed with green

skulls caked with indeterminate crusts
on growths
weird bone structures

in the growing dark skeleton
evening…
men have always been one flesh with

the sun
beneath the window-panes where the snow is
and invisible earth

colored brown with age
and the aged Indian corn
of shirts

grouped under a distant streetlight…
we are the uprights
on which the keys of light and dark

day upon day
are stretched in our heads
out to the spheres
    [*Leavin America*, Coach House Press, 1972]

Before our senses were organized into Homo sapiens, before we had Homo sapiens articulate language, back at our creation, our consciousness was as if stunned into being by the sun.

So the species consciousness I invoke in 'New Moon' is the one at our origin, at Creation, a lost time I identify with the sun: you can't stare into it with our naked senses or it will "disorder the senses," as Rimbaud suggested. Re-ordering requires a physical connection between light and music, between the spheres and what's in the sphere of our heads. It was a way of taking on the cosmos purely with conscious-ness and without an ounce of metaphysics. The resistance we young avant-gardists deployed against the cosmic theater of Psalm 90—its attempt to speak back to the unknowable or supernatural, to have some imaginative connection with the unseen, to have negotiated a *modus vivendi* with Creation—was not shared by an intellectual writer like Saul Bellow. In an essay on Bellow, Jeffrey Eugenides maintains "he believed in, and insisted upon talking about, that very old-fashioned thing: the soul," and in terms of an afterlife. But afterlife or not, the soul is innocent of the Covenant, of history, which is essential to biblical writing. The Hebrew Bible keeps ensnaring God and the supernatural in history, in order to study a border with it and negotiate a covenant; it is not content with or even interested in sublime intimations of the soul and afterlife. All this I hardly understood until facing Psalm 90, in '74, four years after 'New Moon.' But as much as I wanted to, after reading his novel of poet Delmore Schwartz, it would take time for me to find a colleague in Saul Bellow, who seemed equally averse to Baudelaire and the Hebrew Bible.

3.

Bellow's immersion in a man-made consciousness comes clear when he writes about and agrees with James Joyce's *Ulysses*. "For what are we to do with such a burden of information? *Ulysses* is a comedy of information. Leopold Bloom lies submerged in an ocean of random facts... The man-made world begins, like the physical world, to suggest infinity." But no, we can't embody that infinity, that lost condition of Eden. Critically apt as I thought Bellow was, it was hard to imagine him writing a poem, especially not as James Joyce had, a disposition that underlay *Ulysses*. It was as if he considered poetry in eclipse, an art too strong for modernism, proven by the shadow it cast on Delmore Schwartz and even Joyce's descent into the great *Finnegans Wake*. I remained suspicious of Bellow until '76, when his *To Jerusalem and Back* revealed an affection for the poets Schimmel and Silk, whom I had recently befriended. I reread *Humboldt's Gift* and was able to put aside my queasy feeling that Delmore was made more interesting as a character than as a poet, even though Bellow does the same for my Jerusalem poet-colleagues, coloring them up with exotic crayons. Instead, I accepted the poetry of his sentences, each one often a lyrical weaving together of thought and perception—more thought than found in much of the latest poetry.

"The only way I could ever read The Bible was to return to it again and again—by which I mean I started it several times, read about 100 pages each time, gave up, then came back to it." I'm not being fair to the writer Lydia Davis, from whom I've extracted this quote with a slight change: she actually said "Joyce's *Ulysses*" and not the Bible. But many writers have said something like this about the Bible, though never admitting to finally finishing it as Davis says about *Ulysses*: "not until I was actually living in Ireland and also had very few other books in the house." I think Davis is hinting toward her problem with Joyce, a lack of affinity with his sources, especially Irish ones. And I think we could say the same for contemporary writers and the Bible: a hundred pages in and they share no sympathies with the lost authors. Yet were they to live in Israel and pick up some Hebrew, their position could change—or rather, *begin* to change, because the reimagining of the original writers has only just begun.

We're in town for a visit and my novelist-colleague Jonathan Rosen asks if we can meet at the 92nd Y after the Saul Bellow memorial in '05. We're not going, I say. "You don't love Bellow?" "It's not that. It's the heights of adulation. And I won't be able to put aside comparison with the demise of my old teacher, Delmore Schwartz." Once hopeful, at 22, of confronting his legendary mind, I found it turned into a tragicomedy of a displaced mind, one that I encountered panhandling on East Genesee near downtown Syracuse, and soon enough was a dead mind, unclaimed in an NYC morgue for many days after his heart attack, if that's what it was. A couple years later I'm reading Bellow's *Humboldt's Gift*, with Schwartz a thinly disguised protagonist, badly disappointed that the rebellious poet of my graduate school imaginings was occluded by a generic great poet, albeit on a downward slope to madness. Bellow still took poets and poetry for granted, in an age when I already understood it was no longer possible, and that it was up to the post-modern poet to create his or her audience anew. My own encounter with Delmore Schwartz bore that out, as if the lauded poet himself looked into the mirror of tradition and saw a Medusa head, a greater complexity than traditional poetry allowed for. (Freud imagined that the snake-like hairs of the head were actually penis symbols derived from the female pubic hair, serving to mitigate the horror of the complex). So how could I stomach the Bellow eulogies without recalling the end of *Humboldt's Gift*, where the reburial of the great poet came down to: "The funeral director said, 'Does anybody have a prayer to say?' Nobody seemed to have or to know a prayer." I would rather have had a prayer, a cosmic poem, than all the misplaced Bellovian wit I was sure to encounter at the 92nd Street Y.

But now, rereading that novel and its ironic homage to Delmore Schwartz, my mind has changed. I feel the book is a mourning, that Bellow has actually recorded the *loss* of Schwartz, the end of academic idealizations of tradition. For Schwartz to have truly been an epic poet he would have to have written shocking prayers—astounding in their address of creation and Creator—in place of the quixotic faux epic poem, *Genesis*, he banged his head against for many years. It was too literal, his idea of the epic, just as today's poets take too literally an atrophied *anti*-epic stance. In a gesture to Jonathan, I did take a cab to the 92nd Street Y after the event, Rhonda and Michal Govrin in tow, to find him waiting at the curb. We walked in Central Park together and wondered if prayer could be possible (Michal had just co-authored a book on the subject with Jacques Derrida and David Shapiro) without irony, that only the fuel of irony could break through a complex sorrow. We were quite serious; I don't recall any laughter.

It was like the horribly ironic nexus of Eden and the Holocaust as representations of lost time, both realms black as the death I recalled facing after open-heart surgery. On the operating table, my memory sucked into the blackness of deep space, no longer mine, no longer me, it mattered not that the little world on which I'd briefly lived had existed. It was like the *loss* of Eden that we fail to grasp the bottomless despair of, so that reclaiming each of the 6 million names torn off in the Holocaust, retrieving what has been lost in time, can only be provisional. Bellow worked around that, from rescuing Delmore Schwartz in memory to Allen Bloom in his last novel. He mostly steered clear of the black hole of the Holocaust (even in *Mr. Sammler's Planet* and *Herzog*, B's novels plumb character more than lost time). The Bible especially was a huge absence in his work and probably the reason he couldn't develop a serious deadpan. The greatest Jewish deadpan is speaking back to Creation, as in the form of the Creator. You might stutter like Moses, but mostly you were deadpan (unlike Sammler)—no smile, no frowning, no hint of happiness or disappointment, when faced with God. Even Job was stunned silent. One's feelings were one's own, hidden within as if unborn. The feelings of a fetus—what are they? The answer, bordering on the outrageous, fits many of Isaac Singer's characters, but not those of Bellow's, neurotic as they may be, even when acted out as wild and crazy as Mel Brooks. I wouldn't put Mel up against the Holocaust or Creation. Bellow, as much as he thought about the human condition, did not think about the *universe's* condition, which extends beyond mortality and toward the forging of the biblical Covenant as a boundary of Creation. As much as he had sublime intimations of it, Bellow shied away from the Hebrew Bible toward a Mel Brooks-like ear for Yiddish. Jeffrey Eugenides interprets Humboldt/Delmore's last message, "Remember, we are not natural creatures but supernatural," as "the manifestation of higher consciousness not in a trance or moment of gnosis but in language." I forgot to ask Jeffrey—we talked too much of growing up in Detroit—if he realized how Jewish was the idea of numinous *language*, as the Torah's Hebrew may be considered, rather than numinous *being* in the New Testament. I'd argue that his non-mystical human language is precisely what intimidates Bellow from doing anything with the Hebrew Bible, as it struggles to keep the supernatural confined within the Covenant, rather than all over the place via metaphor. And if we can establish some distance from the Creator in a covenantal boundary, then we can speak to him in deadpan—dead yet still mortal, not supernatural; lost in time but recoverable in memory. The deadpan language I learned from Stein and Stevens, Ashbery and Berrigan, I found again, more powerfully resonant, in the great psalms I interpreted. Psalm 90 speaks back to Creation, turning lost time into beyond time, a transcendent blues of infinity.

The Blues giant B.B. King died last week. He was a Zionist (as was Memphis Slim) and played many concerts in Israel. I heard him twice in the '80s, in Jerusalem. He sang in English but his guitar, named Lucille, sang in Hebrew. In the late '60s I heard the equally legendary Lonnie Johnson in Toronto. He was old, aficionados thought him dead; he soloed at a new restaurant on the corner of Huron and Harbord (it lasted but a year) seated in a folding chair in front of the kitchen. Besides Kati and I, the handful of a white-bread audience was disinterested, apparently had come to taste the food. I clapped extra loud at the end of his short set and went up to him. He was a gorgeous old legend in bronze, slow eyelids, outsized hands. I said, "You are a legend to me and I apologize for this ridiculous gig." He looked at the wall and answered, "You can be a legend in Hell, doesn't matter," and then turned a golden-toothed smile toward me. No legend has ever spoken more intimate words to me. I think I put a Canadian orange two-dollar bill in his cup, an extravagance for me at the time.

I'm listening to a recording of Saul Bellow reading *Humboldt's Gift*, an "amusing" passage, as he called it. The Delmore Schwartz character is contrasted with the car he drove, and then the cars were imagined that Henry James, Walt Whitman, or Emily Dickinson might drive. The character of Schwartz is lovingly described in all its exfoliating disaster—of drug addiction, schizophrenia, tremors, and acting out—yet its the loving narrator that scares me, his own addiction to acting out in the form of exploring the boundary between character and caricature. Perhaps are own lives are like that: we secretly see ourselves as teetering on that boundary, wondering if there is any help for it. Bellow's narrator is beyond wonder at this point in the narrative; he's hypnotized by the decadence of apparent genius. But because that apparition of genius is also Bellow himself in his sentences, the surpassing prose artist, I'm torn that he found help for himself in his art but could not see that Delmore Schwartz needed greater help—or did not want to see it, as if there was no help for it anywhere. If so, it was a tragic passage that Bellow read, beyond amusing, darkly recognizing his own impotence as a friend to Schwartz—and no doubt to many others. It was, in short, a passage of the Blues (the audience laughed liberally, as they sometimes dangerously do at the seeming tall tales of Blues lyrics—tales we should know better are as close to the painful truth as we're likely to get). Yet after all, Blues artists make a living on stage, as did Saul Bellow. And even in the Psalms, Hell is other people:...

> but I am a worm
> subhuman
> what men come to
>
> with a hate of their own futures
> despised
> and cheered like a drunk

staggering across the street
they howl after him
like sick dogs

"Let the Lord he cried to
save him"

Before that 22nd Psalm—worked on for many days in the enclosed, one-toke-was-enough smoke-holding cubicle of NYU's red-faced Bobst library, 1974 (I moved down a floor for thermos-coffee and revision)—back in 1969 Toronto, I was accustomed to provincial poetry reviews in Alberta newspapers that complained Mr. Rosenberg used too much white space. I laughed; I didn't expect understanding in print except within the poems of colleagues. Besides, contemporary reviewers tend to need too much drama from poetry books and almost always fail to parse the deadpan, even when presented with one of the two blank-faced masks for the ancient Greek Muses, tragic Melpomene or comic Thalia behind them. It's not much different for film and theater (when it's not obvious, as in Beckett). The NYT review of *Don't Bother To Knock* in 1952 panned it along with Marilyn Monroe for representing a mental case with a blank look and strange voice. The role called for Bette Davis, suggested the NYT. Davis would have chewed the scenery, however, while Monroe more uncannily represented psychosis: convinced that her dead husband has returned in the form of Richard Widmark, pushing a child off a high-floor window ledge, as she is about to do, would be nothing more than an afterthought—just as the death camps were, in the broken minds of the German populace. More than half a century later, Marilyn's uncanniness pays off on TCM. At the time, however, she might have believed the reviews, as did Twentieth Century Fox, who went on to cast her as a comic. But capital-T time reveals the uncanny best, both in art and the worst horrors of life, though time has little patience for anything less. The great kabbalist poets of the medieval *Zohar* knew this in their bones. When I translated principal author Moshe DeLeon in *Dreams of Being Eaten Alive,* I worried that the brief satanic dream of cannibalism was going to appear *grand-guignol,* yet now, fifteen years later, it reads as deadpan as Marilyn Monroe's psychopath: it seems more pathologically true than art.

I don't intend to pat myself or DeLeon on the back for it. Melpomene and Thalia, their masks twinned, compel it, like many of Bellow's daringly cold-blooded sentences. And so did the compelling streets of Jerusalem in the early '80s, when the most likely representative of a mixed English-language/Hebrew poetry scene was as improvised as a fruit stall: Who decided the dessert melons went up front while the grapefruits, that breakfast staple to American eyes, were stuck in the back? Surrounding the Mahane Yehuda *shuk*, Jerusalem's largest open-air market, were former warehouses turned into primitive studios and apartments (lately upscaled). Shalva Segal, an artist and recent American immigrant (later to show in NYC as Sarah Segal) rented three raw rooms (toilet in the hall) scrubbed whistle-clean and fixed up with tie-dyed curtains. The "sitting room" took its name seriously; perhaps twenty cheap folding chairs were lined against the walls. This room would fill up once a month for our poetry readings, in which Michal Govrin, Susan and Allen Afterman, and I would read our latest "unfinished" work, plus an occasional guest like Dennis Silk, Alan Kaufman or Zelda. The minyan of an audience was made up of *baalei tshuva*, recent Russian immigrants who'd been deprived of Jewish knowledge, a few Israeli Kabbalah students and their teachers, and some mystically inspired artists of song, including Australian immigrant Ruth Wieder Magan and Israeli avant-gardist Esti Kenan. The Russians and Kabbalah students had barely any English, made up for by rapt attention to every word, chewing on them as if the Passover *afikomen*. It was a scene of intense honor to poetry; if the Poet's Cafe friend of Orpheus at the beginning of Cocteau's eponymous film (1950) was to show his latest issue of *Nudisme*, where all the pages are blank (he explains to Orpheus that it is more purely absurd than the common journals filled with absurdist works) the audience at Shalva's would have gasped with delight. The most ironic Second Avenue or Buddhist-entranced audiences I've known elsewhere could not approach the kneecaps of that *sefirotic* high in the Mahane Yehuda. Shalva's windows leaned over a row of fruit stalls open until midnight, with a low muttering of its patronage backgrounding our readings. I thought back to Jeremy Prynne's Cambridge rooms in the '60s, where a handful of sardonic postgraduates tried to pick up on Jeremy's verbal moves through the rugby shouts outside. Jeremy provided the tea and cookies as Shalva would, but we were all too full of ourselves then, or rather, empty of ourselves, as Jeremy's cookies were hash-laced. Back at Rochdale College in Toronto a couple years earlier, Victor Coleman and I held our occasional "Poetry Front" readings in the totally bare (on purpose, *vide* Cocteau) art gallery, where the joints making the rounds of the audience affected the reader to the point that I recall David McFadden, that night's guest, slumping his head into his book and rolling over (we were all seated on the floor).

Reading *Humboldt's Gift* again, where all was still alcohol-and-pills in the literary '50s, the real-life manic depression of Delmore Schwartz scared me in the year of his death, when he was nominally my Syracuse U mentor-poet. He started out so well in his writing career that even in his last days no one thought to treat him as an ordinary man with serious health issues. Was that how I was going to end up if I kept at it in poetry? I asked myself not for the first time. How could I know I didn't have a buried mental health issue that would surface later, and that pursuing the poet's path was an early warning indicator? I'd already given up my preternatural left hook in junior boxing, scarred on the lip for life and forever to be mustachioed. Those of us who'd boxed Jr. Golden Gloves were invited to closed-circuit TV coverage of a Sr. regional championship bout in, I believe, Muhammad Ali's hometown of Louisville. It was clear to me at 15, my last ever bout already behind me, that the man with the artist's name, Cassius Clay, was the great artist of my generation—as dancer, deadpan, spontaneous intelligence. Yes, you had to take a beating to succeed, but if not the head, the ballet dancer's feet also take a beating, and perhaps the poet's emotional life. It appeared to be necessary, considering the postwar global nerve-ends. "What is happening everywhere is, one way or another, known to everyone. Shadowy world tides wash human nerve endings in the remotest corners of the earth," writes Martin Amis on the collection of Bellow's letters. Yet, quoting Bellow, "it is apparently in the nature of the creature to resist the world's triumph," the triumph of "turbulence and agitation"—and Bellow's corpus is graphic proof of that defiance, avers Amis. But to resist the shame of it too? If Bellow could, Delmore Schwartz couldn't, precursors of his mania challenging the psychosis of the Third Reich by pitting the grandiosity of the Bible against a modern man's modernist tradition in his epic poem, *Genesis*. Unlike a genocide, which perhaps a later generation can get past, the fantasy obsession with the chosenness of the Jews represents a mass psychosis that is never done away with. The only antidote in history, as Jews and their lovers have always known, is Israel. It's not just that it's inscribed in the Bible, and that the Bible was written there. It's also two millenniums of resistance in exile to the world's triumph.

Amis writes further: "Common sense and a sense of humor are the same thing, moving at different speeds. A sense of humor is just common sense, dancing. Those who lack humor are without judgment and should be trusted with nothing." That doesn't help us with the Third Reich, however. What is more revealing is, in an emotional speech while visiting Israel, German Chancellor Merkel saying "the memory of the prisoners' fates fills me with deep sadness and shame." One hopes she means more than German shame, more than even Western humanity's shame, but species shame. The Jews were not simply prisoners like Marxists and POW's, they were Homo sapiens deemed unfitting and to be cast out of not just society but Homo sapiens history. What would Darwin say? And would Bellow represent his relative silence on the issue as the necessity of resistance? Freud, when asked in the late '30s to speak out against anti-Semitism, said if it's a Jew who has to make the argument, all is lost. Israel, as it were, need say nothing more to the world than that its particularity is one with Creation—that is, in historical terms, the particular creation of Homo sapiens out of, most likely, Homo erectus. If that sounds funny, then perhaps the world, *pace* Martin Amis, has lost its common sense, once again.

4.

In a rare dream I wrote down, the late Joe Brainard visited me in my '70s St. Marks Place apartment, to show me the latest issue of *Art in America*, with an article about his autobiographical work, 'I Remember.' The subtitle said each memory was so intense it blotted out auto-biography. "I think it will be useful for your memoir," said Joe. I couldn't focus on it; I hadn't had an issue of *Art in America* in my hands in so long, I just wanted to skim through the pages and be infused with all the creativity spilled out there, with technicolor illustrations. I imagined how different my life would have been had I taken in each monthly issue over the decades I stopped reading it, so many artistic points of view to process, so many probings of boundaries. "They did a pretty decent job, but I don't think it's going to help sell any of my art work." Only it wasn't Joe's hesitant voice speaking, it had morphed into the more melodic one of Lewis Warsh. As Joe turned to leave, I said, "I'm going out with you," and put on my Navy peacoat. I wanted to get my own copy so I could digest the piece on Joe slowly and see if he was right about its usefulness—but also I was suddenly starving for news of the art world and regretted I'd turned down a request from Joan Simon Greenwald, Art in America's editor, to review a show. We were having drinks at an opening and I was uncomfortable, both because I was attracted to her nervous energy and because I didn't want to trespass against her husband, poet and poker partner Ted Greenwald. Down in the winter street, I realized I'd have to walk quite a way for a copy; the East Village bookstore got its new issues late, as did the Eighth Street Bookshop. I'd have to walk all the way to Brentano's on the corner of Sixth Avenue, or to the NYU bookstore on Waverly Place; there was heavy snow on the ground and I forgot to put on boots. I had to have that issue though, I felt it would change my life, and I thought my memoir needed to be grounded in art. At the corner of Third Avenue I bumped into Ted Greenwald, who was just leaning against a lamppost. I took it as a sign to wake up, to realize I'd already missed the chance that rolls around only once in life, to open the door that leads toward a singular work that will tie it all together, a work too intense for its genre like Joe's—a confession, for instance, that I had slept with Joan Greenwald and the wife of every other colleague I had known and cherished. It would be a short book, a forty-year historical journey like the one recounted with a collage of rabbinic textual interpretations from the longer history of the Jewish people, the Passover Haggadah, illustrated in the dream with collages by Larry Rivers, Jim Dine, Mimi Gross, Lewis Warsh, Erika Rothenberg, David Shapiro, Ann Lauterbach, Barbara Kruger, Bill Berkson, Charles Bernstein and Hannah Wilke, among nominally Jewish friends and art-minded colleagues I'd left behind.

It's also possible that a remorselessly logical thought can get stuck in a dream or a poem. "The thought that this happened and then this happened and then this and this and this, the relentless march of event and emotion tied together simply because day follows day and turns into week following week becoming months and years reinforces the fact that the only logical ending for chronological order is death." The memoirist Abigail Thomas, daughter of science writer Lewis Thomas, is suggesting we need art—or dogs—to break down that merciless order. A time- or space-bending collage could do it; poetry especially disarms order by posing an alternate, equally complex time-bending order, like a miniature mirror of the physical universe, but one that we may internalize. You can observe this, among other elements of the Passover Haggadah's epic poem, when many people stumble over the little poem therein of "The Four Sons." They have trouble distinguishing one from the other, especially "the simple son" from "the wicked son" from "the one who does not know how to ask," in that all three, asking or not, pose the question, "What does this all mean?" If they've drunk the Passover Seder's (*seder* means order in Hebrew) prescribed full cups of wine, the problem may become hilarious. At our last Rosenberg Seder, at cousin Daniel's in Miami Beach, one hard-core rationalist tried to contextualize the problem by referring to our more simple-minded "forebears." From that moment on, we devolved to discussing "the four bears": Was it a fairy tale, a folk tale, or a Rabbinic midrash; were there not actually three bears; were they bachelor bears or married bears, and were there baby bears, etc. Eventually composing ourselves, and on a more serious note, we read a Hasidic take on the problem that complicated it further: "Unfortunately, there is, in our time of confusion and obscurity, another kind of a Jewish child: the child who is conspicuous by his absence from the Seder Service; the one who has no interest whatsoever in Torah and who is not even aware of the Seder, of the Exodus from Egypt and the subsequent revelation at Sinai. We must make every effort to save that 'lost' child, like the other four." Here, to our mind, was a reflection of the literary modernist obsession with absence, one that reaches its apex in the previously mentioned project to inscribe on a monument all six million names of those lost in the Holocaust.

I was once a poor understudy in Sartre's *No Exit*, and if one is dreaming a confession like I just described, of endless sexual betrayals of colleagues and friends, it may remind you of "Hell is other people" in the afterlife/dream of the play's three characters stuck together in an eternal room. Yet it's the particular time of Sartre's scene of writing in 1944 that sticks in my mind as more real than the play. At the minutes and hours, days and weeks, that Sartre was writing, three hundred thousand German camp characters were living out the poetry of Psalm 22, in addition to the Reich's V2 rockets, which were killing a few thousands in London and Antwerp

about the same time, presaging the Cold War I was interpreting at my own
'70s scene of translating:

> ...I am surrounded
> and no one near
>
> a mad crowd
> tightens a noose around me
> the ring of warheads
>
> pressing ravenous noses
> the mad whispering of
> gray technicians
>
> the water of my life evaporates
> my bones stick through the surface
> my heart burns down like wax
>
> melting into my stomach
> my mouth dry as a clay cup
> dug up in the yard
>
> I've fallen into the mud
> foaming dogs surround me
> ghost men
>
> pierce my hands and feet
> my bones stare at me
> in disbelief
>
> men take my clothes
> like judges
> in selfish dreams...

I was also once such a writer as Lydia Davis, the kind who couldn't get very
far in either *Ulysses* or the Bible (past my liberal definition of its poetry,
that is) until there I was, living in Israel and beginning to speak Hebrew—
and having few other books in English in the house. I still needed to read
it with the help of scholar Harold Fisch's faltering (hence human) *en face*
translation beside the Hebrew. Yet because I could recognize so many words
and phrases from Israeli lyrics and newspapers, including the ads, I began
to sense the authors also must have picked up the "news" of their day—and
of their literary history, in translation—in the same language in which they

wrote. To recognize a word, or better yet, a thought, as both ancient and new in the same moment is unforgettable. Since I was also translating some poems by a friend at the time, Yehuda Amichai, the irony of his biblical echoes also reminded me that the original Israeli writers of the Bible had their own ironic echoes, and that many of these were still available if I would read Sumerian, Egyptian, Sanskrit and Canaanite texts (with the help of English translations). I've written about this elsewhere, but here I'm focused on that ineffable moment when I could feel as lost in time as distant ancestors, dizzied by the vast stretch between us, and knowing that rescue was possible. Made possible, that is, via the ancient Hebrew text whose original scenes of writing were right there, in Jerusalem. Unlike it, some survivors of the Holocaust have left documents of their experience but these do not generally evoke the richness of their culture's art and history through the catastrophe's shadow, a lost time that no new translations of Heine or Freud will rescue, though individual works are revived.

In the late '60s I was a conceptual artist, indifferent for awhile to any poetry that was not about language and any art that was not about the viewer. I received grants as a conceptual photographer, using a Kodak Instamatic to make "real-time" series: unfolding street scenes, for instance, in various towns—Prague, Venice, Tel Aviv, Toronto. My first book was a conceptual box filled with pages of innocent Japanese household objects, described in a laconic conceptual poetry. What pushed me in this direction for a time? How did I become uncannily disarmed by ideas, starting perhaps in my personal history, aged 4, when my mother returned home with my new baby brother? I had somehow ignored all previous reference to her pregnancy. The uncanny idea, to my mind then, was that baby brother was a foundling and now the object of the exclusive loving attention that I deserved. While this might at first seem a common psychological fantasy about being forced to share maternal affection, it was already uncanny to me, aged 4, of my suspicion that my father's return from the war as a wounded veteran, when I was 3, was actually as an impostor, and that my real father was an embarrassment, a criminal locked away in jail. A more literal influence, however, was the work of Lawrence Wiener, whose first exhibit was a "book", *Statements,* on view at the new Yvon Lambert Gallery in Paris in 1967. I had an instant flashback at that time to my undergrad years at The New School, where a schoolmate, Gerard Malanga, wrote some imaginary art reviews in the form of poems. I don't recall if Gerry had yet discovered Andy Warhol, but by '67 he was a Warhol collaborator. And by that year I was determined not to have in my life's biography the standard grandiose mush of a "first book," but rather to have it record an uncanny rebellion against an inexorable chronology. No usual kind of poetry could be taken for granted in the after-shadow of the Holocaust, I thought.

Later, my first book of lyric (some anti-lyric) poetry was *Disappearing Horses*. People had been living with horses for thousands of years, and there were still a few left in my early youth, used by scrap men and the last of the ice deliverers. When I visited behind the Iron Curtain in the '60s I saw many horses still hanging on, pulling carts with automobile tires for wheels. In Prague you could see the visible pain of their disappearing, as carts were dangerously shunted aside by the electric streetcars. And then a scene from which I quickly looked away but is still an open wound in memory: a horse and wagon veered over the tracks, crowded there by jittery cars, the horse knocked screaming to the ground by the tram, upended wagon wheels spinning. It's painful to disappear, I understood, occasioning the title poem (and its somewhat pretentious irony toward the cliché of the "dead dog" poem), and painful to watch such scenes strengthen in memory. I've heard of, and perhaps seen, worse scenes—certainly those in wartime documentaries—but this one came as I was still holding on to a shred of innocence, and that innocence attached mirthlessly to the driven animal in the scene—it, like most Holocaust victims, was given no quarter. Angelica Huston, splayed and sobbing inconsolably on her bed, in her father's film of Joyce's *The Dead*, could not put aside the memory of Michael Furie's teenage eyes as he rose from his deathbed to see her once more—a memory from many decades before but only growing more vivid precisely because all hope of changing anything, ancient then or immediate now, is utterly lost. Unless. Unless the "author" of the memory, Angelica, sits up from her bed, dries her eyes, and is galvanized from the moment when ancient and present collide, to rescue the Michael Furie lost in time as an actress. Joyce was hardly so sanguine at 24, when he wrote the story, but I was the more likely romantic at that age, as I averted my eyes from a screaming horse in Czechoslovakia. A few weeks later I landed in Israel for the first time. I think my youth was the horse in that scene, because already in the streets of Jerusalem I encountered time differently:

> …may our hearts live forever!
> and the furthest reaches of space
> remember our conscious moment
>
> inspiring light
> like those disappeared from memory
> returned to the planet's earth
>
> everyone has to appear
> at death's door
> everyone falls to the ground…

In this further excerpt from Psalm 22 inexorable time is measured by
death, the ironic fall to the ground, but also as in genuflecting prayer,
or "dropping dead"—in street language—"at death's door." Somewhere
in his published letters, Saul Bellow describes his ambition as "the
democratic diffusion of high culture….street language combined with a
high style." Of course, American poets had already achieved this, not least
by W.C. Williams; it's a more intuitive thing in poetry, drawing upon a
wider range, from subconscious to classical allusion. In Bellow it's more
academic—in the good sense. Certainly many of his sentences read like
striking little poems, yet he's beholden to many narrative constraints—
plot, characters, description, exposition—that a poet can override. I didn't
need to become an academic master to write poems in my twenties that
collaged Shakespearean rhetoric with Howlin' Wolf's. For that matter,
neither did Shakespeare, when Prince Hal spoke with Falstaff or Hamlet
with Ophelia's father. Although Bellow's point is about American lingo, for
which he found a similar range in his university colleague John Berryman's
Dream Songs, I was put off by what I called in my youth, for want of
a better articulation, intentionality. Telegraphing may be better—like a
fighter telegraphing his punch. In a poem, you might never know from line
to line what sleight of language would redirect or deepen your experience
of the poem. I found something similar in the first Hebrew psalms I
engaged, with the parallelisms creating reverberations more quickly and
often than prose. It's there to, in the incessant wordplay of much biblical
prose, though I wasn't ready to tackle it until many years after interpreting
the poetry, including the Prophets.

The problem with time for a poet, however, is that it so quickly becomes
history that you tend to lump all history together into the category of
"history." Even were I to finish this chapter in a few hours and overnight it
to you, it will still be history when you read it tomorrow. Yet the difference
too often ignored by contemporary poets, between today becoming history
and ancient history, is that today I am still fighting *against* history, thinking
against it, while that has long since been foreclosed to, say, the ancient
capital of Jerusalem when Solomon ruled. Yet I learned to disagree with
myself, as the weight of this book will hopefully convey; a good part of
my project is to reopen that ancient history and render it *unlost*. True, any
historian worth her salt will re-envision the period she confronts, but the
perspective I want to bring includes today with the ancient, so that you
find me thinking along with a history that we share with poets: yesterday's.
Without posing the poet's conflation of history into whatever happened
before this morning—a sensibility in which high and low cross-fertilize—
against the historian's high-scholarly breakdown into periods, I could not
think like a Biblical writer. For him and for myself, nothing about our
human existence is ever completely lost or unknowable. If it isn't buried

and to be dug up one day as a fossil, it may be found on another planet or exoplanet, at least analogously. My Little League baseball uniform still exists in an old photo and perhaps in the mind of one of my old teammates. Then there's my own mind, in which I can be prompted to picture things I normally wouldn't, for instance in a dream or within a psychoanalysis. And if it isn't retrievable in my mind, it may be in someone else's—someone, for instance, who had a crush on me in third grade that I knew nothing about, or someone who wanted to punch me out in high school. One day in 1981 I was waiting all alone for a bus in an outlying suburb of Jerusalem when someone in a passing car flung a heavy stone at me, just missing. I didn't see that person but he saw me and may recall it. No doubt he was from the nearby Arab village and considered me his enemy.

Personal enemies can be among the most lost things, if we've turned the page. But they are still there, waiting in the problematic of lumped-together history, however ancient, unless I confront time as both poet-translator and historian together, to keep that enemy or fellow ancient poet waiting until such time as we can face each other in "street language combined with a high style." It may be a sad coming-together, as when poet Charles Simic writes, "the blues, in the end, is about a sadness older than the world, and there's no cure for that." There may be no getting past the necessity of enemies, yet I'm not sure the lack of a cure is the problem. Expecting a cure can be delusional; instead, better to simply hold on to history and not give up on it. That the blues or ancient psalms are still being sung is a sign of vigilance toward history, even if, as Ben Lerner writes, "What if we dislike or despise or hate poems because they are— every single one of them—failures?" Even the blues singer is not going to get his baby back, the psalmist is not going to be spared the grave, yet contemporary bluesman Robert Cray is still singing from Psalm 137, some millennia after its composition:

> Into the rivers of Babylon
> we cried like babies, loud
> unwilling to move

"I think we're going to have strong indications of life beyond Earth within a decade," NASA Chief Scientist Ellen Stofan said. "I think we're going to have definitive evidence within 20-30 years.". The irony is that such a revelation only increases the need for our particular human history, which, like the particular history of the Jews in the Bible, helps us define who we are today against the sundered history of ancient Greeks, Romans, Egyptians and Persians. How did we manage to survive? becomes a question both for Homo sapiens and Jews, to pit against extraterrestrial species. The Hebrew Bible is full of such ironies as needing history in order to sing, to be fully

alive, just as the evolutionary history of oceanic history on Europa will sing
to us through each species, assuming they can't sing to us on their own.

> Into the rivers of Babylon
> we cried like babies, loud
> unwilling to move
>
> beyond the memory
> the flowing blood
> of you, Israel
>
> to an orchestra of trees
> we lent our harps
> silently leaning
>
> when the enemy shoved us
> "asking" tender songs of Israel
> under heavy chains...

None of this is obvious to conventional interpreters. Even my literary
colleague Cynthia Ozick, who recognizes the ironic Hebrew word-playing
of the Bible, shies away from delving into its historical source within a
Hebraic culture of original writers and other artists. When I commissioned
a collection of essays by 40 literary writers reading the Hebrew Bible
afresh, each on a particular book within it, in *Congregation*, only two, Isaac
Bashevis Singer and Harold Bloom, concerned themselves with an original
Hebraic writer. It was a few years after Singer, in '84, gave the JPS annual
keynote in Philadelphia, while I was editor, in which he identified himself
as kin to Biblical writers. When Saul Bellow gave the same keynote in
'88, he identified instead a loss, an absence of intimacy with those Biblical
writers, and in compensation for that absence—as a form of connection—
he offered his fertile Canadian-American Jewish consciousness in place of
a deep textual history. Instead of the biblical struggle for revelation and
historical redemption, Bellow suggested his own struggle to express his
own mind. And in his novels, it was a kind of epic struggle; he did not take
to the romantic lyrical sublime, which is partly why he and Harold Bloom
distrusted each other.

Bloom thought poet Delmore Schwartz, as well as the protagonist
Bellow made of him in *Humboldt's Gift*, failed because he strove for the
epic gesture over the lyrical one, and Bloom thought the same of Bellow's
novels. He could have been right, if only in the sense that Bellow's epic
ambition approaches the biblical, even if Bellow himself didn't care
to say so. Why was Bellow so reticent about confronting the Hebrew

Bible? Certainly such avoidance is common among writers modern and postmodern, yet it's more striking in a Bellow who could read Hebrew and write *To Jerusalem and Back*. In some perhaps subconscious way, Bellow must have recognized the biblically epic gesture in his novels and wished to draw attention away from it. He didn't want to account for a traditional Jewish upbringing, one that was not readily assimilable in North American culture. Bellow had no problem being an assimilated Jewish-American—as long as that didn't detract from being an *unhyphenated* American. Although not quite a universalist, Nobel notwithstanding, he described himself as a writer of the universal common world. I'd place the Hebrew Bible in the same human commonalty when in its translated form and under-arching a universalist NT. Still, both testaments express an epic sublimity, being familiar with the numinous, no less than Homer. Bellow's epic gesture was to cover over the numinous voice of the narrative Torah with his own. "Cover over"—in the Freudian sense of both protecting and repressing, like a father unacknowledged, left behind. My own father was finally revealed to me, many years after his death, at the Western Wall in Jerusalem, where I uncovered his secret wish to be at home someplace in the world, fully at home. Suddenly, there, his insecurity rhymed with my own. That wasn't yet possible for Bellow; his reading knowledge of Hebrew did not become a spoken one, coming of age in a prewar world not yet having an Israel again, and still far away from assimilating it.

A question for more writers than Saul Bellow: Why did becoming a man or woman of the world, the common world unfolding from the Greco-Roman and Renaissance, exclude wilderness, animals, even the new frontier of space? You'd be hard-pressed to come upon an animal or pet in Bellow, or the nonhuman world in general, and I think it's because the nonhuman represents a biblical wilderness for the common world— opposed to the metaphor of an urban wilderness. The 40 years moving through wilderness in the Hebrew Bible is formative, so it's not surprising Bellow avoided it like other Bible-averse modernists, for the sake of testing the self and its boundaries of social and individual consciousness. Yet absence of the nonhuman, of wilderness, of space—literally, the universe— is striking, especially since the cosmos is never far from Biblical concern, and the Talmud records the endless Jewish thinking about our relation to animals. They no doubt had the science wrong, but so might we, when others look back at us in a further millennium. Ecclesiastes, for example, is shot through with a capacious wilderness mind, as in this passage of Chapter 3, in my translation:

> ...and through the window of a moment
> the opening of eyes within eyes
> to see the ancient perspective of time

painted in a landscape with light
the future the eyelids opening
as of a prehistoric creature

under the ungraspable sky
that was
is

and will be: the airless height
of understanding   pure space we pursue
like fish the worms of conscience

and are drawn to
like a seed to air...

You'll find fish and other creatures in Singer, not least in *The Slave*, where they're lovingly evoked. Unlike Singer, however, who is able to identify with the original Jewish authors of the Bible (and explicitly so, as in his memoirs or in the lead essay to *Congregation*) Bellow identifies primarily as a sociological Jew. Though he rarely quotes from the Hebrew Bible or identifies with its hundreds of Jewish writers, he does acknowledge them as forebears and cites kinship with their worldview while leaving them behind for "the common world" of the Western Canon. Like him there are even some non-Orthodox rabbis who read the Hebrew Bible largely as a philo-sophical or ethical document, though their acquaintance with the literary canon is far less serious than the Bellow who slights the biblical writers for their apartness (even as he sympathizes with the Jewish history of "a people apart"). His book on Israel, *To Jerusalem and Back*, fails to imagine ancient Jerusalem as the original scene of writing for the Bible. The J writer or S, the Court Historian, might as well be from a species of ants that is still keeping clear its pathways beneath the Old City yet goes unnoticed—except by the entomologist E.O. Wilson, who in his memoir contemplates one he has lifted onto his finger: "This fellow creature was working at this site before an early ancestor of ours arrived, by which I don't mean King David, the Jebusites, or Neanderthals, but the kind that could hang by its tail."

If I could have been there in '88 for Bellow's lecture to JPS (I was already collaborating with Harold Bloom) I could have made him aware that he was following in Singer's footsteps, though I can hear his protestations: Singer stood in direct relation to rabbinical stock, while "I had to go up against it, one foot in the Hasidic batter's box, the other outside it at Wrigley Field, going up against Chicago's Great Books guys. Didn't matter to them what religion Plato or Virgil was brought up in, because those sluggers were already in the common world, World Lit. You can't imagine the Torah-writing boys in that world..."). But that's precisely what I'm doing, I might have answered. The theme and variations of the original writers, of origins and the scene of writing, are an underlying passion and measure I hold up against colleagues who fail to acknowledge ancient origins, yet from their standpoint it is as though I might judge them for not being conversant with the history of botany—it just doesn't present itself as relevant to their lives. Yet relevance, I would say, is blindly misleading; what we need to know is not simply what's going on here but how we got to here. The relevancies we are addicted to by the temper of the times shield us from penetrating to origins. How about this for stating the obvious in order to make the movie *Noah* relevant: a New Yorker writer states that "The Hebrew scribes responsible for the Noah story were clearly working, either directly or indirectly, from an earlier literary source." Since, "clearly," the scribes weren't on the Great Flood scene themselves, they *had to have* sources—that would only be non-evident if the word "scribes" did not denote writers, authors. Since scribe is a term used mainly in the literal sense of *copier*, even *The New Yorker* fails to imagine the so-called scribes of the Bible as real writers, authors. One finds the same anti-writerly confusion among translators and scholars who can do all sorts of interesting things with the Bible's text, including mimicking its "Hebrewness" (according to critic Robert Alter chastising critic Everett Fox), but have little interest in its scenes of writing. The idea of a self-conscious Jewish writer of the Bible was just too unconventional for even as sharp an ironist as John Updike, who at least reviewed books related to the Bible in *The New Yorker*, including my own. Of course, I was arrogant to think I was alone in my rebellion against the hubris of the modern writer, one who assumes self-consciousness was a modern or Shakespearean or even Augustinian invention. "What has been entirely forgotten is that the Torah was the first rebellious text to appear in world history. Its purpose was to protest. It set in motion a rebel movement of cosmic proportions the likes of which we have never known. The text includes all the radical heresies of the past, present and future. It calls idol-worship an abomination, immorality an abhorrence, the worship of man a catastrophe. It protests against complacency, self-satisfaction, imitation, and negation of the spirit. It calls for radical thinking and drastic action without compromise, even when it means standing alone, being condemned and ridiculed." A contemporary Israeli rabbi, Lopes Cardozo, is evoking his own isolation a bit grandiosely when he characterizes "what has been entirely forgotten." He's writing today but he might as well have been responding to Bellow's *To Jerusalem and Back*, which originally appeared in The New Yorker forty years ago. In place of characterizing the ancient writers in Jerusalem, Bellow invokes poets Schimmel and Silk as contemporary characters, without any obligation to suggest their poetry's relationship with Jewish history. I came to know them differently, as poets with deeper roots and interests in Jewish history going back to origins in Davidic Jerusalem. In correspondence with them before Bellow's trip, I read issues of Silk's mimeo poetry mag, containing work mostly by him, Schimmel and Arieh Sachs, as if they were time-travelers from a distant past. Harold sent me the first Hebrew book of poems I'd received hot off the presses, *Hotel Zion*, in which he sinks his footprints into an aesthetic soil that holds together contemporary and ancient Jerusalem. Dennis also sent *Retrievements*, his anthology of Jerusalem history, which helps to imagine a future civilization interpreting our own.

Seth Shostak, director of SETI, states astronomers are looking for extraterrestrial civilizations that are far beyond what humans have accomplished. According to current calculations, he stated a Type III supercivilization may use up to 100 billion billion times more energy than humans on Earth." That's a level of technology as hard for us to understand as a Neanderthal with an iPhone in her hand. But what about their poetry? Will it be sincere and bad, as Oscar Wilde asserted all sincere poetry is, or will it be so uncanny that we will *mistake it* for being sincere? Anyway, it will require NASA or SETI to hire a host of poets for interpretive work. Can you imagine that parents will then be encouraging, even pushing their adolescent children to become poets? "Put those science toys away. Here's a book by Allen Ginsberg!" Even better, a book about the poet of Ecclesiastes, who is reinterpreting and pulling together cryptic poetic fragments from another day. Film directors can do it, though they tend to bog down in awkwardly sincere language for their characters.

5.

In Fred Zinnemann's sublime Academy Award-nominated *The Nun's Story* ('59) we are led to sympathize with the initiation of Catholic nuns, including floor-kissing, wall-hugging, and wedding rings. When Audrey Hepburn arrives for duty in the Congo, an educated native asks where is her husband. "He's in heaven," she replies. "Oh, I'm sorry," says the native, whose typically human response gets a knowing smile from Audrey. Yes, these natives still have much to learn about the ironies of being human. Fifty-six years later, in Darren Aronofsky's trenchant *Noah* ('14), Russell Crowe is initiated into the understanding that human-beings have proved a disaster, responsible for the demise of Eden and now a threat to the entire world. Noah understands his mission is to survive the imminent Flood that will wipe out humans, but to survive only long enough to save the innocent animals who will repopulate a new Eden. Noah himself, along with his progeny, must die out, the end of the line, leaving Noah a kind of messiah to nonhuman life. Yet just as Audrey struggles with her love of self ("pride") Russell strives to understand why Creation must devolve this way. Both Audrey's Sister Luke and Russell's Noah come to internalize love of humans as a noble flaw that needs expiation by a lifelong struggle with Biblical text. Unlike Audrey, however, whose Christian struggle with humanism is familiar, Russell embodies a very Jewish character, one who reads the rainbow provided by the Creator as sign that the fate of humans will be left in their own hands, to eventually enter into a more complex covenant with the Creator.

Just as the exotic Congo scenery guaranteed the popularity of *The Nun's Story*, the "stunning visual imagery" of *Noah* rendered it a block-buster, no less than the bawdy pub scenes of Shakespeare's *Henry IV* in the 16th century. Yet it's Russell's struggle to *interpret* the world that uniquely anchors the film, for it's at odds with everyone else, including his own family, who seek authority in their own selfhoods. We can't add Audrey to this equation because her Christian struggle against selfhood is absolute; it doesn't require her study of biblical history, just the incessant purging of self. Noah, prefiguring the Jewish experience, ruminates on history (represented by the most vivid imagery of the present kaleidoscoped back to Eden) and comes into a negotiation with the Creator, the first Covenant. Everyone in the film resents this Jewish Noah for his endless interpretive struggle with history. I call *The Nun's Story* sublime because it acknowledges the supernatural without engaging it: the intimations of immortality are what are sublime, uncanny moments. It's a worldly outlook, post-Christian but also resonant with universal religion, with its sublime moments as bedrock, from Christ's passion to Buddha's perfection. The Jewish resistance to all that entails endless intellectual study, starting with Biblical text; instead of discrete sublime moments it is searching for interpretation of history and text that helps reveal a path back to Creation: the ideal of lost time. Can we ever get back to, or uncover the scene of, our Homo sapiens evolution, an Eden we lost—as if in a Holocaust, a hard and vastly unjust comparison but there it is, undone by the satanic? Myself, I'm stuck in the worldly universalism of sublime moments, lyrical, anti-lyrical, and, when it come to rescuing the Bible, epical and visionary moments. Perhaps stuck is the wrong word; it's more like I'm responding to the moment in time in which we live, and against the advice of W.H. Auden, who, in his *Paris Review* interview says, we should write according to our self-aware age, e.g. 50, and not according to "1973", the cultural age. In 1973 I turned back from my education and lost myself in biblical language, yet always coming back to Auden and my contemporaries' belief that "it's a poet's role to maintain the sacredness of language," and in our case the English language.

Auden is asked, back in '74, "Do you see any spirituality in all those hippies out on St. Marks Place? You've lived among them for some time now," to which he answers: "I must say that I do admire the ones who won't compete in the rat race, who renounce money and worldly goods." Though I lived on St. Mark's Place while Auden was still alive, there were no "Diggers" around, the 17th century Bible-alluding cult, appropriated in name by a handful of non-Bible reading hippie idealists quickly to become disillusioned. We, of the 2nd Generation New York School poetry rat race, stuck to our sacred language of deadpan. Deadpan and the dreamlike language afforded by intense collage. It allowed us to resist the academic and ally ourselves with the enlivening avant-garde of our moment, which was taking place not in literature but in visual art and dance, de Kooning and Porter, Balanchine and Cunningham.

"Most modern masterpieces are critical masterpieces," writes Harold Rosenberg. "Joyce's writing is a criticism of literature, Pound's poetry is a criticism of poetry, Picasso's painting is a criticism of painting. Modern art also criticizes the existing culture. All we have on the positive side is the individual's capacity for resistance. Resistance and criticism." I'm quoting Bellow quoting Rosenberg; I resisted the latter for his intellectualizing of "the new" in art, just as he resisted answering my letters (2), from the putative cousin who it seemed represented the new's anti-intellectualism. Timorously navigating between resistance and criticism, I found myself on the resistance side, among poets I knew personally and who are still working in 2015, Ashbery and Hall, Nichol and Notley among them. Although Nichol was younger than me (and who died at an early age) his "unfinished" finished masterpiece, *The Martyrology*, remains alive, as I've often written about. Like only a handful of others, it makes meaning of its resistance, a representation of character similar to Joyce's Leopold Bloom, both of these writers presenting the unrestricted range of their consciousness as a type of comedy that their authorships are immersed in. Or perhaps it's tragicomedy, both in the persona of "bpNichol" and in Joyce's critique of what literature has become, as it reveals the loss of cosmic myth. I found the biblical side of that critique in the Jewish poets Reznikoff and Sutzkever, Nelly Sachs and Amichai, but like Celan they lose themselves in it, come forward with no Leopold Bloom or bpNichol to disarm and resist our state of being. No Abraham or Sarah, Joseph or Miriam, Isaiah or Jeremiah. The latter prophets do not fail to make of themselves characters in their authorship. I was quite aware of this when, not quite 13, I read from Isaiah for my bar mitzvah *haftarah*. I practiced the text for a year, spellbound by Isaiah's crying, which I heard in the plaintive tone of the rabbi at my Zaydeh's graveside when I was eight, singing "El malei rachamim" to help the soul find its way to heaven. Soon enough, however, I understood myself as a critical modernist, and the Bible seemed so saturated with mythic belief that it was hardly worth critiquing. If you wanted myth you had the poets H.D. and Robert Duncan, an exoticism of myth I encountered as an undergrad, in which the ancient poetic authors they invoked, even when named, were satisfied to remain disembodied—a state their contemporary channelers often aspired to as well.

If novelist Marilynne Robinson were invited to speak about The Christian Writer at Union Theological Seminary, there'd be no expectation she'd have read a slew of Christian books or liturgy in order to talk about Jesus or God. Saul Bellow, however, was unlikely to touch the Jewish equivalent of that subject when he lectured for JPS because Judaism was the religion of the book and he had not made room for it. Back when I was going to Yeshiva kindergarten in Detroit, my parents had a discussion about going to the movies. They themselves were not religious but said the money spent for movie tickets (50 cents for two) would cover the tzedakah box (a charity coinbox, collected weekly, for scholars in the not-yet-state of Israel). So they did not go to the movies (though if I could whisper in their ears from today I'd say the price of the movie would provide a helpful education in American culture for these recent immigrants). Last night, the characters on "Mad Men" were sitting in front of small-screen black/white TV, watching Neil Armstrong's "live" first step on the moon. An argument broke out—and I remember it reverberating across the nation—that the money would have been better spent on helping the poor. Almost fifty years later, what good has the moon done? I don't know how the change came about, but no one is complaining anymore that the money for visiting Mars would be better spent on the unfortunate. Perhaps the knowledge has sunk in that we need an escape hatch from planet Earth, that the crucial "live" picture from the moon was of our fragile globe. Yet the mankind in Armstrong's "one small step for mankind" was thought at the time to refer to the charter of the United Nations, and not the anti-mankind totalitarians—from a US perspective—of, say, the Soviet Union, or better yet, China, which was not a UN member. Nobody at the time would substitute the term Homo sapiens for mankind, though Elie Wiesel had already written: "at Auschwitz not only man died but also the idea of man."

If we're to save Homo sapiens as a precious species, however, it means we have to set civilization aside and think cosmically, not globally. There are no doubt other civilizations out there in the galaxy (or in a hundred billion other galaxies) but we don't seem headed for a Federated galaxy à la *Star Wars*. Instead, we only have to hear from the first one to know that creation is more special than civilization. That contact with another intelligent species—quite possibly one long since extinct, or one extant while it's we who've gone extinct in thirty thousand Earth years ahead—means what counts is species consciousness in deep time, beyond "prehistoric," and not simply mankind. Life itself, in the light of creation, becomes our texts, perhaps to be read in the galactic library of newly discovered ecosystems. The latter are still being discovered on Earth, yet our formative text at home has clearly been the Hebrew Bible for its concern with creation.

The hippie costume I wore for a year back in the '60s was a protest against excess, to put it simply, but it was also a fundamental sympathy with creation. It was hard to be an uncertain hippie, peering through shoulder-length hair; nor did a headband indicate you were still in a quandary. Most of my intellectual hippie comrades would have said the costume merely showed you identified with how weird our history, personal and national, had become. Might as well explore weirdness—and why simple logic, like living in socially responsible communes, could be the answer. So in 1968 I moved into the largest urban commune in North America, though I'd cut my hair and beads by then. Rochdale College was a satellite of the University of Toronto in name only, its small board of hippie sympathizers having raised X hundreds of thousands of dollars for a 12 storied prime real estate building on the backs of its board of directors: architects, grant writers, nonprofit fundraisers, progressive urban planners and UT icons including Marshall McLuhan. Already a university Lecturer, I was entitled to a small though exclusive apartment; most residents lived in "ashrams," rooms surrounding a common living and dining area. There was a 4th floor 24/7 "free store," stocked with food from farm communes as well as clothes, bedding, whathaveyou—all of it taken on the honor system, not even a clerk necessary. I recall taking vegetables and a pair of flip-flops. Ground floor was a free macrobiotic restaurant, at which residents volunteered. It all worked like Eden for about a year, when the garden began to despoil, thanks to drugs and their salespersons, petty crime, suicides, whathaveyou. The honor code forbade us calling in the Toronto police, and even when they arrived to suicide or drug overdose scenes, there were residents offering protest. In less than two years, such protestors were replaced by scary biker types acting as our own police. When original residents, who had been nominally vetted as students, moved out, a harder-edged contingent of dropout-types took their place, many of them clinically depressed. The joyful hippie ethos devolved into a more cautious, if not despondent one. I served along with others as a "mentor in literature and writing" but what was now needed—in fact it was too late for them—was a cadre of therapists. One day I came home to find my apartment broken into; nothing much was taken, but the aquarium with three innocent angelfish was turned over, the creatures who had relied upon me dead on the floor, symbolic of the commune's dissolute condition. There was no use calling the commune police. The border between life and art, which we had ideally been cultivating as a zone of creation, was now lost in time, accessible only in memory of our innocence—though it was never really innocence, more like let's-try-anything-at-least-once.

To imagine no border between life and art, you had to imagine no border between McDonald's and avant-garde poetry, between bog-stage sports events and SoHo (in the '70s) art gallery openings. My old St. Marks colleague, then poet and now art critic Peter Schjeldahl, recently married and setting out to entertain from his and actress wife Brooke's newly acquired rent-stabilized St. Marks Place apartment, a block further east from mine, in the early '70s hosted a Saturday NCAA basketball Final Four TV watch party for a dozen of us, mostly poker players (*vide* my chapter 'The Poem of the Bad Hand') who'd awakened at five in the afternoon after Friday night's artists&poets poker game broke off at nine that morning. Peter ordered two dozen McDonald's Big Macs, fries, and Cokes, something I hadn't eaten in years, its super-fluity of triple buns a threat to taut waistlines and besides, we were semi-macrobiotic. It was Princeton vs Michigan, and you'd think we'd support the under-funded and non-scholarship underdog East Coast Princetonians, with their cerebral coach and style of play, against powerhouse Ann Arbor. But no, we saw UM's African-American star, Cazzie Russell, as more multicultural than Princeton's whitey star, Bill Bradley, and since I was the only UM alumnus there, it suited me. Meanwhile, I just looked it up and memory doesn't serve; it was actually the 1971 NBA final that we watched at Peter's and our Cazzie Russell-led Knicks lost to the Lakers. For the aforementioned college game I was a student writing fellow at Syracuse and the fare was Lapsang Souchong tea. Even then, the road to professional success required that you put your resumé aside and plunge into the art of living off the commercial/academic grid. Along with the tossed resumé went historical memory for the sake of a cultural mashup of high and low that made either socialism or surrealism feel like walking into Brooks Brothers.

A generation later, apropos my telling Edmund White that I played on the Southfield High basketball team that beat Cranbrook the year he was a student there in Michigan, Joyce Carol Oates reminded us that although Princeton was known for more than half its undergraduates participating in sports, she herself dislikes it and never watches a game. We were eating at *Mediterra*, an upscale Euro-funk mermaid aquarium of a "Taverna," abutting Princeton's campus, when Ed asked what I thought of the Cranbrook boys, who we'd just shellacked to the tune of 85-17, something like that. "We thought they were stoned," I said. "Sometimes they'd just stand there and admire my layup. In the locker-room after the game, we wondered if we could hit on them for some weed, a drug we public school boys had only heard about, or rather heard you could be offered it at rich private schools like Cranbrook." Joyce said she never knew a private school until she taught at Princeton, except for U. of Detroit, which was a Catholic school; "secular private school, that is." $50 for a plate of blackened pasta in French. But the "Mediterranean" waiters were wonderfully dour for a small town, and Joyce was her usual deadpan hilarious when conferring with Ed over their latest *New York Review of Books* assignments. "Bob sent me a biography of Amelia Earhart, whose legend always seemed sleazy to me, but I couldn't say no." Joyce turned to Rhonda and me to explain: "I never can say no to a request, like when David asked me twenty years ago to write about Adam and Eve for his Bible anthology." Ed said he was reviewing a Rimbaud biography. "Let's exchange," suggested Joyce. "I'm curious about Rimbaud and you'll love Amelia." It's hardly the risk-taking of tearing up your resumé; in its place, professional legitimacy has become the sine qua non of survival as an artist, while resumé-less computer start-ups live on the edge. A generalization, of course; perhaps the next generation's most ambitious poet, male, female or transgender, has been picking cotton on a Northern California Buddhist farm for ten years or studying Talmud for a decade in a piss-poor Jerusalem neighborhood.

6.

You never know where the most radical thinking is coming from. "FBI director James Comey called the Holocaust the most significant event in history and said that's why a US Holocaust Memorial Museum program on its lessons is mandatory for new agents." If you asked a hundred MFA students, few are likely to agree with the FBI director. Why? Because it's buried in the past, with its factory chimneys of death offering less relevance to the present than the mushroom cloud of Hiroshima. That latter cloud still pertains to vigilance, or one hopes it does. But the FBI director added that "Good people helped to murder millions. And that's the most frightening lesson of all. That is why I send our agents and our analysts to the museum. I want them to stare at us and realize our capacity for rationalization." Liberal Arts students today, however, who consider themselves good people, may not want to stare at themselves so closely. I didn't; I preferred to stare out at the world, not in. What I saw was an aunt Yanka who was a Holocaust survivor, but I didn't see her invisible young daughters who'd been gassed before I could know them. The latter belonged to lost time for me. I could have rescued their memories, perhaps, but I was too young to ask the right questions while my elders were too stunned. The young girls left no text, unlike even the Burgess Shale of 500 million years ago, a huge mashup of species. Liberal Arts students may not comprehend its evolutionary aspects, but its relevance to their present concern with the trendier aspects of climate change will be apparent: climatologists study the fossil records in the Burgess Shale to understand the climate of the Cambrian Explosion, and use it to predict what Earth's warming climate in the future might be. That's a future today's youth can relate to, one that even technology might help us prevent, but what technology could prevent the Holocaust? What vigilance of *other people's* inner lives?

Easier to consider the life of *Elrathia*, a small, rare, and poorly known trilobite discovered in the Burgess Shale. I read: "The adult dorsal exoskeleton is up to 25 mm long, with a large semicircular cephalon occupying about one-third the total length.... Eyes are small and transverse eye ridges are very weak.... The surface of the exoskeleton is variably granulate.... may, like similar small trilobites, be interpreted as a mobile, epibenthic deposit (particle) feeder adapted to low oxygen levels.... The concept of Elrathia is quite confused." However confusing, it's still a puzzle we may eventually work out. When you see a picture of the fossil, the ancient corpse is intriguing, you don't want to turn away as from a pile of bodies in Auschwitz. I can get closer to Elrathia than my gassed cousins. For instance, I am fond of the plants and animals described as filtering feeders, combing through the water for edible particles—like collectors, like archaeologists themselves, alive, or once alive. You might say they were not trying to understand anything with their collecting, just eating to stay alive, but in that drive they remain open to something new, as if their ecosystem acted as a giant brain in which, indeed, their species might evolve. We might meet Elrathia again on an exoplanet, or, as we scan through the galaxy itself like feeders sifting intellectual particles, we may encounter more evolved species, to whom our intellectual feeding seems a primitive form of exploring our galaxy-wide environment. Yet I misuse the term primitive; Elrathia is a fellow species, as we will be to one however more advanced, and we have much to learn from it—if even how rare it was and how confused we are in describing it.

It was at the Royal Ontario Museum's exhibit for the Burgess Shale that I came across Elrathia among hundreds of Cambrian species. It's the shale itself, the complexly stratified rock that humans stumbled upon as an outcropping on a mountain ridge a century ago, in British Columbia, that reminds me of a great precious wall. Specifically, the Western Wall in Jerusalem, an ancient stone remnant from when the Temple last stood, a mere 2,000 years ago. When I saw it last, in 2007, I'd already seen the Burgess Shale exhibit in Toronto, incorporating both walls into my Jewish Writers Conference talk of that year—as personal talismans of cities I'd once immigrated to. In Toronto, in my early twenties, I didn't know what to do with the Burgess Shale, other than groove on it, in the old parlance of the '60s, as if it was the ultimate psychedelic mandala of life on Earth. I wouldn't have had the patience to study the complicated historical evolutionary context. Instead, it's historical to me *now*, just as are the original lost writers of the Bible, though in cultural terms the shale is "prehistoric" and the ancient writers in Jerusalem might as well be, since they are covered over with the prejudicial term "anonymous," more deeply buried than the Cambrian trilobites. Yet less so of late, since textual scholarship has burrowed into the ancient Hebrew and come back with lettered names and numbers for biblical authors, including "E", a designation admittedly less evocative or profound than "Elrathia".

In '07, Rhonda and I walked up to the Western Wall (aptly named, since Western history is embedded in David's and Solomon's inspiration to build the first monotheistic residence within that later fragment of a wall) and touched the stones, feeling a tactile sob from the sorrowful loss it represented—not lost in time but lost time itself, irretrievable. Except that it now represented a new page opened in the ancient book of Israel, just as the Burgess Shale opened our minds to deep history. I just looked up its location online, to see if we could visit and touch it too; and one can, though it's a bit of a trek into mountainous wilderness when compared to modern Jerusalem, where we left the Wall to dine on gourmet sushi a few blocks away. A few days later, back at the conference that sponsored our trip from Miami and after my talk on the two Walls, hosts Martin Kramer and Hava Pinhas-Cohen asked if we'd visited the large scale model of the ancient Temple newly reconstructed beside the scroll-shaped museum that houses the Dead Sea Scrolls. And so we did approach the model of ancient Jerusalem—to be reminded that a veritable fossil, such as Elrathia or the actual scrolls, is worth a thousand breathtaking models. The former actually breathed, to my mind.

At this very moment of writing I note our cat's toy model of a pink mouse on the floor. Louise will fetch and retrieve if I toss it to her, dropping it at my feet as only the rare dog will do (they generally keep it locked in their jaws, wanting a tug). But Louise knows very well it's just a model, not a real mouse. Here in Florida, she catches small lizards on the screened patio (how do they get in?) and brings them into the little ring of our kitchen, positioned alive in her mouth, then dropped like a tiny bull for her sometimes hours of matador training. We feel bad for the lizard, it must know its fate is sealed; or perhaps not, perhaps it knows ultimate humility—of the kind Oscar Wilde espouses in jail, in *De Profundis*—as Louise's teeth flash the *coup de grâce*. She won't eat it, like a true matador, and leaves it for us to do with what we will.

There's a floor-length scale model of the Everglades ecosystem at the National Park entrance. It's nothing you can see in reality, as it's mostly underground, but in the most real of senses and in all its generous reality the Everglades we visit today is a pale remnant of lost time, much of it chopped and buried under Miami. The scale model, in fact, resembles a plaster monument, bereft of the multitude of living species born there. What is left is only a suburban remnant on life support. Like a genocide, we can sketchily document the loss but never recover the soul of the lost, it's *creative* power—for in the living time of the Everglades, some ten thousand years, it fostered the evolution of new species. But not today—unless we count invasive species, which would be like counting Turkish citizens who moved into murdered Armenians' homes a century ago. Nothing creative about that, a cockroach could do it. Still, the tales of genocide tell of our inability to internalize them. What will never be shakeable from the human mind, concerning the Holocaust in particular, is the psychosis of hatred. Today, the descendants of the psychosis are satisfied to say the hatred was irrational, and yet the enabling of it by an advanced European civilization was utterly rationalized, industrialized—as redemption from the demonized Jew. Industrialized redemption: there it is in a phrase, the inversion of Judeo-Christian redemption into a mechanized psychotic structure. Were it simply inhabited by irrational people we could say in concert with the German nation that we are sane today, the rational ones. Yet although the German Third Reich was smashed by the Allies, the psychosis violently broken, we can no more internalize it than be redeemed by our industrious push into the future. It was an irredeemable lost time.

Can I say the same for my 8 hours on the operating table during open heart surgery? Eight hours of my allotted lifetime tacked onto sleep, but no dreaming, just utter black void, outer space. Doc said don't look back, some patients fall into depression, just keep moving forward, take your wife to dinner. (Don't look back, I asked? I'm in the middle of a memoir). My early teachers, poets Snodgrass and Lowell, were of the Confessional school along with Roethke, Sexton, Plath, Ginsberg, showing how to live or survive with the lost time of mental instability, and depression is a form of mental instability. They had no heart operations, though they did have depressing thoughts (and Snodgrass's Pulitzer-winning book was titled *Heart's Needle*). Their confessions could acknowledge lost time as well as suicide. It's more complicated today; being human means having to create a history for yourself that can live with lost time, even if it's not on the popular agenda. Lost time seems not to exist online, hence no need to address its oldest memes: Creation, Eden, psychosis or evil. Why internalize the Shoah when you can google it? To live with it, however, requires a poetics of interpretation that can access history as well as psyche. The Biblical writer J took in the Expulsion, Flood, Sodom&Gomorrah (Hiroshima&Nagasaki), and Dance of the Golden Calf—all while seated in an unplugged room.

Novelist James Salter just died. We were having dinner at *Mediterra* a few years ago, after his Princeton reading of a passage from his novel-in-progress, to be his last, when I asked him if Robert Weil, the editor-in-chief at the time of Norton, had told him—as he'd once told me—that Henry Roth was the American Jewish novelist nonpareil. No, answered Salter, never heard of him: "Is Weil actually a well-known person?" To everyone in publishing, at least, I answered! Robert Weil was the name Salter had given his new protagonist in *All That Is*, a naval flier who became a NYC book editor after the Second World War. On hearing this, the color drained from

Salter's face; I was reminded of his publishing insecurities as well as his
Jewish ones. He actually hadn't realized—so assimilated had he become—
that Weil was a recognizably Jewish name, almost as much so as Horowitz,
Salter's original family name. He thanked me for telling him, and I offered
further that no one at his Princeton reading would have assumed he had
it in for Norton's Weil. Phillip Bowman is that character's name in the
published book now, stripped of current associations, Jewish or other. And
Salter had been so skittish of invoking any connection to the Hebrew Bible
that you'll scarcely find an OT biblical name among his characters, neither
a Saul nor a Sarah, as his ancient forebear J or contemporary Bellow used
(*vide* Moses Herzog). Nor would you find a hint that James is merely the
Greek translation for Jacob.

Saul Bellow's experience of his own individuality was so intense that
it left him skeptical of writers without it, among which he may have
accounted the biblical prose stylists. Without names and biography, not
even a laconic tombstone epitaph, they can seem like medieval saga-
writers, or folksingers in prose. Yet their contemporaries in literary art were
not balladeers but Homer and Hesiod, Sophocles and Euripides, Lucretius
and Plato, writers acknowledged by Bellow even through the character he
creates in his last novel, *Ravelstein*, of his close friend, philosopher and
classicist Allan Bloom. But there was no one in Bellow's day to make this
argument for individualistic biblical writers; instead, the academic fashion
in the latter half of the twentieth century was for textual submersion,
almost a religious erasure of the writer, now subverted into his cultural
surround. Disembodied, you might say, and may find it still said today in
esteemed approval of a selfless pose in some pop iconic work or other—
and no doubt a successful one, for even failure is no longer acknowledged
unless it's a successful one. Besides, disembodiment was not to Bellow's
taste, and it would have been hard for him to look past his early religious
upbringing and find a way into and behind the biblical text. His fellow
Nobelist, Isaac Bashevis Singer did it, but Singer himself (whose stories he
translated from Yiddish) was Judaic enough for Bellow, comic and tragic
in the same breath, as the Bible seemed to me when I translated it from
the writer's point of view. It was a pov you needed colloquial Hebrew to
enliven, or some variant thereof, such as ancient Judeo-Aramaic. When
you had it, you could begin to discern the ironies presented to the biblical
imagination, especially those between linguistic archaisms, clichés, rhetoric,
and the historical vs literary pose. You discover that few of the best biblical
writers could resist a play on words at every juncture.

When they awoke in the morning they swore as a man to his
brother. Isaac walks with them as they turned to go, sent off in
peace. Now listen: on that same day, Isaac's servants approach with

news about the well they are digging: "We have found water," they said. He called it Sworn-oath—"Sheb-oath"—which is why the city is named the Well of Sheba—Beersheba—to this day.

A literal translation is content with "seven" for sheba, designating the putative seven wells in the area. "This day," the day of the actual writing many centuries later, the writer J is playing off the vicissitudes of oath-making against the cloudy histories of place-naming. Or so I've reconstructed the individualistic imagination of the writer.

Further, Hagar speaks:
Yahweh had spoken to her and the name she called him was "You are the all-seeing God," having exclaimed, "You are the God I lived to see—and lived after seeing." That is why the hole was called "Well of Living Sight"—you can see it right here, between Kadesh and Bered.

That triple play between seeing, sight, and living extends to "you," the reader, who can witness the well—and by your witness, attest to Yahweh's presence and Abraham's history in the land and with Hagar. We cannot separate the writer from the history, the history from the place, and the ancient (already to the first readers in ancient Jerusalem) drama of God's presence in the distant past from the appeal to ourselves, the readers even today, to confirm the presence of the well. One can imagine the range of ironies available to the biblical writer at the original scene of writing if even my individual freedom as the translator allows me to interpret ironically—true to the imagined original context beyond the literal text.

Certainly the biblical author Nehemiah was accessing an earlier trope for the irony of combined joy and sorrow, but by the time he expressed it after the return from Babylonian exile, it seems characteristically Jewish—no less so than Bellow's irony that can conjoin laughter and trembling in the same sentence, as in Sammler reflecting "There is still such a thing as a man—or there was." Or: "According to Nietzsche, the Germans, insufferably oppressed by being German, used Wagner like hashish." To laugh—or to cry at that sentence? (Bellow follows it with: "To Mr. Sammler's ears, Wagner was background music for a pogrom.") In the Book of Ezra, the oldest exiles recalled through their suffering the First Temple at the ground-breaking of the Second:

...could see it still standing
fixed in their memories—
these men broke out weeping

loudly, openly
as they stood before this house
rising again in their living eyes

many others were shouting joyfully
a great noise was going up
people in the distance could hear it clearly

and they could not tell by their ears
the sound of weeping
from the sound of joy.

Apropos, a link arrived recently to an obit, sent by a friend and former student of Harold Bloom, for luminous literary critic M.H. Abrams, who had been Bloom's teacher and a litcrit staple in my undergrad years. I'm not a fan of obits; when I hear someone has passed on I prefer to google them and their books online. That's how I came across the necessity to read Bellow's *To Jerusalem and Back* again. A sentence from the Meyer Abrams NYT obit, however, took me further back: "Professor Abrams examined the works of German philosophers and English poets to document the transformation of traditional Judeo-Christian religious ideas into poetic theory in the Romantic period, when art was called upon to perform many of the spiritual functions of religion." "Called upon" certainly has a religious ring to it, but who was it calling? Educated men are perhaps designated, perhaps women too, but consider the creative writers, especially the original biblical writers. They read historical texts that were previously considered religious, such as the Sumerian hymns—but in the palace precincts of Solomonic Jerusalem where they were writing many centuries after the Sumerian writers, those Sumerian texts were read as literary classics, the way the epics and dramas of Ancient Greece are read in classrooms today. What counts is how a creative writer works with his or her sources, regardless of what those sources are. The writer, then, is the archetype of the individual, and the literary business of applying critical structure is like imagining Professor Abrams, whose Harvard dissertation was *The Milk of Paradise: The Effect of Opium Visions on the Works of De Quincey, Crabbe, Francis Thompson and Coleridge*, having no considerable experience of opium himself. A couple decades later and the critic I was impersonating as a student was no longer a "second-hand" individual like Abrams: for my own '60s dissertation at the UK's experimental University of Essex, where individualism ran rampant, it was quite acceptable that my research into the poetic texts of Gertrude Stein would necessitate experience of cocaine. Nevertheless, in those early years of soft drugs in every pocket, cocaine was still rare and I had to visit the continent for it (it was research, of course, not a lifestyle), namely Paris, where I was able to take a scholarly stroll down the rue de Fleurus, past the prior lodgings and atelier of Stein, with a contemplative hashish high, compliments of my Wivenhoe Park, U.Essex colleagues. Cocaine was saved for reading through Stein's voluminous texts in Alice Toklas's privately printed *Plain Editions*, accessed at the Bibliothèque Nationale de France. In other words, the late '60s had turned me into a first-hand individual, one no more or less individually minded than the supposed "religious" painters in the prehistoric caves of southern France, whose sources for painted fauna are too often described by second-hand critics as "the hunt," when in fact, like all true artists, their sources were earlier works, even if cognitively apprehended with the aid of ingestible bits of flora. Maybe even a prehistoric tea or naturally occurring fermented fruit. I'm sorry, but the very first artist, were there even to have been such a possibility, would still have looked back to patterns traced in whatever form by his/her forebears, whatever earlier primates they be. Certainly they were individuals, every bit as much as our cat Louise. It all comes down to history, but for the artist, it is history experienced first-hand.

So what on earth could "traditional Judeo-Christian religious ideas" mean to an artist like Michelangelo or Dante except sources no different than the sexy bodies and garments worn by early Renaissance men and women, or the kooky transcendental theories of some Middle Ages scholastic precursor of Swedenborg's book on the afterlife, *Heaven and Hell*. William Blake sourced the latter, but Blake's poetry was as individual and undaunted by theories as the Sumerian Gilgamesh poets, who no doubt scavenged religious sources but conceived their new works as history-come-to-life, just like the great writers of biblical poetry and prose. What—were they not pious? Perhaps they could seem so to their readers, in the sense of a pious loyalty to their Hebraic or late Judaic culture. The same holds true for Whitman's or Williams's American piety. Would we not be shocked to learn that these red-blooded American poets were in fact Wagnerian acolytes? But so what; so what if their sources were *The Saga of the Volsungs*, the Poetic (or Elder) *Edda*, and Snorri Sturluson's Prose *Edda*? For they would have made them just as American as a Betsy Ross flag (and our contemporary, the artist Jasper Johns, did just that). Dare we ask where Ms. Ross got her particular notion of stars, of stripes? The encyclopedia says she got them from General George Washington, which is as laughable as asserting that the biblical author J got her sources for the speech of God from the High Priest. No, she got them from her individual experience of history, and had it not been filtered through a great Hebraic sensibility, we super-sophisticates would probably be looking down our noses today at the *Eddas* instead of traditional Judeo-Christian religious ideas.

7.

Tonight I watch an episode of the *Groucho Marx Show* (c.1954) and one from *Mad Men* (2014). Why does the show from 60 years ago appear more sophisticated? First, we know Groucho from his past acting-persona and see him now as the mature "himself." Groucho conducts a play within a play, of which he is master of both: the interviewee contestants reveal their inner confusions, but he moderates their embarrassment with his own acting-out of ambivalence toward the divide between public and private, so that we in the audience are charmed to offer up our own inner confusion as testimony, albeit sublimated into comedy. Dan Draper, however, the *Mad Men* protagonist, may serve as a subconscious master of ceremonies, but there's no mediation between him and our position in the audience, other than the narrative frame of a restoration of mid-century culture. Is that concession to historical restoration enough to justify our embarrassment at peeping into the confused inner lives of the '50s characters as they act out? Is it enough to note the carefully reconstructed details of mid-century sets, public and private, as rationale for beholding the often self-destructive confusion acted therein? Is it not restoration for restoration's sake, rather than for the sake of enriching a familiar text? For ultimately there is no significant text to be restored in *Mad Men*, no play within the play. We are made to seem a knowing audience, so that it's we ourselves who offer up our inner confusions—yet there's no public acknowledgment of it, no master of public and private like Groucho to reveal the hand-me-down position our culture places us in. Along with Groucho's real-life '50s contestants, we are pleased to recognize ourselves as second fiddle, and not embarrassed.

Yes, the writers of *Mad Men* are good writers, and there are several comic and poignant moments in their work, but what are we to do with those moments beyond being entertained? I don't think the writers know. We should be embarrassed at our privileged position in the audience but we're given no excuse for it, no mediator of embarrassment, other than the entertainment of enlightened titillation. No original narrative or drama is being restored, no surprising inklings of authorship as we get when an aspect of Shakespeare's life or culture comes to light, or Emily Dickinson's, or even Meyer Levin's, whose narrator of the play within, Sid Silver in 1956's *Compulsion*, is both in it and without. It's just this week that *Compulsion* has been republished in a new edition and allows me to add an aspect to its authorship, by virtue of friendship with Levin's son, the poet Gabriel Levin. Anybody can know that Anat, his wife, is a psychoanalyst, or that Gabi's poems and sinuous prose encode his being a Jew within a larger world. Yet it's not the great common world that Saul Bellow invokes; rather, Levin's is a restoration of a lost region of the imagination, the Levant, within which his Jewishness can thrive as a "worldly" narrator whose Jewish self-knowledge is sublimated into the lost Mediterranean landscapes he investigates for us, all of them standing in for Israel. Reading his father's book now, we see the same sublimation of Jewish landscape into worldly Chicago, a play within a play, where the Jewish murderers and victims (including their families and community) are woven into the larger landscape as distorting mirrors of the breakdown between the public common world and the private psyche, freed of moral knowledge. The real Jew of *Compulsion* is its narrator, Sid Silver, whose moral connection to Jewish history is still intact. Gabriel Levin's own work brings all this to further light: Silver's psychoanalytic framework in the novel is given more significant weight in our world today when you see Gabi's wife, Anat, more firmly planted in the Israeli landscape than Sid Silver was in Chicago, and when you read Meyer Levin's son's elaboration of a Jewish consciousness, which seeks to knit Israel more deftly into the surrounding landscape and history. As for the father, Gabriel has provided a brief Intro to the new edition that hints at how Meyer Levin's wanderlust, which leads him to postwar Paris, where he marries Gabi's mother, takes root in Israel via his son, who confronts a similar though far more complex melange of Jewish culture, ancient and modern, than his father's Chicago.

So I was sent back to Bellow's Chicago (from which he embarked *To Jerusalem and Back*), as he conjures it in an earlier essay: "In a story by Meyer Levin one character exclaims: 'I was a foreigner, writing in a foreign language ... What am I? Native, certainly. My parents came to this country ... they were the true immigrants, the actual foreigners. ... But I, American-born, raised on hot dogs, I am out of place in America. Remember this: Art to be universal must be narrowly confined. An artist must be a perfect unit of time and place, at home with himself, unextraneous. Who am I? Where do I come from? I am an accident. What right have I to scribble in this American language that comes no more naturally to me than it does to the laundry Chinaman?'" And in that same essay, in alliance with Levin, his Chicago-born colleague, Bellow goes further to justify the Jewish writer as a man of the common world: "But Jews have been writing in languages other than Hebrew for more than two thousand years. The New Testament scholar Hugh J. Schonfield asserts that parts of the Gospels were composed in a sort of Yiddish Greek 'as colorful in imagery and metaphor as it is often careless in grammatical construction.'" However, Bellow fails to note—it would not aid his man-of-the-world self-image—that Judeo-Greek, like Yiddish, is far more suffused with biblical Hebrew than is English. Nor did Bellow's son, Adam (also a writer with an unusual slant, like Meyer Levin's son) gravitate to Israel, where he might have elaborated his father's intuition that the New Testament writers were more deeply Jewish than the common world has given them credit for.

In his intro to *Compulsion*, Gabriel Levin refers to his father's Holo-caust-tinged sensibility: "Just how World War II and the Holocaust link up with the crime committed by Judd and Artie [precocious Nietzsche readers] I will leave for the reader to discover in the concluding pages of the novel. Hints are dropped along the way: on hearing of the crime for the first time, 'On that day it was as though the crime had split open a small crack in the surface of the world, and we could see through into the evil that was yet to emerge.'" Meyer Levin, who wrote the first play based on the *Diary of Anne Frank* (ironically deemed too Jewish for universal consumption) in the forties, was still assessing the recent Jewish history in the fifties that Bellow admits to having ignored, at least for awhile; Bellow was headlong in pursuit of a new vision of American literary vocation that would naturalize the cosmopolitan Jew and even honor him for bringing the world to America. Ironically, however, and against his intent, Bellow would often be designated a specifically Jewish writer, along with his younger colleagues Roth, Ozick and several others, all of whom struggled against any hint of marginalization, with a notable exception in the older Henry Roth, who in later life also travelled to, and wrote essays about Israel—though unlike Bellow or Ozick, Henry Roth was trying to find a way to emigrate there.

Time is a poem. All the things and places in the spatial universe are the subject of prose, fiction and nonfiction, description and analysis. Time passes by: it looks at things, contemplates, but passes, as all things pass in time. Sometimes you have a mixture of the two, prose and poetry, as in biblical prose and a psychoanalytic session. So Bellow, a supreme prose artist, looks at two poets in Jerusalem who soon became friends of mine, Harold Schimmel and Dennis Silk, and thinks wistfully, in *To Jerusalem and Back*, how they have learned to push the noise of the world aside, yet fails to notice the muscles they grew in the pushing, along with Gabriel Levin in his poetry today. Their work reveals the strength of holding on to time, as it moves through and past all the noise of talk and violence. These invisible muscles make poets look slightly odd. You see it especially in photos; you can pick out a poet in any group picture. It started for me on the high school basketball team, and when I first saw the team photo in the yearbook I cringed at the otherworldly set of my face, above shorts and Southfield Blue Jays jersey. I wasn't looking at the camera like the others; my gaze was passing by it, having left the occasion. I was like the wind in "woo you, woo you, I blew in to woo you," from a lovelorn poem I'd already written at 14. And it was already ironic: in this poem, written during months of heartbreak over my steady Judy's defection to a star halfback, I discovered that the poem, in the persona of wind, was more firmly at one with change than she. I held on like a cowboy to his horse and it reformed me, made me slightly bowlegged, though less in the legs and more in the face, yet you couldn't put your finger on it. Look at Emily Dickinson or Wallace Stevens, but more to the point, look at the depictions of our ur-poet, Homer: he is blind.

The blind Homer looks back to the lost time when we evolved and were perfectly at home with our original wild ecosystem, as well as to the birth of civilization when a paradisaical origin, as in Dilmun, was sacral for the later Sumerians and reinterpreted as "pardes" (garden in Hebrew) by biblical writers: wild civilization as pure garden, as in Eden. If I may say that early civilizations like Dilmun "domesticated" us, at a time when we still remembered having first domesticated plants and animals, then it's important to continue exploring the meanings of domestication, as Darwin had begun, in the footsteps of Aristotle.

For instance, why did good movies about dogs and cats explode after World War II, as in the Lassie series? Most likely because they were the hopeful scions of civilization, trustworthy, brave, curious and most of all, innocent. There was Spot the dog and Puff the cat in the Dick and Jane readers, making most youngsters want one. They were not pets but, through a youth's eyes, companions. Only more recently have they come to be prized for cuteness, not from the youthful perspective but by adults, and this attribution has spawned detractors. Nobody thinks of civilization as cute, especially not the current Pope Francis, who worries that dogs and cats are replacing children. Better cute companion animals than too-cute children, I'd say. Dick and Jane were not cute, they were enterprising. Their innocence was tempered by alertness and agency. They retained a connection to the natural world through affinity for domesticated animals and plants, as during their regular jaunts to visit granma and granpa on their farm. The land is ancestral, where we come from, was the message, and companion animals ratified it. Not so today's cutification of pets; they seem to come from a fantasy of innocence and are beaten down into loungers and, when abandoned, confused strays or feral scroungers. Not having lived with one, this may be all that the Pope knows. Yet that may be a momentary phase, because in the online craze for pet videos their cuteness has been transcended into uncanniness, a suggestion of our own species ingenuity. And there is now a counter-movement, expressed in books and other media. to see ourselves, the historical domesticator, through the animal's eyes. Darwin had that vision for his many companion dogs and cats, and it may be coming back: a lost, almost edenic time when we began to partner with animals and plants. Yet Eden was innocent *wilderness*, so it seemed, where all that was sentient had its own integrity (they talked!), and it's precisely that wild vision of coevolution that is lost and, in the meanwhile, represented by imagined encounters with aliens on other planets.

That aliens can be thought of as benign at all is ironic, although I argue in my bio of Abraham that he was such a historical creature. Aliens represented the unwanted side of immigration and in modern times morphed into the more common expression, "enemy alien." But many modern artists deeply ironized it, especially an uncommon and complex poet like Charles Reznikoff who anchored the irony of an alien-at-home in the Hebrew Bible. And just the other night, after watching Capra's extraordinary *Mr. Deeds Goes to Town*, I was reminded again there are two kinds of poets or artists (and many shadings in between). Deeds is an amateur poet, in the sense that Winston Churchill and George W. Bush are amateur painters. Basically, amateur poetry is anti-poetry, in that it subverts alertness to language by loading it down with intentionality. Jean Arthur is charmed by Deeds's poem for her to the extent it's about her and not about language. An amateur poem is always ironic about poetry, using some formal aspects like rhyme and metaphor to appear like a poem. In fact, it thrills to the irony of *not being* a real poem but instead a *sentiment*, or any other kind of messaging system. That's why poets often find amateur poems hilarious—as if it is really possible for a poem to be about anything but language itself. To sentimentalists, that sounds like a limiting but it's just the opposite: language itself is a universe, each sound and groupings of sounds reverberating back through hundreds of different usages or meanings, all the way back to the lost time of the first language. It's as impossible to get back there as to Eden; it would be like entering a black hole. But we can imagine it: each sound, each word existing outside the weight of time, having no history, no infinite range of nuances with which to write a poem. Life would make the poem, not language; perhaps a fruit fly experiences life this way, as a poem, and a plant putting forth its flower as well. For us aspirational poets today, however, language is so large, rich and deep that it's all we can do to control it for a brief spell, like riding a rodeo bronco or bull. And those moments of holding on to it, once we're off it, are always ironic, for "riding" the wild bull is an illusion. No great poem, from the ancient Greek or Hebrew to Anna Akhmatova and Lea Goldberg, can be anything but ironic—the less ironic, the more intentional and sincere, the more a poem is sunk by packaged feelings. For the deeper, internalized feelings of a lifetime to be freed up a bit during the poem, there must be a barrier built of language that permits the inner life to become conscious. What can that barrier be but ironic, and the more ironic the stronger the barrier and the more uncanny its protection of the freed-up feeling.

That is the reason the Bible is so rarely read for its great art anymore: we've lost the strength of its irony. Instead, we have the cheap irony of media entertainment and ads, what amounts to amateur poetry. Can there be anything more ironic, however, than the Pillar of Cloud and the Pillar of Fire with which the Creator of the universe (hence Creator of language) marches through the wilderness, a protective barrier for the culture he has chosen to hear his Edenic language of morality, as in the putative ten-line poem of the Ten Commandments? The pillars too, like the words, are ironic because they protect us from confronting the Creator directly. You would hardly want to reduce the Creator's words to the bathos of "sincerity"—in fact, they are barriers against drowning in sincerity, and thus are open to endless interpretation throughout time, along with the rest of the Bible. Rhonda, upon hearing my slant, asked if this could make sense to "believers," to the religious and the respecters of religion. Perhaps if they're self-conscious, I prevaricated, realizing my affinity for the many who are. When I'm in a synagogue, I'm conscious of being in theater within a theater within a theater—the largest theater being the cosmic one, in which my body and mind make up an artifact, a creature that flares to life for a moment and falls to dust. It's powerful drama, you can re-enter it every day or week and still be moved, just as you can witness a hundred productions of a Shakespeare play and still be hungry for more. Under the rather common scaffolding of story, in both Bible and King Lear, lies the universe of language, where not even one word of Cordelia, neither her refusal to flatter at the start or her refusal to breathe in her father's arms at last, still reverberates through a galaxy of language that is the play. As the poetry therein frees up internalized feeling, it protects me from galactic harm. It is the same in the Bible, especially reading the weekly portions within the theater of history, as dramatized within the synagogue. You could say it's an acting-out of reading, the way it's enfolded within the synagogue as liturgy, and that thereby the original irony of the text is safeguarded.

But if it's irony, how can you "believe" it, how can you trust it? I have another word for irony in this context, namely poetry. Trust the poetry—its reliance on the world of language—the way all sentient beings trust the poetry of life. The latter is no amateur poem like the ones written by Mr. Deeds in the movie; its reverberations are infinite, ridden or played out for a moment by the specific poem of the bird's or the bee's life. However, Mr. Deeds knows his poems are amateur ones and he's consistently ironic about his status as a poet inspired by tuba-playing. The movie reveals that the real poem is the one in which Jean Arthur and Gary Cooper show their inmost delicate feelings to each other. At that point, there is no more acting-out, as amateur poems are made of; there's a complete absence of acting-out, a helplessness that resembles "falling" in love, with each other and the world, while protected by the irony of language gone silent. No acting-out language now, but rather the unpeeling of language. What can be more ironic than words within words within words—an endless need for interpreting—so that the act of becoming conscious of the universe of language is the one that counts, leaving all the possible acting-outs of daily life by the wayside, at least for a moment. In that moment, we're also conscious of lost time—of having to live with it. It may seem like a jarring leap now to bring back the memory of the Holocaust as lost time, but there it is: instead of re-creating Eden, Europe was capable of creating Hell with a very bad poetry of sincere tropes of purity and extermination—bad tropes that blot out the creative world along with all innocent feelings, driving them further inward.

True, it's the acting-out that kills us, which is why Christianity and Christian Humanism proved a weak defense in 20th Century Europe, privileging what's in the heart over moral deeds. In Judaism, interior cleansing is not determinative; what counts is how your interior life is reflected in actual deeds. How you fulfilled the "mitzvot"—inspiring moral acts derived from the Bible and Talmud—is how you were embodied at your funeral eulogy. It mattered not that you were a spiritual person with spiritual inner feelings if you could not refuse the horrific anti-Semitic deeds your society enacted. On Sundays in Germany and Austria under the Third Reich, spiritual people went to church while their Jewish neighbors were pulled screaming out of their houses and sent off to death camps. I couldn't have articulated this before my thirties because my sense of Jewish history was overcome by the '60s imperative to act out social and personal liberation, though I could hardly disentangle the two. One day I dropped acid and the next day I was at a Vietnam War prayer vigil. I doubt that most of my colleagues at the vigil would have disagreed with the thought experiment in which the war could be stopped by passing out tabs of LSD to combatants on both sides. Yet no wonder the deep history of the Jews was vilified just twenty years before: the liberation it embodies demands the vigilant study of a lifetime, while you could drink the Hitler Youth Kool-Aid in a day and be transformed. It was too much for me to enact, the Jewish moral culture; I was more taken with Saul Bellow exploring the boundaries of Americanism, or Zionist pioneers feeling out the boundaries of democracy. It all pulled me toward a boundary I constructed of my own: the one between poetry and translation, which I explored by studying Hebraic history and trying to lift the biblical text off the page—in the experimental act of poetry.

8.

Rhonda is being celebrated at a party, along with three research colleagues on a high-scoring National Institutes for Health grant to help adolescent kids with AIDS in Haiti. Spouses are in tow, and I've been enticed with the knowledge that one of them, a psychiatrist and psychoanalyst, has written on a psychiatrist-poet whose work parallels that of William Carlos Williams. Where the latter was an obstetrician who sometimes wrote of delivering babies, the psychiatrist-poet invoked clinical sessions where buried thoughts were pulled into consciousness, or so I hoped the analogy would go. In fact, what Eugene says bolsters the image of psychoanalyst as poet, one who listens intently to the language of the analysand for signs of uncanny discontinuity, a word or phrase that evokes a deeper layer to the story. Unlike a poet, however, Eugene is talking about helping the patient build a narrative. He's arguing for the conventionally sincere memoir, in which the author can step outside the resulting narrative and see himself in it. To which I offer a favorite Oscar Wilde quote, "only bad poetry is sincere." This startles him (can an analyst be insincere?). "To be good," I add, "it has to be playful enough to forget about itself. To pick out the surprising detail from a widely unfocused lens or unintended thought in an otherwise coherent train of thought." "Like a psychoanalyst!" exclaims Eugene. "If the patient internalizes the analyst," he continues, "she's not seeing simply herself but a hybrid kind of thing that includes the analyst. Am I following you? Aren't you poeticizing the transference?"

I started to wiggle out of the conversation at that point; poeticizing was coming too easy. I was missing Eugene's clinical necessity. He is dealing with seriously disturbed patients who cannot even construct a simple narrative within which to see themselves as victims of circumstance, if not worse. They are already modern poets of discontinuity, though it will do them no good to continue that way. And few out of a hundred overly focused, graduate writing-workshop students will make a living from their works. And who can blame them for their anxious focus—they may be paying the equivalent of a thousand dollars per workshop session in tuition, or even more at Columbia, Stanford and NYU, over the two years of striving for an MFA. Seriously though, what makes us creatively anxious? You may laugh but I offer, more than symbolically, our loss of a tail. You see it in our fellow household mammals, dogs and cats, with that wavy, antenna-like extension of their nervous systems into the surround that keeps them in balance with it. We, however, are more closely bound into our self-made cultures, and like some animals in the zoo, some cultures most tightly bound are prone to madness. A psychiatrist like Eugene would not have survived in the Third Reich, but like Freud in the years that preceded it, his willingness to think outside the box might range even to the evolutionary history in which we lost our tails. But that's the poet in me talking again. I don't have Eugene's clinical responsibility to deal with mental disease—you don't joke around with someone deeply suffering in your presence. In the same way, I circumvented the communal responsibility of a traditional Jew. The result was perhaps a creative anxiety, one that left me exposed on the savannah. With no tree to climb for safety, I had the poetic practice in which to imagine one. And then came the crucial realization: I had no tail to anchor me among the branches. I'd now need not only the tales of my ancestors but the biblical irony toward them by my ancestor-poets. They were the analysts of family myths, who refocused them into the historical context needed to survive in an often mad or dangerously ambivalent world. But it wouldn't have worked unless the reader could internalize the poet; the writing had to look past a desired sincerity and erase the boundaries of time, uncannily lifting the reader, like the poet himself, into the realm of origins and lost time, where our spirits, such as they are, were formed. Not just transcendent Eden and the Promised Land but also the trauma of slavery and the terrors of exile.

I went directly from translating J's Garden narrative to Fairchild Tropical Garden, where I was presented with lost time as a silent paradise, sans humans or any other animals. It was imaginary, of course, so I'd have to animate it; you couldn't have fruits and flowers without animal pollinators, including the extinct dinosaurs who munched on, and carried afield the seeds of cycads. The book I came away with, *The Lost Book of Paradise*, contrasts the specifically historical time in which the early Bible was written with the lost time of Eden, in which everything, including the plants and the subtle serpent, had a question and used the same language to express it: Who am I? It takes a poem to evoke a restoration of that lost time, because poetry's origin, like music and dance, precedes speech: as energy, or light, from a star. Thinking again about Eden and the vicissitudes of time, I'm corresponding with a young Miami artist who was recently invited to "express" Fairchild Tropical Garden in her work, twenty-some years after I'd accepted the challenge:

Hi Naomi,
Sorry to miss your recent Fairchild art talk where, as first poet-in-residence, back when your dad was on staff and I could touch "his" palms, I began to understand, after many years locked up on the island of Manhattan, that nature docs were similarly far removed. You couldn't even ask a film questions, and then feel silly, like when I asked Jack Fisher the difference between male and female palms. "Morphology," he answered, not without irony, but the bashful kind that botanists reserved for those who had skipped Plant Sex 101, a course unheard of in the East Village—not for our shyness about sex but for the uncertainty of just what an unpotted plant was.

After we moved into Fairchild's old director's house and were married beneath the male and female African Borassus palms, Jack and Karen, your parents, had us over for dinner while you scurried off to some youthful pursuit that had no patience for our intellectual distance from the starfruit dessert: "They're indigenous, so they won't stock them at Publix supermarkets, too hard to keep fresh." "But why are they shaped like a perfect star?" I naively asked, wondering if there was some more than morphological relation to starfish. Even though this was not the kind of question Jack was used to answering, he was comfortable saying "We don't know," leaving it to me to interpret the "we" as anything from the human species on up toward the more specific botanists at Fairchild. Earlier, after all our questions had been answered about the mated Borassus couple, with their anatomically penile and vaginal-shaped fruits (though titillatingly outsized), few would have thought of hugging them, as Rhonda and I did during our wedding, she the female palm and I the male.

A while ago I read your piece in *The Miami Rail* about a Martha Graham Dance Co. restoration and the comparative value of seeing it live vs. video. But I thought instead of a video of a 1940s filming of a Graham Company performance, because there's no chance either of us could have attended it live. The video makes the event historical in a way different from a contemporary restoration; there was less room for creative reinterpretation, of course, but on the other hand it's more up to us, the video audience, to imagine ourselves into the context of a '40s audience; and because the dance makes you so bodily aware, I began imagining what kind of clothes I would have worn to the performance (suit instead of jeans, oxfords instead of sandals, neat haircut instead of distressed layered styling, etc.) and what brand of cigarettes I'd have no doubt smoked during intermission. You yourself were sent back a few years to Wenders' 2011 film of the Pina Bausch Company, which we saw in a Coral Gables arthouse at the time, while you are just watching a video in '14. It's only 3 years difference, yet not only could we not have watched the film on our home devices then, we weren't yet meant to see Pina as historical, a wave of avant-garde already passed. Instead, her company was presented as if of the very avant-gardist moment. I chafed at that, having seen her perform live in NYC 25 years earlier; now, her work was no more or less historical than Martha Graham's, and ditto for Wim Wenders. And now I see in your piece that you've absorbed that, and that you can view Bausch and Graham side-by-side as historical. You contextualize Bausch's advice to a dancer to "get crazier," which might have still seemed *au courant* in 2011 (the word of choice then was "weird") but is now eclipsed by an *au fond* cultural attitude of "nothing seems shocking," so why not literally live in front of a screen (only the elderly would be shocked by that). Yet you still argue for *live* performance, of "history colliding with the present, bodies ever aging, ever changing." I'm charmed to recall how my body has aged between '11 and '15, between having sat in an audience, even if a movie audience, and just checked YouTube on my device, sitting in the car while Rhonda gets some stuff at Publix. An audience reminds you of a cultural moment through which you are passing, but what does an empty car offer? I'm shocked to say, like your father long ago, "we don't know."

Meanwhile, I'm attaching some pics, including the "Field Bridge Map" of our seminar with literary writers in the Everglades. Could there be anything more pathetic than watching a PBS Everglades doc instead of wading out to a dry season alligator hole in Everglades National Park? Not the danger (there is none, with a Park Ranger guide) but the layered liquids of sweat, humidity, water, and clouds so close you could almost touch, through which you watch a brood of baby alligators swim out from mama to eyeball you. *You* are being looked at, not likely through a screen on a device. (True, there's Skype, but no curious alligators on the other end, at home in their natural environment. Maybe some human slackers, zoo-like in sleepless Seattle.) So we look forward to catching up, and though we could do that on a video chat, there'd be no necessity then for Miami. It's like Miami is our audience and we can only exist as artists if we're historical in it, lost in time, and in need of rescue.

—David

The ultimate translation of "Who am I?" is: What is missing. Or, simply the *nature* of a question: Is there a question? In a specific historical sense, I'm thinking again of perhaps the great questioner of modern American literature, Saul Bellow: a questioning lies behind almost every sentence he writes. Yet that's also his weakness. The great biblical questions and deal-makings of the cosmos are in the margins, almost lost in a welter of everyday critique. If we judge Bellow a post-Holocaust success in rescuing the image of poet Delmore Schwartz, for example, in his novel, *Humboldt's Gift*, it equates to six million novels required to "pull out of the fire"—as it were—the Holocaust.

From Judith Miller's *One by One by One* (1990) to Michal Govrin's Van Leer Institute studies of Holocaust memory during the last few years, arguments are made for recalling the former lives of each of the millions of victims. I reviewed Miller's book favorably in the *Times*, criticizing only the inattention to the cultural loss, namely European Jewish culture. As soon as I read it in the paper I was ashamed; it was a callous caveat on my part. If I'd had room for a hundred more words I might have expressed how I intended the blackest irony, though the words would have failed me. Here I have perhaps enough room to ponder a new usage for even "laxative attracts romance." In *A Letter to Three Wives* (1949) Kirk Douglas, the English professor, sneers: "radio writing, as far as I can see, is to prove to the masses that a deodorant can bring happiness… and a laxative attract romance." But coming so soon after the war, I consider it a deeply Jewish dig at German Romanticism. The latter period idealized the Middle Ages (absent the Jews) and stood to recreate that absence for the Third Reich. Meanwhile, Florian Huber, the author of *Child, Promise Me You Will Shoot Yourself*, a literary examination of the mass-suicide phenomenon that plagued Germany in the aftermath of the war, claimed history has paid little attention to the suffering of ordinary Germans during and after the Nazi regime. "There were literally tens of thousands of cases of suicide. Many people have told me they felt relief that someone had opened up Pandora's box. It has been forgotten for 70 years. All this time, we have been talking about history focused on Nazi killers and concentration camp victims."

Today, I can't help think of this as literature for the masses, as panned in Joseph L. Mankiewicz's *A Letter to Three* Wives, a major Hollywood film that is unafraid of its own design on the masses. It's 1947, radio is still king, and a network executive is invited to dinner by her hit show's editor, the Ann Sothern character. After Ann's husband, the Kirk Douglas "literature professor" is told that "Myrtle Tippett has become immortal through her dramatic episodes of *Linda Gray, Registered Nurse* and she's only 32," Kirk politely offers that "Keats, Shelley and Marlowe were immortal before they were 30." "That's just classroom stuff," comes the reply. "Radio writing attracts the masses." By now Kirk has had it with his wife's boss, even though he promised he'd "lay off the radio wisecracks." When asked as a literature expert which of the *Linda Gray* episodes were the best, he sneers "They're all the same and have the same noble purpose: to prove to the masses that a mouthwash guarantees success and a laxative attracts romance." Editor wife Ann collapses. Nevertheless, she gets credit for being the realistic one and, through her, the cachet of editors is uplifted over writers and literary critics.

Mass entertainment-wise, a request for rights to my *A Literary Bible* describes its cable project as an "erotic Exodus serial of the love between Moses and the Pharoah". When I write back that it's quite weird to edit God out of the story, the Hollywood writer/producer says it's for a secular audience. Still, when reviewing Ridley Scott's misadventure, *Exodus: Gods and Kings* in 2014, A.O. Scott of the *Times* describes what's missing is "a kind of love story, about the often contentious relationship between the Israelites and their god, who is a complicated literary character, by turns compassionate and stern, steadfast and fickle." On the other hand, any hope of attracting a Judeo-Christian audience is stymied by what critic Scott calls "a New Testament sensibility at work," i.e. an absence of a sense of humor. Christianizing the Torah won't work, because the absence of the father, God, neuters the text. So the message from the TV exec arrives, who is "a fan of all your translations. I am interested in knowing who owns the film/TV rights to your translation. I intend to use the words as dialogue in a TV show set in ancient Israel that I am pitching." He continues: "I have been mulling this project over for at least a decade, ever since *The Book of*

J." I message back for more info and receive this: "For me, the purpose is to show how the Bible might have come to be written down, how it was made more masculine and patriarchal in later edits, and how the feminine side of religion and politics works, even while the history books may highlight the masculine contribution."

I reply again: "That the actual Bathsheba, in a joke perpetrated by Jack Miles, could have been an 'oral storyteller' who was 'written down' by J or anyone else, as you assert, is ahistorical. The Bible was not a transcription of oral stories but clearly and carefully written narrative by writers in an artistic culture. They used older sources, just like Shakespeare used them, and just as most writers do. And, they were largely older *written* sources— even the Sumerian ones were written documents in cuneiform from over a thousand years earlier. So what you need is not a rollicking cartoon of Bathsheba but rather a serious great writer figure. More to the point, there is little suggestion in your film treatment of such a thing as Israel's God, who after all is the great unifying character of the Bible. Again, it's crucial to understand that the Bible was not "written down" but in fact written by a multitude of writers, in the literary sense. Ergo, there were no masculine/ feminine (to cop a title from Jean-Luc Godard) "edits". Few scholars would consider the biblical stories "fiction" in the way you are using the term; rather, they might consider those stories a form of historical writing by scholarly (in the ancient sense) imaginative writers. True, they were Jewish writers, and therefore had a deep sense of irony, but that doesn't mean they were comic à la Philip Roth. Perhaps think Freud on Moses. And why will reinterpreting the Bible with a "female approach to spirituality" get you closer to proving it is fiction? The patriarchy provocation will just prejudice your audience against the show, as it already does against reading the Bible, even if, like you hope, they'll be attracted to Bathsheba for her aura of sex and violence.

Misinterpretations of Bathsheba remind me of Rita Hayworth's singing prostitute in *Miss Sadie Thompson* ('53): she has an audience of little boys who she likes to have touch her, arms and waist, understanding they never would dare to, in the forbidden places. The villain is true love, bringer of great pain, and the heroic theme is Sadie's acceptance of her fate as a sinner—in the larger sense, her acknowledgment of death, as she listens attentively to a complete rendition of Psalm 23. If Sadie is sin personified as sexual joy in life, she's straight out of the Hebrew Bible, where sin is death personified: "Sin croucheth at the door in wait." Seemingly in contrast, Audrey Hepburn's nun, in *The Nun's Story* ('59), finds true love also brings great pain, but in the form of a renunciation of sexuality. Enmeshed in worldly physical pain as a nurse in the Belgian Congo she finds death can also be a villain, crouching at the door. This was the '50s, when culture could deal with those things, however tentatively, or masked in the issue of sexuality. Today, sexuality is itself, no more no less. If rock stars overdose, the villain is time the miser, and the psalm reduces to "Forever Young." My TV exec fan, who seems to not have much time to read the Bible, might do well to at least watch '50s films—and I'm not demanding classics like Bresson's *Diary of a Country Priest* ('51)—to see if an evocation of biblical writers can be subtilized.

Unpretentious is a word you rarely hear applied to popular art anymore. Most melodramas are happy to be pretentious forays into issues of social responsibility, relationships, or identity problems, as even found with the robot in Alex Garland's sci-fi *Ex Machina* (2015). You won't find those themes prominent in Audrey and Rita's films of the '50s; they're there as background, but the real issue is the physical body and death, subjects too large for today's version of verisimilitude. They were still possible in the '50s because religion, sin and morality were still thrashing themselves out. Walls with crucifixes weren't weird yet, and the idea of horny men with erections fully repressed—for a lifetime if need be (vide the inventors of flight, Wilbur and Orville Wright, whose seeming lack of sexual needs raised nary a question in their day)—was still normative. Fortunately, gay marriage is now fully with us, but not the Hebrew Bible's original authors, whose dramatization of sex in the Sodom and Gomorrah passages we should be able to see as deftly ironic, if we can look over the writers' shoulders. In my translation of J's narrative the ambiguity is stark, involving angels confused with humans; rape is the sin of the mob, as it expresses its hatred of married domesticity, gay or straight. It's the intolerant mob that's indicted and not the angels they wish to abuse, who might today be sympathetically personified as trans persons.

9.

"I am not trying to reach some divine/ ear," the poet Brenda Shaughnessy declared at the beginning of her reading. "Imagine. Where once/ was mercy trash now crunches/ like leaves under stars." But that was already true for my granpa's Bible reading; he had real, imperfectly human authors—not a divine ear—to get the scene down. Shaughnessy, my brief colleague at Princeton, is demythologizing the New Testament, but the Hebrew Bible had already done so for itself: nothing angelic about the writing prophets; they're as shocked to hear an otherworldly voice as stuttering Moses, or First Isaiah stunned by the Temple's incense before he records *his personal vision*:

> ...and the House was filling
> with white smoke

clouds
and I heard myself
I was saying

Oh my God!
this is the end of me
my lips are a man's...

Yet in most ancient representations, divinity is authorless. In Kurosawa's *Throne of Blood* (1957) the pair of warrior protagonists are discussing the effect of confronting an oracle: "The life of mankind is meaningless," one concludes, "meaningless as the life of insects." My instinctual reaction is to recoil at the slander of insects. They are tillers of the soil, pollinators of tree and flower—the landscape would be dead without them. On the other hand, our species has despoiled a good percentage of that landscape; we've exchanged complex, colorful ecosystems, in which new forms can evolve, for monochrome crops and killing factories for animals. Most of what we've invented has been insatiable gadgetry, right up to the latest space telescope gobbling up the earliest galaxies. We have helped a portion of mankind to live longer and think farther—so what? But am I just another cog in the techno wheel of greater communication, even poetic communication? Maybe not. I'm concerned about what ancient Eden we were once born into, and then lost, leading up to the Israelite drive for a covenant with Creation—the unknowable fact that made us possible. This Hebraic metaphysical contract, which enacts mutual respect with the unknowable, and the interpretative commentary of that covenant down through history, entails an understanding *with* (not simply *of*) my origin. It needs writers, starting from origins. It's the Jewish difference, even for modern poets: take Wallace Stevens, who agrees with my vision of history and the crucial instrument of language enlarged by poetry—but who privileges the vision over the history. That missing history in modernism includes the several writing Isaiahs who historicized their (or their precursors') visions. We might say as well that postmodernism makes modernism historical—but even postmodernists are loath to say it, or to admit the paltry human history invoked.

To give Stevens his due, in his vision poetry strengthens from line to new line, poem to new poem, as we lift ourselves into position as witness of lost time. But what are we to do with this witness? There's nothing to do, there's no going back for what is lost *in* time, as I am going back to perhaps rescue Stevens for the Hebrew Bible—because all that is lost to history is still in front of us, whether it's distant, extinct galaxies or the Torah. The Stevens I hear is working toward a confrontation with our unknowable origin (rather than sublime Wordsworthian intimations of it), but I have no idea what he'll do when he confronts that unreachable lost time, other than turn from the lyrical to the epic cosmic theater, to which Psalm 90 is prologue. The poem of lost time is the physical scene of confrontation, the scene of writing: a dying man in his insurance co. office, in Stevens' instance, a glass of spirits in hand. I can bring back the scene, but I can't do the same for myself—as a living creature who's a moment ahead of memory, of history—except in a poem of lost time, one that aligns me with the Jerusalem poets of the Bible as "translator," interpreter.

In the twenty-first century I'm watching a major news program in Hebrew via the international channel: a man who lost his wife yesterday in Israel, in a horrific crash, is being interviewed. He's articulate and soberly answers question after question. What have you learned that led up to the accident? "I'm not interested in the accident; I only want to share the life of Shira, how life-giving she was to her family, her patients and to everyone she met." The life of Shira and her two young children is now told in pictures, with commentary from her husband. This is not the kind of reportage we're used to in the States. There are too many who died yesterday on the roads, in train, plane and boating accidents, in homicides and suicides. In a conversation a few years ago with novelist John Irving, who was passing through Princeton, he was being interviewed on German TV, where he's a big hit in translation, and was asked about the Holocaust. "I don't want to think about that when I'm in Germany," he told them. "It's like a colossal accident by a nation of mad, drunk drivers. I want to talk about their children, the Germans who are alive and who I meet here."

I wanted to remind John he was talking to a Jew, so I shot back my experience of waiting in the Green Room before an interview on Israeli TV. The poet David Avidan, who for a while was the Jack Paar of Israel, was interviewing a couple who survived a horrendous car crash (pictures of the demolished car were provided) and who said they had no memory of it, only of an out-of-body experience that suggested the afterlife. "It was a very different response than you get from Holocaust survivors," I told John Irving. "Not out-of-body events. Most of them can document their experiences in some detail. They'd rather talk about that, even more than what they did before the war—this I know first-hand from aunts and cousins. Their lives seemed to have taken on a historical meaning greater than they could have ever conceived: the meaning of Western civilization, or even more than that, of the human species. They didn't have to philosophize about that; all they had to do was describe as exactly as they could how they came to, and through, Auschwitz-Birkenau. Nothing about our lives or the afterlife could compare, yet it wasn't the intensity of confrontation with the deep space of death that we all must enter that mattered. Rather, it was as if the details of the Holocaust didn't matter at all, that the years that were lost could never be retrieved, that their lives had been sucked into the black hole of lost time, and the recounting proved only that the accident was not over, that it could never be over, that the very inexplicability of the hatred that abetted it insured that the shadow of unfathomable gravity would not lift. We today may be innocent of that, including the lively Germans who Irving encountered; we may be happily whirring on the outer arm of the galaxy held together by the supermassive black hole at its center; nevertheless we are lost in space if we can't recognize the shadow of the creation story that still hangs over us, the catastrophe of losing Eden. That's what my family survivors were urgently denoting by their Holocaust experience: the shadow.

Of course, the conversation with John Irving never was that heavy; we were downing the party drinks at Princeton, becoming progressively lighter, bordering on Dadaist anarchy. My memory of it is like that too; it's suffused with the daylight on my Florida poolside patio, permitting me to write only so much before being overcome with awareness of the scene of writing. Just as to my cat, watching nearby for birds overhead, my writing is a form of waiting. The birds of my memory, as for instance this one of John Irving, move too high and swiftly past, but there are always more to come until nightfall. Our Colombian next-door neighbors encourage us to talk as much as we can about the Holocaust, including to their children. True, they've told us there's a distant Jewish ancestor somewhere in their family, but that might hold true for a large portion of the population, and not just our former Secretary of State, Madeline Albright, who didn't even know both her parents were Jewish. "We cannot forget the Holocaust," said Ruth Gertner Frohman, the honorary president of the Jewish Foundation of Belgium. "But the people of Europe are fed up with hearing about it. When they're nice, they'll listen and say, 'But in Israel, today you're doing the same thing to the Palestinians,' said Frohman." I don't know anyone that simple-minded—or wait, there was the professor at Princeton, the spouse of a colleague with whom we were having dinner, who said, "Israel is murdering Palestinian children every day." I googled and couldn't find any verification of that, except for a *Guardian* op-ed. Probably the professor reads the *Guardian*, but still, we all know an op-ed is debatable. Maybe I shouldn't say that. Many journalists and former officials in Europe brought testimony to London and Washington during the war, even verifiable proof that Germany was perpetrating the Holocaust, only to be ignored: it wasn't even debatable.

If there's an antidote to anti-Semitism, perhaps it's shame. There's no Other toward whom to feel shame, no refocus of history in which to attach our shame. It's a species imperfection, the kind our ancient writing ancestors mythologized in the shame of Eden: the indelible loss of Eden, of sensing we are outcasts, no longer entitled to feel at home. What's necessary is vigilance, alertness to how an infectious disease like anti-Semitism or racism becomes a psychosis—there's no appeasing of it, just breaking of it. While you can't make a rational deal with it, you can cut a covenant with a Creator, who represents all that's unknowable to our species. It allows us to think about more than the human condition, to think about the universe's condition, as it manifests in the Bible, from Creation to the lost time for all sentient beings, the loss of timeless Eden. And the lost time still burning in the Holocaust—how to assimilate it, creatively, as in the struggle for a perpetual writer's room in Jerusalem, reconnecting to the ancient one of Solomonic J and the myriad others, or like the one at 13 King David Street, in which I began *The Lost Book of Paradise,* back in 1991.

The Poem of Authorship

I stand in a 19th-century graveyard, my friend and poet-colleague having found his great great great grandmother's grave. I'm in my childhood summer honky-tonk beach boardwalk town, sprung up in Prohibition days for Americans flooding in from dry Detroit and Buffalo. Not long after, in the '40s, we Jews were allowed to rent in the thin plywood-walled cottages and beach hotel, a decade ahead of most summer places open to Jews, though we couldn't be buried there. One day on the beach I saw a bald man with sunburnt top have a heart-attack and then die in the arms of his wife screaming his name, "Morty! Morty! Morty!" He had to be shipped by train to Detroit where there was a Jewish cemetery, but it was late Friday afternoon and there'd be no train going back there until Sunday, toward a deadline-worried Jewish funeral, past the allotted hours to be gotten into the ground.

I'm in Canada again, more than forty years after a professoriate in literature at York University and an editing gig at the major Canadian publisher, cut short by a dryly worded telegram from the U.S. Attorney General, one John Mitchell, absolving me of any and all guilt—though I still feel it, more intensely during the past fifteen years since my African-American Vietnam-serving former student and poet-colleague, Lorenzo Thomas, died. I think he might still be alive if not for that harrowing experience in uniform. Survivor's guilt, however, is a much older story with me, embedded in early childhood when my father left his infantry unit, post-Normandy invasion, to make certain that his mother had not survived Auschwitz and returned to her Hungarian farm.

I was alone with my own mother when, in 1947, we first summered in the Hotel Orion on the beach of Port Stanley, Ontario. It's gone now, though a remnant of the raucous boardwalk I loved remains. Frank Davey, the Canadian poet I hadn't met up with in more than forty years, my wife Rhonda and I sat by a portal window in Mackie's ("since 1911"), once known across Canada for the richness of its Orangeade drink and its Quebecois "poutine", and still vibrantly painted in orange. From there I could recall the nearby smoke-filled tiny bars, where Patsy Cline singing "I cried a river of tears" was familiar as psalms, and the drunken bathing-suited sand-encrusted adults were as solicitous of us free-floating babes as those in the synagogue pews had been, an arm drawing us close under the ancient tallit, the prayer shawl of Israel. It was from there, on the honky-tonk boardwalk, and among my later childhood customers in inner city Detroit that I first imbibed the Blues. I say customers because, as I collected payment every weekend from some of them on my *Detroit News* paper-route, I was exposed to sounds that eventually acquired the names John Lee Hooker and Junior Wells.

In the entire Port Stanley church burial ground, dedicated in 1845, this was the only tombstone with a Jewish motif, as I pointed out to Frank. More than Moses's decalogue, I could make out Noah's dove over one tablet and King David's crown over the other. The Jewish Temple Menorah was clearly engraved in miniature between the two tablets. "Davey" might have been an anglicization of "Davidovich", for a Russian Jewish family emigrating to England in the 18th century, I said to Frank, teasing a bit. He had seen this tombstone only once before, not noticing its Hebraic uniqueness.

In New York's East Village, a year or two after having returned from Canada in '71, I was walking down lower Second Avenue after a post-poetry-reading party, a bit high, when the ruin of a small orthodox synagogue struck me. I'd passed it many times without stopping before. Now, the weathered Hebrew letters engraved over the boarded-up doorway beckoned me to read "Beit Midrash," House of Study. It took me a few minutes to make out the warn-away letters, a December wind stabbing through my surplus Navy peacoat. It's as if my eyes were pried open to ancient history: the same scene could have occurred 2,500 years before, on a Babylonian street. When I got home I opened a compact Hebrew-English Bible from a brief visit to Jerusalem in '69—bought more as a souvenir than something I intended to read—and read a psalm for the first time as if it were a poem, which indeed it had been. But in the poor English translation it read more like Blues song lyrics, taking me back, once again, to a lost inner city youth. I spent the next few days, sometimes not more than two or three lines in a day, translating a psalm into a more strict and resonant Blues format. It was then the cosmic theater linking ancient Israel and African-Americans hit home.

"Lord, I done wrong, help me…"—this typical blues intimacy with the supernatural, talking to the Creator, was something I felt some kinship with, as in the first psalms I translated that year, after stopping at the ghost-like Second Avenue House of Study. Listening to the Blues as well: "Baby, baby, baby/ won't you please come home." She's his baby, of course—loss of early childhood recovered—but he also knows he's lost it again. As it happened, my last book of poems before the psalms was cast as collaged letters to such a lost "baby." The afterlife of a relationship was there, lines spoken as if to someone dead already—dead to me, that is. And there was Big Bill Broonzy, singing "Lord, help me find that woman," in an other-worldly voice, as if he might, like Dante, enter the supernatural world to search for his baby. There were traces of that ghost-voice in rock, back to Bob Dylan's shaman-like nasal chant, though it was too far from

Creator-consciousness to evoke such a Lord, and "cosmic consciousness" had already become a psychedelic cliché.

Lord, I'm just a worm
don't point to me
in frozen anger

don't let me feel
I more than deserve
all your rage

but mercy, Lord, let me feel mercy
I'm weak, my spirit so dark
even my bones shiver

my shadow surrounds me—I'm shocked
how long, Lord, how long
till you return to shine your light

return to me dear Lord
bring back the light
that I can know you by

because those that are dead
have no thought of you
to make a song by

I'm tired of my groaning
my bed is flowing away
in the nights of tears

depression like a moth
eats from behind my face,
tiny motors of pain push me

get out of here all you
glad to see me so down
your every breath so greased with vanity

My Lord is listening so high
my heavy burden of life floats up
as a song to him

let all my enemies shiver
on the stage of their total self-consciousness
and all their careers ruined in one night.
                                    [Psalm 6]

Lord, My Lord, you disappear
so far away
unpierced by my cry

my sigh of words
all day My Lord
unheard

murmur of groans at night
then silence
no response

while you rest
content
in the songs of Israel

in the trust of fathers
you delivered
who cried to you

they were brought home
warm and alive
and inspired

but I am a worm
subhuman
what men come to

with a hate of their own futures
despised
and cheered like a drunk

staggering across the street
they howl after him
like sick dogs

"Let the Lord he cried to
save him
since they were so in love"

you brought me through the womb
to the sweetness
at my mother's breasts

no sooner my child eyes
looked around
I was in your lap

you are My Lord
from the time my mother found
me inside

make yourself appear
I am surrounded
and no one near

a mad crowd
tightens a noose around me
the ring of warheads

pressing ravenous noses
the mad whispering of
gray technicians

the water of my life evaporates
my bones stick through the surface
my heart burns down like wax

melting into my stomach
my mouth dry as a clay cup
dug up in the yard

I've fallen into the mud
foaming dogs surround me
ghost men

pierce my hands and feet
my bones stare at me
in disbelief

men take my clothes
like judges
in selfish dreams

make yourself appear
My Lord show me
the power

to free my life from chains
of bitter command
from the mouths of ghost men

trained on my heart
like a city
save me from mindless

megaphones of hate
you've always heard me
from my human heart

allowed me to speak
in the air of your name
to men and women

all who know fear
of losing yourselves
in vacant cities

speak to him
Israel's children
sing with him

all seed of men
show your faces
amazed in love

he does not despise them
he has not disappeared
from the faces of earth

from the ground of the worm
or the ear of the victim
I will always repeat

this song of life
with my hand that is free
from men who need victims

may our hearts live forever!
and the furthest reaches of space
remember our conscious moment

inspiring light
like those disappeared from memory
returned to the planet's earth

everyone has to appear
at death's door
everyone falls to the ground

while his seed carries on
writing and speaking
to people still to come

who remember to sing
how generous My Lord appears
to those hearing.
                    [Psalm 22]

Much later, in his last years, my friend Lorenzo Thomas published his deep study of the African origins to Blues that confirmed my earlier presumption. It's rare to live long enough to have one's untamed speculations validated. Well-grounded speculation is way out front of scholarship, the latter being generally in the business of confirming or denying ideas—and usually tone-deaf to the wilder poetry of ideas, the kind that might yield interpretive strength. Lorenzo being a poet, his study backed up speculations of thirty years before, and in my case I arrived at my own scholarly backing-up forty years later in authorship studies. Yet before I could complete my late works of ancient biography, I became engrossed in yet newer speculations of lost authorship. "Where are his footnotes?" cried some critics.

In Port Stanley of 2013 I picked up some footnotes in the form of "ancient" photos of my childhood town, sixty years gone. They confirm my early speculations: that the incline railway, for instance, went to another world. The hill it ascended would have been too steep for a San Francisco trolley with its weak historical frisson of the "Gay Nineties". The heaven I discovered at the top was a previously unknown world of adults foreign to my family and Detroit neighborhood. These people gathered in large communities of fifty or more on sets of picnic tables canopied over with wooden roofs like old European railway stations. The Sunday-suited adults were singing foreign songs, probably in English, as appropriate to their imaginary lodges of Elk, Moose, and Lions Club, denoted by easels hung with the emblem. How does one enter such a world, I wondered, or rather I was scared, realizing it was too late for me—as if such a scene was about to be wiped out in full-throated mid-day celebration, like my families' hometowns in the war, or at least the Jewish sections. I quickly went back down the railway, enriched with inarticulate speculations about heaven as a lost world.

Now it is all gone, so that the old-timers I meet in 2013 can't agree on where exactly it was located, no trace left either of railway or vast pavilioned park above, the hill now wooded and condo'd over. My memory too overgrown with further encounters, as of the Haifa incline railway on Mt. Carmel. I rode to the top in its last creaking days, circa 1977, among elderly patients (so it seemed to me) dropped off on derelict streets. Hardly a heaven, more at purgatory.

Another new footnote: the folding drawbridge, formerly an integral part of the inland waterway, now a tourist snapshot. It works just as before, lovingly restored, and as I cross it sixty-year-old senses are enlivened: sound of echoing footstep on the hollow steel grating, sight of open water just a few feet beneath, and the walking on water smell. My tread heavier now, yet they remain my own feet, attached to my youthful speculations about the world to come: it would all be a restoration of the losses behind it, as of the blackened copper plaque I read again: "22 men lost their lives in the building of this bridge: [names and dates follow...]" confirming my original speculation about danger that the bridge might open at any moment, without warning, yet I would be saved.

"He led a charmed life"—I didn't know what that meant, nothing was magical to me though rather full of portent. I remember the numbered metal fish lurking at bottom of Lucky Fishing Pond at the end of the boardwalk. You bought a small "fishing pole" with a numbered magnet on the end, and eventually you could come up with a fish attached; if its number corresponded to your pole, it yielded a same-numbered prize arrayed on a shelf. I don't recall my prizes, just the wonder of fishing without worms or dying fish. A portent, to me, of restoration: you could re-create the past as art, as if you're there, fully alive in nature, but without its harm and danger. At one point, rummaging through the restored little "Port Stanley Library", I tell Frank and Rhonda that I used to read Nancy Drew mysteries here "on rainy days," early 1950s. I wanted to be a sexy (bisexual?) detective when I grew up. A few minutes later, Rhonda brings over to me a pile of those same old books, though the copyright page notes the last reprint as 1998. To be a detective of the past, to restore it, was my rainy reverie; to keep it alive, to survive.

On returning to Miami, we bought last year's already out-of-date discount floor model of 55" Smart HDTV. We can now watch the canon of 20th-century, mostly black-and-white classics in 16:9 format—it's as if the actors come out of their graves to act again as living dolls. In other words, another dimension to re-imagining a cosmic theater for the literary near-future, based upon a "not good enough" critique of the present. For instance, the best poetry today revels in consciousness but is still not good enough; it can't evoke the supernatural deep time theater of the Odyssey or the Bible, Dante or Blake… Dear Frank, Stepped further back into my childhood, literary-wise, after leaving you in London—in inner-city war-zone-like Detroit, and at its suburban Holocaust museum. Instead of the historic museum-like restoration of Port Stanley, Ontario, the Prohibition-era Lake Erie honky-tonk town of my childhood summers turned into air-conditioned walk past cases of old newspaper front pages with 1930s pre-war headlines like "Nazis Outlaw Jewish Names in Bible" and a restored actual boxcar used to transport human sardines to the canning factory, to be gassed and smoked rather than eaten. The new museum was "good" but not good enough, since I would not have survived, would not have been born in 1943; the only sign I am alive in the museum is my own consciousness, my own memory.

I need to retrace my footsteps, though once is enough, only the site in memory valid now, especially the memory of things hidden, as in Port Stanley: the dead men of the bridge, the lost people of the hill, the dead people hidden in the church ground, already 175 years in the ground, including one responsible for my friend Frank getting born. The Jewish menorah stamped on her weathered, leaning, frightfully thin tombstone, like a page from a book, the rest lost.

We know even less about Shakespeare. No grave, no DNA to dig up, yet the age of his lifetime is Edenic for a writer in English today, the golden age of a David and Solomon. They once lived in a honky-tonk town like Port Stanley, where literature was known solely as entertainment, playwright equals Patsy Cline. 'I Go to Pieces' might shiver the spine of one sitting on a barstool today or standing with the groundlings in ancient London. Still, I was there, a secreted writer, waiting to age. Could have been there, also, in small town Jerusalem, writing earliest psalms as laments for lost King David. Imagine if Shakespeare's plays were anonymous, came to us sui generis, contemporary translations from a language and culture unknown. Would we know if written by male or female, gay or straight, white or black, yellow or brown, Renaissance or early Modern, atheist or believer (in disguise)? Imagining it was me again, in similarly lost ancient Jerusalem, driven to write psalms or historical (prophetic) poems after my wife, like Bathsheba's husband, was murdered and me complicit, or so it seemed. Or a couple centuries later, writing in Jerusalem as an exile from the ancient northern capital of Samaria, most of my family slaughtered by Assyrians in pre-figuration of the Holocaust. A Jerusalem like New York City first seemed to me, richly a-historical, hardly a trace of vivacious

Yiddish Broadway (lower Second Avenue) to be found. One could write great honky-tonk here, like the poet Frank O'Hara did, or supernatural New Yorker fiction, like Isaac Bashevis Singer. Forget the great writers of Genesis and 2 Samuel—in fact, they are already forgotten, along with their Hebraic Renaissance Jerusalem. NYC no Renaissance yet, though it's American melting pot bubbling away in the arts, or rather simmering, any Melvilles or Reznikoffs still dying in obscurity. Just like 7th Century Jerusalem, B.C.E. We've got *Moby Dick* and Reznikoff's *Testimony,* but we don't have *them,* we don't have those widened margins with those writers coming out of those margins. Instead we have their texts and movies, Gregory Peck more alive than depressed Melville, Charlton Heston more alive than depressed Moses the writer. Yes, it was depressing to be writing Exodus in the desert, a sacred artifact perhaps but who was going to read it? Did our actual writer centuries later in ancient Jerusalem have a high time with all that pregnant semi-mythic history, like Homer's "transcriber" in Athens, or Shakespeare of the history plays?

A history of Canada, of course, would start post-colonial, the bright red maple-leaf flag standing for natural roots in the land, the ancient land of dinosaurs and oil, the innocent land found by human immigrants, "First Nation" or Second World—well, enough of that. Suffice to say, no one is rewriting the British-American war. In London though, having two hours to kill before the train to Detroit (Windsor station), we walked over to the Museum. A huge Kim Ondaatje retrospective, still working in London in her eighties. And the bio on the walls: married Michael Ondaatje a year or so before I met him myself, teaching at York, '66, and then lost track. They moved to London, then divorce, then Mike returning to Toronto. Photos of their life in London, documenting her age, almost twenty years older than her husband. How did I forget that she was old enough to be his mother? Didn't do the math in those days, up the 401 in Toronto. It works more often for women marrying older men, but in his twenties at the time, Mike's parallel younger wife would have been a toddler... Summer of '67, Summer of Love, summer of no math. Dying was out of the picture; her body—like all of us avant-gardists—was out of the picture, a disembodied consciousness encountering fragments of the world on canvas. Post-dead, angelic, a cosmic theater of one, without a Covenant. That is, missing a contract between human and supernatural (representing all that is unknowable to the Homo sapiens species), where each could safely meet, on a cosmic stage of at least a literary agreement. As in Israel's Covenant with the Creator. A "Canadian" Covenant? This show might be her afterlife, in that next week, Kim herself will give a talk on the first floor...

We were sitting by the window outlook on a new world Thames when Rhonda said she was going to the rest room. Some time later (women to be allowed any amount of powder room time they wish) she returned a bit agitated. "Come with me," she urged. Ah yes, I aver, the old Canadian flag with the Union Jack, in a historical nook. No, closer, read the text. It's shockingly anti-American, 18th century-wise. Is that what these people are mentally harboring, asks Rhonda? That's a forgotten text, I reply, the new one has authors with names like Ondaatje—though Mike's and Kim's names bound to be lost in three thousand years, as have Israel's biblical authors. Yet we have text, at least one cosmic text, a record of the Covenant. In a language, Hebrew, that is now inscribed on bus stops, gas stations, and fast food ads. In other words, ancient Israel is no longer lost but in the process of being found, a Duchampian artifact plopped onto the non-cosmic world stage.

Canadian consciousness today comparable to European, or to Western consciousness: it's all a nuanced (or not) denial of the cosmic, except for Judeo-Christian exceptionalists. If there were to be a strong cosmic being, God, then he needs a heroic human being to contend with and to make sense of him, and that sounds too much like its anti-image, a Hitler, Mussolini, or Stalin in Western consciousness today. Instead, we want strong consciousness and weak leaders, or at least the appearance of the latter, so that a Maharishi Yogi will do, or the Dalai Lama. We have no interest in heroic characters, only active awareness of the tricks consciousness can play, or the lack of tricks, lack of play. No Homo sapiens historical point of origin is required, to trace our unique being back to. Instead, we're grandiosely tethered to the web of human cultures (not *caught* in it) even when their arrows of progress have turned into missiles. Best to ignore them—call them "popular cultures"—and let the movies and music and poetry, or perhaps the latest software, turn them inside out if they can, so that we can exercise our modern consciousness, art-wise.

Still, without an initial point of cosmic embarkation, there can't be a cosmic arrival. The way out of the postmodern is blocked to even scouts and trailblazers; any path to a point of origin in history long muddled by a levitating consciousness, thrilled to be here and now, personalities free of character. Authorship today is not about knowing a person but apprehending something more complex: a particular sensibility—though at the cost of anything we'd call a soul. In the same way, authorship of a historical text is occluded by textuality. In any case, our immediate predecessors in literature and art are still with us today: Ashbery in his eighties still writes poems perhaps best confronted with hashish—which is not to make light of them but rather to indicate that the leading edge of contemporary writing remains a study of consciousness and its possible dimensions. Anyway, we don't need drugs or alcohol anymore, we can simply imagine we do, and Ashbery's poems help us. Are they merely texts? Is consciousness itself a text that needs no particular author's life to embody it? There are vivid personalities still written and especially portrayed in movies—but our anxious inner life is at best quieted there, the soul relaxed in darkness, and in our inner darkness.

"Ashes," the American poet John Ashbery, once my mentor, is well known for being a "cinephile," with much movie content leaking into his poems. It is the movies with all its behind the scenes huffing and puffing of image, sound, language, and style, an intensity of verisimilitude too great for a particular consciousness, a character, to swallow whole. A movie can act for or stand in for consciousness itself, in a way that Aristotle would call tragic, though no one, including Ashbery, seems to think of that. If it's anti-heroic or anti-cosmic, it can't be tragic—though surely it can be depressing.

I want to see the canon of movies differently, as historical artifacts that unspool a theater of the limitations of consciousness. We can't go there, we can't travel backwards, a movie exists to stretch our memory beyond the conscious—and back to a sense of the supernatural, in that we are the higher beings overlooking the cinema of the lost humans up on the screen. The Blues has that too, overhearing the music of the Spirituals. Honky-tonk of Port Stanley at ten, Patsy Cline singing 'I Fall to Pieces,' *pace* Psalm 6—the white blues. And with such visual and sound tracks, our memories can conceive of the lost Gospel Q and the Book of J. They had human authors, the more conceivably human the writers the better, whether or not they sensed themselves being overlooked, invisibly.

Perhaps a place in cosmic time can yet be found by an art that lets go of "all we thought we knew." In 1939, when it came out, and for a decade after, *Gone with the Wind* was thought to be the greatest Hollywood film—which meant melodrama. Nobody was calling it a great work of art. But today, in it's re-contextualization as an historical artifact, we can see it transcends melodrama and has become tragedy. It gives us the tragedy of the Civil War, the tragedy of slavery, and the tragedy of deaths and divorces that didn't have to be—and it does so unironically. There is no more tragic figure in modern drama than Hattie McDaniel's Mammy, who is the mother figure for both Rhett and Scarlet—a mother they are fated to miss, because she is black, a slave mother. Mammy contains the opposing "cross-purposes" of Rhett and Scarlet within her; she knows it but she can't become conscious of it; it can't enter her consciousness. And yet, in her very unconsciousness, we get to see just how limited the claims of consciousness are today. "Tomorrow is another day" no longer rings with melodramatic hope but rather carries the tragic baggage of warring armies and egos. cultural hatred, and the most brutal fact of the human condition: tomorrow will also be a day in which the gorgeous, magnetic visionary that is Scarlet will "lie, cheat, steal, and kill if I have to." But that was just before World War II, before the death slavery of the Holocaust, so that now it takes on a perspective of cosmic tragedy, of time freeing a ravishing time-bound art, transforming its melodramatic gospel into a timeless Blues.

How much of it is about memory, then, the good and the bad? A phrase from Isaiah or Genesis concealed within a contemporary lament about peacemaking—and then revealed, in a later context, as an irony of and about memory: "Oops, I remembered Dylan's 'don't look back' or the 'do not turn to look back' from my college days reading Hemingway's *The Sun Also Rises,* unconscious of its echoing provenance in biblical Naomi turned to stone, or as contradicted by the cable reality TV therapy sessions of *In Treatment*—"where did the problem start?"—while its original Hebrew version on '90s Israel TV forgotten.

The original Hebrew writers of the Bible themselves used versions, sources, ancient to their own ancient (to us) times. Sometimes unconsciously, but most often consciously, ranging from what seemed to them the archaic epics of Sumer and Akkad to the more recent proto- and early Hebraic, and on up to their immediate predecessors. The Bible's writers, then, like writers today, were living the dream of a poet, though the culture today lives in the dream of a "text," where writers themselves can't be heroic and can barely be identified; at best, they can be celebrities. Even an allusion to "the world's foremost living critic," for example, elicits a chuckle. His or her own text criticizes her very being, her over-reaching.

Driving to Canada's version of Stratford. Walking to River Avon, its pedal-boats. High school girls after the play: "I had a boyfriend like that, all talk. Talk, talk, talk." In the last surviving Tea Room: the Shakespeare-branded engraving of the writer himself on the wall, framed. What would be the Bible-brand? Moses smashing the tablets. Me: "It's too precious to be like it used to be." It being the tearoom my mom brought me into, circa 1950, as if in white gloves—though not necessary, I was unconscious in summer bathing suit Port Stanley. Innocence exists only in the past? The seagulls startled us, they owned Stratford, not the swans. Where did they come from?—first question of experience. Forget it. Forget "Better to die…" speech in *Measure for Measure.*

> Claudio:
> Ay, but to die, and go we know not where;
> To lie in cold obstruction, and to rot;
> This sensible warm motion to become
> A kneaded clod; and the delighted spirit
> To bathe in fiery floods, or to reside
> In thrilling region of thick-ribbed ice;
> To be imprison'd in the viewless winds
> And blown with restless violence round about
> The pendant world; or to be worse than worst
> Of those that lawless and uncertain thought
> Imagine howling—'tis too horrible!

The weariest and most loathed worldly life
That age, ache, penury, and imprisonment
Can lay on nature is a paradise
To what we fear of death.

But a celebrated conceptual poet this year (i.e. thought equals feeling), Kenneth Goldsmith, wants to give poetry back its "loathed worldly life" and its history-making. So he goes on the Colbert show, Comedy Channel's parody of news-making, to read his documentation of an AM radio station on the day Kennedy was shot, pop music and all, a version of how it really was to be unprepared for tragedy on an ordinary day. The radio soundtrack like the mind idling, waiting in line. For what? Just waiting. Something is bound to happen someday. But if it does, there won't be no blues, just mediocre pop. No loss of the cosmic, since it was never there, and not even loss of mind. Contrast Robert Johnson on a different, tragic station: "When the train pulled out the station, it had two lights on behind. When the train pulled out the station, it had two lights on behind. The blue light was my baby, red light was my mind."

"I didn't write it," says Goldsmith. "So, it's not your book?" asks faux newsman Colbert. "It just came to me," the self-deprecating, post-T.S. Eliot poets used to say in the '50s, to emphasize their receptivity rather than their expressivity. It was all in fragments anyways, as in *The Waste Land*'s "These fragments I have shored against my ruins."

My first book came to me while I was at the recently opened Japan Cultural Centre, picking up a catalogue of the "Small and Medium Enterprise Agency." Meditated upon and cut out fifty objects, blew up and photo-offset to equal size—each "page" a flat artifact of image, language and context gone haywire in another culture, even if out of the best of intentions. I needed a few hundred boxes to lay them in, finding them at a Chinese shirtbox factory in Toronto's Chinatown: small book-size for scarves and ties, etc., perfectly white, snugly latched cardboard. A re-contextualizing of "coming to me."

Best to make of history's fragments a museum, a box of a book, I thought, Duchampian. Make Eliot really real, in a museum of cons-ciousness. We *were* here. He—they—were *trying* to be here. Almost fifty years back to it now, and fifty years further back to Duchamp's suitcase museum. In it were miniatures of his own "found" works; and in my shirtbox, artless or artist-less photos, authorless description. Context, history was the element enlivened by this art, yet it was as if no artist needed to exist before it, before Duchamp or Eliot (there was Laforgue and Dante, but in fragments, not bodily). A museum of modern art even before there was modern art, since Duchamp and Eliot were already relics when I was in my twenties. It was the '60s, Japan interchangeable with

Germany for me, I was so *post-moderne*, all of me text, all of it figment of consciousness. I wanted to make my "first book" historical but self-deprecating, all consciousness. After that, exotic poems, documents of letting it come, and then translation. Disembodied. All of it, career-wise, a waiting. Where is the author? When is he coming? Where are we in this lost history of waiting?

Eventually, retracing my footsteps, any footsteps, a gas chamber of history turns out to be *my* history, complete with pre-gassing photographs in the Holocaust family albums. A world of creation does precede us, there's a script behind us, DNA, footsteps. Like mine in Port Stanley, the year Auschwitz-surviving aunts Yanka and Pepi arrived in Detroit and I saw their tattoos. Their fatter, pre-war selves I'd already seen in the albums. Though that's just me; I don't want to make memory itself exotic—don't want to privilege it over consciousness, of which it is part, yet more like a back alley than a boulevard. Memory's just stuff that creation needs to make a body, or body of work. So it had to be there to begin with, there has to be a memory behind origins, created without acting, without acting out—even if I, or we, needed footsteps.

CODA
or, "Resistance"

The best of the New York School poetry, or of the Yiddish giant Sutz-kever & the Canadian giant Nichol, poets of my time, was a resistance to post-Holocaust knowledge of civilization's black hole, a resistance to poetry as usual. It drew a line under the past, aping "the good German," but it was a cartoon line. Funny to be sane, the world a shambles of our ideals, can it be enough to eat, drink, and reproduce? Yes, but... by now the context of resistance is lost, as if it were a matter only of poetics. Or worse, personal or political grandiosity. The Holocaust is lost, Hiroshima is lost, Stalin & Mao are unmasked. The great avant-garde faith in capital "s" socialism is passé. What passes for post-Holocaust today? Survival, and restoration: Duchamp's museum turned into a Holocaust museum of bittersweet, funny restoration. Each poem a delicious memorial, each fiction a delicious memoir of losses, each essay a record. A document of historical context seems all that's possible, in which one can be swept off one's feet, if the floor keeps level, the walls hold. Though it's an art not good enough, what Adam Phillips calls a recognition of our helplessness—our helpless infant state anchoring our consciousness of being lost in time, in a weird universe, "the world is the world."

The Chinese shirtbox holding the yellowing pages of *Excellent Articles of Japan ('69)* is falling apart—45 years now. Encapsulated it in a glass box frame, an artifact preserved. Harder now for the critics to "read" it as a text; it's a memory of a text, my memory. I was an author, I was a child, looked after, looked over. Though seemingly free to roam in '50s-safe, honky-tonk remnant of Port Stanley, and though in memory I am all alone, unafraid, and culture-less—no Canadian flag, no immigrant parents, no homework—I am no more lost in time than Frank's immigrant great great great grandmother, both of us capable of waiting, of being found. Not by art alone but by what I'd call a soul, looking over the shoulder of human consciousness, hearing what it is feeling.

"Not by force
not by power
but by my spirit"
—ZECHARIAH
[c. 5th Century BCE]
[trans. 1977]

Although it may be a history that assimilates myth, the Bible's cosmic theater ultimately accounts for its metaphysical Covenant as an authored text. My maternal granpa was animated by a muse-like Creator, just as was his acceptance of the authors David, Moses, Zechariah, *et. al.* However inspired, these Jewish writers were no more or less human than my granpa, and the term "prophet" no more superhuman than the "immortal poet" ascribed to Homer. I didn't rebel against the spiritual idea of authorship—I rebelled against the scholarship that shrunk the pseudonymous authors (the actual writers in Jerusalem, conveniently erased by tradition) into "text". If you erase the history of imaginative writers at its core, you're stuck without a map to Eden—to the core sensibility that internalizes lost time, as in the loss of Eden. All you'll have is text as a map to braininess; you'll have history too, but one that splits hairs about what constitutes truth, and that's on the verge of neurotic because it can't imaginatively hold in mind at the same time the truth in myth and the single-mindedness of fact. Neurotic is okay if you're self-aware, it's where we're at today, but it's clueless to the future. We're kind of afraid of it because we're mapless; we figure forth codes of honesty that amount to bravely holding hands as we push into the darkness. My maternal granpa had a millenniums-old map; my paternal granma had Auschwitz, though some descendants somehow made it to Israel, with granpa's map internalized.

Anyway, I rebelled against the map; I was interested in the explorers. A couple years out of college, writing in the ascendent postmodernist vein, my object was to see myself as the human creature working at his writing desk. The poem that follows has me looking out the 8th floor window of Rochdale College in Toronto, out over the adjacent Coach House (where

I studied the graphic arts under the watchful eye of fellow Rochdale mentor Victor Coleman) and down the street of TV aerials on Huron. The headlights I see turning the corner and flashing on a Bloor Street billboard are similar to the eyes in my head peering at the page in my typewriter, reflected in my study's picture window. I am a writing creature; I want to know how I got there, the way granpa knew he could flee Lithuania in one night while keeping his most ancient books in his head. Maps are no help; their perspectives, which we oversee like giants, make it even more difficult to see ourselves. Our minds won't stand still like the page, and in the end the headlight of the cream Rolls Royce of the moon, dimmed by dawn, is still suggesting where I sit: the scene of writing, the moon has finally having turned the corner into the daylight aligned with the white background of the page, the black letters like edges, what's left of the night's intellectual repast. *Headlights* was published as a small book in early 1970, from which I excerpt these passages:

> Little car runs around the corner
> leaves more certain a tree
> tube antennae
>
> running from Harbord to Bloor
> more cars pass at the tip
> as telecasts in heavy oil
>
> higher up a chimney
> smokes a cigarette
> because I want one
>
> when everything closes for Christmas...
>
> ...boiling an electric kettle
>
> as unconscious of despair as aluminum
> in a climate pinned to maps
> piano wire of highways
>
> pubic hair of nerves the nets
> of desire perfectly match
> & long after fishermen packed up
>
> for the season ice dots
> the lakes like small towns in Ohio
> disappearing refrigerator lights

as the hinge that holds
this line to this
obsolete no lights shine

meaningfully in the dawn
moon that fading question
a cream rolls royce

turns the corner
the print   crusts
on the billboard the desk

The Poem of Zaydeh's Soul

In the 1970s, poet Donald Hall, my former mentor at Ann Arbor, quit academe and moved to a farmhouse in New Hampshire. Around the same time, I taught my last writing classes at CUNY and signed a three-book contract with Harper for translations of Biblical poetry (I insisted they be called "interpretations" in the subtitles). Don wrote to congratulate me on deciding "to live by your wits" in place of an academic career. He couldn't quite say "live as a writer," as he might have were I writer of prose. Serious poets were not known to make a living from their work, nor were there as yet big cash prizes for poetry. But Hall intended more than that; his word "wits" was a cover for "ancestors." "Live by the light of your ancestors is what you meant" I wrote back. Hall's farmhouse had been in his family for centuries, just as the Hebrew of the Bible was ancestral for me. In a later letter, Don refers to ourselves as "explorers" of history. At the time, I was thinking he's too literal about family history. I would have preferred he had written "explorers of existence," for I thought I could break down historical barriers by digging up out of their graves the ancient Hebraic poets whose palpable existence was buried under two to three millenniums of tradition. Unlike Don, my family's equivalent of a farmhouse had been ransacked in the war, my grandmother and aunts pulled out and shipped to a death camp. And yet, the renewed existence of Israel beckoned as a culture in which I could walk a semblance of ancient streets and speak the language of ancestors when I entered the neighborhood bank branch for a withdrawal. First, however, I had to stand in line and listen to the frustration of the other customers as they libeled bank, unions, and government. Finally, an old woman pushed her way in front of me. After I stammered polite words about the faux-pas—not to her but to the man in back of me—the old woman turned, letting out a stream of high-pitched invective. And just as suddenly, loud angry words were flooding out of my mouth, ancient Hebrew words, unmediated by a previous need to first translate my English thoughts into appropriate Hebrew, in my head. Shocking to me, no one thought I should be embarrassed for shouting at an old woman. She herself turned away, unmoved from her stolen place in line. And this was just one of many shocks at being thrown back into an ancient melting pot bubbling at a high temperature. I don't think Don Hall had such jolts on his New Hampshire farm. He did have plenty of "shocks of recognition," as were common in literary textbooks, but aside from getting advice about the cows and the old well, living by your wits came down to correspondence: a daily struggle to get poems published, with reviews, essays, and books about poems paying the monthly expenses.

Don and I continued to correspond while I was in Israel, he offering to shop my newest non-biblical poems stateside. I was stunned to get an acceptance from *Virginia Quarterly Review*, a journal I'd always considered too genteel to even read, yet there it was, among the current periodicals of Hebrew University's library, its traditional subdued orange cover outwitting my flight from academe. It was the color of a shrunken orange, in fact, the kind left too long uneaten in the fridge. Now, more than thirty years later, I may get paid something for writing about it, just as Don had capitalized more immediately on a poem about New England root vegetables on his family farm, turning it into an essay on farm work. It was not, back then, the kind of exploration of existence I was after; I was instead eking out a living by editing translations of modern Hebrew writers who recalled relatives and European culture left behind. They had escaped the insistence on Jewish nonexistence, and that was the beginning of my adult study in how to imagine existing before or after one has lived.

You won't find it in much writing today and its concern with the irony of consciousness. That irony is played out in a vision of personality that remains what it was in Saul Bellow's novels, where every layer of possible ambivalence is turned inside-out. Social situations are still acted out on a grid ranging from Balzac to Kafka; personalities and sexualities placed under the microscope become a comic or tragicomic distortion. Gertrude Stein, however, who I'm rereading in *Wars I Have Seen* (in a rare 1945 "Random House Wartime Book" recently gifted to my wife Rhonda) remains an exception. She meets ambivalence so directly, so head-on, that it will probably take another decade or more to appreciate her deeper theme of species consciousness. She writes of "the dark and dreadful days of adolescence, in which predominated the fear of death, not so much of death as of dissolution." And what is dissolved is not so much personality but one's sense of existing. The fear of it goes back to early childhood, where the late English psychoanalyst Winnicott had it pinpointed:

> "With the care that it receives from its mother each infant is able to have a personal existence, and so begins to build up what might be called a continuity of being. On the basis of this continuity of being the inherited potential gradually develops into an individual infant. If maternal care is not good enough then the infant does not really come into existence, since there is no continuity of being; instead the personality becomes built on the basis of reactions to environmental impingement."

Those "reactions" are the precursors to neuroses—the adolescent fears Gertrude Stein describes. Bear with me as we look back toward origins. Even though we've learned to laugh off neurotic behavior, Stein was focused on deep history, throwing us back to the primal days before human civilization—back when we first opened our eyes as Homo sapiens, our first experience of consciousness. That was a time when we could not yet reflect on our existence; it was all just happening, no story could yet contain it. Without a story we were still on the edge of nonexistence, and that is where the soul comes in. As far back as prehistoric totems and taboos, and then through religious and metaphysical refinements, the concept of a soul allowed us to contrast nonexistence with our existential life-and-death struggles: the soul came to us from outside existence; it exists before and after our brief little lives.

At least that was the soul in which my Zaydeh (Yiddish for grand-father) and European ancestors believed. I'm 5, and it begins with morning and what I hear: the splashing of water on his hands, three this way, three the other, and the verbal blessing of creation, water, universe, and the poetry that accompanies it. It's a poem in which the Creator speaks; not only speaks but commands: like rhyme and meter in a poem, the constraints can be a joy to obey. This waking-up blessing with water is an intimate speaking to a universe that is in the room; in this case, the bathroom.

I'm stirring in bed, hearing him. He never completely closes a door. Next I am dressed, downstairs, reading Rice Krispies box. Which hand puppet, for six boxtops plus quarter, to choose: Snap, Crackle, or Pop? Pop—in the white chef's hat—a pliable rubber head a dog could chew. Zaydeh bends over me: "Vielst du redden?" Reading out loud, that is, the cereal box: we are both learning to read English. Can't tell where border of English and Yiddish lies or which I speak—all mom's family visiting house speak both, or only Yiddish. My father and his kin understand little of Yiddish, even when I'm speaking; yet only dad, of all of them, went willingly back to The War.

There was more family there than here, over there in The War. I watch as their as-yet un-affixed album photos are sifted through in the big candy box. If alive, they were still in grave danger over there, as is my war-wounded G.I. father, pale-faced as a white man to an Indian, thin, weightless as the cork-filled wooden Indian by the cigar store. At some point the danger turns into "these were killed in the camps." Not all. Yanka, Pepi, and Shari, daddy's sisters, survive Auschwitz (mother gassed). Those smiling girls are Yanka's teen daughters—gassed.

I remember reading that Charlie Chaplin, after denying he was Jewish in the late '40s, said "But after the Holocaust, we're all Jews now." Aren't we? Yet in a generation that sense has been lost; few would say such a thing now. Nor would they think like D.W. Winnicott and Melanie Klein did back in the 1940s, that we're all in crucial ways still children at our mother's breast. The child can only tolerate the mother's absence for brief periods, after which she stops existing and the infant struggles to hold itself together in the face of hunger. When the mother returns to re-enter the child's world, only then does she re-exist in her care and feeding. It's not that the mother's breast holds meaning for the child but that the child fears that he or she ceases to exist without it. That primal fear of nonexistence is similar to meaninglessness, however, when it takes hold of us as adults, even for a moment.

Eternity is a more hopeful way of describing nonexistence. Stein wrote, "Everybody knows even though anybody flies higher and higher they cannot explain eternity any more than before, and anybody can persecute anybody just as much if not more than ever." Eternity is not simply outside spacetime, outside even an infinite multiverse; it reflects what is unknowable to our sapiens brain and its computational prostheses, such as A.I. And the talent for persecution is built into our DNA and its interface with the world: we're frustratingly competitive, yet the totality of human wishes are circumscribed by the evolutionary principle of competition. Were we to do away with competition, as opposed to domesticating it, we'd be erasing our species, and by extension, threatening all other species. Our dogs and cats, especially, would be scared.

A fox in our backyard, staring at us over the screened-in pool. We know she lives in a wild remnant next door, hearing her little ones jabbering. We make similar noises to her now, non-threatening ones like to a cat, and she does not scare. Eventually she walks away, satisfied for the moment we're not a danger. There have been many encounters with exotic animals in our yard, an endangered great horned owl and a Cuban bright yellow lizard the size of a toy poodle that acted like he belonged to us and would not scoot away. But it's the everyday species around us that keep the blood pressure down, dozens of them I can identify within a few minutes, breakfast coffee in hand, and dozens more of wild plants. Amphibians, crustaceans, birds, insects, mammals, marsupials, reptiles. Listening to them reminds me of midtown Manhattan in an air-conditioned taxi—a mild cacophony, punctuated by parrot screeches. It's a domesticated, southern Miami suburb however, fifteen minutes from the all-night university library, thirty minutes in the other direction to Everglades National Park.

Nature was marginalized in my early years until, at the age of 34, I discovered the ancient echoes of the wild Judean hills surrounding Jerusalem. Funny it should be that city, but the other big ones I've lived in, Detroit, Toronto, San Francisco, New York, Paris, London, kept me occupied with cultural amusements—Shakespeare-in-the-Park more than Central Park itself, for instance, and landscapes: Golden Gate Bridge, Jardin des Tuileries. Of museums, I liked Margaret Mead's pearl, the pre-gentrified Natural History Museum in New York, though it was the artfulness that excited, the suspended blue whale, the architectonic dinosaur bones. Yet when I enter my memory bank, I see mostly people—

good, bad, and indifferent ones, interesting ones, unstable ones. The remembered landscapes too are anthropocentric, even lakeside honky-tonk childhood Port Stanley.

Now I'm in the late-night virtually empty Baron de Hirsch Meyer Quadrangle Law Library, in "Area of Relaxation," in front of a wall holding a 55" canvas (i.e. sports-bar-TV sized) with a painted sunset of a northern wetlands (no palms). Could also be a screen-processed photo—can't really tell, no signature or label attached. Ambiguous, it agitates rather than relaxes. If this were a dentist office, you'd have a clearly delineated cheap nature poster, in a dollar-store frame, and would try to ignore it. So to relax now, I imagine it's a Neil Welliver or Fairfield Porter, hip blue-chip New York School-favored painters of abstract-inflected super-real landscapes. Actually, the intrusive fluorescent lighting works to its benefit, forcing my eyes to squint at it, as they would in an abundant natural setting.

As I write, my eye falls upon *Etz Hayim* in the adjacent "Jewish Law" bookcase, a book I was the acquiring editor for, a decade before finding Rhonda (whose cultural ambition matched mine but who was coming from a different direction, science not poetry). You were talking so brilliantly about that highly annotated Bible just last week, I imagine saying to her. I suddenly notice, I continue, that the image in my mind's eye is of you with the curly hair of twenty years ago. That can happen in dreams, but why now? It has to be because I'm pushing ahead and seeing what opens up, as one does earlier in life and as I was doing when you found me at the JCC in Houston. At advanced age now, I'm standing back, surveying the path that brought me here—or am I? Averse to summing up, this work proceeds like a caterpillar on the ceiling: Why does it need a hundred legs when a six-legged ant moves faster? Am I anticipating a butterfly moment? Or is *The Tree of Life*, the translated title of that Bible book, so patently a metaphor for the pleasures of the text that there is no caterpillar in it or on the ceiling? But there is, small and fuzzy gray, a potential moth. And we met by the bookshelf, you with *my* book in hand—*A Poet's Bible*—already purchased. "I liked the way the Bible metamorphosed back into poetry," you said.

How would I have been different had I been familiar with nature in childhood? My father managed the farm before he emigrated yet rarely mentioned it. My maternal Zaydeh ran a dry goods store in the old country; in Detroit he was retired, but now I sense how his life of cosmic connection with all of God's creatures, mediated by Talmudic study, might have gotten under my skin. It was the intensity of his examining gaze— upon the chickens hanging in the butcher shop; the wine glass, the seltzer glass, and the forks, lifted before his eyes before he would use them; dogs and birds in the neighborhood; and I was aware that, unlike anyone else, he consciously smelled the air, took in the scent of everything around him.

2.

Last night we were at the ballet. Two Balanchines and a Wheeldon, the latter described in program as "bracingly contemporary," though the Balanchines of '35 and '78 were more bracing without a need to be fashionable. A better description for the Wheeldon would be "sadly contemporary." He has some lovely translations of the clichés of modern dance into classical ballet language, but many more examples result in too heavy an emphasis on body rather than space. It was the grand consciousness of space that Balanchine carved out, as it were, around the moving body. And it was Balanchine who anticipated the sense of soul for me, his cut-outs of space (imagine a page of paper cut-outs after the bodies are cut out) like the invisible places, or place-holdings, we are born into.

I think of Zorro, our late cat, whose first yahrzeit we honored with a candle last week. For surely he was possessed of a soul: you could tell by the way he moved, as if choreographed by Balanchine. Unlike most humans, who walk around unconscious of their bodies, the grace of Zorro was that he was always conscious of the space his body moved through. On a bigger scale, I'd say the same for our neighbors, the alligators, who we visit in nearby Everglades National Park on weekends when, had we stayed in New York, we might have been instead at one of NYC's museums or on an art-gallery crawl. Watching an alligator walk on dry land seems to come straight out of Balanchine's *Scotch Symphony* ('72), with all its slow strutting around—even the bagpipes echo alligator bellowing. I was there at the launch, using the extra ticket that dance critic Edwin Denby owned, as on many other occasions when his partner of the moment was missing. He'd give the ticket first to Rudy Burckhardt, and Rudy sometimes to me—Rudy had other fish to fry. Edwin was happy to see me in the seat beside him, especially because of my taxi-hailing skills, no small feat outside Lincoln Center among hordes bent on a cab downtown on a cold winter evening. During the performance I mentally prepared to prompt Edwin's droll critique at intermission, thinking up questions for him when he was not besieged by his handful of admirers. One of them, Philip Roth-ex Maxine Groffsky, was often available to me, as she was far more critical of the evening than Edwin, and especially could not stand to hear mention of the Jerome Robbins ballet she most likely detested, and at least one of whose ballets were always on the cards. But I do recall the grace with which Maxine carried herself, and now in memory I realize it was enhanced by the pointy high-heels. Balanced on them as she was, Maxine projected disdain for Robbins's body-heavy choreography (when compared to the soul-pointing of Balanchine). There was no telling her of Robbins' purposeful satire. I'm afraid the epithet "bracingly contemporary" would have been, in retrospect, scathingly applied to Robbins.

I ask Rhonda why she thinks remembering an evening at the ballet may be more intense than the original. "Because there are no distractions when you remember," she offers. She means things going on around the edges, interesting or irritating people, a flute of champagne, a bathroom break, etc. While I was swept away when watching the original, the difference in memory is the personally satisfying struggle to give it shape—call it the *art* of memory. And then there are the layers of memory upon memory, present upon past, and past upon history, official history and cultural ones. It's the layers that help make it art; even the simplest haiku is laid against a complex backdrop of nature, weather, paintings, literature. The layers fold in on each other, until the art flows through like the unfolding landscape on Japanese screen panels. In the real world, I can't remember the thoughts or memories I may have been having at the time of the original event, nor would they have meshed seamlessly with the art onstage. Did the faux marching in *Scotch Symphony* remind me in 1972 of the Vietnam War? And so what if it did; it might have lessened rather than heightened the impact of Balanchine's art layered over Mendelssohn's music, in which matters of life, death and the soul are deftly submerged.

You simply could not take in a Balanchine work without thinking about the soul. Someone will argue that traditionally the soul is encompassed and defined by a sentient being's body. But no, the soul is also observer of that person, within and without. How is this possible? As we've seen, the old religions, back to Sumer at the origin of civilization, made much of a "guardian angel," a spirit parentally bonded to a person. The soul, however, cannot be pinned down; except in art, you can't "talk" to a soul, or hear it talking to you, the way religion envisions talking or praying to God, or to angelic intermediaries. Nevertheless, all of such communication, imagined or, like talking to one's soul, "impossible," takes place in a cosmic theater where natural and supernatural interact, each from its own standpoint. Yet the soul, having no standpoint—the place it opens is filled by us—is also the ideal of what might be an observer *to* the cosmic theater itself; not quite outside it, but as if in the wings, like a writer. To the soul, all that it finds in the world is performance, a movement in spacetime. It watches over our shoulder as we perform in poetry or painting, philosophy or science; it watches the theaters and films we create no less than it watches the performance of daily life on earth.

When it comes to a poem, the soul is on the lookout for its representation. In our day, as in every former one, performance is at the forefront of the arts. In literature, it's likely the performance of the narrator, "I", or variation thereof, in a poem with which we identify as it paints a picture of the world in which we are moved. It may be an inner world, or it may represent states of consciousness, as in our time or another. The "I' may be split between narrator and character, or split in myriad ways. The point is, we vibrate to the performance, even on the page. And the result is, the more captivating the performance, the less we demand a representation of the soul as integral to it. Most of our art today might appear soulless except that, in its reflection of the absence of soul, it suggests a poignancy, and sometimes sublimity, that asks, "Where is the soul?" in this, and by the asking it holds a place for it.

But how will this place-holding be filled without a cosmic theater, as was accessible to Dante and Blake, and also to Emily Dickinson and her Bible? It can't be, no matter how poignant the absence, so in place of it we wish greater physical intensity, more profound performance of our arts, words broken open, which, as I've said, translates into even the best poetry being "not good enough," not as good as the bodily poem of my Zaydeh, his self-awareness as a created creature. Take for instance the recent sympathy with Sufism as an avant-garde hermeneutic, one that reflects the medieval origins of a metaphysics of absence that Zaydeh would have understood, via Kabbalah, as too anxious to make literal in words what is already poetry in the physical world, i.e. creation. Here's the biblical angel Gabriel, appropriated by the Quran, relating a dialogue with Deity:

> "There is a veil that is not unveiled, and an unveiling that is not veiled. The veil that is not unveiled is knowledge through me, and the unveiling that is not veiled is knowledge through me.
>
> "No veil remains: Then I saw all the eyes gazing at his face, staring. They see him in everything through which he veils himself. He said to me: They see me, and I veil them through their vision of me from me."
> *[translated from Arabic by Elliot R. Wolfson]*

Without Zaydeh's irony of being a mortal creation with a deathless soul, hence always half-alive, half-dead, you're stuck with hermeneutics, a poorer, long-winded poetry of absence (the half-dead part). Decon is a recent example. I hear Zaydeh's poetry, however, in a New Year (Rosh Hashanah) lecture in Brooklyn by Rabbi Adin Steinsaltz of Jerusalem, via YouTube: the entire lecture is about how the world is a poem to our emotional life, which hears "new year" as not the scientific imagining (he explains) of longitude and latitude, nor even the rational facts of equator and solar system—all of which tells us that all years are alike, no new year is different from an old year—but new year as a one-year-old finds him- or herself at its factual birthday party. The child struggles unsuccessfully to understand what it's about; really, it's about the adults who are in celebratory mood, and he, or she, the one-year-old, is the chosen representative of it, or so the child may comprehend, even though not yet within language. Emotional life is like that, as if one year old and the world exists for it as a celebratory mirror, in which good and bad can be dressed up and participated in according to civilized longitudes and latitudes and hopes. But only if the new year starts with our species creation is it possible to hope for a "better" year ahead; human creation is as unknown to us as the day we are born and we can know it only in a poem, a creation in which our emotions participate with our grown up intelligence. Steinsaltz uses the term "symbolic world" in place of poem. In the civilized world, our best year may have been the twelfth, the year before adolescent angst, or the year of our wedding day—there's no hope for a better year than that, though perhaps one as good. In a poem, however, it's possible to wish for a better year—"even just a little bit better," says Steinsaltz—because the old year, if we face it openly, as in the "trembling" days between Rosh Hashanah and Yom Kippur, were filled not only with hope and accomplishment, but disappointment, hatefulness, tragedy, magical thinking and bad thoughts. We know the diurnal, solar and sidereal year will remain the same (or at least they have since human consciousness evolved); the Jewish new year, however, since it is celebrated as it was when humanity were one-year-olds and did not "know everything," can imagine each new year as a newly created one, so that what unfolds can be read anew innumerable times, like a psalm or a sonnet by Shakespeare, and especially like the Torah, as if there is more to be found there.

It's as if Steinsaltz is a throwback rabbi in the Talmud, where the world is described and disputed, in lecture and dialogue, as if rational and irrational are bound together in a way that makes sense to one-year-olds but needs continuous elaboration for adults. We're not always aware of the deep irony behind that. Let me explain again the cosmic theater: natural and supernatural meeting for moments on a common stage. Those who are living religiously within the cosmic theater of course see it as literal, with its fullness hidden from us because, as one-year-olds, we can't yet know its language. All this is understood as symbolic (Steinsaltz would refrain from descending into confusing terms like metaphor and imagery, i.e. confusing in terms of what they might ultimately mean) which is exactly why a life requires a lifetime of study, of poetry (as divinely created, in the case of our world) parsed out by reality. All of this is interesting to the soul; although it has been there before we were born and will be after, it's curious about the *study* of life—and not all the distracting acting out, the violence, misogyny, *et. al.* Nevertheless, the soul cannot speak in our civilized world. Like a one-year-old, however, it knows when it is celebrated and is representative of itself, an older world hidden behind, and framing, ours.

Besides, Steinsaltz's glorious yellow-white unkempt beard reminds me of a one-year-old memory, of twisting Zaydeh's smaller beard in my tiny fingers. Also of the poet from the School of Isaiah who wrote down First Isaiah's hallucinatory visit to the Jerusalem Temple, when the clouds of white incense smoke wafting up to the obscured ceiling reminded him of the Creator's beard and robe reaching down from heaven—that is, I imagine the Isaiah poet twirling his beard as he wrote, and as both Steinsaltz and myself do today, unself-conscious as children. The soul prefers one-year-olds because they do not burden it with the multiple meanings of language, though it is calmed by the multiple layers of a poem (and perhaps even a blackboard-filled equation by Einstein). Poem and equation are only *using* language to express apprehension of timelessness, of nonexistence, which is dear to a soul's heart (though a soul can't have a heart, of course, apart from our own).

Let's return to dancing, perhaps in its deeper origins. Consider Edwin Denby's cats, and his remark to me that their uncanny grace was worthy of Balanchine. So too, people unconsciously walking on the streets, who in Denby's eyes could equal or even surpass the level of modern dance, if it were properly framed, as in Rudy Burckhardt's documentary films. A scene my mom never tired of documenting attained the level of dance in my eyes—where the movement consisted of a highly compressed one of merely standing up on a moving train. It represented her fear and wonder at surviving (and hence, my potential existence) the escape from Lithuania through Nazi Germany in the last train authorized to conduct foreign nationals through the Reich. At one point, with Nazi officials aboard to interrogate Jews without visas, Zaydeh slid out of his seat, stood upright in the aisle, affixed his tallit, and began to daven the morning prayers. Mom recalls how she and her brother screamed to him in whispers, pleading that he sit down and not draw attention. He, in fact, intended to calm them, mom says, by showing no fear, though later he intimated that God had protected them. I replayed the scene many times in my head, and each time Zaydeh stood up I tried to as well but couldn't move: he was the cosmic dancer, swaying in the swaying train, and I the modernist audience, frozen in the middle of the 20th century; he was conscious of a soul, and I was aware only of its absence.

In a hundred years no reader will remember Balanchine or Edwin Denby, perhaps, but most will still have access to the Bible, and even to the interpretive work of previous centuries. While the soul is addressed as a distinct entity in the Bible, it's taken for granted. In later books it can go missing altogether, even in the Bible's Apocrypha. It is striking that in Judith's psalm in *The Book of Judith*, where there is no concept of soul to interpose with existence, there is instead the appeal of selflessness—like Winnicott's infant before its sense of "a continuity of being." It is, in other words, without a self, selfless. So Judith's "selfless words" enter the same timeless realm of pre-existence or nonexistence in which humans are thoughts of creation, of a Creator unbound by time. Her Creator's past and future stretch beyond existence; Judith's selflessness, unlocked from "self-embrace," puts her outside of a time-bound existence and on equal footing in her words with the Creator's thoughts. Without Creation, she would exist only in the moment—as in the moment of the Assyrian's slaughter of her people. Yet her words are outside the moment, outside existence, as if it is her soul speaking.

> Lord, my Lord
> now hear this widow's selfless words
> you gave shape to the past
> and beneath what is happening now
> is your supportive hand
> you have thought about the future
> and those thoughts live as men and women
>
> 'Here we are!' they say
> your thoughts are alive in the present
> and you've cleared paths for them
> into the future
>
> Look, here we are, exposed to the Assyrians
> parading their well-oiled muscle
> preening in the mirrors of their polished shields
> bullying the hills with their herds of infantry
> vanity worn on their sleeves: tin armor
> their spears thrusting forward
> their trust in their legs and horses
> their pride in the naked tips of their arrows
> their hope in thoughts of total domination—
> so locked in the embrace of themselves
> they can't know you are Lord over all
> fierce in your shattering of wars themselves
> great armies of the past are dust in your presence
> they were lords in their own eyes as they marched on
> blindly
> but there is only one 'Lord'
> …
> Please hear me, God of my father
> Lord of Israel's heritage
> Master of the universe, Creator of earth and sky
> King of all creation
> hear my psalm

It's a long way from there to here, yet reformed American Jews and Christians still address the soul, if at all, as casually and ambiguously as in soul music. In a recent article in the *Times of Israel*, Raphael Ahren refers to most Americans as ambivalent: "they live to exist"—an existence, he implies, that is based purely on social identity. On that score, Rhonda and I decided to try falling for the Fathom hype about *Unity*, the "live" documentary for millennials, in a thousand theaters around the world for one time only—with "a hundred Hollywood star narrators," progressives among whom many identified as vegan. "Identified" is a key word in the film, where all social identities are dismissed as tribal; instead, we are to identify with the unity of all sentient beings, an unstated Buddhist and Hindu theme. Fine with us, especially when titling its last of five parts, "Soul". Just what do millennials think of the soul today? Not a thing, it turns out. The concept was never actually mentioned in the film, and further, all stripes of thinking were gently derided. Better to let yourself "become conscious" or *feel* part of the universal unity of all life forms and thereby evolve a higher consciousness in which nothing comes to harm. "How could there be any harm," explains Rhonda ironically, "when there is no separation, and to make the point in the film the Jews are offered as a prime example of 'primitive' thinking: they're separate from and better than others, by calling themselves (did they?) 'The Chosen People'." *Ipso facto*, for the unity people the soul is not separate from the body, and it means little to say the soul has always existed because we all "always existed" since the Big Bang, where the atoms created are the same atoms in us and in everything. Talk about primitive ideas dressed up as universalist chatter; but anyway, there it is: the soul is now a meaningless concept, applied equally to food and to the starving. "What am I going to eat tonight?" gasped Rhonda afterward, terrorized to tears by the film's tortured, innocent animals? "It's too late," I offered, "the cattle and cows have been domesticated, and the chicken in the fridge has already been killed." That was over-thinking on my part, and it only led to more anxious distinctions later that night: chocolate is ok, chocolate is a plant, but *milk* chocolate—no, not vegan. Perhaps that's *talmudic* thinking, after all, and the millennia of Jewish talmudic thinking—too much thinking!—is based on the separateness of things (though all God's creatures). It wouldn't matter, however, to Zaydeh's soul; outside of existence, it's also outside of thinking. It is we who are thoughts of Creation, as Judith says, and we in our physical existence have to think our way back to Creation, to Eden, as in the thinking in our poems and psalms. The unity people would like to deny there's thinking in poems—unless, of course, the poem unifies all thoughts, like a mantra. A mantra might have emptied all thoughts from Judith's mind, but that would also have led to the ancient Assyrian slaughter of the Jews, Judith (meaning Jewess) included. She and her people had to think and act in their serious separateness.

It was the same for Esther. She and cousin Mordecai had to think hard, in *The Book of Esther*, of a way to reveal the plot against her people, so that the king would understand it was more than a matter of her word against his most trusted minister. She prepared a banquet, wine flowing, just as Judith had poured out wine for the Assyrian general: the revelation, in other words, required a "normal" situation, a private party, a staging artfully thought through.

And the king
and Haman came
to drink with Esther the queen

the king again said to Esther—
while they were drinking wine
on this second day of banqueting—

your petition is granted, Queen Esther
even if it means half the kingdom
your request will be fulfilled

and this time Esther responded
if I am worthy in your eyes
of the king's favor

and if your majesty pleases
grant me my life
it is my petition

and my people's life
it is my request—
we wish to live

for we have been sold
I and my people
to be slaughtered

murdered and destroyed
yet I would not have spoken
had I been sold merely

for a servant girl
and my people for slaves
I would not have troubled the king

with news of a plotter
whose hatred outweighs
his concern for your honor

Who is it? the king exclaimed
and speaking to Esther he said
who would dare turn his heart to this

and lay a hand on you—where is he?
An enemy, a plotter! she was saying
no other than this bitter Haman

as he sits before us...

The poetry here is what holds both in time, Esther and her would-be murderer, as well as Creation itself, which takes nothing for granted: the good must be *chosen* from the bad. Why? The moral universe, like the soul, exists outside of spacetime: we know it by choosing it but not by why that choice exists. It can't be taken for granted like natural law. Zaydeh could not take it—take Creation—for granted; he had to acknowledge it every morning. And thanks to him, neither could I take poetry for granted. Too much academically-filtered poetry might have dulled my spirit for the shock of the ancient thing, poems as unsettling as Esther's and Judith's original scrolls.

3.

I'm looking in C.K. Williams's poems again, 2 days after his death. He is considering belief in a soul: "Why, as many I cherish—Herbert, Hopkins, Weil—have believed, shouldn't there be a substance/ neither thought nor matter that floats above both..." (from "Brain"). It's not the *substance*, I'm thinking, it's the self seeing itself—the writer in his chair—and if we're to stick with science, then the meeting of two such entities negate each other—albeit with a feeling of something uncanny having happened, a sense that we have seen ourselves as only a soul can, and lived to tell the tale. Since there is no substance within ourselves, however, that can see us from without, we might write it off and come up instead with a faux out-of-body image, as a really good poet like Charlie could: "...that floats above both as mist at dawn lifts from a lake".

I'd say to Charlie, as we're nursing our decaf lattes at *glatt*-academic Princeton cafe *Small World*: "But that's an out-of-brain experience, not out-of-body. The poet still takes his chair for granted, rather than questioning the whole scene of a small-c creator writing his poem—a creature in imitation of a big-C Creator, even if we want to identify the latter with the universe or, in recent physics theory, a multiverse." I'm reconstructing the conversation, although the original one lacked the quotations from our poetry I'll add in here. "If I don't go all the way," I'm saying, "to see myself writing in the chair itself, then maybe I'd feel no affinity with the Bible's writers and the cosmic poetry of Isaiah, when he's speechless before the big-C Creator on His throne of cloud:

> ...in horror of my darkness
> in terror of inhuman space
> exposed to a private death
>
> totally vulnerable on the surface
> of earth's
> material matter...
>
> then one of the seraphim
> flew toward me
> a live coal in his hand
>
> a fire from the interior
> of the earth
> the core of my being
>
> it was a burning stone
> from the fire
> on the altar
>
> with the priest's tongs
> he reached in the holy altar
> and took it
>
> and touched my lips
> with it
> and he was saying
>
> you are seeing
> the purifying fire of creation
> burn up your past
>
> and abstract fear and guilt
> of light   of losing yourself
> your small and only light

now abstraction turns concrete
on your lips
to feel the universe

the private guilt gone
purged   lanced
like a boil

erupted around your body...
and I was clean
and whole

and I heard the voice
of my creator
it was saying

who will I send
to be a witness—
here am I   send me

I heard myself saying
and he said
go and say to this people

hear over and over
and understand nothing
look again and again

and again you don't see
the whole body:
of language, sound

of action, history
of memory
imagination

of matter, light
they can't even feel
the energy inside them

the material of their being...

But Charlie was not without biblical affinity. He was always ready to question me about how—or actually not how but why—I translated the Bible. For example, "Why be stuck within a framework where you have to take God for granted?" I'd answer: "Because God is unknowable. You posit the same for your brain in 'Brain,' but how many poems did you get out of that? One. I'm saying the hundreds of Hebraic poets who wrote the Bible got a lot more out of a Creator than a Brain."

Of course, that answer didn't really satisfy either of us. For one thing, the concept of hundreds of self-conscious ancient Hebraic writers is not yet part of our common education, and further, our modern sensibility does supply a context for the *absence* of a Creator, which might be equally poignant—except that, like the negative of a photograph, the image is a ghost, uncanny enough though hardly soul-satisfying.

I was still quoting Charlie to myself only recently. "I wanted to enter areas given over to prose writers, I wanted to talk about things the way a journalist can talk about things, but in poetry, not prose." This, in answer to an interviewer asking why he developed such a long line in his poems. I turn this inside-out for myself, substituting "poets" for "prose writers" and "prose" for "poetry." Why couldn't I pursue the circuitous and layered building of an intimate theater—in prose, and not only in poetry? But there was no time to see what Charlie's often deadpan comeback would be; no likelihood of his typical ambitious questioning. (In a friendly argument with poet Susan Wheeler and myself, at her house for dinner, about the irrational in poetry: "I'm always rational about the irrational, aren't I?" asked Charlie.) And Charlie's emails, after his diagnosis, were getting shorter and shorter. His last, a few months ago, said he almost dreaded telling me of the book of his that would be published this month, *Selected Later Poems*, the title sounding too posthumous. He passed two days before its pub date, which is today.

As a boy on weekend family drop-by's in Detroit, I heard but put out of mind the dread tales of recent history. I still haven't visited any of the death camps in Europe, though young cousins have. I was much younger, probably younger than my first memory of it at 4, when I entered the Cabot, which included an encampment of family Holocaust refugees spread across several floors of a 1920s post-Beaux-Arts (minimal in ornament though its wings enchantingly spread-eagled) Alfred Kahn knock-off of an apartment building in midtown Detroit. Dad and I, and later with young brother Sanford, came every Sunday, through less murderous deaths and divorces, for a dozen years until no one was left, including cousins Walter and Joyce, with whom I had played hide-and-seek (shades of the Holocaust) through the twisting halls and labyrinthine basement. That last visit was about the time I walked into a suburban warehouse converted into a weekend rock venue, so overwhelmed by drums and electric guitar that my loins vibrated and the private inner life of a fifteen-year-old was blasted open. Finally, my interior life had its own culture, with beatnik life in jazz and poetry just around the corner—in fact, it was down on Dexter Avenue, the neighborhood I grew up in and included the Cabot, where I could now spend weekends camping out in a gutted supermarket that was being transformed into a jazz club. As flooring and new walls were installed, we painted those walls with surrealist jazz "visions" in exchange for bedding down overnight on mattress "crash pads." A spattering of paint on my clothes was a sign of this new culture I took home and wore proudly in high school. Eventually 'The Minor Key' opened with major jazz groups like those of Coleman Hawkins and local Detroiter Yusef Lateef, though with small cover charges we kids still couldn't afford. But those of us painting the walls, mostly suburban white kids, got free passes; until the liquor license kicked in a year later, you didn't have to notice our ages, though we stood out among the uniformly black patrons. This was the only volunteer coffeehouse strictly jazz scene I've heard of; the others were folk-based, with best example perhaps the 18th Street Coffeehouse in Santa Monica, financed by Bob Dylan and built, painted, and run by his cronies. A few minutes walk from the Cabot, where at that late date the last of my relatives was holding out, Auschwitz-survivor Aunt Pepi, I soaked up the death-defying "free jazz" of John Coltrane at The Minor Key.

No trace of it was left a couple years ago when I revisited inner city Detroit with Rhonda, Pepi's grand-daughter Joyce, and my brother Sanford, our driver, who still lived in a nearby suburb. The area was wasteland, no stores, only an occasional wholesale depot (masquerading as 'Auto Parts') of stripped junk from trashed buildings, gleaming cracked toilets in front of silver-painted radiators, pipes and wiring. Someone I knew in junior high must have sat on those toilets; meanwhile, the Cabot retained a handful of aging tenants who'd learned to live with sporadic lights, water and heat. I spoke with one over the phone, asking if he'd buzz us in when we came, explaining we'd grown up in that building. He said there was no buzzer or any way through the entrance unless you had the giant padlock key, nor could his aged, disabled body make it down from the third floor, which he accomplished only once every few days to journey for supplies. No manager or super on premises; Mr. Clark was the only tenant still paying phone bills, with none other listed for this once solid Kahn imitation (no one had yet though of prying off the faux escutcheons below the roof)). Most surprising, once we got close enough to peer through the still-unbroken window atop the front door, was the Moorish domed lobby-ceiling mural remembered from childhood, cerulean blue upon which myriad gold stars twinkled. Presumably dust could not settle on it, the daily door openings blew away cobwebs, and nobody nowadays looked upward.

My father's parents were gone, my grandma in Auschwitz, before I
understood my mother's first words about me, "er haut meira," in Yiddish:
"he's afraid." Maybe of being abandoned in playpen while mom ran off with
another man. All of mom's Hebrew high school classmates were rounded
up and executed in the forest outside of Lithuania's third largest city; three
of my father's sisters survived Auschwitz because they were taken late in
'44. I visited the third in '69, in her flat in Kosice, Slovakia, recording each
day in poems:

GETTING TO DARK

high in Slovakia
are some mountains
it is cool in this chair
some blue comes to it
from a large glass vase
above a Slovak typewriter
above all are 4
or 5 flies
persian raga
why do 3 portraits on 3 walls all face
counterclockwise to a persian tapestry
dragged into my family 70 yrs back
a garden of eden surviving children
in death camps where friendlier
insects return to anonymous
mild cheeks of small flowers
sewn with an erratic patience
only a poet exposes
when he is clubbed by invisible flies
from burials so fast
a tongue is ripped
into the flow of small volcanos
smoky afternoons
in a room where life is really felt
as light reaches in
for its keys to drive simply away
25/7/69
    [from *Disappearing Horses*]

A breathless urgency here echoes the lost memory: too terrible to remember,
or too soon. In time, however, no terror goes unremembered in Bible and
Talmud, though that set of books from the house pillaged for—for what?

Shoring up an outhouse. Nothing to remember, says the doorman of the Grand Hotel. "Grand Hotel. Always the same. People come, people go. Nothing ever happens." Garbo, Crawford, Barrymore—all out of the silents with subtle posture and gesture—faces expressively moving, holding still, in exquisite timing. My memory of the Sunday visits to the Cabot is like that, seeing it now like Aunt Shari's desolate iron-curtain Kosice, coming out of the silent, impossible expression of the Holocaust, to an equally impossible irony: as if nothing ever happened. Nothing does really happen in memory, by then it's too late. Aunt Yanka died in bed in the Cabot, with a book in her hands—she read all night, sleeping fitfully, the author coming to life in her hands like her young daughters in memory, the ones murdered. For a few years after the war the family intellectual, Yanka often nannied me, and I recall her joy (so it seemed) when at 10 and 11 I read aloud to her from a book she was reading. What was it? Walter Scott's *Ivanhoe*. I recall Isaac, who Wiki describes as "the Jewish money-lender, Isaac of York, who is equally passionate about his people and his beautiful (Jewish) daughter, Rebecca. The book was written and published during a period of increasing struggle for the emancipation of the Jews in England, and there are frequent references to injustices against them." A remnant of soul still there today, in the Cabot, a few apartments still hung onto by aging African-American residents. I told Mr. Clark on the phone that I was an author writing a book about growing up in Detroit and would very much like to visit the building again, to say hello and walk the corridors, and to bring along two or three relatives who also used to live there. I did not meet him in person, but when we had talked—he had the solid diction of an aged Sidney Poitier—he filled in some history. The unique Dexter-Davison supermarket, gutted the year after he moved in: yes, they had incomparable Jewish bagels there, he said, the overwhelming black poppy-seeds stuck to your lips and face when you bit down deep into the soft white dough, beneath the dark crust. It was a new thrill for him, now a distant memory. "Haven't had one since." That would be fifty years. "You're the first Jewish person I've talked to since."

4.

For many years toward the end of the 20th century I had weekly dinners in a Tribeca sushi restaurant with poet Grace Schulman. *Zutto* was a Polynesian-like room layered over with jazz tracks by local musicians who ate there. It's not that our conversation was spontaneous, any saki-fueled talk could be, but ours was usually layered on a narrative thread, so that after dessert (intricately sliced oranges on a narrow ceramic tray) we were ready to walk out with a finished story. It might be about New York poets or Israeli women, but it often turned upon a resistance to therapy, for which Ted Hughes was poster boy. Everyone knew that Sylvia was in therapy, which did not prevent her eventually laying her head in an oven, and ditto Ted's next lover, poet Assia Gutman-Wevill, but the assumption was—and Hughes bore this out in his autobiographical work—that Ted was too straightly-strung to require therapy of his own. There were no alarm bells in his personality, and yet that should have been the tip-off. So that was often the unsolved mystery of the evening, the lack of alarm bells in artsy society, although in Grace Schulman's poems that silent high note permeated all society. Grace's poems might seem formally conservative on the surface, but they were a combustive layering of narrative detail that turned them into explosive flash-fictions. There is probably nothing like it, nor did I know another poet (excepting lay analyst bpNichol) so Freud-conversant, building on over twenty years of psychoanalysis. Grace could laugh off faux tragedy like no one else—Ted Hughes becoming British Poet-Laureate for instance, which we determined put a nationalist crimp (how could it not?—*vide* the long list of American poets reduced to poetry-sales-persons in Washington)—in the tragic nature-haunted vein of his verse; or Robert Creeley becoming an academic in middle age, which too preciously slipcased his compelling wanderlust—yet Grace pursued a transcendent agenda of imaginary peace-making in everything: Why not imagine lions lying down with lambs, since it is all storytelling anyhow, everything is, and all stories end with the utter, if not bitter reality of turning out the lights? *For That Day Only* is the title of her book that collected poems from those days.

During the same lonely years before finding Rhonda, my gay cousin Walter and I also met weekly for dinner. Walter mentored me in ham radio in early youth, when we lived close by in inner city Detroit; later, in high school, one night he confessed his sexuality fears and his contemplation of suicide. A year away from my own license, I convinced him to drive to *O Sole Mia* pizza (Quanno fa notte e 'o sole se ne scenne,/ me vene quase 'na malincunia; When night comes and the sun has gone down,/ I start feeling blue) in his 2-seater Italian Isetta (a proto-gay statement in car-chauvinist Detroit). It wasn't our first emergency dining; that happened back in pre-teen inner city in the middle of Yom Kippur. It was a fast day spent in synagogue that mom and dad still observed, and Walter was there with divorced mom operetta singer Adele and grandma Pepi. Up in the balcony, Walter and I could not suppress our usual hilarity at every adult irony in sight (for instance, the canvas shoes of the rabbi, avoiding leather's reminder of slaughtered animals, were the Keds brand that only kids wore, but what sent us into paroxysms were the demands to rise, which would often leave the elderly tardy, and then to be seated, which some didn't hear) until we were chased from the auditorium. Instead of hanging around the front steps as usual, where several eye-averting adult smoking-addicts were palming their cigarettes, we crossed forbidden Dexter Avenue and ducked into Eagle Dairy, which presented no outward sign of food purveyance, having been converted from a Depression-era neoclassical bank building. There, turning guilt up to the max on hot-fudge sundaes, we calmed down among the blasé non-Jewish patrons. But now we were meeting in SoHo, and after the failure of *Food*, a capitalist interpretation of commune fare, we took to a low-profile Australian cafe, our conversation slanted toward the futility of straight society as if it was a religious orthodoxy, though Walter's light parody of it betrayed a desire for greater respect. How outré it seemed (in the dead-end years of *Whole Earth Catalog*) to wear an untrimmed beard, or to imagine a God without one— and the seeming transcendence of sex, to further the religious analogy, was belied by the large amount of progeny. Straight society adopted orthodox values, it seemed, just a clean-shaven version with trimmed pubic hair; everything erotic was domesticated to the point of hysteria: bottoms, male or female, were wiggled strictly for laughs. Yet could they not, bottoms, represent the soul? That is, the soul's attraction to the body, even though souls came from, and returned to, an eternal nonexistence? Why did souls need bodies, why does Creation need our witness? The answers require stories that precede origins, representations of the prehistoric. Science may tuck the latter into evolution, but why not bottoms as our species' civilizing representative of our lost prehensile tails? Anyway, so might go our conversation, Walter's and mine, back in not-yet fully gentrified SoHo.

For Zaydeh, however, nonexistence could be studied for a lifetime, in a yeshiva, woven into the open-ended narrative of Bible, Talmud, and ancillary commentaries like the Midrash and Kabbalah. It was not the soul that needed a body so much as a body needed a soul. Especially the human animal, for "there is in nature an overriding sanity and often, in humankind, an undermining insanity. We, among all animals, are most frequently irrational, distortional, delusional, worried," writes MacArthur Fellow Carl Safina in *Beyond Words*. The worried humans, of course, are unlikely to have a narrative that evokes nonexistence or species consciousness, though they may have ancestral narrative histories. My parents, who loosened the grasp on their parents' belief in a cosmos greater than themselves, still found the biblical stories ancestral when they heard them read out in their conservative (reformed) Detroit synagogue. I might compare this to a film I just watched and that my parents also once saw, *That Hamilton Woman*. In it, Lady Hamilton sacrifices her life to England's existence, to an ancestral story, although she is not harmed and does not die. It is her affective life that dies, in her love for an English icon, Lord Nelson; she is self-extinguished by her imaginative dying with him. It's not a suicide; it's a pledge of belief in the religion of undying love. Of course, either of my parents could have found other Jews to marry were they to become divorced; they had not vowed marriage to biblical Abraham or Sarah. Yet they had avowed a belief in romantic love for themselves and were therefore open to thinking about it in modern movies (their English still too new for reading books)—open, but reluctant to trust fiction. However, *That Hamilton Woman*, their first movie stateside, like so many films of the golden era, is an historical story, if not history, just like some biblical stories written by ancient poet-historians. And although it may seem Catholic, in that undying love admits no mistake or divorce—not even the adolescent misunderstanding of a Romeo and Juliet, who might assume their undying souls could reunite after death—the Hebrew Bible allows for all sorts of mistakes, from Eve's to Jacob thinking he was sleeping with Rachel when it was in fact Leah. Besides, Leigh and Olivier were adulterers (although married in real life); their Lady Hamilton and Lord Nelson could only have made sense to my broken-English speaking parents as escapees from traditional religious practice.

"For the masses it was practice that mattered, not the correct theological formulations of a few literati (including those idealists who wrote the Hebrew Bible). Thus we cannot look to the textual traditions…" writes William Dever in his recent *The Lives of Ordinary People in Ancient Israel*. Let's substitute Shakespeare and the English poets for "Hebrew Bible," and the English translators of the King James Bible for "a few literati"— what then becomes the point? Not merely that it's easier to find household archaeological artifacts than the writing implements of "idealists," but that the literati of any nation are irrelevant to history. Alas for such scholars, movies have made literary history available to "ordinary people," and it was probably the same in ancient days: instead of celluloid or digital, they had poet-storytellers in even the rural villages. Love at first sight between biblical Isaac and Rebecca—via Isaac's literate foreman, or what today might be a matchmaking site—made the filmic coupling of Vivien Leigh and Laurence Olivier familiar to my parents even while still illiterate in English.

When Shifra Glazer and Herman Rosenberg met at English language night-school in Detroit, 1938, they were recently arrived immigrants. They did not speak each other's language (Yiddish and Hungarian) so their incentive to learn English speeded up. In the realm of my nonexistence, a hole that needed filling opened when they were married the following year. The war had not yet started, it was after "Peace in Our Time" appeasement, so I could expect to exist soon in a family. (No such luck: the London Blitz and Churchill's "Never Surrender" were around the corner, in 1940). But in '39, my father's older brother David, who would become my namesake after his shocking early death, was already Americanized and insisting my parents take in their first ever first-run movie. It would help improve their English, he claimed, and this particular film, *That Hamilton Woman*, would also uplift their souls.

Nevertheless, the film opens with this striking image: battered by age, Lady Hamilton (Vivien Leigh) looks in a mirror and says, "It's always the same. I will never be looked at again by the one who made my life matter." A dungeon-mate eggs her on: "And then?" "There is no then, there is no after." That kind of undying love, then, does end in death, is almost noirish, and probably too complicated—English history combined with a confused Christianity—for my parents, who responded to the English language and to Hollywood as an escape from history. Escape, that is, from Nazified Europe, anti-Semitism, and religious obligations. Vivien Leigh was also escaping her girlhood, as was mom, not looking back—until our heroine sees the wounded Nelson, who can also personify my mother's war-shadowed past. At first flush, Mom might have seen a sturdy Nelson in Dad; later, however, a reverse ending to the film played out: When dad returned from the war wounded, mom's resentment at his having left her and volunteered (while over-aged) for the draft, was vindicated. By then I was already speaking, conceived on Dad's last furlough in '43. I had gotten myself born out of nonexistence—just as had baby Horatia, Lord Nelson and Lady Hamilton's illegitimate daughter, talked about but never seen. Horatia lost her parents by film's end; what will existence allow her to become? I felt similarly parentless growing up. When dad came home a spectral shell from the hospital, I knew I'd have to live by my wits, way before starting school.

Yet I was a reluctant Jonah. I knew nothing of my parents' earlier romance, would never have imagined them going downtown to a first-run movie, nor embracing *That Hamilton Woman*'s idealism: evoking Churchill in Lord Nelson and Western democracy in Lady Hamilton. Then the war cancelled out Shifra and Herman's youthful escapist ideals; I would be the one to play it out, escaping from their historical responsibilities (Auschwitz-surviving relatives had to be brought over) into a postwar world of unburdened youth culture and skin-deep soul searching—"body and soul" now implied a woman's body dressed in a soulful, braless, refurbished granny dress. At best, the equally retro Billie Holiday cover of the song, 'Body and Soul,' revealing the hole inside the heart through which a soul might have escaped—envisioned by the now heroin-fueled great talent—would become diffused into our whole generation, aided by less harmful, softer, cheerier drugs.

But the original soul song was Jonah's Hebrew psalm within the whale:

Water was all around me
penetrating to my soul: I was almost gone
devoured by a flood

Seaweeds were tangled
around my head
I sank to the depths

I went down to the roots
of mountains
the earth shut her gates

Behind me
it was the end of the world
for me....

My soul was ebbing away within me...

This soul song of 2,500 years ago takes place within the body of a whale—as if Jonah's body, like Billie Holiday's, were swallowed by ineluctable despair. But who is the lover Billie is singing to? How could he or she be worth her surrender of body *and soul?* Unless it's her maker her soul itself is singing to, creator of both her life and the whale together. How would her Creator wreck her life, except by asking the seeming impossible—to speak in his name, in the name of creation, of her existence—when she is on the edge of self-doubt?

"I can't believe it, it's hard to conceive it

That you'd turn away—
Romance are you pretending—
it looks like the ending
Unless, I could have one more chance to prove, dear

My life a wreck, you're making
You know, I'm yours for just the taking
I'd gladly surrender myself to you
Body and soul"

Jonah, however, a prophet in the sense he embodies all of Israel, is like a soul fleeing its body, ending up at the bottom of the sea. But the Creator can make a request of the whale, just as he had of the man. The great fish-mammal responds, as will Jonah in the end. The first sign of that response is this psalm/song in the whale's belly: it's his soul prompting him to respond to his maker, from the belly of death.

And a great fish was waiting
the Lord had provided
to swallow Jonah

And Jonah was a long time
within the fish body
three days three nights

and Jonah prayed to the Lord
within the mothering fish body—
he prayed to his God, saying

I cried out within my despair
I called to the Lord and he answered me
I implored him within the belly of death itself

Yet he heard my voice—
I was flung into the abyss
swept into the sea's bottomless heart

Devoured by rivers
all your waves and walls of water
fell over me

And I was saying I am lost
cast away, driven out
of your presence, from before your eyes

How will I see
your holy Temple again
if I am gone?

Water was all around me
penetrating to my soul: I was almost gone
devoured by a flood

Seaweeds were tangled
around my head
I sank to the depths

I went down to the roots
of mountains
the earth shut her gates

Behind me
it was the end of the world for me
—and yet

From destruction you brought me to life
up from the pit
Lord my God

My soul was ebbing away within me
but I remembered the Lord
and my prayer came up to you

Up to your holy Temple
as if I were there
in your presence

Those who admire mists of illusion
to hide their fears
abandon the compassion of openness

But I with a thankful voice, not fearing
will make of sacrifice a thanksgiving
I will pay with gladness every vow I make

It is the Lord who delivers us
alive
he is the captain of our praises

I will pay my fare gladly
I am
his precious cargo

And the Lord spoke to the fish
and it vomited Jonah out
onto dry land.
     [Chapter 2]

Does one have to believe in a Creator to hear Jonah's song? Let's say we can believe a neurotic and depressed poet like Jonah exists, and that a whale exists. What else exists here? The sea, land, seaweed, mountains, temples, language—all these we take for granted as existing in reality, not fantasy. But Jonah, like Billie Holiday's voice, conceives "the end of the world," his ultimate nonexistence. Although Otto Rank, in *Psychology and the Soul,* says that humankind's wish for immortality has always required a version of the soul, Jonah, like secular people today, seems to have sidelined such need. Yet it's one thing to disbelieve in our extension into nonexistence and another to doubt our own existence. Can we go so far as to not believe in our existence? Of course we can, though not without a level of anxiety that equals Jonah's, as he seeks to escape "to the end of the earth". When your despair reaches that deep, you have no need for society. Jonah's anxiety about believing in the Creator's words is finally resolved in the psalm he offers within the belly of death—because you can't sing if you don't believe there's an audience. Billie Holiday in her stylings or the original Dada poets don't stop making poetry; their work intuits creation and a belief in their existence. So I would ask, Is there really much difference between belief in existence and belief in—or wish for—immortality, i.e. a soul that comes from and returns to nonexistence? When classical psychoanalyst Otto Rank answered this question, he suggested that a modernist belief in the *absence* of a soul or a Creator still contained the seed of its wish. I'd add that wishes are also prayers, poems, songs—so that all our human creations require belief, if only belief in an existence bounded by nonexistence.

I don't mean to get into a thicket of post-coital existentialist thinking here. After sex, one can feel so rejuvenated that I recall often riffing on existence while my partner fell asleep. One reason Rhonda and I knew we were soul-mates, however, is that neither of us wished to stop extending a conversation, either before or after sex, and sometimes during. So let me bring in the Reform rabbi who just edited the new High Holiday prayer-book, *Sanctuary of the Soul.* "What rabbis have had a long time coming to grips with is that Jews are a prime example of people who live and feel their lives to be secular. And our basic texts were written by people who took God's existence for granted. That is the defining issue of our age." I'm sorry, rabbi, but if you'll read my preceding paragraphs you'll understand that the difference you pose between big C and little c creation is wishful thinking. Secular creation requires a belief in existence no less taken for granted than a Creator is by biblical writers who put words in His mouth, or who speak back to Him as a representation of what's unknowable to Homo sapiens, namely the conflation of existence and nonexistence.

5.

My own secular Bible-like text as a young poet was the great six-volume anthology edited by W.H. Auden and Norman Holmes Pearson, *Poets of the English Language.* I read through it during two semesters as Robert Lowell's assistant at The New School, including half an entire semester of Lowell reading *Antony and Cleopatra*, which Auden and Holmes inserted in its entirety. Lowell loved to drawl out the names of characters before their speeches, especially Dolabella (Do la bel la) and Enobarbus (E no bar bus), so that when their speech consisted of just a phrase, the pronunciation of their names stretched even longer. Although I couldn't articulate it then, I now understand Lowell's fierce battle against silence, which in his case entailed the withdrawal into manic depression, or what we now call the bipolar pole of inertness. Sitting next to him all those weeks, reading over his shoulder, I saw evidence of the struggle in his trembling forefinger as it parsed out the text. His reading voice assigned a dire urgency to every word; even Shakespeare's endless punning was spun by Lowell into a flashing weapon. So that was my youthful community, writers still living like Lowell and those long dead, like Sextus Propertius, a Lowell favorite I imbibed through Ben Jonson's 'Propertian Elegies.' I also took in poets Philip Sidney and his sister, the Countess of Pembroke, luxuriating in their sinuous translation of the Book of Psalms, though it would take almost a decade before my attention bore through the Elizabethan Sidneys and down to the ancient Israeli poets of the Hebrew psalms. When I began to translate them, I sensed the same anxious struggle against silence that Lowell represented, the same communal tradition of biblical poets that constituted *Poets of the English Language*.

By then, however, I had joined the junior congregation of New York School poets who drew a line under Guillaume Apollinaire (1880-1918), beyond whom into the past we cared not to go. Some of us had graduated from the Black Mountain School aesthetic of breathing with and within the line, as in Robert Creeley's parallel urgency to Lowell's: lighter, however; less literally anxious, though just as tense—and even more so in Charles Olson's work. Still, it was the language itself that was tensed-up, and we NY School poets lightened it, relaxed it, as evidenced by our master, Frank O'Hara. Relaxed is probably the wrong word; it was anxious, in a sense, to catch ourselves in the act of writing, self-conscious, photo of a Homo sapiens body rather than mirror of a mind. On the surface, picturing a higher primate performing the grandiose task of writing and thinking, was often comic; underneath, however, was the tragicomedy of having no choice, a species consciousness. What else were we going to do with our hard-earned musical intelligence?

And I do not choose the word light, lightly. Lightening an understanding of a biblical verse, for instance, means disarming an overdetermined meaning and removing its layers of interpretive varnish. It's harder, in fact, to resolve or focus a biblical work than to overlay it with dense meaning; to lighten it, to translate it imaginatively, you need a vision of history that cuts through commentary, a sense of historical context. Whose vision; whose context? The author's, both the ancient one and the living one, each seated in a chair with a writing implement, each a higher primate uniquely talking back to creation—not simply in a cultural but in a species consciousness. A poet speaking to a Creator is performing a species act in writing, one that has been domesticated from acting out an anxiety of self-consciousness into holding onto it, creating a formal frame in which to consider it. "The Lord is my shepherd" begins to create a scene more natural than supernatural, one in which we can consider how we're talking and with whom, less alone in our unique species. It's a domesticated talking back to creation, just as it is in O'Hara, whose poems embody the natural, daily talking back to life. It can be the sun or it can be a friend on the phone; in either case, O'Hara's audience is both in and outside of the poem, as the Hebrew psalmist's shepherd and Lord also are.

When you get up close with the writer at his or her table, you realize that the transformative act begins in silence: writing flares up from a ground of silence, even more so than speaking, which is accompanied by the sounds of the immediate world, the ambient noise of nature and society. More than before, the modern movement became self-conscious about this silence, already a hundred years ago, as in the early Imagists and Ezra Pound. Instead of speaking to the community, the modernist poem, generally speaking, created its own community of fellow poets and readers, eventually subsumed into academe. That's where I found it, though I was still in high school and heard first the louder sound of Beat reaction. The Beats wanted to speak to the wider public anxiety about losing the soul; they amped up a tradition of modern experimentalism into public theater. It was still, however, a wrestling with silence, though it asked for a paradoxical letting go of selfhood, which can look foolish—except in the great tradition of Fools like Lear's Fool, and on up to Rimbaud and Emily Dickinson, unafraid to sound dizzy on a visionary jag. In place of society, the individual could become a metaphor of soul; belonging to the realm of nonexistence, beyond existence, the soul is oblivious to society. But how to trust the individual outside of a communal society? The Shakespearean Fool, for instance, was attached to the royal court. Yet that was the question that evoked my affinity for lost writers, whose community and culture were suppressed by later tradition. My case for the lost biblical writers could depend on their individuality because the character of their entire Hebraic culture was cut off historically from tradition. And the paradox follows: these were the writers of a Bible that is read by world-wide Jewish, Christian, and secular humanist communities. If I were a critic making that case, I could be accused of wearing Fool's motley; as a translator the charge is more dubious, for translation suggests letting go of an interposing individual self. To properly challenge me, I'd have to be accused of *mistranslating*. So I didn't wait for such closed-minded charges; I inscribed a transparent yet nevertheless rebellious translator-self. My rebellion was in favor, thereby, of biblical writers—falsely accused of being invisible—who were actually poets in rebellion against the surrounding idolatrous world. And I found myself in what I sometimes thought was a similarly counter-intuitive community of contemporary poets, found first in my '60s Toronto colleague bpNichol, for whom no literary tradition could hold authority without its own exploration of the origin of writing. Out the window went T.S. Eliot's sweeping statement that "It is in Christianity that our arts have developed," largely because Eliot not only took writing for granted but failed to explore the writers of the Hebrew Bible. I would find rebellious authorship there, from J and E to Isaiah and Ecclesiastes, including the author and character of Jonah the prophet, who was Creation's Fool: the whole world turned out to be the Creator's royal court for Jonah. There was no escape, in other words, from the counter-intuitive, from "knowledge of the unknowable," so that following Nichol I'd have to ask where in the world the Bible's words come from.

> ...and so I turned again
> blind as a hurricane
> against the sea of life
>
> where all works sink
> like jettisoned cargo
> under the lidless eyeball of the sun
>
> the whole cargo of civilization
> was a weight on my shoulders
> my life's work dead weight
>
> all life depressingly empty
> hollow as cardboard dumbbells
> in a bad circus...
> [Ecclesiastes 2:13ff]

The biblical poet here, in my interpretive translation, is a kind of Jonah exploring civilization at its edges. In the scroll or book that bears his name, Jonah's desire to escape to the end of the world—the furthest known city of Tarshish (and possibly Baudelaire's Lisbon in 'Anywhere Out of the World')—evokes a frontier. It's the same common theme you find in the golden age of screen Westerns, where an independent guy, for a myriad of reasons, was heading further west, to lose himself in California or Oregon, or like Wyatt Earp, to escape the frontier lawlessness of southwest America, Dodge City to Laredo, embodied by the mid-America cattle drive and its attendant cowboy adventures in frontier towns along the way. Usually the cowboy had a dream of one day owning a small farm or ranch, and sometimes he was enticed to settling down wherever he found himself on the frontier, rather than pushing onward. Either a gold field or a free land stake, as in Oklahoma, would entice. Post-cowpoke, consider the film of Steinbeck's *The Grapes of Wrath*, where Henry Fonda's Okie family is pushing on to California. The question embedded here—to stay or to move—haunts me: In my parents' generation, the operative word was not "move" but escape. Although they had to leave their possessions, their graveyards, their ancestral history behind, they brought with them in their heads a Jewish history that went back not to legend but to a historical land, ancient Israel, in which all their immediate travails were prefigured in ancient migrations, wars and exile, and especially in books.

My mom was educated in a liberationist Hebrew *gymnasium* in Lithuania, my father in a liberationist political movement while a student in Budapest. But they escaped to Detroit, partly because of family there, yet it also seemed easier to push westward than to settle in the turbulent frontier of the Middle East. They didn't fear losing the Bible and Jewish historical roots wherever they went—yet within a single generation it was gone. Until the late age of 28, I and all my siblings, cousins and newborn nieces and nephews, were wiped clean of Jewish historical memory. For me alone it flooded back as a fateful choice: stay where I am, as a Gertrude Stein American (for whom exile in Paris was no less American than Wyatt Earp in San Francisco) or push onward to more fertile—and fraught—underpinnings in the modern metropolitan frontier of Jerusalem. As a newly-conscious explorer of Jewish history, I still could not escape my education in Stein's *Wars I Have Seen*, the last of her several autobiographies. "You keep on thinking how quick anybody can get killed, just as quickly just as very quickly, more quickly even than in a book even much more quickly than any book." Stories and histories have context but an actual death is more shocking because there's always the question of the soul and what will or will not happen next. And if *nothing* will happen, that too is anxiety-provoking. Even Rebecca Newberger Goldstein's insight into Plato's various conceptions of the soul in her new book, *Plato at the Googleplex*, says she is "hoping to get a glimpse into the soul of the man." Speaking for herself, Goldstein is using the word soul here metaphorically, playfully, and in contemporary ironic doubt about the worth of thinking beyond death. If there's something beyond an intellectual Boot Hill, it's not in Plato's thought but in the uncanny shock that he indeed can have a soul revealed in his writing. It's the same for the newest life of modern Jerusalem, built upon literal layers of earlier iterations, and it's the same for Gertrude Stein's revelation of the flaw in literature, that no loss of life there can equal the sudden finality of a human death.

Death—and suddenly the issue of space is gone and only time remains: memory for the living, and for the dead; it's something we can think about. Thinking requires time, not space. You can do it in a coffin with a breathing hole. The Homo sapiens flaw is in our tendency to confuse fantasy with reality. We can conceive of a soul, however, as a witness to our confusion, an anxious soul. How to calm it? That's the question we've been studying since the prehistoric cave painters: those miniature animals on stone, wild but harmless there, calmed the prehistoric soul. Yet whatever fantasy of nature is played out, the prehistoric soul was no doubt witness as well to catastrophe. It may not have been until the Hebraic Garden of Eden narratives, however, that the human flaw and tragedy was dramatized for the entire species. As I reimagined it in one of the Hebraic books that preceded Genesis, *The Lost Book of Paradise,* no fantasy can elude the crushing reality of having lost the Garden. The way back has to be as clear-eyed a witness as the deathless souls of Adam and Eve.

> Adam:
> Then two worlds here, one
> the world of feelings only mine
> each thing with his own
> mirrored in his mate
> meanwhile the plants must speak to everything
> to be tended, shape their leaves to catch
> the wind and shape it with their need
> You need learn, they say, to understand us
> beings from another world
> come to inhabit
> a world of feelings as within yourself
> a tree will grow within you
> like a mother or father, and all around
> lovely trees to eat from
> and lively to the mind of man
> "Listen to the wind among leaves"
> echoes in my bones
> Each plant needs a world of others
> to find its hidden mate
> animals are already being taught at each bush
> drinking deep of nectar
> more is all they want and fly
> or walk or crawl to another flower
> These plants must be the priests of life
> also its prophets, pointing the way
> while setting a table
> and busy in their workrooms making
> the air we'll need to breathe

How do I listen to the air itself
except through the trees dangling
tongues of branches and leaves
while the hair of the grasses is ruffled
by restless winds: my breath—
the breathings of all the animals—
mimics the mothering trees.
    (*from* Chapter 24)

As Adam recalls being in the Garden—and the more he does, which is half the book—it dispels the memory of a fantasy by paralleling it to the real world. Not that his soul from deathless Eden, like our own, calmed by recalling the Garden, would be calmed for long. Once it realizes again that Eden has been lost, the soul's profound depression returns. Poetry may work for awhile, but neither lyric sublimity nor anti-poetry, which attempts to de-anesthetize the lyric with shocking cross-sections of brain content spilled into language, is going to last any longer than railroad track laid over a frozen lake that begins to thaw in spring. No, as Baudelaire reminded us in 'Anywhere Out of the World' (translated in my chapter 'The Poem of Lost Time') nothing will satisfy the soul, except perhaps talking directly to it, as in many psalms. It requires a not-feeding—the complete absence of form and content, as if having broken through it. That would be a welcome acknowledgment to the soul of its emptiness outside Eden. Of course, it's impossible; so the next best thing is dramatizing the situation of the soul—of existence and nonexistence. This superhuman effort is the best in us, like all great representation of loss and human flaw, from Bible or Sophocles, Shakespeare or Gertrude Stein, and I'll come to the latter again shortly. Meanwhile, recall Steinsaltz's one-year-old. We must talk to it as to the soul, and as if, being but one year old and without complex language, it is surprised by our intense attention. We might also recall Aristotle, or Kierkegaard's quotation of Aristotle's "fear and trembling" as the best outcome for tragedy (or "baring the soul," as we say) and some merit in catastrophe, if that can be said. The catastrophe in question is the loss of Eden to the soul, the ultimate reality, the *sine qua non* of reality.

    There's no escaping at least the surface of reality tonight, because it's Clarence Brown week on Turner Classic Movies channel. We watch Brown's profound direction of *A Woman of Affairs* (1928), where the 19th century obsession with scientific reality is still going strong (and will continue until after the Second World War, when strangeness, as in film noir or the nucleus of the atom, intrudes, as it does in our present day). Greta Garbo is betrayed in love by John Gilbert; as a result, her later husband leaps out of a high window, his best friend who's also her brother commits suicide by alcohol, and so does Greta herself, by car crash. These people take reality very seriously; it's not weird or absurd or accidental, it's hard-edged. True, Garbo has an ironic edge here, but its more existentially bleak than humorous. The direction and cinematography, however, do border on the strange: we see the characters from unusual camera angles and in almost 3-D settings, where their figures seem detached from the background. By the time of Brown's *Song of Love* (1947), a firmly 19th century biopic of Clara and Robert Schumann along with Johannes Brahms, the 20th century's primary trope for the strange—madness—is center stage. It's no longer a romantic madness, as it was in the 19th Century, but a debilitating one that suggests the flaw in the human species, our dependence on fantasy. In the end, therefore, composer Robert Schumann can't tell the difference between fantasy and reality.

Fortunately, he's institutionalized and isn't murdered or doesn't murder anyone. And his soul is "immortalized" by Clara, who promotes his music 24/7, so that her soul too is put in jeopardy by artistic fantasy. When Moses came down from the (as it were) soul-writing of the tablets, he was faced with the art of the golden cow (not calf; see Egyptian poetry or my book, *An Educated Man*) and the dance. How could you argue with it (and Aaron couldn't), this joy in fantasy. But Moses and Aaron fashioned the counter-art of the Mishkan, with an ark for the cosmic tablets that had written upon them an antidote for human fantasy, the Decalogue's Moral Law. We covet, we steal, we murder—out of our fatal flaw and fantasy—and it puts the fate of our soul in jeopardy. Clearly those tablets are not enough, hence the unfolding of the Torah and Hebrew Bible. In the Talmud, which comes later and is an effort to adjust to the reality of a flawed psyche, the Torah is used to create a template for behavior and meaning in society, one that can ameliorate the flaw and counter the fantasy in our species and society. To be more specific once again, that flaw in a nutshell is the element of fantasy in knowing what others are thinking. In psychological terms, at bottom it's the threat and fear of nonexistence, of the one-year-old's conception of murder. From castration anxiety to having in some way been responsible for a death by not preventing it, it's the child's fantasy of not being cared for enough; or, in terms of the adult, of not caring enough. Anyway, that's the beginning of it. Even psychology still has a long way to go, to assimilate our evolutionary origins in an edenic ecosystem. It's a long way back to Eden, though it's not as long a way back to the original biblical writers of the Eden story—and, as I attempted to uncover in *The Lost Book of Paradise*, back to the earlier sources used by those ancient Jerusalem writers.

6.

Except perhaps when coming from a funeral, few writers are thinking about their souls. Read any writer's professional bio and it seems we are born into it, as if the cited experience that reveals one's calling is more significant than our natal birth. I read online that Lerner has won a MacArthur grant today, good for him; if it stresses the ambitious part of me (I'm not getting younger), another part is relieved. I'm the reader, but Lerner the grant recipient will now have even less time to read, under the burden to produce work that validates this award to his ambition. I don't know Ben Lerner but I've been interested in his writing for some time. He is quoted in his newly happy state as thankful for this "like": "It takes away all your excuses to not be doing the most ambitious work," he said. "It means you don't have to take on more things. You use the money to make space for the work." It's a common sentiment among grant-winning writers, this gaining more time to write, but I've never heard one say it will buy her more time to *read*. As if that sentiment might snub the prize's purpose: to simply read and not produce product. To read—and to reflect on how mortifying it is to a soul to be trapped in existence, including such ambitious creations as literature. As I've suggested from page one, the way out, or through existence is, *pace* Socrates, to "see thyself." There is nothing in the journalistic notices to suggest Lerner can't help but not see himself *as he writes*—or preparing to write, seated at his desk, a creature who is lost in time but bound into the Homo sapiens history of tool-using, from flint to keyboard. The former no less than the latter helped a body to eat. Seated there, by campfire or backlight, the creature may think of, or even know itself, yet fail to see how time has other plans for it. That it ages minutely is put out of mind; all that counts is what consciousness can bring to bear on the task at hand, namely to please that compartment of the mind we used to call self-deprecatingly "useful."

Ever since the first scribes in the Indus Valley, however, writers have worried they are not as productive as other artisans, and are poorly compensated as such. Ben expresses this in his forthcoming book, *The Hatred of Poetry*, which is quoted from on Amazon (the book itself being many months from publication) as his attempt "to explain the noble failure at the heart of every truly great and truly horrible poem: the impulse to launch the experience of an individual into a timeless communal existence." Well said, my soul might respond—that is, well said for an existential or postmodern evocation of the absence of soul, and thereby making for it a useful place in our current literature, if not in society in general. But I would answer how that timeless existence to which Lerner alludes, or what more specifically we may call nonexistence, already exists, as it were, in us—so that we don't have to be launched toward it. It is the biblical soul that causes the failure of poems because it is misnamed the heart. I would rephrase Lerner to read "the noble failure in every great poem is the impulse to override our soul—our representative of nonexistence—as if we completely exist. What can be more poignant, more sublime, more

Shakespearian (in, for instance, new King Hal's rexdom), than to wish for our complete existence. No, the soul reminds us, the part of us that came from and will return to nonexistence is always with us.

It is to Lerner's credit that he would not deny this, which is what makes him more comic a writer than tragic. His characters are often depressives but their circumstances are self-conscious and potentially hilarious—unlike those in which suicides Josef Roth or Walter Benjamin found themselves in imploding Europe, their works taking on a tragic dimension. We doubt that either could have written poems in the '30s that weren't bleak, if they could write them at all. However, if we already live in a poem, which is the biblical perspective, it's more important to read than write, which is why Jewish scholarship is so heavily weighted toward interpretation. Hebrew poems until the modern era were most likely to be *readings* of biblical and post-biblical Hebraic works. Furthermore, the poem in which we live is a failed one, it goes without saying, holding a mirror to Eden or Mt. Sinai at best. Adam and Eve were created noble but I don't know how noble was their wish to be completely knowledgable of their situation. Can we call the loss of the Garden noble? We can, of course—which is why we are gifted with irony.

What our writing poets must fail at is to recreate a connection with the soul, a connection that is severed by worldliness. That's the situation. Plenty biblical writers were worldly, if not all, but they lived within the poem of Creation, so that their ironies implicated the soullessness in a worldly rejection of Creation. In the cosmic poetry found in the Bible, or in Dante and Blake, or in neo-visionaries like Stevens and Ashbery, the communal existence we share on earth and in visionary literature is already a poem which the writer recognizes as a cosmic creation that one can only fail at imitating, though one can succeed at dramatizing this larger human situation. That means for us today, as once held true for the ancient biblical poets, we need to engage and retranslate our sources. I started with Rimbaud as source of the modern and was propelled back to the Bible. John Ashbery, still writing today, also starts with Baudelaire and Rimbaud, but the noble failure encoded in his poems is one that takes consciousness for a text. Were his work to be typical, we might find only the absence of soul in it. But its visionary quality allows us to hear the soul ambiently, in its often hysteric (and hysterical) clash with existence.

News of Limmud Jerusalem comes today, a city-wide seminar over several days, with hundreds of classes and workshops that study Jewish texts, history, and politics of all streams. Such Limmuds, which derives from the word study, have been held in cities around the world, a Jewish semi-antithesis to Christian prayer gatherings. It's what's missing, however, that crushes my spirit: the original writers of the Bible, most of them working right there in Jerusalem, go unmentioned—as if a conference in

Athens on the Western canon failed to mention an ancient Greek writer; no Homer, no Sophocles and Sappho, no Plato and Aristotle. Acknowledging the speculative nature of Bible authorship is hardly an excuse, since study of biblical sources has a long history, yet that is the excuse proffered, that it's too complex and scholarly a study for the general public. "Who wrote the Book of Jonah (and in what Jerusalem neighborhood)?" is too hard a question to ask? Too imaginative a question? And yet we're offered self-consciously creative classes at Limmud Jerusalem in 'Teshuvah, Drugs and Rock and Roll,' 'The Rabbi, the Teacher and the Vibrator,' and 'Approaching Troubling Torah Texts.' What troubles me in the latter is not the "troubling" texts but the focus upon them as disembodied *texts*, bereft of authorship. Can't the fundamentalists in the class suspend their disbelief in human authorship for even an hour? And can't the atheists and secular humanists in the class suspend their disbelief in the Jewish cosmic theater of a divine 'Shema Yisrael' (Hear O Israel) for an hour? For if we're to hear words of the Bible's poetry in human language, then certainly the authors matter. Yet where's the thought of a Jewish culture in which such poets and historians were educated? Instead, we have a class in 'Jerusalem Culture' where "three key players in the cultural scene of Jerusalem will discuss how the city's distinctive demographics, history and atmosphere influence what is created here"—without a mention of the original key players, the writers who made the word "Jerusalem" a world-wide touchstone. There's also a class in 'Art as Resistance,' i.e. art-making in concentration camps. What about making art in the literal world we all can feel trapped in, either by mortality or human fantasy?

However, Ray Kurzweil, director of engineering at Google, believes we'll be able to upload our entire brains to computers within the next thirty years. And then, our "fragile" human body parts will be replaced by machines by the turn of the century. According to Google, "we" would run on a kind of software for consciousness; reports *Huffington Post*: 'The first company that develops mindware will have [as much success as] a thousand Googles." And further: "We do need a body, our intelligence is directed towards a body but it doesn't have to be this frail, biological body that is subject to all kinds of failure modes." A sadness inherent in such news is its non-awareness of the loss, the terrific loss of history. Oh, it's all still there in the brain, Google might answer; but it's there for mere *access* rather than internalizing. "What internalizing? That's old stuff, going back to a soul encased in a body." I'm writing this with a half-eaten slice of pizza at my side, at an outdoor table of a strip mall: "The Visiting Vet" sign flashes catty-corner, where the late "Professor Zorro Buber," our cat, was caged for a week during a hurricane, ten years ago. He comes back to me as I write and then is gone. Or wait—as I smell the pizza and consider another bite, he is still with me, intrepid sniffer of all that he surveyed. He may survive in my brain, but what of feral cats; is someone going to download their brains and replace their organs? I realize how easy it is to satirize Kurzweil by bringing nature to bear, as in the missing complexity of a wild ecosystem, another order of complex over a brain. But what about sexuality; can we imagine a poetry of the future without the problems of sexuality, let alone minus soul?

Actually, I'm reintroducing sexuality here and now, in the form of what I'd call orgasmic thinking, in which writing is an artifact to be framed and distanced, as in a museum—so that we become more aware of ourselves doing the looking and the writer-artist seated at a scene of creation. That would be too fancy a wish, anyway; the reality is artists overload their work with conscious intention—with pointing, that is, to the fact of the art. Hey look, it's art—rather than it's work, a job. Does a salesman stand in front of his sample cases and say look, I'm a salesman? A fishmonger in front of his dead fish displayed in a glass case, saying hey, this is fishmongering. No, the artist and writer have a job like anyone else. They should be able to go home like anyone else and have a private sex life, or even an ambivalent one, even post-Google. The same for ancient biblical writers. Although human history and a speaking Creator were big subjects, they were rarely as preciously grandiose as those back in my high school creative writing scene, with its semi-tragic dead bird and dead dog poems. "My dead bird carcass was flattened to the pavement like a charcoal drawing..." etc. Now it's a cliché that can be dissed in every university writing workshop. The only birds in my own workshops, the ones I was a student in and the ones I later taught, were accidental signs of nature in the linguistic complex—jay-walking, pigeon-toed, duck (your head) etc.—not accidents of gross human intrusion in the natural landscape. Or actually, yes, linguistic intrusion. Either way, something gets lost: birdsong! The one accompanying my waking this morn, our chimney-top mocking-bird, recently returned from up north. You can't stop listening for when his/her song-loop begins, yet I couldn't find it; among the various birdcalls she recorded is the screech of tires but it didn't seem to come round again. Instead, sound of an ice cream truck jingle! One that she must have picked up in Atlanta. No more ice cream trucks around here—an awareness I would have lost, save for mockingbird. It was the same for the poetry of creation in the Bible: the biblical writer held on to an awareness of being a created creature in most every chapter. One way he or she might have accomplished that was by having internalized the connection between creation and Creation. You won't be able to google that; Creation requires a real mockingbird, wild, free. And (if her complex song were considered human) wildly neurotic.

Rhonda sends me a link to an article and asks, faux plaintively, "How neurotic are we?" Another semi-psychological study in the *Times*, saying neurosis breeds imaginative work. This, based on the false romantic assumption that artists (and children), including writers, need imagination above all else. It's the difference between what makes an artist vs a scientist. But no; unread, I'm ready to argue with it. There's no difference between artist and scientist. Further, imagination is at the bottom of the list of qualities and in most cases needs to be restrained, not encouraged. What does make a serious writer or scientist is the drive to explore, interrogate, and experiment, even if it's all done in the mind. Within her territory, however, the same applies to Louise, our young cat. Besides eating and grooming, she is exploring her surroundings daily, as if something new might be discovered. It often is, from butterflies and opossums to rain puddles. Yesterday Rhonda brought home a large plastic ice chest in case of a hurricane. Since the first thing to go would be power, soon the food in the fridge would rot if not transferred to the ice chest. Now, Louise can't know all this, she's just one and a half, hasn't experienced a hurricane before. She explores the chest to find it's inert and hollow inside, which she determines by jumping in. She interrogates it: What can you hide in there beside yourself? She brings one of her dead toy mousies in. Then she experiments by jumping out and walking off disinterestedly. Soon she jumps back in, retrieves the mousie in her teeth, and jumps out. Some misguided folks would call this a game, or imaginative play, yet it's more serious than that. She needs to be in control of her territory and this new object elicits an interrogation of her whole world, by virtue of its usefulness. She discovers you can put something dead in there and take it out, that it will remain in place. And when we do have to use it ourselves, she won't be surprised. And that's how a poem gets constructed by a human. You find a provisional form; it can change, depending on how much space is in it. Is there enough room for all of you to jump inside? Can you bring in a familiar object?— here's the only part where imagination comes in, since that object is in your mind, as in a love object or things that remind one of death. Will it all hold?—try removing your lover as an experiment, see what happens. Reading/experiencing the poem will tell you something about your whole world, your life's territory, and not just what's in the poem. Now finally, we can walk through these three steps—explore, interrogate, experiment—for a scientist rather than a poet. The difference is minimal.

I'm translating a poem that turns into a car whose motor's gone dead on the railway tracks while a train is bearing down, whistle screaming. In the seat beside me, Rhonda says life is great if you smell the roses by the tracks… "Rosenberg, wake up!" Those roses were in a dream, in my brain, while Rosenberg is in the world. The work I am actually translating is like that dream; it's as if in my brain and I'm trying to make it alive again, in the world of my language. Although he wonderfully dramatized it, Oliver Sacks had a more conventional view: he said we see with both our eyes and our brains, and then he called the brain-seeing, imagination. Where we disagree is I'm disinclined to privilege imagination. You have to translate the brain's work just like a literary work, for it's dead within the brain, shaped by a dead language like the plot of a dream, and I must make it live again in my language. I fear Sacks, like conventional wisdom, is still anti-Freudian; it, conventional wisdom, doesn't want to face why Freud recognized that we are not dream-tellers but dream *translators*, and that we can learn much about ourselves from the nature of the translation. His seminal book, *The Interpretation of Dreams*, often cited as the most influential book of the 20th Century (though an argument ensues over whether it is a scientific masterpiece or a literary one) puts the emphasis on interpreting or translating the dream in order to enliven it. The "it" is basically a lost thing, to be found in translation. If I don't have Russian, *Anna Karenina* is lost to me unless I have a translation. Anyone can learn a human language, even an obscure one spoken by a tribe of indigenous forest people, but inner brain-language is lost within an individual until it's translated. So what if that individual itself is lost? We have a translation, say in ancient Hebrew, but it's my contention we don't have a living translation unless we recognize the writers. Instead of their ineffable imaginations, I want to insist we privilege their physical brains and acknowledge that they lived and breathed no different than ourselves. Then, the task becomes one of enlivening these writers in our own language. We already have, in the English King James version, a great translation of the *text* of the Hebrew Bible, or *Tanakh*, as it's called in Hebrew. It's still just a text, however, without writers: dreams without dreamers.

Considering "officialese" used by politicians, a pundit on Israeli TV last night (via US access) ticked off various other jargons, including one he called "Tanakhy," by which he intended a certain Bible-sound, for instance the equivalent of Elizabethan-sounding language to us today. But there was no such thing as Elizabethan-sound in Shakespeare's day, nor did his writings sound like Ben Jonson's or like the Psalms translations of the Countess of Pembroke—all of them Elizabethans. It's the same for Tanakh, only more so, since here we're talking about centuries and not decades in which most of the writers are ignored or erased. So let's imagine the pundit was blasé enough to mean anything having to do with the larger context of creation or a cosmic perspective. For instance: "I believe that God is (and must be) a transcendent presence in any worthy work of art." Those are the words of US fiction writer Joy Williams, not known for religion. The latest NYT profile calls Williams a "misanthropic genius" who is "one of the greatest chroniclers of humanity's insignificance." According to the *Times*, Williams "sounds the alarm for literature itself, [because it is] doggedly focused, as Saul Bellow wrote, on 'the human family as it is.'" Her words are "a call to arms for a new kind of literature, one Williams sounds doubtful that anyone, including she, can write, due to contemporary language's inability to cope with the grandeur and tragedy of the natural world."

Accounting for Williams' wicked humor, why doesn't it occur to her or her profiler to step back for a cosmic view—if not biblical, at least considering the prehistoric cave painters? True, we don't have the language of the early Homo sapiens, but everyone has a Bible nearby, no farther than the nearest bookstore, synagogue or church. The grandeur and tragedy of the natural world is what Adam and Eve face after leaving the Garden, as do their progeny up to the tragic First Century A.D. Other religions have their later cosmic texts but I'm focused on Jewish books, where the Creator's presence does not sit so easily transcendent, as Williams may or may not know. I've found the uncomfortable power of her stories in their vortex of absent transcendence, hope for it so utterly missed that they suggest nervy Jewish books, from the Bible's *Job* to Isaac Bashevis Singer's *The Family Moskat*. For contemporary literature to find the language Williams imagines can cope with cosmic joy and tragedy, the ongoing struggle with his absence since the death of God in the 19th Century will have to be heightened. Darwin and Freud have yet to be surpassed in literary art, though many, like the Franzes, Franz Kafka or Jonathan Franzen, have paralleled them. Struggling with translation of the Bible is what came to me—but only after many years of ironic toying with its cosmic absence.

Zaydeh's disappointment in America startled his sons and daughters. I hardly noticed, of course, taking in his joy in Jewish books, but my mom and her four elder brothers (and her sister locked behind the Iron Curtain) had no time for Jewish history. In Zaydeh's cosmic equation, "no time" equalled no memory. And no window for the soul. They had no time for Singer or Kafka either; that fell to me.

I Know that You're Dead, but I Still Worry About You is the title of an online and unfortunately pedestrian memoir of grieving for a deceased spouse, five years after. The posthumous worry is funny because of what it suggests about those we care about who are alive. I may worry about friends, relations, colleagues—and writing projects. Seven years after publication of a book, I still worry about how I let it be altered by editors from a literary work to a "general reader's" volume. I had to, in order to keep my six-figure advance, which allowed me to write more literary works after. Yet the original literary form of that compromised work still lives in my nervous system and I worry that its unhappiness affects what I feel today. If that sounds like I'm worrying about myself, in fact much that I do is an effort to set that book free. Three decades ago, an analyst with whom I worked might have said it's a repetition of my fear of abandonment, projected onto the book. In other words, it *is* me I worry about—except it's a me long ago deceased in early childhood, whose little body is still carried around internally. When I think about him, that body was abandoned by Zaydeh when I was 6 and he allowed my parents to pull me out of yeshiva school and send me to the secular jungle of public school. He would still live another couple years, but once in public school I no longer spoke Yiddish and I saw that he withdrew almost completely into his books. The main book, of course, remained the Bible, though it could be reshaped in different books appropriate to the time and season: *Siddur, Machzor, Chumash,* et.al. When I ask myself, I see that he had no choice but to abandon me: I was singing "She'll Be Coming 'Round the Mountain When She Comes" in school assembly, instead of "Hinei Matov U'Manayim" (Psalm 121: "How much better to sit here together as brothers..."). I was lost to cowboy six-gun pop culture instead of three thousand years of focus on how to satisfy the soul. It came down to allies, of whom he had none in house or neighborhood. Like King Lear, he no longer controlled his finances to where he could pay for my private yeshiva school. I don't know if he wandered the heath—he still had his books. Passed his age now, I see I've let go of my colleagues, contacting them less and less. It was always an effort, anyway; I was the one involved with this *mishegas* that smelled like religion—which to friends was like bullfighting. Why bother? What we had in common were careers and art and the struggles of the writing life, not bulls. How could I explain it was not a bull, it was a canary? A canary in the mine of dark questions: Who or what is in control of creation? Why did Zaydeh have to abandon me (my father for WWII I understood)? Could I reach the point of self-control where I could abandon my inner child—and abandon him without guilt? Finally, knowing that at some point I will abandon my whole life for the grave, why not become the happy abandoner?

If, before we're born, the soul waits for us to exist, it is best apprehended as a place for waiting. And what is longing but an anxious waiting? And where but in the margins of all we're capable of perceiving, as if the fourth witness to our existence, after memory, thought, and feelings. The poem of the soul is thereby a view from the margin, at the edge of non-existence. It waits there, for poets to find. In any case, it is waiting for something to happen; it may have already happened, perhaps many times, but it didn't make an imprint in memory. Perhaps there's nowhere to find it in the world, except in the far margin, the one just beyond what we consider a margin worth inspecting. Certain great artists look there, occasionally, or imagine the looking, within their works. What they may glimpse is the soul, but it has no way of being apprehended by the senses, it is simply waiting. What must happen to move it is... or rather, it is constantly moved, every moment that we exist, but it is waiting for us to be aware of it, of the place it is.

From the standpoint of the soul, all that it sees through the medium of its physical host is a grand performance, the workings of time and space intertwined, exploring each other, creating and deconstructing beings, ecosystems and landscapes. The soul may be the ultimate observer, the ideal of human omniscience—different than the gods, not seeing the future but simply of holding a place for the prophetic imagination, a high point. After all, distance is the ideal vantage from which to encompass reality, but even that ideal requires a "standpoint," a place in which one cannot see oneself. From the standpoint of the moon, the earth is a glowing ball... but one must physically be somewhere, as on the moon, to say this. Then there is the human imagination, where we can say that the earth is actually a square but its corners are physically invisible, etc. Still, we are talking about reality here, the one into which we are born and die but once. Religions can use the metaphors of dying and being reborn endlessly, but that is precisely why they are called faiths rather than sciences. They are like poems, and their closest approximation/approach to us is the soul.

7.

Lee Harwood, the esteemed British avant-garde poet, a friend I may have abandoned (or vice versa) died last week. His poems were a mainstay in my poetry magazine, *The Ant's Forefoot*, for several years in the late '60s. In 1970, while sharing a house near the U of Essex where we were graduate students, the poet Paul Evans and I began a series of chapbooks, *Voiceprint* Editions, under university auspices. The last title, in '71, was Lee's, a translation of father-of-Dada Tristan Tzara's poems, *Destroyed Days*. I'm reminded of it as I look again in Lee's *Collected Poems*, where even the most serious matter became "the lightness of the hollow bones in a bird's skeleton," said August Kleinzahler in *London Review of Books*, a very Dada reduction. By comparison, Lee himself could write:

> "The orchestra had to be slaughtered—they put everyone's nerves on edge. It was only through luck that Stravinsky escaped. That would be funnier if it was a joke. Insanity is always terrifying and illogical in its own logic."
> [from 'The Nine Death Ships']

It's hard to think of Dada disconnected from the 20th century's world wars ("At this crowded exhibit, war is never far from the picture," wrote Robert Polito of MoMA's major Dada exhibition in '06) but even here, in Harwood's disembodied voice, the light logic of slaughtering the orchestra presents a psychosis subverted by art (art = "joke") and Stravinsky's talent for dissonance. Yet "you are struck by the delicacy, even the sweetness of much Dada," wrote Polito, and it was the same lightness subverting grave danger that I first sought to translate in the original Hebrew psalms, at the same time as Harwood was translating Tzara.

you set a table before me
in the presence of my enemies
you give me grace to speak

to quiet them
to be full with humanness
to be warm in my soul's lightness

These stanzas from the 23rd Psalm evidence my desire to lift the primitive-sounding previous translations of it to the level that Tristan Tzara (née Samuel Rosenstock) accorded African art. One of his final public activities took place in 1962, when he attended the International Congress on African Culture, but all his life he'd worked to imbue so-called primitive art with the highest aesthetic. A famous researcher of Yiddish literature, Salomon Schulman, argued that the combined influence of Yiddish folklore and Hasidic philosophy in Tzara's youth shaped his style, while the literary historian George Călinescu wrote that Tzara's "early poems deal with the voluptuous strong scents of rural life, typical among Jews compressed into ghettos." Whether ghetto-bound or African, Tzara distilled strong scents into the perfume of Dada, driving European art insane and revealing how its competing nationalisms "shit in different colors so as to adorn the zoo of art with all the flags of all the consulates." It was modern Europe that had embodied its own slander of the primitive. Of course, not all Europe took this lightly. A Fascist colleague of Ezra Pound attacked Tzara as a representative of the "Judaic spirit," and another critic charged that Tzara's "visions of social change continued to be inspired by Arthur Rimbaud."

It hadn't occurred to me, when I was translating Rimbaud in the late '60s before turning to Hebrew psalms, that he was a social critic, nor did it occur to Lee Harwood when translating Tzara. We responded instead to the sweet tossing of conventional poetics into the air and lightening them of overdetermined historical burdens. Tzara, who once stated that "logic is always false" and that it failed to comprehend a "final dissolution"—or nonexistence, as Gertrude Stein would have suggested—was in line with Rhonda's psychoanalytic probing of science: it can't account for fantasy, not even the fantasies to which logicians are prone. We're glad that Kant pushed fantasy out of the philosophical picture, but Kant the human being, and not simply the mind, had to expend human psychic energy to repress at least those of his fantasies that might have hampered his work.

Harwood lets the fantasy back in, though just enough, and through his own work making of Tzara a figure of species consciousness, one for whom the seeming absurdity of Homo sapiens is actually a revelation of unbridled fantasy. That is, our flaw extends into the fantasy of logic—a logic that admits no fantasy at all. Freud recognizes it as our civilized lives

lived as post-modern witnesses of the fleeing soul. How to catch it—that
too a question for the ancient Biblical writer:

...I was desolate and empty
he had gone
my heart leapt from my breast

I ran to the door
my soul overwhelmed me
my hands were drenched, as if with perfume

it was my love for him—
the lock was wet with the myrrh
of my devotion

I opened for my love
I alone was open to him
but he had gone

the one for whom I trembled
heard it from my lips
how I had turned from him when

I thought I was alone—
suddenly my soul no longer knew me
just as I had forgotten him

I was riveted with anxiety
I was as lifeless as an empty robe
I couldn't move

my feet were a statue's feet
I was lifeless clay
I was naked earth

then I wandered through the streets
looking for signs of his nearness
seeing nothing

I called, I cried
desperate for his closeness
hearing only silence

only my enemies heard me, like watchmen
patrolling my city's walls
who found me in night gown

who saw me vulnerable and alone
who struck me down
I was wounded for my distraction

my robe my dignity stripped away
I could not even pray
my heart was in my mouth

but now, nations of the world, I warn you
when you see my love
when you turn toward Jerusalem

you will say I bore all for him
the pain and loss was for him
I was his to the core

"But what makes your love any better than ours
what makes you so beautiful
that he leaves you, and you search for him?

How is your love better than any other
that you stoop from your ivory tower
daring to warn us?"
     [*from* Chapter 5, *Song of Songs*]

Tristan Tzara was focused on the fantasy-life of nationalities, yet wished to be rid of them via an extracurricular socialist idealism, as if layers of history could be tossed off like bedcovers. The biblical *Shir* (Song) was far too lost in history—though it was right there for him in his Jewish childhood. To lose history was like losing your memory and that was Zaydeh's despair for his children in America as well as cause for Tzara's absurdism. His mother tongue in Romania was Yiddish, an echo of it heard later in the black humor of his poems, for Yiddish was a language of an impossible exile—going back two thousand years. It is peppered with biblical Hebrew quotations, syntax, turns of phrase. It reflects a domestication of exile if ever there was, and I think Harwood's translations of Tzara—but especially Harwood's own poems—are a kind of domesticated Dada, softened into a lighter vein, though at the same time stronger for their accommodation of a postwar life.

We could say that Tzara and all moderns had exile internalized; Tzara, for instance, coming too early to consider an end to his exile with the recovery of Hebrew in Israel. That is, if any non-Israeli moderns, then or now, are Bible-conscious. Likewise, the modern and postmodern commitment to exploring consciousness as if it was a post-exilic territory left no room for interest in Eden, the cosmic home on earth where consciousness was once at one with creation. Call it at home too with nonexistence, for there was no birth and death in Eden to demarcate a human consciousness. The Hebrew of my Zaydeh, however, still contained a connection to Eden via the soul, most clearly in the midrashic and kabbalistic books depicting the soul's yearning to return to *Gan Eden*. In modern existential terms, it's a soul looking through our brief, tenuous lives—as were my grandparents' lives, on the edge of extermination yet with an ancestral connection to the Garden representing home: the world in which our species first opened their eyes and were unafraid.

This knowledge came back to me when noting a teensy scandal in the poetry world last week, where the pseudonym "Yi-Fen Chou" got a poet published more easily as a minority Chinese-American than as the white guy he actually was. Although hardly as ambitious as the critiques of authorship embodied in the pseudonymous Japanese poet Araki Yasusada's books in the '90s and early aughts, the fate of Yi-Fen Chou quickly became an urgent meditation by *Atlantic* online that "raised hard questions for editors, writers and readers: How important is an author to the meaning of a poem?" No poet is likely to use "Anonymous" as a pseudonym, however, since it has no identity-cachet at all. Still, we're expected to be happy with that for the hundreds of Biblical writers—that way, we don't have to identify them as Jewish, to say the least. So how important is it to know the origins of a poem or a species, whether J's re-imagining of Eden in Genesis or the latest Homo erectus/ Homo sapiens link suggesting where we first opened our human eyes? I've long argued that this is much more than an Identity question, which is all that concerns those commenting on last week's pseudonymous little poem. It's a cosmic question even in Darwinian terms: All those who derided Darwin's animal genealogy for humans were no less grandiosely dangerous than those who claim today that it's insignificant how the Garden of Eden history/story got written. Unlike the disciples of Rabbi Jesus, there was no one taking notes in Eden, nor do we have the textual knowledge of bones and fossils. Yet the words come down to us in a language, Hebrew, that served a complex culture of poets and scholars—to say it's of no importance is like saying Jesus is of no importance, or Darwin and Einstein. It's precisely by probing Einstein's mind and imagination that we continue to learn more of what time might mean. And Zaydeh had his version of J in the context of Moses as a writer/historian; telling him that an author of Genesis was insignificant would be as meat-headed as claiming that we should be satisfied with an attribution of anonymous primitives, which is what the anti-Semitic German Bible scholars in the preceding two centuries suggested in their Documentary Hypothesis. Several "strands" or authorships were differentiated in Genesis and other books, denoted by initials, as in J or E, but no Jewish author—or any author for that matter—was to be reckoned as a flesh-and-blood writer.

To return to our invisible elephant in the room: "How important is an author to the meaning of a poem?" I'd say it comes down to the soul. Since the modern view tends to discount the soul, a writer can seem superfluous. Yet only the writer has a soul, not the medium he's writing on and not a disembodied text. Sure, a text can seem to have a heart, passionate or not, but its soul is obscured by the entanglements of language. The reader may have a heartfelt response, but a reader of such an overdetermined text may also be unaware of her soul's predicament. How is it to see through the aleph-bet to the corresponding soul of the writer—if no writer at his writing table is acknowledged? Zaydeh might have felt the hand of Moses moving in the latter's desert tent, even as I sense the breathing of a Deuteronomist, D. So that even with the mere initial J, I'm granting permission for my soul to peek between the letters of the text and imagine the bodily writer confronting my own soul's embodied writer. For souls don't write, themselves; neither do texts. But let *me*, your author, change your text's tone for a moment, no differently than when J transcribed the exchange between Sarah and her Creator.

Bearing on the subject of those pseudonymous initials J, E, and the rest, "SB" is the Hollywood starlet who conducted interviews with me in the 2000s. In addition to acting classes, she was taking night courses in philosophy/religion at UCLA and freelancing for the literary mag that commissioned the interviews. I've integrated some outtakes into this book; the following one came in the middle of an appraisal of Marilyn Monroe's art.

DR—...Too many academic scholars hate the Marilyn Monroe stereotype, and I'm their Marilyn nightmare. I can't read the rules because I forgot my contacts, you know? They can't tell if I'm winging it or really have the lines down to a tee, so they'll just make up lies. Slander is easy for the authorities: you just say it with authority, that's all that's required. For instance, an academic scholar reviewing *A Literary Bible* writes, "he just makes these subjective assertions without any evidence." It's plain to see I have several introductions and appended essays, but intended readers of this review are not going to ever look in the book. They're busy minding their p's and q's. The reviewing scholar doesn't have to engage my arguments, because they enervate him—and enervation leads to passion, passion to subjectivity... Now the charge of "subjective assertions" will be projected outward onto me.

SB—What is the Documentary Hypothesis? Is it a full-length documentary with subtitles?

DR—Great to hear that question because it's hardly ever asked. Too many assume it's already been disproven, or partly so, like Darwin's "theory" of evolution. You can't see an animal evolve and in the same way can't see the original authors of the Bible. That is, you can witness the results, the different styles—but they're like fashion to dowdy scholars, mere clothes. However, the text of the Hebrew Bible is made up of the clothes, so you can tell earlier from later writers by what's in fashion for them, what's old-fashioned. Men in the 20th century generally wear ties; men in an earlier century sport ruffs or ascots. Since you can't tell a lot about the author from the clothes he wears, you tend to dismiss him. When I asserted along with Bloom that the author called J was a woman, that really opened some eyes, because nobody had thought about what women wore three thousand years ago, especially educated women at the royal court.

SB—Let me get this straight: Is it sort of like a costume drama documentary?

DR—Exactly! That's what it is for many academic scholars, only there are no bodies in the clothes. Pretty weird, no?

SB—Not even mannequins?

DR—No. It's got to be weird for academics to swallow it. After a while, it seems almost normal, so then they have to weird it up again with linguistic skeletons and academic fashionistas who worship a great designer like Vidal Sassoon or Yves St. Laurent—they'll call this designer-type an editor or "redactor." Yet even these redactors are not flesh-and-blood but rather ghosts—you could call them ghostwriters, since in academic biblical theory today they stand in for the real writers. Actually, it's even weirder than that, because the original writers are sometimes referred to as makers of mosaics. That means they didn't really write anything, just pieced together stuff they took from "oral tradition," aka "campfire tales." So in this way the writers are not only marginalized but swept under the carpet.

SB—But aren't they Jewish writers? I can understand why the carpet if they were pagans or Christians, but why would they deny ancient Jewish writers? I mean, the same thing happens to Hollywood film writers, nobody even remembers their names, but if Russian critics were theorizing about our movies, I hope they wouldn't deny the writers were American.

DR—Terrific. I think you've hit on the nub. Many academic scholars just don't want the writers to be too Jewish. These critics and scholars, even in Europe and Israel, are secularists. They think religions can't be even-handed, though the secularists themselves are biased in favor of ghosts and ghostwriters. No joke. That's why they switch the subject as fast as they can to purely textual matters. Since they have no physical "evidence" for the flesh-and-blood writers, let's talk about their clothes and fashion statements, they say. That's something we can tell from the way the words hang together, they say. The words are the clothes and in place of styles they call their fashions "genres." There's oracles and laments, legends and songs, etcetera. And behind it all is a big fashion show called a "vorlage." That's where all the genres got mixed together, one big mash-up.

SB—It's funny because we're fashion conscious in LA, but it's all about who wore what, not what is what, not what for it's own sake.

DR—And that raises an interesting question. Here in Miami we're mostly stuck in our embarrassing short pants and wretchedly simple sandals. Only the bathing suits are high fashion. Ancient Jerusalem was probably like that, sans the bathing suits. No doubt there were Egyptian styles and Babylonian styles, but Jerusalem styles? Judean fashions? The writers in Jerusalem, where most of the Bible was written, were less into literary fashions than literary imagination, pure and simple. That's why the Bible is so rich in narrative and poetry; there may also have been accounts of gorgeous Egyptian sphinxes or colorful Babylonian wall friezes, but they had to be left behind, just like the Egyptian province of Goshen and Abraham's Ur.

In his book *Charisma* (2007) the late Philip Rieff argues that we've replaced a charismatic culture with a therapeutic one: the latter desires to rub out the former with the irony of a deeper memory. But it's the ancient cosmic theater of the Bible that first embeds the oldest Homo sapiens memory of being born as a unique species. I've addressed it for many decades and Rieff denotes it in his chapters 'Covenant and Charisma' and 'Prophetic Charisma': We're now failing to suspend disbelief in our cosmic origins and earthly imperfection, compounded by science as it explains away our species' tragic flaw. According to the social sciences, for instance, it's the civilizing process where our flaws may lie, and that problem could be ameliorated by further study. But in the biblical cosmic theater, the Garden of Eden represents the wish for a social fix as fantasy. Acquiring such knowledge over our mortality—or eating from the Tree of Good and Evil—is to ignore the nature of our species as limited.

Since 20th century culture tends to vitiate the charismatic poetry in the Hebrew Bible, we view Genesis ironically; the deadly flaw of original sin is reduced to the strange. And that extends contemporaneously to the mad psyches of Hitler, Stalin, Mao, *et. al.* and, in caricature, their zombie-like followers. I argued with Rieff one 1990s summer in Jerusalem; I grandiosely claimed that charisma might make a comeback when it becomes domesticated by a historical, species-conscious awareness. Those weeks of conversation, when Rieff and I had adjoining rooms in the urban art colony *Mishkenot Sha'Ananim*, were formative for me, putting an exclamation point on my drive to reimagine the historical writers behind biblical text. Were they, the writers themselves, charismatic in their day, like a Tolstoy or Twain? I doubted it; it's hard enough to write history and poetry in private, let alone with acolytes at your feet. And once biblical text itself became charismatic and even sacred, memory of the original writers could be dispensed with—as easily as ghost writers. Yet ghost writers, like any other kind, are historical; they exist in time, and if we go back for them as scientifically and imaginatively as we can, we get a new cultural adventure that takes some strangeness out of strange and returns a cosmic (or to be edgy, species-conscious) sensibility to the arts.

Rieff, who had just delivered the Martin Buber Centennial lecture, humored me: "I'm afraid it's too late for an ironic impersonation of Bible-centric Buber. He's secure in the Jewish pantheon and you're so insecure in the American one that you barely find an audience. I think your *The Book of J* was a blockbuster because the public thought it so strange and humorous, not historical. If you continue to insist J was a woman you'll disenchant the ironists, embitter the scholars, and turn off the general readers, who don't really want to entertain a female authorship; they just wanted a good joke." Not surprisingly, Rieff proved prophetic, and it was modern women in particular, including women scholars, who seemed indifferent to the possibility of educated female writers in ancient Jerusalem. For how were they to identify with J when her texts formed the backbone of a patriarchal tradition they wanted to eclipse? Yet there it was, the pre-21st Century problem in a nutshell: the problem of with whom to identity. We're on the way past that now, I would have argued with Rieff; on the way to a new century's comfort with rethinking any epoch as if it were our own—and more comfortable with the understanding that the minds of the original Homo sapiens explorers, a hundred thousand years ago, are not a whit inferior to our own. But I couldn't articulate this for Rieff back in the '90s. He was just putting the finishing touches on his three-volume masterwork, *Sacred Order / Social Order: My Life Among the Deathworks*. By "deathworks" he meant the unrestrained desire of writers in the 20th century to remove morality from its charismatic hold on human aspiration; in short, to ironize morality if not savage it. Even science gets into the picture, by virtue of explaining morality away as a social adaptation, though it does so with less humor and probing strangeness than modern and postmodern literary writers. Only Freud gets a pass from Rieff, in his *Freud: The Mind of a Moralist*, where he turns out to be a paragon of the misunderstood writer, i.e. a kind of rejected biblical prophet. Unlike Jonah, however, Freud didn't run from anything, though it's not hard to see how his ideas were swallowed by the great whale of Western culture, to be vomited out in often misunderstood forms. I wasn't thinking of Jonah when I translated his book, I was worried about myself as Jonah's psalm interpreter: Was Jonah my internalized father-figure that I had to let go of? How to accomplish this, how to spit out the wound and nurture dad's memory back to health? It was as if he was the plant shading me in the desert—but how long could you depend on a plant?

> And then, the sun already shining
> the Lord had provided a desert east wind
> blistering
> and the sun grew fierce, attacking
> Jonah's head, he was falling
> into a daze, wishing he was dead
> already, saying
> for me it is a good thing to be dead
>
> And the Lord said to Jonah
> can it be a good thing
> that you are hurt so deeply
> and because the castor-oil plant
> no longer can shade you?
> and Jonah was saying
> it is a good thing to be hurt deeply
> until I am dead like it
>
> And the Lord said: *you*
> may feel compassion, may identify
> with the castor-oil plant
> for which you did not labor

to bring here, did not provide for its growing
into a great plant—a sudden child of a night
yet in any one night it could be gone...
(*from* Chapter 4)

I'd have to let my soul speak, which I found in the next book I encountered,
Ecclesiastes, where it was as if the soul from outside existence was speaking
of my father:

rain has fallen on the history books
and the sun bleached it dry
for the new generations

which are endless in number
as were the ones preceding him
and for both alike he is unknown

the living page of his time
bled white out of memory
another page lost in the sea of the present

where even the beautiful craft
of inspired imagination
have their sails reduced to tatters

and their vain hopes discolored
like old photos
by the vague tears of sentiment

the memory of that star
like any moment of triumph or despair
is cut loose from the mooring of its time

adrift like a lifeless raft
after an explosion
after the countless explosions of moments

and the photos a living mind has made
in fits of hope or doubt
forgotten utterly as the sounds

of shutters clicking open
spoken words
a wind has blown away.
    (VIII: 4:13ff)

9.

Still in the shadow of mainstream novelists, Gertrude Stein, whose many autobiographies, biographies, and intellectual memoirs could be considered postmodern novels (*Four in America, Wars I Have Seen, The Geographical History of America, Ida*) presents the antithesis of Saul Bellow's soul behind bars. In her narratives the soul speaks, and the personality as well as the conventions of language struggle to get out of the way. And yet she steals a march on writers whose theme and variations on the absence of soul are still at the forefront. How could the soul's absence possibly trouble the soul itself?—which is why her narration is so gallingly exuberant and vivacious. Meanwhile, Bellow's harder-edge irony is still our own, having bubbled up into pop culture in the form of Jon Stewart and his successors, who allow those who can't think for themselves to feel that thinking is less necessary than exposing the seeming absence of thought. Either way, thinking or it's absence, it can only be given it's proper weight when confronted with the soul in modern exile, from Proust and Kafka to Bellow and Joy Williams. I'd call it a Jewish exile, in the tradition of Gershom Scholem, although the current haut historian of Kabbalah, Moshe Idel, still refuses to accept it. After lunch one day in the Hebrew University faculty lounge on Mt. Scopus, we walked over to the newly built Mormon campus to consider its view of Jewish history, as represented in its lobby models of Jerusalem cityscapes through the centuries. But I was stuck at the first one, the Jerusalem of Solomon's Temple and the royal palace archives. The main street leading to that royal library, lined with shops and teahouses, was empty—where was everybody? I realized the Mormons were at a loss to represent the ancient Israeli intelligentsia. According to folk tradition, the only intellectuals who could read and write were priests and officious scribes. Yet the royal family alone numbered in the hundreds, and it's impossible to pretend they were not educated. Who educated them, along with the thousands who made up the literate class? Even if a million were partially illiterate, the educated and civil servants would have flooded that empty ancient street with its shops for writing supplies and cultural artifacts. It's not only the Mormons who did not know how to populate that street with Jewish intellectuals; religious and historical traditions of all stripes shy away from it. As I was still expressing dismay, Moshe Idel laughed. "Today no one is illiterate and everyone in the street has an educated opinion," he said. "Maybe that empty

Jerusalem street of long ago signifies something purer, with more emphasis on the spiritual than the social." I didn't have a comeback for Moshe at the time, but soon after, when I began my biography of the first historical Jew, Abraham of Ur, I was determined to explore the origins of Jewish writers (certainly Abraham was educated and his son Isaac, as an adult, would have kept the family history written down). Of course, I'm imagining, but unlike that empty main street of ancient Jerusalem, the scrolls of ancient Israel are teeming with words that have been honed by hundreds of original writers, and pored over by hundreds more of ancient scholars and historians.

Down to its first written strands in Jerusalem and Samaria, the Hebrew Bible is, by current standards, strangely postmodern—too much so for the modernists, which is why it was so often ignored in the 20th century. What gave it a postmodern sensibility in ancient centuries was the way it took mainstream myth and rendered it newly and ironically self-conscious, mining it for history and realistic drama. The historical Abram of Ur was fleshed out, turning the legendary aspects of Abraham and Sarah into humans you could identify with. And even though she is intent upon elucidating modernism and her writing remains strange to most, Gertrude Stein may have been precursor of a 21st-Century sensibility. In *Wars I Have Seen*, Stein elevates a common trope in her day of characterizing decades, such as the "Gay Nineties" and the "Roaring Twenties," by attributing qualities to centuries. The Nineteenth Century progresses from romanticism to realism by her trope, including realistic novels, reportage, and science: Dostoevsky, Tolstoy, Dickens, Melville, Darwin. That century's hopes for realism extended into the Twentieth, from "The War to End All Wars" to institutional socialism and communism. The 19th century began falling apart, however, with Stream of Consciousness, Cubism, and Dada: a progression from the real to the strange. 20th century culture goes on to abstraction and the uncanniness of psychoanalysis, so that even today our leading thinkers and poets domesticate the strange (Ashbery still writes). It was long ago packaged for academe in the '80s, when the late philosopher Jean Baudrillard explained how "the distinction between reality and representation vanishes. There is only the simulation, and originality becomes a totally meaningless concept." It seems no one told Baudrillard he was unoriginal. Besides, he merely noted a return of the absurd, from repressed Dada earlier in the century. Now it's domesticated, some of it hilarious and even poignantly despairing, when it's not strangled by political theory.

The obvious question, then, is what will emerge as the dominant quality of the 21st century? In my own work it turns into the neo-historical: an understanding that no instance in spacetime is lost, although Homo sapiens, like any species, has a limited history. No longer can we get by with characterizing the "prehistoric," as in the 19th century, or the weird and mad in the 20th. Now, we are lost in time only to the extent that we've lost the wonder of thinking and invention that the first humans deployed. Neo-historically speaking, I find traces of that sensibility, in terms of civilization and art, in the revelatory account of the universe on Mt. Sinai. It says we have progressed from Adam and Eve mainly in our ability to study the past, in which we've discovered that there's a moral law within natural law, as there is a soul within the body. What to do with such knowledge? In the Jewish history that's come down to us, it's mostly writing and study of what morality can or cannot mean, and how the soul represents all that's unknowable to our species, expanding our physical cosmos within the poetry of a created one. That cosmos spoke to us in early myth and, later, in the biblical study of myth, as the Bible's poet-historians distilled the historical from myth. But not simply boiled down to "fact"; they still needed the poetry of a cosmic theater in which our creaturely history can be imaginatively restored, flaw and all.

So what does that portend for the quality of my 21st century? It suggests our dominant art can be one of restoration—parallel to the science of restoring endangered ecosystems along with discovering them on other planets. For me, that's a life of restoring the historical culture in which the Hebraic writers of the Bible lived and worked. Since an avant-garde remaking of the word "historical" is going to take time in this new century and no doubt sow confusion, I like to use the term species consciousness in its place. It reminds me that the present is already historical when we take the next breath, making us artifacts of the present. To focus on breathing is to encounter the world as another species does, even as a tree does through its leaves and roots, and to find yourself in it, like a mouse in a mouse-hole when a cat sniffs it, or like myself through the eyes of a domesticated species like Louise, a cat, who, when she seduces me into playing hide-and-seek, honors my interior life, though I doubt she shares the human fantasy of imagining she knows what another is thinking. No fantasy, however, in our having a consciousness of being created like all species have been, though perhaps uniquely aware of it, and of having a connection to nonexistence called the soul.

Here's what that's worth according to Zaydeh, who acted it out ritually rather than articulating it, as I do. When we die our souls return to their home in nonexistence. That is, in the Jewish understanding, to the Garden of Eden, which no longer exists except in poetry. That's my version, giving voice to my grandfather. King David had his history of the *Mishkan*, in the sanctuary in the Sinai wilderness, where the nonexistence of former slaves became hallowed; and we have our history of the Civil War, after which former slaves became a *raison d'être*. Sinai and Appomattox are history, unlike Eden, but souls do not return there. In our lives too, souls resonate only to poetry, horrific tragedy or sublime comedy: the great poetry written in the shadow of Mt. Sinai and the great African-American music from spiritual to jazz and soul. And all the written progeny down through time, from Jonah and Psalms to Whitman and Zora Neale Hurston. But my soul doesn't thrill to hear this; it rejects grandiosity. It's just as content with the irony of being denied or laughed out of existence—because a soul's power to shock us, in the inarticulate babble at death's door or baby's birth, remains intact. The charisma of birth and death belongs to the soul, our non-existence before and after life, a force of personality we know best by its absence. In poetry and history, it resonates as uncanny.

Even without the mythic, or consciousness of the soul's connection to nonexistence, we try not to be shocked by death. Not long ago, the cherished neuroscientist and writer, Oliver Sacks, facing death, contemplated a Jewish Sabbath without Creation—and hence without the unknowable, without a stress on the limitations of species consciousness. Instead, in a final publication, it's as if the Hebrew Bible, which goes unmentioned in his *Times* article, does not have greater themes and poetry than an ironic "one may, in good conscience, rest."

"I find my thoughts drifting to the Sabbath, the day of rest, the seventh day of the week, and perhaps the seventh day of one's life as well, when one can feel that one's work is done, and one may, in good conscience, rest."

When I was a child and afraid I'd never know rest if I became like my father, whose recovery took two years, I was glad to grow up and find work that could be done with the mind and not with my back. My father, a stretcher-bearing medic, came home after the war to live in the VA hospital for over a year. I was scared to look at him when mom and I visited, he was so pale and gaunt. Even later, after he was home, mom and I "stood" (her Yiddish locution) in the Hotel Orion on the beach in Port Stanley, while dad remained home, first recuperating, then working. I was fearful every night, sleeping in the narrow hotel bed with mom; she was such a large bundle of nerves and emotions that I had to somehow care for by being a good, attentive boy. But I was taking my father's place with her, in what psychologists call an "Oedipal victory." I did and did not want to be in this position: I wanted my mother to myself but I also resented being responsible for her. Yes, she cared for me, took care of me in my physical and social needs, but she also worried a great deal about my safety, more than I worried about hers. First-born, I had this gorgeous young woman all to myself, for awhile. Dad got better, my brother was born, and it was all a receding memory by the time I was five or six. Such first semi-nightmares, however, are indelible. In mom, I had a woman by my side way before I was ready. Later, I was comforted by the ease with which I found girlfriends, but when the time came to really know them I was lost.

Knowing Zaydeh, however, saved me. In his old age, mom took care of him too, in the bedroom next to mine. He showed me how to treat her as if she was a grown-up child: reassure her by pretending to know exactly how to grow up. Zaydeh wasn't pretending. Having learned to care for his endangered soul on earth within the Jewish cosmic theater, his body was easier to manage; he was a creature at peace with other creatures, even though most of the others were unaware of being created and were anxious in their skins. I was such a one, but knowing Zaydeh allowed me to understand that the world in its essence was unknowable to a human creature, that relationships were fraught, yet the more you studied it, the more you were at home in the universe. He didn't mean "study" the way his six surviving children would understand it, by getting ahead in business. Only I, apparently, learned from him that his study and prayer were forms of cosmic poetry.

Of course, my aunts and uncles were 19th century realists. Their dire reality in Europe required that they save themselves and leave their mother and father's cosmic poetry behind. But Zaydeh and Bubbeh came too, into the strangeness of the 20th, so that I might find the thread. We are born into a literal history, as I see it, that can only be fully interpreted with the history of poetry, including the Bible and the prehistoric cave paintings. It's not simply the history of our birth weight or family history, not that of city or country, culture or religion, not that of our era or century, not that of our species or genus, not that of our planet or star or galaxy. We are born into the universe at a specific time, so that all that went before is history, and all that is to come is another history to add on. I used to think "my" history was different because it was open to change, but it turns out all history is changeable with the power of interpretation. We can get it right or wrong, or in between.

In the same way that a disinterested outsider might miss all this, the majority of secular readers of Zaydeh's texts—the Bible being the one most well-known—miss the complexity of its poetic composition. This includes especially the academic scholars for whom divine authorship and divine inspiration has been reduced to pseudo-divine text—a divinity of textuality. Here's one example of the kind of thing that drove me to rebellion: misapprehension of names, whether of people, peoples, or towns. I was told that my name, David, meant "beloved," but then most other names were just as soporific, like Isaac, "someone laughed." Whole tales seemed to be built around the names of wells, villages, groves, burial sites, and mountains. Upon closer inspection, however, these names were occasions for authorial punning that we've lost the references to—though known to the original audiences. It's not a matter of simply one pun, but a whole series on many layers, spun out into the wordplay that typifies ancient Hebrew in particular, but all ancient languages as well. Here's what we lose: Let's posit a character journeying to the city of New York—what does it mean? What is a york? Even delving into the OED, I assume few know. As a writer for whom the story is cosmic, I'll tell you what I think:

york meant dawn to the Stonehengers, hence our character is journeying to a new dawn. As a poet-scholar, like the crucial Bible writers, I'm free to play upon what I think. And to be more specific, I'll explain that it used to be called New Amsterdam, and we know what that means. Amster is a wall, and dam is a hole. New Hole in the Wall is what it was, but we are now in the story of a new dawn...

You might think the pun on hole in the wall is too egregious for the Bible, but there are many that are yet more exotic. To start with, the name of God is pun-filled throughout the Bible, including the inescapable one of its ineffability, and the life-threatening one were it to be pronounced. He has answered Moses that his name is "I am that I am," a punning etymology for Yahweh. He's also know in a perhaps more devastating pun as Elohim, the plural for gods—among other names as well. To strengthen the ineffable pun, the name Yahweh is pronounced in Hebrew, in one variation, "Adonai," which means our Lord, just as it does in English. Yet in both languages, a lord is a common term, as in landlord. If the Creator is our landlord, it's an appellation too marvelously subtle for most of us. Even more common, lord can be a cute diminutive, as in Little Lord Fauntleroy.

The western outer wall around the ancient Jewish Temple is all that is left of the Creator's physical connection with Earth, and yet neither He nor Israel remains daunted. His Son, pronounced as the biblical Joshua among Jews of his day (it translates as Jesus in the Greek) never connected to any other land or people than Israel, yet He gained a Vatican in Rome. The stories spun out of names in the Bible are legion, but my point is that their echoes are largely lost, along with their original referents. The biblical writers were serious about history but if they didn't know the Sumerian derivation of a word or name they could make an imaginative guess. As old as the city of Jerusalem is, long before the birth of King David its name had a Sumerian root, the "foundation" of Salem. But the same consonants for Salem could be used to spell "Shalom," peace (and more simply, hello or goodbye), hence "City of Peace." Whether or not the original biblical writer knew the Sumerian root, he preferred to deepen the echoes of the name, and not because he wished to erase the earlier history; on the contrary, his early Hebraic audience would probably have known that history. Or not— just as we today are innocent of the meaning of New York.

What is the purpose of poetry, if I may continue to ask? I'd begin again by suggesting that it teaches us how to live in a poem, as my complexly-pious grandparents did. You could turn it around and say the purpose of life is a poem. Not only a journey through time, from birth to death, or through the stations and roles we assumed, or a journey to knowledge. Instead, a poem for which no explanation, however brilliant or nuanced, is a final answer. Could this just be another way of posing an ancient riddle-poem and getting a poetic, sphinx-like answer from the oracle? Or could it be the suggestion that a poem is like a prayer in a cosmic context, with faith or hope or despair underlying its lack of need for an audible response—not from a God and not from a silent reader?

One way to consider it is as a Poem of Holding On to a Thought. Of course, thoughts can't be nailed permanently to the mind, but we invent all sorts of ways to keep them close. For instance, we may attach them to an object or a sentient being, so when we notice our household cat each day we're reminded of that thought—that life is dangerous, that we don't have nine lives. Or we could sew a thought into a homily over the fireplace: "a penny saved is a penny earned." Still, thoughts don't stay put, our minds are a flowing river, just like our bodies changing and aging in time. Holding on to a thought, however, considered as a poem, would mean that there were places for the thought to move or hide among or behind other thoughts and yet always be there when we read or remember the poem, sort of like quantum mechanics, where indeterminacy resembles a physics poem. Whenever I remember that I live in a cosmic poem, the thought comes back to me that I am a created creature. Somehow this always calms me; it allows me to feel that I'm not responsible for everything, something else shares my body's commitment to time and space.

There can be similar thoughts, but no two poems are exactly alike. They are tiny universes: at one glance, a star of apprehension flares up, but at a further glance, another star or word takes on new significance. Look too long at any star and the meaning can drain away—"to be or not to be" can become a burnt-out cliche. Then, if we pull back, reconsider the context, and rediscover Hamlet himself, he appears as knotty as a poem within a poem. The psychoanalyst Adam Phillips spends much of his book, *Missing Out*, on getting at the difference between "getting it," as in the pursuit of knowledge, and "not getting it"—as in a poem. In other words, if you "get" a poem you're missing something, assuming of course that it's a good poem. What are you missing? The soul, the indeterminate—to our physical apprehension—soul. After all the ironies of meaning, sound and rhetoric, a poem or prayer without its wordplay comes down to the missing soul. If the author can remove the clothes of wordplay and help us sense what's missing, it's there, as in a moving poem or prayer: all the richness of existing that language can allow for is only as good as our sensing the nonexistence that frames our physical life. I extend "poem" and "prayer" here to Zaydeh's weekly passages of Biblical dialogue between man and Creator, as well as the internal dialogue of Talmud he meditated upon. The soul here luxuriates in its witness of imagined eternity. But it also must enjoy the imagining of its absence, as in our modern arts. My dad, from a less pious tradition, went from synagogue to Gypsy violin Budapest coffeehouse—and like the Blues channeling Gospel, Gypsy bands channeled Jewish folk klezmer, at least it did so for dad. He was lost in Detroit culture, pouring the absence of Hungarian coffeehouse into suburban chess club meets, but I recreated his youthful music obsession in weekend late nights in the black neighborhood's Baker's Lounge. Its live Blues and Jazz expressed the soul's sublime absence, evoking the clipped wings of a secular angelology. Earthbound technology and science can hypothesize about nonexistence, from the innards of black holes to downloaded brains, but it's the absence of a cosmic theater in poetry and poetic historical narrative that can still remind us of what's missing and stir our dispassionate soul. James Agee's *A Death in the Family* did that for me in high school. Now, seeing again the '63 film based on it, *All The Way Home*, I'm struck how at that late date it could still ask us to sympathize with those who take a Judeo-Christian (plenty of "God" but no Jesus) cosmic theater for granted. The movie, in its pious mistranslation of Agee's prose, is more ironic than it intends. "Why is papa here?" the boy cries beside the casket. "You said he was in heaven." Jean Simmons explains to her young son in 1915 that it's not papa in the casket, just a likeness to remind us of him. "His soul is in heaven." This is the only mention of a soul in the entire film and the moment quickly passes. No question about it from the boy or anyone else. Heaven, on the other hand, oft-mentioned, is a happy realm that takes the place of all that's unknowable about life and death while covering over the deepest dread. There is no apparent interest in knowing anything more about it; the priest has only mumbly words to offer. No Judaic cosmic stage on which great questions of grief and loss can be biblically dramatized; no presence of a cosmic Jesus to feel close by, to talk to. Although the boy would not yet understand our species-long traditions of acknowledging death and loss, his confusion mirrors our own modern absence of a cosmic home. Our lives are basically a road movie, our family life an off-Broadway medicine show that runs for decades, a la *The Fantasticks*. Jean Simmons, in her halting attempt to translate eternity into a child's understanding stands for our own loss of a believable translation of cosmic meaning. And just as the boy can become distracted by things to do, so are we in our secular world, until an Agee or an Art Tatum reminds us—happily as in heaven—of the absence of soul.

10.

Rhonda has come home from the bookstore with *Black Earth*, a new Holocaust study by an Ivy League historian. She's ambivalent about it, first because we're trying to downsize our overflowing physical library by preferring e-books, and second, because she was upset, upon a cursory reading, by the author's intrusive political ideology. "Am I right?" she asks me, about the undercurrent of distaste for Israeli politics, possibly unconscious to the author. She's got post-its on pages the author deploys an academic microscope on Polish-Jewish prewar relations—in order, Rhonda underlines three times on her post-it, to re-focus some of Israel's old Polish-born leaders as "national terrorists," even though it has been a trendy commonplace of Israel-bashing for years. Yet Rhonda's generous nature is worried—for, as much as about—the author's unconscious; he seems unable to name a psychosis although he's passionate and powerful in describing the European one that engulfed the 20th century. Further, a blurb describes the author as "now our most distinguished historian of evil," although he appears not only psychologically-challenged but metaphysically as well. If human nature is susceptible to murder, anti-Semitism and bestiality, as the author warns, then it always has been. The book, however, is as weak on religion as on depth psychology—especially so on Judaism. There's no historical insight of the kind that might recognize the fountainhead of Jewish books, the Torah, as a healthy though neurotic reaction to ancient Israel's experience, oppressed by the state-sponsored religious fantasies of Egypt and Mesopotamia. Much of the latter—as later under the equivalent ideological fantasies of Hitler and Stalin—was psychotic. Neurosis can be a salubrious reaction in that case, perhaps the only feasible adjustment to a murderous reality. According to *Black Earth: The Holocaust as History and Warning*, Hitler could not stand the Eden story in Genesis because, along with Judaism, it perpetrated the lie that "all humans are created equal." Not to mention, Thou Shalt Not Murder. That last commandment may contain a neurotic hope: if one must kill in order not to be killed, then the overcoming of anti-Semitism requires a self-defense of cosmic proportions, as in imagining the Creator's co-authoring of the Ten Commandments with the Jewish Moses. At the least, call that neurotic hope a sound basis for moral living.

A new global crisis will aid anti-Semitism, says *Black Earth*'s author, because it unleashes free-floating anxiety. In turn, a mental state tending toward psychosis is desperate for consensus and fears its resistance, among whom the Jews are usually found to be the ultimate demonic destabilizer. Nazis simply called this resistance "cosmopolitism," but the book can't quite articulate its source as a mental state. "It's trying to," Rhonda says. "The author appears to be heroic for taking stands. But he doesn't know himself; he leans too hard, maybe unconsciously, on his political ideology." Jewish history is sidelined, perhaps also unconsciously, argues Rhonda, while there's a suggestion that Holocaust memory-projects might be more neurotic than necessary. How? Memorials are too much concerned with remembering the victims instead of the perpetrators; only by understanding the genocidal perpetrators of past and future can we hope to be realistic. So goes the book's objectification of history, a realism too fanatic in Rhonda's eyes, especially when the book insists the psychic disease of anti-Semitism is but one instance of human madness—as if such insistence is healthy in a book *about the Holocaust*. Better to be a bit neurotic, or even paranoid, than claiming relative health for a study of the Homo sapiens creature—when that creature is known to be inherently flawed. Of course, you can't be healthily neurotic either if you're not in possession of the brutal facts facing you, so in that sense *Black Earth* and other Holocaust histories are necessary. There's never enough to think about when it comes to humanity's tragic flaw, and that flaw has always been best faced with the consciousness of neurosis we call irony. *Black Earth* is plenty ironic but doesn't want to or isn't able to admit it. That's been my literary theme in my disquisition on the soul, the necessity of irony, yet Rhonda points out how doubly ironic is the book *Black Earth*, in that its highly paranoid author is unaware of his justifiable paranoia. I worry about him. He says it's all about reactionary politics and our need to understand it, but he also says that Hitler was "in certain ways a madman." Those are the marks of paranoia: fearing psychosis yet saying it's all rational if we can just understand the political dynamics. I hope he has a good therapist, says Rhonda. No, he doesn't, I reply. "How do you know?" I read the Acknowledgments pages, where lots of help is appreciated, yet no one resembling a therapist and no Bible-related assistance is apparent. The man is unconscious of his soul. He fears another Holocaust could be around the corner, due to global warming and "the politics of ecological panic," yet when he ticks off a long list of "disturbing," additional flash points, including China, Russia, "a United States where citizens sometimes deny climate change"—three states, by the way, he considers rational—he fails to mention Iran, as if theocratic Iran is among the "stable states" that are nobody's nightmare. It's hard to believe there is no dread of Iran in his soul (in later interviews he corrects that impression). The soul is not neurotic. And since it's unable to take flight from its human host's psychosis and fantasy it is frozen in horror by threats from the Supreme Leader—or it would be, if we didn't calm it with our neurotic Western books, built upon the grand ironies and imperfect idealisms of Genesis, such as those, post-Eden, culminating in the Decalogue. *Black Earth* continues that necessity, even as it marginalizes its Jewish sources, from a neurotic Adam (self-involved, he fails to notice Eve's openness to experiment) to a neurosis-hunting Freud.

The author does, nevertheless, provide an epigraph that quotes the late Israeli poet, Zelda, who was as Biblically-rooted as they come. "Every man has a name/ Given by the stars/ Given by his neighbors." It's the second line here that invokes the Creator's words—"Your seed multiplied/ immeasurable as the stars in the sky… for it was you who listened/ and heard my voice"—spoken to Abraham, a promise of many in place of the one son, Isaac, he feared to lose, within the nightmare dream of sacrifice.

Although the soul has no such need of a name, unlike every Jewish descendant of Abraham, it recognizes the nightmare.

"The Jews were not simply prisoners like Marxists and POWs, they were Homo sapiens deemed unfitting and to be cast out of not just society but Homo sapiens history." That sentence comes from an earlier chapter of mine, and though it could have come from *Black Earth* it reminds me now of the recent discovery of *Homo naledi*, a pre-human species that buries its dead ceremonially. These people appear to be aware of nonexistence—of an abyss of time through which their dead are carried to further life. It holds true for ancient Egyptian mummies too: we today are that ironic further life, the receivers of Homo naledi skeletons three million years later—and their revivers, in Homo sapiens thought. Of course, they'd be surprised to discover that we too are existential, that we still know not much more than the Bible of nonexistence and the soul. If these prehistoric people were to be found alive, would we fear them as the Jews were feared by Hitler—as people whose belief in equality of the races negated Hitler's own, which *Black Earth* remarkably succeeds in driving home? Only we'd need to ask Homo naledi, who lived at a time when several other Homo species co-existed, if the word "species" could supplant the word "races". Did they rage to unnecessarily murder fellow species? And if not—if they were as well-adjusted to reality and as non-psychotic as most wild animals—would they not be horror-struck by the Twentieth Century? Surely our human souls have been.

The Poem of Audience

After the midterm elections, Obama is now understood by some to be presiding over a lame duck administration. Everyone knows that "lame duck" is a political cliché and does not impugn the president personally. And yet, as we watched the nightly news from Israel on the international cable channel, they used the Hebrew term, which, when translated into the English subtitles, reads "limping duck." If lame duck were a term in the Bible's text, that's how I might also translate it, "limping duck," because it enlivens the original usage by the biblical writer. I may assume that writer is not cliché-ridden, based upon his or her acute ear for anachronisms, officialese, and other clichés. But after thousands of years of commentary, we don't see the limping anymore, just as we do not think of the writers. Furthermore, the biblical text has come down to us over-invested with signification and under-imbued with context. Every word or phrase is expected to have a life and death reverberation.

"What do your poems say about death?" I once was asked. "It's not for me to say," I answered. "Who then?" "That's where poetry comes in, the art of stepping aside, along with our grandiose need for truth-telling, and letting the unknown speak, and in the case of cosmic poetry, the unknowable. This can take the form of imagining a creator more omniscient than myself, as in this chapter of the poet behind First Isaiah:

> It was the year King Uzziah
> died and the year
> I saw the Lord
>
> as if sitting in a chair
> the true throne
> as it was very high
>
> so high
> the train
> of his robe flowed down
>
> to fill the Temple
> where I was standing
> the sanctuary
>
> seraphic beings burning
> shone around him
> six wings

each had six wings
two covering the face
enfolding it

two covering the torso
and enfolding the sex
of its body

and two unfolded
in space
flying

and each was calling
to each other
and the words were saying

a chorale   a fugue
an endlessly unfolding
hymn

Holy   Holy   Holy
is the Lord   beyond
all that is

and filling the world
with the substance of light
unfolding creation

the doors the windows the foundation
were shaken
moved by each voice calling

singing out
and the House was filling
with white smoke

clouds
and I heard myself
I was saying

Oh my God!
this is the end of me
my lips are a man's...

Or the problem becomes who it is, beyond your personality, that's ultimately speaking, so that it takes the form of representing the unknowable (what is beyond the limits of our human species) by language itself: the endless complexity behind even the simplest statement when the context changes, a multiplicity of contexts. Any moment can entail a shift in context. Yet the comedic avant-garde poet Cathy Park Hong takes exception to the desire of her colleagues to push context to the brink, knock any particular "I" off its pedestal, and pose pure consciousness in the place of a particular Asian self like hers in America, which still feels constrained by racism:

> "But even in their best efforts in erasure, in complete transcription, in total paratactic scrambling, there is always a subject—and beyond that, the specter of the author's visage—and that specter is never, no matter how vigorous the erasure, raceless."

Concerning that last word "raceless" (and we shouldn't be put off by "paratactic"—just press or google) I would pose the ancient Judaic authors of the Bible, similarly erased of identity by the reverse avant-garde of biblical scholarship, in accord with tradition (except that tradition actually retains the placeholder of flesh-and-blood authorship, ascribing the writing of the Hebrew Bible to biblical characters, from David and Solomon to Isaiah and Jonah).

But I don't mean to go on like this, as if I could be writing an essay in the field of poetics. Meanwhile, already I've shifted context and might continue by planting simply the word "field" with any number of puns. Puns are crucial to poetry, not just by their use but by resisting their usage when they most suggest themselves. It's the same with images of the Creator, which is why the most common image is nothing more than a pun, picturing an old guy rather than one in the vigor of youth. The original Hebraic pun, of course, was vigorous in its irony, in that it lent to this aged figure a protean creativity, as if old men make the best and most fecund lovers. Actually, no picture-taking of the Creator was allowed.

Psychoanalysts who've lost the thread of Freud's great ironies have a bee in their bonnets about this Creator. They hate even the word, in any context, such as "creative" writing, because it may reference the writer as creator, small-c notwithstanding. But it's impossible in the end to avoid, because the mere avoidance entails its suggestion. You could become a mathematician, I suppose, but sooner or later you're going to have to explain yourself creatively, if only to your wife. Or to the love of your life, as Dante does to Beatrice throughout his *Paradiso*.

So let me keep it simple, like the divide between public and private. A poem, once it's published or even merely heard, is public, and its meaning or lack thereof a legitimate area of inquiry. But when I've written a poem, though not yet decided it's finished and may come back to it later, it's still private, unborn. Next, I finish it. Next, I publish it. And yet, unlike any other means of knowing, it retains a measure of privacy, even though I'm now on the outside looking in, just like any other reader. So to whom, or to what, does it retain its privacy, its indeterminacy of meaning? It comes down to the issue of borders, the border between public and private in this case, which at any moment, in any context, might suddenly shift. It's a border you can't ultimately fix, although you can appreciate it. That's what a poem allows you, to appreciate a border you can't nail down, inasmuch as the appreciation itself is private. You can admire the rhyme and rhetoric of a Shakespearean sonnet, but none of it will answer the question: To what end?

That is a private matter that is objectified, or made public, in most human endeavors, including creative writing. Except in a poem. Who does the poem serve, what audience? This may be obvious if the poem is serving a political or erotic end, but even there we can ask: Is the poem serving that end or betraying it? Because if it is obvious, it has already betrayed its privacy: the poet is revealed to be self-serving and the poem's privacy will be lost. The poem of Isaiah's that I quote from above can be ripped out of context and used by anyone's politics or religion, but in itself the poem contains words and imagery, rhetoric and rhymes that effect a larger echo of mental rhymes with other poems and other histories. So that's why its privacy must be taken for granted, to the extent we come away with a grateful recognition of how much the poem exudes an awe and respect for privacy itself. Because if we fail the poem and consign it to the public cultural noise of whatever themes or imagery it suggests, then the nutrient threads into history and memory are drowned out. This may not have been the case for Isaiah's public readings of his prophecy-poems or even the public occasional poems of Tennyson, yet the writing of them, when they are good, still evoke a scene of writing where the poet is alone with his interior voice. It's hardly any different for the most avant-garde conceptual poem today, where the word "conceived" may be interchangeable with "written". However conceived, the poem still must proceed line by line, or word by word, with the poet listening. "The poet listening," then, is key to the poem's audience, as it takes place in a scene of writing, poet at her table. I would say it's the soul's listening, as I've posed elsewhere in 'The Poem of Zaydeh's Soul.'

"S.B.", let me remind you, is the Hollywood starlet who conducted interviews with me on these subjects in the 2000s. In addition to acting classes, she was taking night courses in philosophy/religion at UCLA and freelancing for the literary mag that commissioned the interview. Before SB asked me about "soul," or anything else, I queried her about where she was in her acting career. What follows is another excerpt that didn't make it to publication, this one again touching upon soul, revelation, and the poet's interior voice as having a cosmic parallel, an internalized Creator.

SB: I was called for an audition of a Shirley Temple remake—I was supposed to play Shirley as a twenty-something who's lost her charm and has to go on in name only. They said if you get the part you have to put on some pounds, pretend to be nearsighted, and act like a prima donna. I never was that so I wasn't sure what it meant. They said come in early tomorrow and watch a few old Shirley Temple movies with some other girls and then we'll audition in the afternoon. So that's what I think you meant by a professional historian, right? Someone who wants to do a remake?

DR: Historians and journalists, Syd. The journalists have to write a story out of some new facts and appending yesterday's contextual paragraphs, but they don't have to worry about having told the same old story, decade after decade. You can read an item about Afghanistan and then go back forty or a hundred years in the archives and read the same story in *Pravda* about the Soviet adventure or in a London paper about the colonial army. For today, however, there's no such thing as a remake because everything has to pretend to be new. So it's a different "pretend" factor; the pretense of being new versus, for the professional historian, the pretense of reinhabiting the old. Actually no, the historian and journalist are about the same. The historian also pretends his history is "new" by virtue of some new facts he's drummed up. Here's an example for Bible class: There's the young biblical scholar who claims Abraham really killed Isaac in the earliest account and that's why you hardly see anything about Isaac as a grown man.

SB: I don't know, in Hollywood nobody is ever "really" killed. So maybe it's the same in the Bible, because if it was real than it's really old news, the same old violence. It's only on the local TV news that people are getting killed every day so it's never new. You turn it on every night and you expect people to be killed. If one day no one is killed or injured it's a shock—what happened, you think. It's maybe a shock like that when Isaac's father doesn't kill him. Unless the Bible really is like Hollywood and nobody here's seen the original that the remake is based on.

DR: Great idea, Syd, you picked up on my "original writers" agenda. And even if the "original" was five years ago—not three thousand, as in the Bible's case—nobody remembers, because the actual film original is almost always a silent film. Just about everything after 1930 was a remake. Within a few years in the 1930s, the silents were like ancient history.

SB: Yeah, really ancient history. When some old woman is pointed out as a famous silent-movie star, I can hardly believe it, I'm in total awe, like seeing a Civil War widow. The silents are older than the Bible to me. So is that what you mean about the Bible? That it's too old to have writers like we have today?

DR: No, a writer is a writer, just like a silent-film actor is an actor. The silents had writers too, and before there were movies there were writers of plays and stories. But yes, you're right, scholars think of the Bible like the silent era in reverse. The characters could speak, even God could speak, but the writers didn't have voices. Though that's just a small part of it. The whole cultural era of silent films doesn't seem to exist, like the biblical writers. Great authors exist in the same epoch, like Homer then, and like Joyce and Proust in the twenties, and great composers like Stravinsky, great nonfiction writers like Freud and Wittgenstein—but they seem to exist in a world apart from silent films, as if writers have nothing to do with it.

SB: I get it. Like writers have nothing to do with the Bible.

DR: Correct! It's like the original that the remakes are based on: nobody want's to think about it. Actually, those that read the Bible usually don't want to know about the originals it is made up of, the original writers.

SB: The ones God spoke to? But why did he stop speaking? After Jesus, I mean.

DR: That's a more important question than you may think. And so is the answer: It's because there are no more translators of revelation. What is a revelation, you ask? It's like if the silents start talking—*before* the invention of talkies. Once you get talkies and color, you start to expect the advances, like Todd-A-O, 3D, Imax and holograms. But back in the silent era, the expectation was you only needed to read what the character says. And the *revelation* was that you almost knew what he would say before the dialogue card appeared; you saw the lips moving first. So that's the way it is with God in Sinai: you, the living reader, already know what he's going to say, the general drift at least, because you've internalized the character. Same with

Moses, same with Pharoah, same with God, and Jesus too. Then when you read the words it comes as a revelation: you knew it and yet you didn't quite know it. It's uncanny, but more than that, it tells you you're not quite who you think you are. That is, you're a character too, a created creature, in a larger, unknown drama.

SB: But why did God stop speaking? You didn't answer that.

DR: No? The talkies, that's the answer. Once you have the talkies, you lose touch with the internal voice. It all becomes human drama, what passes for "realism" with us, and it's further heightened with all the tech advances. The silents were more real: they were like dreams. When you remember a dream, even a black-and-white one, it's more real to you—it's part of you; it came to you, not to anyone else.

SB: So if God stopped talking, is he still listening?

DR: We don't hear him talking because we've replaced him with our own self-conscious talky reality, and our artistic creations mimic it. The great commentaries on the Bible, like the Talmud and Aquinas, try to keep the Bible alive in its revelation. The revelation is about his existing, his talking to the original writers. He talked for them because they wrote it like a dream, like the great silents—their words were the dialogue cards!

SB: OK, do I have it? You're saying he's not interested in listening anymore because the writers after Jesus are making up their dreams instead of having them, and that the dreams are pretending not to be dreams but real?

DR: Why would our made-up dreams be interesting to him? They're made for us and only interesting to us. He already knows everything about us. But we don't read him anymore like the words are a revelation—so what should he listen for?

SB: You mean we're that boring?

DR: Well, not exactly. We still have great writers, or at least we used to. Their great works are the ones that critique the situation we put ourselves in. They actually have a revelation of their own about how limited we are, how foolish. It's a tiny revelation, compared with the Bible or the silents. Our art today rarely stretches all the way to all the universe out there. It doesn't make a stage for us and the unknowable—like the Unknowable Creator—to meet, or to dialogue.

SB: It's true we never feel foolish when Charlie Chaplin or Buster Keaton are on the screen because they do it all for us, acting the fool.

DR: Very interesting point! Their comic silents aren't about us—it's just between them and God. God loves them—he doesn't even have to forgive them. You can almost feel he's watching, listening. That's why somebody called Charlie's little tramp a holy fool. You know that God would never let him die, at least not in the dream. The writer will die of course—the writer for most of Chaplin's films was Charlie Chaplin, who died. Now he is an historical artifact. But the little tramp can never die—not because he's always the same in the film but because he is God's fool. He exists both in and out of human history.

SB: But isn't that the same for Snow White or Little Mermaid?

DR: No. The difference is that White and Mermaid never lived in the first place. They don't exist without an audience. They're just like the talkies, where the audience is a witness and so the writers are self-conscious, always thinking about the people in the audience and what they're thinking. In silents, like in dreams, it doesn't matter so much what the audience is thinking. It's all a kind of revelation to them. Sure, they're supposed to laugh or cry—but it's as if the characters in the film don't know it, don't know there's an audience out there. They're in another realm. It's the same for Abraham and Sarah. They don't know we're eavesdropping on them in the Bible. Well, we're not; it doesn't matter if we live or die, but they will always be there—because they die in the Bible.

SB: Wait a second. Didn't you say God wouldn't kill Charlie but now you say he lets the people in the Bible die?

DR: The important thing is that the writers died, including Charlie. They are historical artifacts that can be enlivened, brought back to life if we think hard about them—what they did and how they did it. But Charlie and Sarah as characters, you can't kill them, even when they die.

SB: That's scary! It's like vampires and zombies. Oh, but you'll say the vampires and zombies are like Snow White, they never lived. But aren't they historical artifacts too?

DR: They're human artifacts, but since we created them, they're ahistorical. Well, I can't really say that; they have their cultural lives. What I mean is that their authors are historical, they lived and died. Since they were created creatures, the human backstory can extend out into the evolution of the universe. But their histories are mostly like talkies, too talkie. I don't know what I have to learn from the author of Little Mermaid, except what I already know: that I too am and will continue to be an historical artifact in creation.

SB: I see I got off topic—namely, you! You and the Bible courses I take. What would my professors say about why they don't talk about the writers?

DR: Okay, wait a minute while I get this blurb off Amazon for a new book by a supposedly with-it scholar... "Through a work of extraordinary 'literary archaeology,' Zakovitch explores the recesses of literary history, reaching back even to the stage of oral storytelling, to identify sources of Jacob's story that preceded the work of the Genesis writers." I have to add: So what? What we want to know is how the Genesis writers *used* those sources. Literary analysis helps but we still have to *imagine* what kind of writers they were, how they lived and breathed. You know very well from your courses that thinking of them as "religious" is useless, just like thinking it's crucial whether James Joyce was a Democrat or a Republican—if he was an American, that is. What too many biblical scholars don't want to know, however, is how imaginative writers write. If would be great if they could even just talk about it with some contemporary writers, but unfortunately too many writers today are way too talkie. Genesis is an ancient silent film for them, one they'd never rent from Netflix, even if Netflix offered it.

Now here's an example I should have offered S.B., except that it came later; it's when I responded to a review by a Bible critic who also claimed to be a poet:

Dear Professor Mincer,
Although several years have passed since your review of my *A Literary Bible* appeared, I now have the flexibility, immersed in a memoir-in-progress, *A Life in a Poem*, to look back and regret my impatience with your comment, as well as that of your review's editor, to whom I wrote a message of disappointment. One of my mentors, the art-critic Arthur Danto, has just died, and I read an obit that describes his graciousness in replying to critics of his essays and reviews, taking

special pains to "educate" them, just as he did with his Columbia students. Although I recall instances when his patience gave out, so that I'd be careful what I would say in correspondence, I learned intimate things from him, especially about how to translate one's gaze on a work of art to a work of poetry. I say "intimate" because, as one gazes upon a poem as if it were hung on a public gallery wall, it can appear naked, undressed against its will, its private, innermost compact between poet and reader (or auditor) violated. Of course I'm talking about an erotic intimacy that today, in the wake of performance art and showy poetry readings, has somewhat dissipated into the tamer event of an orgy of elocution in front of an audience that was subconsciously required to strip naked of literary history as an admission policy. Not counting audio as an art in itself, of course, for which members of the audience are critically tuned-in like the organist at an old-timey burlesque house.

Sorry to start off topic. First, let me say that I regret not having taken the time to reply to your criticism of my thirty years of biblical translation/poetry more benevolently. You noted that you had been a student of one of my favorite poets, Gary Snyder, and yet it seemed to me from your comment as if Gary's influence upon you, in his later role as literary legend, was filtered through an academic constraint he himself had never known, at least in his earlier and middle periods. When I read *Myths and Texts* as an undergrad, I felt free to also consider biblical text in terms of how its original Hebraic authors worked with mythic sources, thanks in part to Gary. That freedom didn't manifest in me for another decade, but it was simmering, along with similar encouragements from other poets I studied, including O'Hara and Ashbery, Creeley and Olson, Stein and Reznikoff, and in particular Cid Corman, with whom I corresponded from Ann Arbor to Kyoto. The books of translations he sent, Basho especially, along with the issues of Origin filled with poets' translations from all kinds of languages (except Hebrew), inspired me to think creatively about translation as intertextual. So my youthful intertextual poems, engaging modern French poets, prepared me for the shock of encounter with a psalm—as *periplum*.

Studying Pound's *Cantos* in grad school, I'd internalized his concept of periplum, just as your teacher Gary Snyder had. FYI, here's a recent Wiki definition:

"In his book *ABC of Reading*, Pound describes the geography of Homer's *Odyssey* as 'correct geography; not as you would find it if you had a geography book and a map, but as it would be in "periplum," that is, as a coasting sailor would find it.' That is to say that Homer's geography is understood from the point of view of a sailor who is actually 'in periplum' or in the midst of the voyage itself. In *The Cantos*, Pound similarly perceives space [and time] from the point of view of a poet in the midst of experience."

It was a periplum I struggled to embody in my biblical translations, graduating from intertextual to experiential translation. What experience? That of the poet at his or her ancient scene of writing, and to get back there I'd have to immerse myself in millenniums worth of scholarship, especially the "Higher Biblical Criticism."

Now let me get back to your critical review, especially to your charge that my translations seemed "curiously slack" for a poet, although perhaps you used another word than "curiously". Let me begin with biblical parallelism for just a moment, the element of ancient poetry that corresponds to what we might call collage today—in the sense of how the step-down lines of William Carlos Williams ask for a kind of caesura between each break, as if the lines were collaged. They sometimes are in Williams, but more often in the following generation of poets. For Snyder, the periplum is closer to haiku-like, whereas for myself it is biblical parallelism, in which the repetitions slow down the lines and cause you to notice the wordplay ahead of the syntax or narrative. This attention to slow-motion wordplay is so prevailing in biblical text that the centuries of tradition that follow strive to emphasize it, both in commentary and in the reading itself. If you go to any synagogue on a Saturday morn and listen to the bar mitzvah boy or girl read their *haftarah*, you will hear how greatly the text is slowed down by the addition of cantillation, the chanting.

Unfortunately, most translations of the Bible do the opposite, speeding up the reading and losing the poetry. The recent translations of Everett Fox and Robert Alter, for instance, lead one to think the originals roll along like primitive chariots, with respect to Fox, or chug along like school buses, with respect to Alter. Of course, these translators are not poets themselves, but even so, how many translators of the Bible do you think might have had their sensibilities tutored by Pound or the contemporary Howe sisters, Fanny and Susan? Or Snyder, for that matter, and that's why it could be helpful if you'd carefully consider the term "slack." It used to be that you'd go to a store and buy a pair of slacks, which implied that the trousers hung loosely and allowed greater sway of movement. One certainly wouldn't buy some jeans today and ask for a pair of slacks; ditto for women, who would most likely prefer a pair of pants. The lines of biblical poetry, however, and even the wordplay of its prose, requires a slower, looser embrace, one in which the mind dials down to the level of contemplation. You don't want to read a psalm or Isaiah as fast as a Marianne Moore or Robert Duncan, even though the latter modern classics are intensely listening to the line. I'd suggest, once again, that you go back to Basho, whose classicism is more clearly aligned with the biblical poets—and I include the biblical prose poets as well, the writers of Genesis *et. al.*

This might seem strange to you especially because the biblical translations you know are quite antithetical to the original Hebrew—and yet, even the Hebrew text is, itself! How can that be? It starts with the earliest Christian translations, which expected the Hebrew Bible to coast along like the New Testament, so when Jews became acclimated to any Christian or Muslim society, they looked back to Tanakh (Hebrew Bible) as if it were written in a similar state of sacred holiness. But of course, it was not; the biblical texts are largely cultural works written in cultural contexts spanning more than a millennium. Only later than their composition were they appropriated as canonical religious texts. And for those Jews still reading in an unbroken tradition back to the beginning, you can hear how slowly they hear each word and phrase by consulting either of the Talmuds, where one line of biblical text might entail pages and pages of hearing and rehearing.

What about the psalms, you may ask; surely the Hallel was chanted fairly speedily up the stairs of the Temple precincts of yore? I don't think so, particularly when you remember that their recitation was accompanied by lyre and flute. I would think of lyrics of the Blues by way of comparison, where phrases and stanzas can be repeated many times, as well as "paralleled" by lines that re-echo and harmonize with previous ones. My second volume of psalms translations, back in '74, was titled *Blues of the Sky* (from Psalm 73) for a reason, and when Ashbery and Creeley in the U.S. or Amichai and Schimmel in Jerusalem asked for more, they were wondering if I could slow them down even more. So you see, when you wondered why the entire oeuvre was slack, I did not know how to respond to you slowly enough, as your review's editor, Dan Friedman, asked of me. Now, however, the passing years have done their work (where did they go so fast?) and I hope I've caught up with you in time to be of use.

Let me go back now to an earlier paragraph, to my imagined scene of subconscious sexual arousal at a poetry reading, something I'd agree with Arthur Danto can displace or cause an erotic diminishment of intimacy to the art. Danto fought to show how art is as intimate with philosophy as lovers, and needs to be as much an unexpected thing of beauty as an uncanny quest for truth. Sure, truth and beauty can be a heady collaboration, and it may require taking one's pants off subconsciously, but we're not talking about the generic acting-out of a rock 'n' roll concert. Unless, of course, you are the writer and the original model of fecundity. In that case, think of the biblical poet at his or her table—the scene of writing—in ancient Jerusalem, whose model, say Moses, may have existed centuries before, and whose character he or she took from history and stripped bare as new life, or shall we say, slowed down to the years of a life in real time, his or her own, from naked birth to naked death.

Regards to Gary, whose publisher we share, and best of luck to you in your literary endeavors—DR

Returning to the present, it's always seemed to me that too many modern and postmodern poets are too committed to *knowing* something, too literal-minded about both their careers and what they put forward as poetry. They would claim, with notable exceptions (Stevens, Stein, Spicer—for the S's), that they are the opposite, dissidents of literalism. Yet they stand behind their poems, stolid before their audiences at the lectern, as if they are trading in horses. Poetry was to be taken for granted. To me, it seemed too late in the day for that, too late too for horses: you can go years without seeing a real one anymore, not even in city zoos. A poem, I felt, had to now go deep in disguise, like our inner beliefs, clothed in ancient garb and sandals. There used to be, in Manhattan, a few homeless souls who wandered midtown in such apparel, and of course you'd notice them because they stuck out. Just as quickly, you'd brush them from your mind, because they were not "really" ancient figures or archetypes, such as our psyches are based upon. In the same way, I could walk around the literary landscape as a stand-in for an ancient biblical writer, with only passing notice—and therefore no great need to expend vital energy on the marketing of my poetry. Sans the self-promotion, what is left of the poet behind the lectern? There is a poignant answer: What is left is the absence of self, acted out in various interesting strategies, so that the poems themselves are like wondrous vessels, magician's top hats into which the fearful rabbit, our innocence, is placed. And then it is gone, in an instant, and the hat remains empty, a powerful statement—if the poem is really good—of absence. I don't mean to belittle poetry, in whose world of a longing for great poetry (and the poetics of its absence) I also breathe, along with aforementioned avant-garde poet Cathy Park Hong, but just to say, it may take years of searching and effort to find a face, an existential disguise, that is less crowd-pleasing and thus more original, more unchangeable—like that of any creature, say a horse—than a magician's. A disguise as natural as inhabiting the life of an ancestor, as natural even as fur. My second book, published when I was

26, *Disappearing Horses,* has a cover designed by artist colleague Jim Dine, envisioning a horseless bodiless world of creaturely longing. Jim was living in London, England then, as was I, and I can't recall whether it was dogs or cats, but wife Nancy and kids had gone to the seashore, with Jim left behind to care for the animals.

In this regard, and on a lighter note, or so I first thought, I came across a piece in an art mag a few days ago, one I didn't bother noting or think more of than a good cartoon, ephemeral. But now I see it won't slip from memory that quickly, that there's another level beyond humor. It was a report on an avant-garde artist's exhibit entitled 'Great Works of Art Made Better with Cats.' Take Da Vinci's 'Mona Lisa,' the meme-like image of it anyway, for example: the domestic tabby is placed against her breast. Hardly a new concept, it echoes Duchamp's famous 'Mona Lisa with Mustache' of a hundred years ago. Yet there's a crucial difference: the cat is looking out at us too, along with Mona Lisa, adding the subtle impression that she—both of them—are imprisoned in the canvas. It's ironic, of course, but only ambiguously cute, like conceptual artist Wegman's famous dolled-up dog photos. It's unsettling. And it's not the cat that's unsettling, it's the accompanying figure that is, as in Manet's famous reclining nude, with the cat resting against her. The cat here, as well as in the rest of the collaged repros of famous art (even an Andy Warhol and a Russian Futurist poster) is always itself, comfortable in domesticity—that is, in any representation of human civilization, which it has adopted. We believe in her (or him) because she is innocent of our nuanced purposes, our art, though quite aware of the obvious motivations, such as the pleasures of looking, or of resting, or of cuddling, or just the fact of being in each other's company. Cats don't look at paintings, it's true (unless they move), but I'm sure there's many an artist who's worked long and hard at a picture on canvas, with kitty lying about as company, who has returned to the room inadvertently to find kitty rubbing against the canvas, or at least the legs of the easel, "possessing" it, as it were, which is not so different than a human gazer saying to a companion, "I like that," in a parallel form of appreciation.

Nevertheless, the cat's comfortability in the picture brings out a subtle sense of discomfort felt by the artist's model: she is "posing," whereas the cat is simply herself. Without the cat, we accepted the figure's artless pose, but the cat question's our willingness to suspend our disbelief, or rather disarms it. We may laugh, yet we the art consumers are also made uncomfortable.

What is brought into question by this fellow mammal, albeit one of a different species, is our species consciousness—or lack thereof. Suddenly there's a spotlight on us as we view the painting, the spell of disbelief is broken, we're made self-conscious, so that the whole enterprise of art-viewing becomes suspect, and perhaps even the whole venture of human civilization. Certainly the original viewers of the great paintings discovered from over 30,000 years ago in the Chauvet caves of southern France were not attending an art exhibition, at least not in the sense we do today, as consumers of culture, if not buyers. How is it I surmise this? After all, the ancient Sumerians had their own museums in such cultural seedbeds as the city of Ur. The Ur-ians were collecting works of the past, however, with both historical and cultural context, while the ancients of 25,000 years earlier at Chauvet were depicting images of nature without any thought to "collecting" them. Even if they killed and ate the bison, literally consumed them, that would hardly represent an aesthetic convocation. No, we might better say that they swallowed their art for sustenance, and that the paintings of bison in the cave sustained them in some uber-aesthetic way, which I do not hesitate to call religious. Well, I do hesitate a moment, because I want no inference that these people of thirty millennia ago were in any way primitive, or any less human or sophisticated than we are; they had the same DNA we do, the same Homo sapiens brains and brainpower. All they lacked were art stores—yet they did well enough by making their own supplies direct from nature.

So what do I mean by their religion? The animals, plants, and even the human hands depicted in the Chauvet caves are *numinous*, like Adam and Eve when they're speaking with the Creator, or Abraham questioning God on the way to Sodom and Gomorrah, or Jesus addressing God the Father from the cross. We have paintings of all these scenes, mainly from the Renaissance, but that is because the painter is challenging us to hold an uncertainty in mind: the ambivalence toward whether we are embracing the painting or embracing the numinous scene. Same goes for the bison: they are more than simply images, they are also in some serious sense real, hence super-real or supernatural. How could a bison so realistically encountered in the wild also be supernatural? Because they are literally *alive* and images at the same time—and that is what I mean by religion: encountering the world as if it is more alive than oneself and one's images, that we are but one among a multitude of species, and that we cannot view them, the bison, as simply representations but as *equals*. In other words, we are creatures, created beings, and the value of representing this, of imagining the Creator, is to create a vantage outside of our limited understanding of the world, a way of seeing ourselves from outside our world of life and death, of understanding or imagining that as created creatures we too can be viewed as existential representations of something more than ourselves, like the figures in great art.

That is what I mean by religion. But what of the cats in the paintings, who are simply themselves and are most powerful not because they are numinous but because they cannot be anything more or less than themselves? The bison, recall, are wild creatures, whereas the cat is a domestic one, subsumed into human civilization. The cat knows us, or at least something of us; the bison and horses of Chauvet simply accept us as fellow creatures, if they notice us at all.

Yet there is a sense in which we can consider these works of famous art with cats akin to a religion, even a bit more than an aesthetic religion, if we want to fully account for ourselves as an audience, and not simply a gaggle of ironic meme consumers. When I was in elementary school and we went to assembly programs in the auditorium, we were an audience, yet when I sat in a similar theatrical setting in synagogue on Saturdays nobody called it an audience; it was a congregation. What's the dif? It's that disbelief had already been suspended before you walked through the synagogue doors. I'd say we art consumers today are also a congregation albeit one of ironists, that we're already believers in irony before we walk through the turnstiles of the Tate Gallery in London, where Russian artist Svetlana Petrova, who's become known for her online artwork of famous portraits featuring her big ginger cat Zarathustra, has brought her internet meme into a physical setting. We the viewers, who have brought our physical bodies out of our office chairs and into these public rooms, are a congregation of ironists who, at the very same time, have been marked and counted as an audience of consumers as each of our paid admissions has been added to the till.

Yet what does Zarathustra see but a congregation of humans who have collected for no immediately apparent purpose, like a group of feral cats in an empty, after-hours parking lot, who soon are revealed, however, as a hungry audience when the human feeding them at the hour appointed has arrived. Yes, they too are consumers, yet sans irony they are also an audience of species-conscious beings, acknowledging the human creator of the scene in which they are eating as a species whose motives may be unknowable but whose desire to bring together this purring congregation is acknowledged.

It was kind of like that as I stood on the synagogue's stage chanting my bar mitzvah haftarah (portion of Isaiah, etc.). At not quite 13 I was proud to be accomplished in the performance and in the approval of the congregation qua audience, yet I hardly knew how the cultural context in which I was standing came about or even what the motivations of the human creators of this congregational context were. I was proud of myself for being able to perform while at the same time disbelieving in the ultimate Creator who was being addressed. I was inside and outside at the same time, balancing these incommensurate worlds and holding down the nausea of doing so. That's a term the late poet Armand Schwerner used, the nausea of holding in mind incommensurate worlds, when he created his poetics of translating and interpreting cuneiform Sumerian tablets—and at the same time knowing that it was all his creation, including the imaginary tablets. But by mid-life, I came to a dark wood, so to speak, forced to allow myself to be guided out of it by Shakespeare, whose "all the world's a stage" fell into place with my understanding of the original biblical poets as working within a cosmic theater. So it was more than entertainment; there was a purpose to the cosmic stage in that it allowed for a contract, a covenant to be written between us and the unknowable Creator—who, like the human feeder of feral cats, creates the scene but whose motivations are not knowable to the subjects. Stepping back to work with this in an art context provokes a sense of nausea that has to be overcome, like that felt by the usurping King Claudius watching Hamlet's play within a play—or felt equally by the astronaut, our contemporary, in zero gravity. Eventually we adapt to it, outer space that is, we "translate" ourselves into it via protective prostheses, and then we forget about the nausea we've overcome, or King Claudius the dizziness he suffered at the "play in which to catch a king." That's how it was for me at almost 13, on the synagogue bimah, pretending to believe and also sweating from the double layer of clothing (in the '50s, such large spaces were not yet air-conditioned). Underneath my blue wool suit I had on an additional suit of striped flannel, my Little League uniform, with the team's name, "Stars," emblazoned across the chest.

I would sneak into the men's room while the synagogue service continued, remove the outer garment like Clark Kent, and run out the side door toward the ball field where I was scheduled for the catcher position at a 1 p.m. start. I missed the national anthem and the first pitch, but fortunately we were the visiting team that day and I was only batting 7th, so I wasn't yet missed. But I was sweaty, not just from running over a mile to the field but from having to carry my duffel bag (earlier stashed in the men's room) of catcher's paraphernalia, dubbed "the tools of ignorance" by professionals, further stuffed with my discarded bar mitzvah suit. On top of that, I recall a sense of existential nausea or unacknowledged guilt, which was not helped by my hitless afternoon that included an error behind the plate when I missed an easy popup by nervously discarding my mitt instead of the mask.

Would Svetlana Petrova have felt a touch of similar nausea for trying to hold together the tradition of great art and the natural integrity of her cat Zarathustra? Was not the dignity of each brought into question by the impropriety of bald-faced irony? Probably any trace of it disappears when Petrova is forced to defend her work as legitimate experimental art, which like Duchamp brings the audience into the field of the work by provoking questions. Once you're defending the integrity of "art," an artist or poet is on solid ground, the nausea left behind, because one is defending one's right to be on the stage, period, and this coalesces with a defense of the stage altogether, the necessity of it, the necessity of an audience, which in cosmic terms is our entire species and its questions about how the covenant with creation is to work, or to be adapted in different contexts throughout history.

But the whole story was there at 13, if not much earlier, as I was met with the silence of the audience when finished (this was a congregation, after all; applause is secular). My father told me later that night how everyone appreciated my "singing" and my following speech (he didn't ask about the game, pretending not to know). Yet half of me was missing there, the half whose natural integrity was compromised: I knew I was going to lose that feminine voice register any day now, and I knew I'd bluffed my way through writing the speech, using phrases and concepts more hi-falutin than anything I knew to believe in. Perhaps the feral cat feels that way after it's accepted a meal but walks off as if entirely independent. The baseball game proved my independence but actually it didn't; it proved the opposite. I didn't know why the whole cosmic theater business was necessary, yet it jibed with my knowing I was never going to escape my life as it was given, never escape my unsophisticated (so it seemed to me then) parents, not escape the cosmic audience for my life and death that would always be more discerning of my inner life than anything my writing career could evoke, never escape the feeling that an unknowable audience is missing—even if I didn't question its existence, as many contemporaries don't hesitate to do.

Perhaps I'm not fair to my contemporaries. Their babyish questioning— call it ironic— might actually be a defense of their art, in the way that a refusal to acknowledge the cosmic stage actually confirms our holding the concept of a cosmic theater. Petrova's cat may destabilize our comfort as an audience for art, but the ensuing artwork and its public success shows just how fiercely, if helplessly, we hold onto art. It's our own complex way of being ourselves, just like Zarathustra.

The African-American drama was something *I did* understand, better than my own history in the synagogue; it was a culture apart, yet still engaged in racial struggle with the dominant caste, a history in black and white, in which the "game" is to become color-blind. The loser, ironically, is stuck in black-and-white, stuck in memory like the history of the world series-less Chicago Cubs, though our memories too get lost. The winner is truly lost, but in the best sense, like an explorer, with a chance to see what's next. So here we are on the field, playing a larger game where winning and losing matters beyond the season, with the managing adult, the facilitator, standing in for a higher meaning. The audience was always white, except for the rare times a team would venture into the inner city, like on the day of my Bar Mitzvah. They were the enemy at one with their team, they shared the same memory, yet it was impossible for us on the Stars to think of them as anything but the "opponent," thanks to the moral character of our African-American coach.

Nothing matters, he says, except how you adapt to the game and your opponent's weakness. Think of them as Bears, he says (the team's name that day), it's our job to tame them. He is way beyond political correctness, more like an Ethiopian rabbi in a flannel cap—a return of the repressed Rabbi Fisher, in whose lap I sat, age 4, for blessing. He was my father's Jewish sage, Whitmanesque girth and beard, Einsteinian white hair, Sinatra's blue eyes. I was surprised by his unaccented English, otherworldly, compared to my Zaydeh and pre-kinder yeshiva teacher, likewise white-bearded, who spoke in Yiddish. Later my dad tells me Rabbi Fisher was confined to his bedroom now, too old to go out, and yet I identified, since my bedroom was my new place of intimate privacy (I was happy to stay in there all day, smoke Prince Albert in a pipe hidden in my rarely worn, hence rarely cleaned Bar Mitzvah suit, read Greek mythology in secondary school editions). Like Rabbi Fisher and King Oedipus, my baseball coach also had an authority that preceded him, tragically ennobling, since I understood a Negro League player, however local, was most likely superior to a white one. Coach's English was the most articulate I'd yet heard, his bearing more serious than any Caucasian. He never joked, baseball was no laughing matter, and as a team the Stars were on a mission to the suburbanites, showing that Negroes were more cultured. After a bus trip to a night game in rural Ohio, where the team we played was composed of literal hicks, I began to see white kids' racist slanders as a sign of classlessness, especially since I got the worst, as in "Hey, black boy, wipe that powder off your face."

I was exotic enough as the white boy that my Jewishness melted into it: I was applauded by black parents at our practices when I grounded into a double play. It was an unearned audience, like the one in after-school Hebrew School, where you got praised and promoted even when you skipped class to play pingpong in the lounge: the school needed your body to survive. The Holocaust survivor who spoke to our class was a hero because she survived, that's all you had to do as a Jew, survive. Or else, in our lesson about Israel's War of Independence, fight to survive. I already understood this as a fight for meaning, unlike the dominant culture that took itself for granted. When I discovered a modern poetry anthology a bit later, poet pix of Pound and Stevens appeared to be stunned Holocaust survivors, fighting to recall a meaning somehow lost and marginalized, exotic for all that.

The meaning in the Book of Isaiah, from which I read for my Bar Mitzvah portion, was explained to me as "being a witness." You didn't have to go to school to be one, it just happened to you, like living in inner city Detroit. It happened to my aunts from Auschwitz, living nearby. And it happened to Isaiah, as I found when translating his poetry some decades into my future: all you had to say was, "Here I am."

All he had to do was have a dream.

These are the words
Isaiah found
before his eyes.

One day
far away from now
distant as the days of creation…

…even the finality of holocaust
will melt away
like lowland snow

the military hardware
translated into monkey bars
where children play

the hardened postures
crumbled
like ancient statues

children will wave through the gunholes
of tanks
rumbling off to the junkyard

people will find hands
in theirs
instead of guns

learn to walk
into their gardens
instead of battle…

…the highest imagination
will be shimmering sand
on that day

when only the Lord
like a blue sky
will be above us

that will be the day
a day
over the heads of all

that stands
and by its little height above the earth
is proud

feels endowed with highness
and tall words for what stands
merely upright   in its image

human or inhuman
or the giant Cedars
of Lebanon

all the upright oaks
of Bashan
all the straight-backed mountains

and high-rising hills
the skyscrapers
and sheer walls

the Super Powers
and their walls of missiles
stockpiled

the huge launching towers
of the Saturns
the incredibly tall masts

of the ancient ships of Tarshish
sailing to the edge of the world
all the beautiful craft

all the inflated art
the high-priced picture frames
and gilt-edged imitations

all the high-sounding ideas
and high-minded poses
will fade to nothing

on that clear day
will melt away
like dew on the ground

men and women
in the statues and masks
of their pride

will topple over
like carved chess pieces
in a gust of wind

the little board
on which they lived for power
swept away with sand

when only the Lord
like a blue sky
will be above us

and the idols of dark thoughts
like dreams
passed away   utterly

Go back and clarify your good fortune, I say to myself, when the white families on your block, Jew and Gentile, seemed to arise en masse one year and flee to the suburbs, especially the one suburb where Jews were now allowed, Oak Park. (Your family was the last holdout, for another year and a half). Then it happened you could sign up the blacks moving in, to be "new customers" of your paper route. Thereby you win in your precinct the all-expense paid week-long trip to NYC, to fly American Airlines and stay at the Taft Hotel, where Errol Garner played. You felt comfortable, enough to sneak into the over-21 Lounge at night, to listen to his whirlwind of jazz notation, whilst the other newsboys stayed in their rooms, playing blackjack.

In Little League when you return, still 12 and in your last season, it's not just that you're the only white player (there's another, a boy with a Southern accent and thus with his unique freight of unconscious reverberations, hence undependable, doesn't show up at times, kept on the team nevertheless as a heavy hitter, unlike you), although you're also the only Jew on the field, the suburbs we play in all Christianized.

You fought family and Torah to survive on those ball fields, where you were exceptional merely by default, where you survived purely on your meaning. You survived by showing up. The others could take their audiences for granted but you had to invent them by becoming yourself, by making a meaning out of that. The ancients were listening, they held a place for you in their dusty congregation of extra innings, you were their catcher, you just had to survive, you had to crouch there and catch their meaning. It was an invisible audience and you had to invent it every day.

So consider this poem by Abba Kovner (1918-1987) who fought one day at a time to become himself, to survive as himself, later to find his audience awaiting him in kibbutz cowshed and NYC cancer ward, hanging on his account of fighting off history by sitting in the bullpen, in the game but also waiting for a place in the game, the Jewish paradox, for the call to save the game, if he can think.

Like a Computer Screen, Like Life

You had no need to make an effort
to avoid pretense.
You did not pretend,
laughing or crying,
for forty-three years.
Wedded to his bed,
your face was as legible
as words on a computer screen, clear and sure.
His wretched, irksome needs,
the dough of his distorted lineaments,
each sign, each life-giving gesture
you recorded like a phosphorescent graph
without pause, morning
and evening.
                                    Never give up!
For him and for yourself, no frost
only the rising sun—
it's hard not to sound sentimental, but that is how
it is preserved in a man's memory,
only the potter's clay
not a nude exhibit, not
a computer screen
but the genuine
fact of life.

I'm nonplussed at the last line, the "fact of life," because it seems so flat—unless it's an echo of "not a nude exhibit" representing the sexual "facts of life." But in between that line and the last, a most lovely and uncanny rhyme: "screen" with "genuine," belying the otherwise inert last line. As this is a translation perhaps the original Hebrew, which goes unprinted in the English rendition of the book (Sloane-Kettering, 2002, translated by Eddie Levenston) has a more complex, even biblical, resonance. Few other

contemporary poets would leave such an unadorned phrase hanging—
or else it must be ironic, standing in for the will, and begging the post-
Nietzchean question, Where does this will to survive come from? Except
the poet is on his death-bed, so how is it also about survival?

It must be the surviving poem *is* that "fact," as ironic a characterizing as
ever there was, since in most cases a poem suggests a heightened reality, one in
which consciousness is stretched, however minimally, however linguistically
or avant-garde. So I ask further, who or what is the audience here? Clearly
it's us, the survivors of the poet, but then we too are no more than facts of
clay. Yet if we imagine ourselves a congregation, i.e. having meaning, then
"it's hard not to sound sentimental"—there it is, the hardness, perhaps,
of the unsentimental facts of sun and life, no rhymes or metaphors to be
wrung from them. A last poem. And yet even here, the "last" entails there
having been a first. It's simply impossible to get away from it, this will to
meaning (an avant-garde irony or anti-meaning amounts to the same).

So I would say the audience for a poem is actually a congregation,
that a poem resembles a prayer to "the potter." Laugh or not, that's the
risk the poet takes, identifying with a potter-creator, turning himself into
one. Right there is the struggle with sentimentality, with wanting to avoid
it by addressing merely an audience—even an audience of computers or
frogs—but without the burden of a congregation.

Does Kovner's poem seem too simple to hold an audience that
demands some kind of complexity to match its complex brains? Certainly
life appears complex, the cosmos incomprehensibly so, yet what can be
simpler than the moment of death, like a plug pulled and the brain turned
off instantly, like a lightbulb. That is what he allows for in his poem,
balanced against a life, a memory, of overwhelming life-and-death struggle,
surviving the Holocaust in starved-out ghetto and frigid forest, and then
guerrilla combat against fascist forces armed to the gills, followed by Israel's
war of independence, also against implacable odds. More than ten years of
daily combat, more losses than one can count. True, none of that's in the
poem, but the poem's in a book, and the book includes that bio elsewhere,
even were the author anonymous. Yet how could he be, unless our whole
age were to become so, anonymous, lost in time. And if that were to be,
any one of us could still walk onto the ball field of the Stars and simply say,
"Here I am"—witness to... (it's not for me to say).

Meow. Does that mean, "What's next?", when our cat tires of watching
me write? I'm thinking it's a quantum meow, indeterminate, contextualized
by our need for meaning, our being an audience. It's the perfect compliment
to where we've arrived as a Western culture: we are largely resistant to
meaning, and in its place we have a craving for knowledge or information
of all sorts. On the internet we can "feel a connection to a vast body of
knowledge of which I am not master, much as I am able to live in a society

bursting with information," writes Jonathan Rosen about the ancient Talmud, which we might study for a lifetime but likewise never master. Jonathan, who like a psalmist craves an image for every statement—in contrast to his emails to me over the years, in which he complains it's too hard to write them because images are superfluous to the message—offers several, both found and invented, in his *The Talmud and the Internet* (2000), such as how it is so "complicated that even God, who presumably has a good working knowledge of His own book, nevertheless has to devote a portion of every day to studying it." That's a rabbinic found one, adding to the complications that make one self-aware, or so says Adam Phillips about how psychoanalysis works. You don't come to a final meaning but rather grow to be aware of how complicated you are in the context of a life. Jonathan has said the same for the Talmud, that we become self-aware creatures as we experience or engage it, rather than progress to meanings.

Meanwhile, in just 15 years (2029), Ray Kurzweil predicts that "In the future people will be able to directly connect their brain to the cloud so that they can expand their knowledge and memory." And why not, as long as we aren't inhibited by necessity to know what meaning such access to knowledge entails. But where's the point at which knowledge seems an addiction, losing its grasp of self-awareness? Where anything can change into something else via the literary quantum of translation. So exclaim the poets who contribute to *Telephone*, the online mag of translation-for-translation's sake. Before I translated my first psalms, I might have bought in. The year prior, in '72, I "translated" several Shakespearean sonnets; you couldn't call it adaptation, for every line was re-phrased from the Elizabethan text. I'd also begun the same with *Love's Labor's Lost*, and then tried this experimental method with a Hebrew psalm, which took hold and wouldn't let go: the "meanings" of the original Hebrew poets were cosmic, so that unlike Shakespeare for us moderns, they could only be translated within a cosmic theater—and that theater of man and Creator in communication had to be re-enlivened. It was as if the Jerusalem Temple, rendered almost meaningless in modern poetry, like a hapless, parochial man's version of the aptly named Globe theatre, would have to be imaginatively rebuilt. It did, after all, hold the original cosmic drama of man vs. meaning.

2.

Please don't worry if the names of poets that follow are unfamiliar; the poetry world is a small one, even if riven with struggle over what constitutes the most authentic poem today. In the same way, most of us fail to recognize the names of important scientists, though we've heard of their achievements, or their honorifics, such as the Hubble Space Telescope.

It's not important here that you know who Hubble was, or who the poet Gary Snyder is; consider their names as placeholders. What counts is that you are an audience for the bigger issue of what an audience can mean, depending on how we view the existential questions about life and death.

More than forty years after my own little Shakespeare inventions found no audience, the editors of *Telephone*, Paul Legault and Sharmila Cohen, asked over a hundred poets to each "translate" a Shakespearean sonnet. They conjured an audience by composing a manifesto aimed at the postmodern multicultural affectation of globalism. It doesn't amount to all that much that's new, since the subversive nature of translation had already been assimilated, back in the theory-mad '80s, as a subtle form of "intertextualilty," another iteration of collage. Grandiose, to be sure: "The *Aeneid* is so contemporary in a way—it's frequently thought of as political/ imperial propaganda, and certainly there are elements of that," writes the translator of a new version from the Roman poet's Latin in progress, David Hadbawnik, "but I believe it is also pretty subversive." Or at least it better have been—otherwise, why would a postmodernist bother to re-translate Virgil's epic?—or so goes the excessive literary inference. Subverting meaning is another brand of knowledge, perhaps an unacknowledged addiction to meaning, but whether it's Philip Morris or Herbert Tareyton, it's still more books for the library, if not more smoke in the air.

MANIFESTO OF THE NEW TRANSLATION

1. We want to sing the love of translation, the habit of renewable energy and reconstitution.

2. The essential elements of our translation will be change, augment-ation, and the remixed.

3. Translation has up to now magnified pensive immobility, invisibility, and slumber. We want to exalt movements of originality, feverish repetition, the double click, the perilous link, the syncing of devices

4. We declare that the splendor of the world has been enriched by a new beauty: the beauty of translation ... an ever-expanding browser which seems to depict itself ... is more beautiful than Parmigianino's 'Self-Portrait in a Convex Mirror.'

...

7. Beauty exists only in repetition. There is no masterpiece that need not be remade. A viewing, a reading, a rendering has to be a translation of what's there into what it's like that it's there. Nothing exists without translation...

By now you can see in this the origins of a literary craving for knowledge: with all its irony it remains anchored to the Socratic aim to "Know Thyself". And tethered as well to probably the 20th century's strongest writer, Freud, as he's brought up-to-date by my old panel colleague on the meaning of translation, Adam Phillips, in his new biography, *Becoming Freud*. To a certain extent *like* Freud, Adam strives to keep meaning at bay, as in the way he describes the psychoanalytic session: it's a process of becoming aware of oneself as more and more complicated, rather than leading to a particular meaning. In the same way, he characterizes Freud the Jew as an outsider in Viennese society, occupying a role in that society made more complicated by his "not fitting in," rather than the church's attribution of embittered meaning to the Jews.

"'When, in 1873, I first joined the University,' Freud wrote, 'I experienced some appreciable disappointments. Above all, I found that I was expected to feel myself inferior and an alien because I was a Jew. I refused absolutely to do the first of these things. I have never been able to see why I should feel ashamed of my descent or, as people were beginning to say, of my race'. He did not refuse to do the second of these things, to feel an alien—'I put up, without much regret,' he adds, 'with my non-acceptance into the community'—but seemed rather to enjoy, as he did throughout his life, the status of being an outsider, of never quite fitting in."

If you start with an audience of one, of yourself as unassimilable in your society, it becomes more compelling for your reader to collaborate with you, as if you both, reader and writer, are a society of your own, as in the common misunderstanding of a psychoanalytic session or a postmodern poem, yet nevertheless you are in the process of becoming self-aware and attuned to context; in other words, becoming more complicated.

An outsider, however, is already someone who is in a sense more complicated in becoming aware of the society he's excluded from. So, contextual knowledge, by virtue of being applied from outside, helps create an audience of outsider cognoscenti, for whom meaning begins to inhere for each person in being no more than a self-aware member of the audience. No card-carrying in this audience; one contributes by one's craving for more knowledge, more context of what it means to be excluded from a society (especially one unconscious of itself)—to be alienated from its meaning, or any meaning. Of course, one psychoanalytic session is like one poem: once you feel complicated by a poem, you need to read more, volumes and volumes, until you've become a poem to yourself as well. But let me tease out further how crucial context is to meaning.

In my own sessions, I said to the analyst "I feel like an exile." "From what?" he asked. "From love," I answered, feeling rather silly as soon as the words came out of my mouth. In subsequent sessions I tried to give the feeling of exile other, more specific contexts, like from the university; from the literary community; from my colleagues, etc. And even the strangest: "From myself." "What does that mean?" he asked. "It means the guy my family, my high school debate coach, my JCC boxing instructor, my creative writing teachers, and my college girlfriends all thought was someone who was going to amount to something, is someone who got locked inside me, and I can't find the key to let him out." "Do you want to let him out?" "Not sure. I'm in exile from knowing what I want. There— that's it," I said, feeling as if I'd finished a short poem, then realizing right away that my poems were about the same thing, not-knowing. I said that, and the analyst asked, "Why can't you live with that, be satisfied with that accomplishment?" "What accomplishment?" I replied.

That's how it goes, wanting meaning while working against it. It can be funny: old friend Ron Padgett has leveraged a career on that dark humor, just watched him in an Academy of American Poets video. I once thought of Ron as the fiercest of postmodernists, yet now he's matured into the role of a literary psychoanalyst. The poem he's been asked to read and discuss consists of the opening line, "Nothing in that drawer," repeated 14 times, the equivalent of a sonnet. What does it mean, you may ask the psychoanalyst, to which he replies, "How does it make you feel"? Like it has no meaning, like there's nothing in all the drawers, you may think. But it's the search that matters, implies the analyst, the desire to keep looking through all 14 lines. And then there's the matter of emptying out the grandiose pretensions to meaning of the sonnet. Moreover, continues Padgett, "I was young and crazy when I wrote this," suggesting that madness can be caught and tempered in a poem. "There are many kinds of poems in the house of poetry, just like the drawers in my desk," he goes on, advising his audience to accept some craziness into their lives, not get their underwear in a twist as they scavenge for meaning. But it's not at all simple, we have plenty of complexes, matched by many contexts with which to take in his poem, offers Padgett, gently. We've already mentioned the venerable sonnet form going back to Petrarch in the Italian Renaissance; then there's the avant-garde context in which repetition is explored (Padgett suggests we consider Gertrude Stein, who opened mental drawers no one knew were there); there's also the context of the quest, quixotic or otherwise; and perhaps most fundamentally, the context of disarmament: not only the disarming of grandiosity (and its stockpiling of missiles) but also the rush to knowledge in the gentrifying of one's identity.

"It's even plausible to think that God might have made a huge and complex universe as an object of knowledge for intelligent creatures," says a scientist in the *New York Times*, bending over backwards to religion. Nevertheless, it's not meaning that matters here but instead "an object of knowledge." We're on the arrow of progress to getting smarter and smarter, more "knowledgeable"—all of it complicating, if not expanding, our consciousness. What there might be *besides* consciousness is something we're no longer conscious of. Yet what, after all, exists beyond our limited Homo sapiens consciousness; what is it that's unknowable, outside spacetime? Here's how that most sympathetic of scientists in the NYT answers the question with another one: "Does there need to be a nonmaterial cause as an explanation for the entire material universe?" But isn't that on the order of explaining algebra to a dog: Does the dog want to know if algebra is material or nonmaterial? In that sense, our scientist may be as lovable as a dog whose bone of contention, "a nonmaterial cause," might really be no cause at all, no principle, but instead a poem. "Nonmaterial" can be an elegant representation of what is unknowable, because if we have representations then we can write a poem, especially a cosmic poem like the Book of Genesis. Better to read that than the NYT religion or science blogs, which barely rise above the standard for greeting card verse, albeit a greeting card for the anniversary of Einstein's birth.

Anyway, Einstein himself did not write greeting cards, scientific or not. Yes, he wanted to know what can be known of thyself, at least the material part, regarding which, if enough can be known, then perhaps the nonmaterial can be materially inferred, like the atmosphere of an exoplanet. Certainly he knew that to know thyself is to be human, and that there is nothing more human than to have to die—but does that mean he wanted to die, looked forward to it? Possibly, in the sense of Freud's concept of the death drive. Really, though, wouldn't he rather have lived on, at least long enough to follow newer theories in and of the universe—wouldn't that be a more human wish? So there's the point at which dogs and humans converge: no species wishes to fulfill its destiny simply by dying (aside from altruistic individuals) yet death is a scientific fact. It is not, however, a poem; at least not until we create an epic poem for it, a cosmic context in which what exists beyond spacetime (if the word "exists" may be applicable here) can negotiate a meaning, however imagined, with us limited beings. The standard poem has no ultimate meaning, but captured within it are meanings we can discern by their agency. Death, that is, may have meaning in a poem about paradise, eg. Milton's "Paradise Lost," but there is little that we can meaningfully say about either Milton or his dog's death outside of a cosmic poem. Outside of any poem, all we have is info interpreted, i.e. knowledge. Yes, to be human should be to want to know thyself, but among us postmodern cognoscenti, we're too weird a species for that, too grandiose, so it's knowing *per se* that's worth pursuing, and its corollary, unknowing, unmaking the tropes about ourselves and our appurtenances, from language to behavior.

One of the first adult books I read, about age ten, seemed to do that in title alone: *Portrait of the Artist as a Young Dog*, by the Welsh poet Dylan Thomas. I was surprised I couldn't understand that book, even the part about a dog's life. There were too many fancy words and phrases. And poses: it's hard to tell the dif between a pose and a genuine riff when you're ten, especially when you've loved a dog whom it was impossible to imagine as a poseur. My girlfriend in junior high would tease my puppy love, still blushing at a dirty word, especially when mouthed by a girl: f-u-c-k, if you see Kay, tell her I love her. It got to the point where Nancy asked me to fuck—pretend, of course—and pretending to unbutton her blouse, but before I could swallow the inhibiting ideals of prepubescent innocence she had moved to the suburbs along with the rest of our Jewish neighbors. Abstract thinking had already come to me when I later found the bestselling poem 'Howl,' which my first thought conjured to be about a dog. Ten seconds into the first page I understood that poets could howl because they had a poetic license. They could also suicide, but the poet Ginsberg still talked to them as if they were here. I'd experienced the death of my Zaydeh and Bubbeh, they died even if I didn't want them to, but especially I didn't want to hear that they were elsewhere: I wanted them here, period. That's the problem with death, you can't have them here, except in a poem.

Nor could you know you'd have to die also—until you kept on knowing until you knew thyself. I already knew that poetry was the best way of knowing because you could be a novice thinker and still write a good poem—as long as you admitted it in the poem, attested to your own ignorance. (Feelings, on the other hand, remain the same on your deathbed as they did in your bassinet; they don't get smarter, just more wily at eluding apprehension). Another scientist has figured this out and takes the poet's stance of admitting to knowing less rather than thirsty to know more. "We are able to observe only a tiny portion of what's 'out there,'" he avers of the material universe, and reaches a provocative conclusion: "science, the main tool we use to find answers, is fundamentally limited." So too are "our own limitations as an intelligent species." However, recognizing limits in this way, argues Marcelo Gleiser, is not a deterrent to progress or a surrendering to religion. Rather, it frees us to question the meaning and nature of the universe while affirming the central role of life and ourselves in it. Finally, science swallows philosophy, though sexually blind to its auto-eroticism: "Science can and must go on, but recognizing its limits reveals its true mission: to know the universe is to know ourselves." Nevertheless, not only is the truly great poet of modern science ignored (not a single citation in 500 pages) but so are Freud's colleagues and modern psychology altogether. This in a book my own publisher, Basic Books, describes as "an authoritative, broad-ranging intellectual history of our search for knowledge and meaning [*ed.* though not necessarily finding them]. Gleiser's 'The Island of Knowledge' is a unique view of what it means to be human in a universe filled with mystery."

So, is it enough to evoke mystery in order to seduce readers on the fence between science and poetry—to evoke it but not to capture it, as within a poem? "Not necessarily finding" are within my brackets because the entire book attempts to persuade us that the *search* is everything, while knowledge is but the catnip. As for meaning, that was once the addiction of Plato and Kant; now we are going on the simpler, cheaper fuel of adrenaline, with scientists posing as poets. But why require Newton to turn over in his grave? Is it merely to entice an audience in love with its own consciousness as if it could be an objective "other?" An audience dying to find all that consciousness can contain, admitting its limits but never stretching to consider what it can't contain and why, such as the unconscious psyche and the creative motives behind spacetime? An audience, in other words, engaged by the chase and paying only lip service to its meaning, a mainstream audience dressed up in postmodernism?

Thus we get just the pose of wanting meaning in this bestselling book, this "Island of Knowledge." Posing the *context* of events, as in the smashing of atoms or the evolution of our brains, we become less needy of meaning; just context is enough, since the complexity of any context can be infinitely expanded, depending on your theories and access to the benign quicksand of information. I'm not knocking it—I've imbibed it, to the point that I'm chasing down the origins of this pose of complexity-sans-meaning. It's interwoven in my life and time, interrupted for a couple decades by the Holocaust, but long since back on track in the casual clothes of irony. There's something species unconscious about it, fascinated with other species only as stepping-stones to us or as themselves innocent of contemplating consciousness. Meanwhile, our cat says to herself, "Why do I need to know what those big beings are up to? I'd rather go outside and smell lots of other species. Maybe I'll scent one of my own species, but it's just as interesting [*ed. vide* consciousness-expanding] to root around in the organic smell of dead leaves that dropped from heaven."

Most organisms, as Daniel Dennett put it in *Darwin's Dangerous Idea*, seem to have "hit upon a relatively simple solution to life's problems at the outset and, having nailed it a billion years ago, have had nothing much to do in the way of design work ever since." Our appreciation of complexity, he wrote, "may well be just an aesthetic preference." I don't think Dennett realizes how a wild feline's or any organism's "simple solution" is a misnomer. It's their connection to the super-complex "brain" of their ecosystem that allows them to explore their territory fully, unselfconsciously, without fear of having a nervous breakdown; their brains rely upon a brain far more complex than ours. And it's that "brain"—the ecosystem that evolved not only them but an infinite number of other species—that continues to have much to do "in the way of design work." Our miniature brain, a kind of simple imitation of a wild ecosystem that apes the latter's creativity with "ideas" instead of beings, is more a fearful than an aesthetic preference— afraid we might have lost our way, so that science and art, preceded by religion, becomes a complex tracking of our place in the universe. But not to make too grandiose a point of it; however comfortable our seat in the audience of the universe, our connection to it is more unstable than any other animal's. Actually, that's what makes us more grandiose than a lion, and also more interesting to ourselves: we think we know something that a tiger can't know, which is true, except that there may be nothing special about it when we too are up against extinction.

The Biblical writers, for instance, did not pretend they knew something but rather allowed that something to play with them—or they to play with it, in the art of their writing. I mean "it" in the decisive sense of their cultural heritage, which thus has become ours. I don't feel put upon to validate their knowing; instead, I enter their cosmic theater without fear of being browbeaten. Even the slightest browbeating makes me nervous, and it usually comes from writers who have "something to say." The fine poet Peter Gizzi's recent title, *In Defense of Nothing*, worries me that he may think he knows something about nothing. If his poems convince me he does not, I'm charmed. For it's the *loss* of something to say that most needs saying. When did we lose it—back in the caves, when the cave artists registered the loss by painting animals? We don't need to know a thing about what they may or may not have known about the animals; it's the beauty of the painter's attention that holds us, and in that attention we register the truth of our Homo sapiens limitations: what we lost when we evolved away from gorillas was our mothering ecosystem, its "big brain" that provided all our needs and cues for thinking.

The gorillas are still there, quite calm, far more calm than us—except when they hear us encroaching. Once we lost that ecosystem and were forced to become alert to every possible threat, our big brains took over, turning us into the most nervous creatures on the planet. So we tried to calm this nervousness within culture, often leaving the impression that we have not lost anything. In the Biblical version, we've lost the voice of the Creator, yet we can find our way back to it through centuries of complex commentary and interpretation. "Finding our way back" is what we want from all great art, and from our contemporaries as well—if not to the loss of the mothering ecosystem in which we evolved, as represented by the Garden of Eden, then to the loss of the symbolic Laws of Nature handed down at Mt. Sinai, for though we still have their written form they don't bring us calm but rather make us nervous that we can't embody them. Scientists thrive on this nervousness, and so do poets, but what is great about Einstein's theory of relativity is how much more it reveals to us of what we don't know than of what we do, and what is great about contemporary poet John Ashbery's 'Self-Portrait in a Convex Mirror' is how much it reveals that the origin of our complex consciousness, however "advanced" we've become, is graspable in our being made aware of its loss, like the receding mirror-images that are reflected back to us in a complex mirror. Those refracted images become an abstract language that we postmoderns can make into a new art, yet that art is valid precisely because we can read our original loss into it. If you can't "understand" Ashbery or Einstein then you will see their work as "weird," something beyond what you know, and that feeling of weirdness will at least proffer a key to re-read them for the loss their work encodes, a longing for knowing something that can only be satisfied when we acknowledge the longing. It can seem wondrous or hilarious, that longing for having a purposeful origin, but the loss of knowing it can be bullied from our minds by artists and scientists who speak to us as if they know something, appealing to our desire to wish the loss away. Yes, we are explorers of the universe-wide ecosystem, as the movie *Interstellar* shows us, but it also tells us what even a gorilla knows when it is caged in a zoo: don't trust your keepers, whatever the truth of your dependency on them reveals, for they too are created creatures who've lost their way and can only partially know it.

My thought as it unfolds is usually circular, in this case circling in an orbit back to the Biblical writers who I am always wanting to "call back"—a phrase inscribed upon Emily Dickinson's gravestone in Amherst. Although Dickinson was called back from life, our encounter with her, through her writing, calls her back to consciousness. To get to that calling back of the Jerusalem writers, however, I first must circle through some recent cultural totems. But why, you may ask? Your critics may accuse you of rambling. I'd say: an explorer must risk rambling, so that you in his audience may come to know more clearly how he thinks—and why he thinks it—rather than what he knows.

Watching the 1947 noir, *Boomerang*, the other night, we focussed on Arthur Kennedy's character, the "jobless drifter" who gets mistakenly fingered as the murderer. While the plot centers on Dana Andrews, the DA who uncovers Kennedy's innocence like a gorgeously analytical scientist, Kennedy's character stands out as the only one truly lost in the film. We want to know more about him, to go back in time and commission a sequel, because "jobless drifter" seems perilously close to a description of an artist or writer. If I say I'm a writer (let alone a poet) the clichéd question still is raised, "So what do you do for a living?" And without an anchoring job in the city where I live, I might as well be a drifter. Yet because Kennedy is an *honest* jobless drifter, we can understand how vulnerable he was to being charged with murder—and how *necessary* it is for an artist to be that vulnerable. It was Rhonda who latched on to the contrast between Kennedy's potential-murderer honesty, and the corruption of most of those with solid, respectable jobs in the movie: the politicians, policemen, etc. "The murdered priest was the mirror image of Kennedy, since he too was presented as honest. Honest to a fault, it's implied, because it got him killed and it got Kennedy threatened with the electric chair for killing him."

"I still like Kennedy for accepting his victimhood, when he shocks DA Andrews: 'Yeah, sure, I'm a murderer, call me anything you want, throw the book at me.'" It's precisely this mock confession that changes the DA's mind about his guilt, as if only an innocent man could afford such irony— or an artist. He's more complicated than simply honest, though the movie hasn't enough time left in it to spin this out."

We're not arguing about the film, just playing off each other, like lovers do when they tease, especially in bed: "Do you have a headache, nurse?" "No, I'm just sick of checking your erection. Why don't you put it in your mouth yourself?" etc. We're both mock confessors like Arthur Kennedy, we've both got something to say, like when we were safely driving home last night from the Imax wild ride of *Interstellar*.

Everything is everything, an ironic encapsulation of relativity theory, is quoted in the new film biopic of physicist Stephen Hawking. To simplify, everything is bonded by gravity, which is why nothing is flying around random in the universe, even if some orbits, from rogue asteroids to rogue exoplanets spewed out of their solar systems, are hard to figure (quantum theory may account for that). In other words, there is an erotic bond between everything (though the eventual discovery of dark matter and dark energy may complicate that), including between ideas. Rhonda likes robots, posing the benign ones in Kubrick/Spielberg's *A.I.* and Nolan's *Interstellar*, while David worries about HAL, the banality of evil computer in *2001*. And so it goes, until we can get to the bedroom and rip our clothes off, like any erotically charged couple who make love with words, as does even Joan of Arc with her God in Shakespeare's *Henry VI, part 1*. Her God, that is, who is pulled into the universe by her, just as He was by the Hebrew Bible's Covenant, although the God of Israel, also being the Creator, must represent what is unknowable to our limited species. Yet the imagined dialogue with the Creator began in Eden, where our erotic bond with everything was created—including a bond with a Creator outside of the universe, outside the box, which poetry may still pursue, if not science, and for which we remain the prime audience (so far as we know).

So when we were driving home from the Imax *Interstellar*, noting that poetry was not forgotten in it, we still regretted that barely a shred of cultural reference appeared in the film, other than a bookcase and the couple lines from a Dylan Thomas villanelle of the early '50s. Why that, we wondered, unless it signified a remembrance of the last poet in English who was commonly held to be a demi-genius. Just the week before, we were watching a sour new docudrama about Dylan on BBC TV, on the occasion of his 100th birthday, in which he manifests a Swiss army-knife-worth of self-destructive behaviors. Clearly the British have had enough of "genius," a term attributed anachronistically to Dylan several times during the film and widely discredited in our day when applied to artists. Perhaps the demystification began with Dylan's death-by-alcohol suicide at age 39, followed by too many suicides among poets, most notably Sylvia Plath's just ten years later, in 1963. Today we prefer the self-deprecation of Clark Kent's representation of genius in the Superman franchise (about to be reprised for a 2017 release date) to the oratorical Dylan Thomas. Clark Kent read no poetry and rarely uttered a three-syllable word, nor did he drink. Yet we appreciate him for his widened consciousness, which besides inexplicable compassion for our species, includes X-ray eyes and deep-range hearing, and we regard him all the more because he is unpretentious about his cosmic superpowers. But if he were a poet, what would he read? Being cosmic in origin, would he read the Bible today for its cosmic poetry? I think so. I think he'd want to know of the greatness we've left far behind with the lost biblical poets, the actual ones in Jerusalem, who took on all of creation without the need, apparently, to flaunt their superpowers. Rather than Dylan Thomas, they were more like anonymous Clark Kent (or so religious tradition would like us to believe).

Yet the ultimate species consciousness, the thing that makes us a bit different, is the wish not to have been born. However much an animal or plant suffers stress, it is not wishing that. It's the most complicated of self-knowledge, and it begs the cosmic theater in which we are un-self-created beings, back to the ancient Joban poet's opening speech for Job:

> Rip up the day I was born
> and the night that furnished a bed
> with people to make me
>
> the pillow from every night I lived
> smother that day   cover its light
> so God can forget it
>
> let death's shadow
> hold the ether mask there
> clouds obliterate it

A Life in a Poem

a total eclipse
blackout
swallow it a tiny pill

and that sweat that night beginning me
black oil absorb it
a hole drilled deep in calendars

shrivel that night in the hand of history
let it soften in impotence
turn off its little shouts of pleasure

every science unsex it
genetic biology   advanced psychology
nuclear bomb

no next morning shine on it
through the afterglow
singeing the eyelids of dawn

because it didn't shut the door
of the womb on me
to hide my eyes from pain

why couldn't I have been
a lucky abortion
why were there two knees

waiting for me
two breasts to suck
without them I could have stayed asleep

I could have melted away
like spilled semen
in transparent air

wrapped up in quiet dust
with gods of power and influence
and the emptiness of their palaces

with rich families their money
paper houses
for plastic children

with criminals who can't break loose
there they rest with tired workers
no more hell from bosses or jailers

who all fall down
under one blanket
not the simplest machine to serve them

why should someone have to live
locked in a miserable spotlight
bitter inside

waiting for a death far off
they search for it restlessly
like the final person in a late-night bar

they can't wait to see the iron gate unlock
and the little grave plot
comforts them

why should someone have to walk around
blinded by the daylight
he can't wave off

that God throws on him
waiting at every exit
in front of me

a table of sighs to eat
and moaning
poured out like water

every horror I imagined
walks right up to me
no privacy no solitude

and my pain
with my mind
pushes rest aside.

Here you get (Chap. 3, Book of Job) what seems total emotion, total feeling, and yet Job's not-knowing the context of his suffering (the test of his trust in the unknowable, as played out in the prologue by God and His satanic prosecutor) and his not-knowing the limits of knowledge, creates a complication vividly postmodern, at least in ancient terms. You can't be speaking if you can't get born! Job would wish to withdraw the meaning of existence, while nevertheless not calling for an apocalypse. Others could exist all they want; the universe could go on as it is; but Job wants out of spacetime, out of meaning. And that made perfect sense to me, as a postmodern poet in '74-'76 when I was translating the Book of Job, because the subversion of meaning, the avant-garde simulation of "pushing the boundaries," was the most ironic of tropes: it was as impossible for a poet or artist to actually accomplish (in "meaningful" terms) as not having been born.

And I felt it as a painful irony that stood in literary parallel with the Joban poet's representation of suffering. That's how I got started on it, engaging the poem on postmodern terms, but it wasn't long before the fact of Job's suffering became palpable, overriding my literary bearings: it was testimony, like the testimony of a Holocaust survivor, and testimony only makes sense if there's a court—an audience—to hear it. Perhaps the Book of Job had such an audience, akin to the progressive religious context in which I read from my translation during its Yom Kippur placement in an upper West Side synagogue's liturgy, but I found that the biblical Hebrew was really all that was wanted there—while a need to further the progress of postmodern poetry was not on the communal mind. The poetry world itself was apparently unperturbed by my work, and had no place either, or so it seemed to me, for such meaningful complications that subvert meaning. Or that's how I took it, undaunted, not considering whether my poetic skills were sufficient enough to bring it off. How could I imagine such a deficient situation, when I already had fifteen years of training in poetry and the aesthetic complexity required to keep meaning at bay?

3.

Postmodern meaning, then, is what takes the poet from behind the page and sets him down in front, with the audience of his poem, just like the Hebraic Joban poet as he watches the classic, ancient gentile character of Job—a "dead" memory he reanimates in league with his audience. In point of fact, all memory and history is dead; it's one thing to access it, but another to animate it. The latter is the job of living poets. In the 1980s, it was the animating voice of the poet in performance that suggested a cosmic perspective on life—we die every day, are reborn every morning, sang Ted Berrigan, as if it was the poem that remained constant, animated by the poet's voice. It paralleled my own program at the time, "rediscovering the voices of the original text," my subtitle for *A Poet's Bible* in '91. While ancient biblical poets could imagine reaching out to empty space in supernatural terms—terms already so archaically mythological that they become reanimated in Hebraic terms—Ted and his coterie, of which I hung on to the fringe for awhile, did it in what he, echoing Ginsberg, called the Bardic voice, disembodied. The body stood there at the podium during a poetry reading, but the poet's voice wandered out from it into the eternal emptiness around us, or indeterminate spacetime (or what passes for the cosmic for a Buddhist poet). It was the same as Job's voice speaking/arguing across that boundary to the eternal signifier of physical creation, the Creator.

So I would estimate that a complex context has been arrived at in literature and art during the past century and a half by virtue of withdrawing from meaning in order to watch the mind moving, "greeting" whatever is encountered in the empty space that surrounds us. That's why modernism thought it needed new forms, as with Pound and Eliot, Picasso and Stein, in which the variable textures of collage could take over from meaning. Let me explain it in the way I first learned it: Collage disarms meaning, takes it apart, and what results is the epiphany of knowing; that is, we gain knowledge of how complicated are our resources, from cogitation to language itself. And that's the sublime whoosh we get when rereading Stevens' 'The Blue Guitar' or looking again at Picasso's 'Guernica'. Some tried to enhance the latter with the meaning of anti-war anguish, but "anti-war" itself is contextual—you need war to give it meaning. If it's ever discovered that humans can survive as a species without war, then "anti-war" will become a historical relic, as envisioned in the ancient poetry of Isaiah. The same might hold true for modernism and postmodernism, if meaning is found once again to be a necessity for our survival. Meanwhile, pushing back at meaning, pushing it to the sidelines, remains our ecstatic goal for art and science: just take a look at any episode of Neil de Grasse Tyson's *Cosmos* and its breathtaking recontextualizing of Carl Sagan's original PBS *Cosmos* of the 1980s. Meaning becomes a bore, replaced by the excitement of pushing the boundaries of knowledge for its own sake, the making and breaking of scientific theory, including the "story" of science and its addiction to testing, also known as exploring, and also best exemplified by the aesthetics of collage, where two or more randomly unrelated thoughts or events are brought together to produce an "experience" of meaning rather than meaning itself.

I was a master of collage—not a grandiose master but rather the ordinary kind, as in "Master of Fine Arts," a creative writing degree I came out of grad school with. There are now something like half a million MFAs in the U.S., so it's hardly any more of an accomplishment than the one million Ph.Ds that populate our cities and countryside. I gained insight working with collage in poetry and joining the joint program of trying to make it a tradition (back to Rimbaud) and even hook it up with traditional tradition, as in Pound's echo of Dante in *The Cantos* or the sadly not-yet-well-known Canadian poet bpNichol's echo of Sumerian, early Anglo-Saxon and ancient Asian poets in his late 20th Century epic, *The Martyrology*. I got a strong whiff of each: Pound in the form of MFA grad work, Nichol in my brief but formative friendship with him in late '60s and early '70s Toronto—all of it coming back like a shocking peal of thunder when I heard of his early death in a botched operation in '88. Ultimately, my own drive to keep meaning at bay, in the collagist poems of my early books, collapsed when I expanded into the Hebrew psalms, attempting to co-opt their ancient form of poetic parallelism into my personal vision of collage-as-narrative. The "appearance" of narrative, that is; the lineaments of it, holding together what are otherwise indeterminate fragments, the sources of which create further resonance. I was playing at developing my own omniscient narrator, with a typically postmodern precociousness that would reveal the folly of any such thing as an omniscient creator.

In my mid-twenties then, on the New York School poetry scene, my avant-garde colleagues clapped at this, an audience of anti-congregationalists. I got an encouraging blurb from John Ashbery for my first "mainstream" Psalms collection (*Blues of the Sky*, Harper & Row, '76). By then, however, my whole program had fallen apart and the strength of the ancient psalms themselves had opened for me a new meaning of meaning. Whereas I thought I was co-opting ancient sources into avant-garde practice, those sources had co-opted me: their meaning constantly overflowed the parallelism of their formal making, as if a poem could be constructed of meaning alone. "As if"—because it was not a refusal of poetry by ancient Hebrew poets but rather a gorgeous enhancement of it by virtue of proposing an omniscient narrator, the Creator, who was both the writing creature's creator and thereby also the inspiration of the poem's creator. And thus began my descent into biblical scholarship and Hebrew language, forsaking if not puzzling my audience of fellow avant-gardists— yet only because I thought it might nurse poetry into re-joining the ancient congregation of cosmic inspiration, or what I came to call the "cosmic theater." I can imagine being a "nurse" somewhat in the path of my father, who was a medic in the Normandy invasion. A nurse, too, in service to my poetry doctors, Pound and Nichol, who hoped to re-embody a humanized cosmic epic in their singular lifelong poems. At least Nichol did; I'm not sure Pound wasn't out to foreclose any possibility of the cosmic.

Postmodernism, however, still holds us, even if many critics are self-importantly claiming it has slipped away. Will postmodernism (whatever it comes to be called in the future it will forever represent what comes after modernism) ever get over its will to destroy its sources, as scientists destroy a theory with a new one? I'm not saying we love destruction, although "disruptivist" has penetrated our vocabulary right down to the squarist mainstream ("our disruptive frames will give you a bold new look" it says on the poster at LensCrafters, where I pick up a pair to prove to the youngsters and our cat that I'm still in the game), but rather that pushing back, even viciously, at meaning has been domesticated. It hardly sounds ironic anymore to say we live in a meaningless society, which at least is preferable to a communist, socialist or fascist one, given what overwhelming destruction they wrought in the last century. Even after 9/11, the powerful avant-garde composer Stockhausen was quoted as saying that no performance art could top it, which might also account for a certain desire to criminalize terrorism instead of uprooting it; to normalize it, like a rape or mugging, rather than contemplate a state that could support it, even an evil state opposed to us, otherwise filled with nice, innocent, sympathetic bystanders.

Can anything be more freighted with meaning than evil? It doesn't have that wonderful contemporary irony of what's inside an atom is not what's inside an atom. Or, that quantum particles form a collage rather than a coherent meaning—an experience of matter and energy rather than a coherent picture. Thus, according to *Science Recorder,* today in 2014, "Scientists have long struggled to identify realistic ways to manage fragile quantum states. In pursuit of this goal, the researchers have confirmed theoretically that contextuality is an essential resource needed for realizing the benefits of quantum computation." We might also say that contextuality can be neither good nor evil; it's just frameworks of knowledge, or lenses, that might help us one way or the other. And since the evil scientists of science fiction and horror movies of the '50s are no longer relevant, I would have agreed for the longest time that postmodern contextuality is only for the good.

Dear Adam:
I don't know if you plan to review it, but I'm reaching out because I'm reminded by this bio of what puzzled you in your review of *A Literary Bible* five years ago: "What is gained, besides unnecessary complication, by considering some of the biblical Prophets as writing poets?" (I paraphrase). In his new bio of Freud, another Adam (Phillips) ignores the complication of racial resentment lying at the root of an unbalanced psychic economy—whether it be the burning of Freud's "Satanic Jewish Science" books in the '30s or political Islam's resentment of Israel in our new century. Once resentment attaches itself to a psychotic meaning, logically enough, it requires a counter-meaning to confront it. And yet it's precisely the keeping of meaning at bay that Phillips identifies with, like a poet in tune with the current zeitgeist, especially the literary

and artistic culture that prevails as postmodern. I'm hardly in the position to criticize, however; my lifework of "A Literary Bible" also strives to keep meaning at arm's length. That's the best we can do, I thought, until an epic poetry is re-conceived; meanwhile, it falls to us to scout the way by building a bridge to the great epic poets of the Bible. Because that way lies an ore of meaning, along with the centuries of Midrashic and Talmudic commentary, and we can gaze at it through our postmodern lenses of art, as if to "find" it, a found library of sources with its own daring resourcefulness in confrontation with meaning. I'm saying "we" as if an audience exists that I can't say I've found, except inasmuch as I identify with the poet as his own audience-in-the-making, toward an eventual congregation of meaning, a future we have little control over. The poets of the ancient school of Isaiah spoke to that future in the cosmic voice developed centuries earlier, one they ground into a lens that worked in the present. Yet their contemporaries were listening, collaborating with the writers as if they too were in the future, poet and audience anxiously looking back at themselves, their past fraught with glory and desolation.

But were the biblical writers *performing* their work? I doubt it; they were invested in getting it written down. Today, however, the emphasis on reading or performing one's writing looks back to a nuanced Bardic past, preferring the disembodied voice to the seated author at her scene of writing. How anchored the writer is to her writing table is a question of cultural context; it begs the question of audience, since there is no one there in the room with the writer besides her cat, while the classical Homeric bard, no less than Ginsberg or Ted Berrigan, performed their poetry as if it was written extempore, fronted by a public audience, however small. Yet at the scene of writing, at his lonely table, the writer's private audience is the past, the largely dead writers and readers of tradition, even if it is only the modern avant-garde tradition going back to Baudelaire.

And that is how I imagined the biblical writers, surrounded with their own cultural past of sources and traditions, of dead voices wanting re-animation. This goes against the grain, the public image of mythological "scribes" who are envisioned as secretaries to oral bards, prophets and psalmists. The closer you read the biblical text, however, the more you see writers at their tables, with scrolls or even wet tablets before them. Or rather, you don't see them, because the weight of Judeo-Christian tradition is against them, presenting them instead as ordinary or even primitive men "inspired" by divine voices. In that view, no audience is necessary, anymore than one is necessary for an individual's dream or nightmare. Nor is there sensitivity to what the Elohist writer in Genesis wrote in the ancient style of a dream—and in the case of the Binding of Isaac, a nightmare. Abraham is woken from the dream by the very real bleating of the ram caught in a thicket, as I was awakened this morning by a less felicitous leaf blower that nevertheless chased away the voice of my angelic mother telling me I would not have to go to school today, I could stay home and listen to my crystal radio set. My dream is not an ironic comment on Abraham's; it's simply a reminder that individuals have dreams and that the biblical author of the Binding passage envisioned Abraham as an individual, not a mythological instance of divine intercession—although we're free to imagine divine voices, like the angel's message to Abraham to put down the cleaver. We all have heard such voices in our nightmares, absolving us or waking us. In my childhood, I had a puppy-love fixation on radio's *My Little Margie*, who I nervously listened to, late at night under the covers when I was supposed to be asleep, fearful of being found out and deprived of my beloved crystal, sometimes falling asleep with earphone still affixed.

In postmodern terms, then, would Abraham be a character or a consciousness, disembodied? If the latter, he would certainly crave a public audience of physical bodies to stand in for his own. But in the biblical text he has none, and no further evidence that his wife or son mentioned a word of it. He has had the dream of a bodily individual, and his Hebraic author could only write it in the style of an inexorable nightmare, Abraham plodding forward, unable to stop or reflect or even ask "Why?" We might also say he is lost within a poem, so that he remains a consciousness that an individual reader like my postmodern self might stand in for. And once I'm in the dream, where creation is timeless as in the supernatural, I can accept a disembodied audience within or without the universe.

"Poetry will never have the audience of *Game of Thrones*—that is what television can do," says William Logan in a tongue-in-cheek fluff piece this week that may placate the *Times*'s conscience at too rarely reviewing new books on/of poetry. But this is the cliché of audience as consumer of entertainment, with Logan harking back to the days of the Brownings (totally ignoring the 1950s bestsellerdom of Allen Ginsberg and Sylvia Plath, among others who followed Robert Frost and the latter-day publication of Emily Dickinson) when poetry indeed could have the audience of cable's *In Treatment*, if not *Game of Thrones*. We're not interested here in entertainment, however, or with Professor Logan's narrow idea of academic poetry; had he been a contestant on *You Bet Your Life*, Groucho Marx would have asked him why T.S. Eliot, who'd sold over a million copies of 'The Waste Land' and was still alive at the time, wrote more commercially unsaleable essays than poems. Logan would strive to give a witty answer but Groucho would cut him off gruffly, saying "Enough with this snake-oil of no-nonsense essays and its ailing audience, it's time to play *You Bet Your Life* and a chance at the $10,000 dollar question". Groucho was right, a commercial audience is one that needs to be distracted from its ailments, such as watching television. Why do you refuse to write a best seller, my mother used to ask, "Is it so hard for someone like you who's writing his whole life?"

Mom has no sense of a discriminating audience who might ignore the "minute steaks" and make for the local organic food. Yet neither could I try to satisfy the foodies, because such self-conscious attention to public sensibilities would lose touch with my internalized reader, the one like myself whose fundamental context is solitude, and who, in that solitude, may be more deeply disarmed by the inner life, where consciousness cares little about frozen processed french fries because it hardly believes in the need to eat at all.

Anyway, mom has little idea of a book-buying audience; her friends play cards, golf, shoot the breeze at the gated senior community's pool—though that's not fair, they don't need to buy books on the Holocaust, most of them have lived it, and anything else seems a bit spurious, though mom's not judgmental, just worried that I don't have an audience that respects me, and how can they respect an author who is not selling? Everyone wants to be part of something bigger, something successful. Your grandfather (mom's still talking) had his Chumash and all the years of Jewish history; your father and I came to a big America where who knew what you could become; yet you seem not to care for success, you joke that all you need is a minyan, but such a small congregation is not an audience for you to make a living.

Mom was always surprising her children with how American she'd become in half a lifetime. Still, she remained half-universalist, half-particularist; half Woodrow Wilson, half Chaim Nachman Bialik. She had broken out of her parent's Jewish ghetto by graduating from the first Hebrew High School in Lithuania's 3rd largest city, an entree to the larger, universal world. Who would have expected that Israel's success would translate into the world's suspicion of Jewish particularism all over again? Although mom did live to see my bestsellerdom in *The Book of J* and the high six-figures publishers bid in the auction for *Abraham*, she remained ambivalent about these successes. "Who is reading these books but Jews?" she worried.

Meanwhile, in the fall of 2014, there are two audiences of roughly equal size for the Met opera *The Death of Klinghoffer*, one outside Lincoln Center protesting its performance, the other inside, offering a long standing ovation, according to the *Times*. Some of the latter, as they spilled out of the opera house doors, said they were Jews and found themselves—since the work had transcended politics into art—vigorously offended by the desire to censor. Those who remained outside throughout, however, said art cannot transcend politics if the issue is murder and the murderers are still calling for blood, as is the case with Palestinian terrorism. In countless murder stories that can be called art, the murderers, even if they are not killed themselves and go undetected, are not a direct threat to the audience. And even when it may seem they are, as in a Nazi or Communist spy story, the vantage point of the audience has rendered the story historical. Not so today, when anti-Western terrorists seem to be more bloody-minded than in the days of the Achille Lauro hijacking. As the critic Paul Berman writes of the opera, however, we're swayed by the simple-minded "root cause" theory to identify with the victims who seem most helpless to move on. Was that why the appeasing of the Germans before World War II, handing over Czechoslovakia and Poland, and even before, turning a blind eye to the Nazi rearmament, could be accomplished, sympathizing with their inability to move on from their losses in World War I? Yet consider the Jews: In two thousand years, they couldn't move on from their loss of ancient Israel. Why, then, so little identifying with their plight, especially from the other monotheistic religions? And who better to address this conundrum than the Jewish librettist of *The Death of Klinghoffer* turned Anglican priest while writing it, Alice Goodman. If the opera were a medieval Passion play, Klinghoffer's murder—bound to his wheelchair as if to the cross—would be transformative, and the bystanders on the Achille Lauro, terrorists and vacationers alike, would be condemned for not saving him, like the Jews in the New Testament. Un-Pietà-like, Mary/Marilyn Klinghoffer's closing aria of grief is not only not suggestive of redemption but stereotypically Jewish, stubbornly unforgiving. The Jewish rejection of Christ goes on, even if unconscious and postmodern in the libretto of convert Alice Goodman.

In the interview with Goodman that critic Berman points us toward, she decries the "romanticized state of Israel" handed down by her "observant" Jewish parents—*both* Israels, ancient and modern, the latter associated with her charge of "state terrorism." The opera that counts in this story of authorship is the anti-psychological one, in which Alice's unconscious rage against her parents is repressed by a love of art—which becomes, as she explains, the art of a Christian sermon, her only form of operatic writing since Klinghoffer a quarter-century ago. Although I haven't heard the sermons, I expect they're infused with modernist anti-romanticism. My mom was a kind of modernist too, for whom I was postmodern; she believed in the Hebrew Bible but only as the good book, not a plan, while I believed it contained the fountain of Western art, in that nothing could be more postmodern than its myriad writers in service to a self-conscious dramatizing of history. Where are these writers' "selves" within the text? Hiding in plain sight, I'd say, a detective story still not much past its beginning, requiring a deep dive through millenniums-long confusion about pious anonymity and divinely-inspired primitives. This goes as well for the disaffected Jewish authors of the New Testament, anxious to supersede their parental Hebrew text. Goodman has further postmodernized both texts, supplanting Jesus with the American Jew, Klinghoffer, but the unbearable weight of her artistic parricide caused her to convert to Christianity before she'd finished the opera.

We don't have to imagine the story of writer Alice Goodman, anyone can read the interview in the *Guardian* online, and perhaps I'm not alone in preferring to enlarge the opera-specific audience for the ambiguous libretto with the underpinning cultural story of authorship. In Jewish historical terms, the true authors would be Goodman's parents, for having her and for giving Alice a Jewish education. But her artistic and probably subconscious parricide in *The Death of Klinghoffer* also reveals the common wish to abolish the story of the historical authorship of the Bible. Even in two thousand pages of the latest commentary, no mention or imagining of these bedrock writers is made in *The Jewish Study Bible*, since after all no tradition ever studied their art and culture—only the great, miraculous fossil of a text that has survived. Instead of putting words in the mouths of non-exemplary Jews like the opera's Klinghoffers, the Bible's original writers didn't flinch from putting words in even God's mouth. They're just too stubbornly Hebraic as poets and prose artists to be contemplated at the scene of writing. Alice Goodman's good name, however, has not yet been erased from her esteemed text; she can still be championed for an even-handed separating of the Jews in her story from not only God but Israel. But I'm probably too hasty, since it's their hatred of Israel that galvanizes Klinghoffer's killers. Yes, perhaps Klinghoffer is also a stand-in for a wished-for, crippled Israel. All the more reason to widen the opera to the cultural story of its author and her times.

Did J, the earliest known biblical writer (vs. earlier ones whose texts are lost or cannot be discerned) imagine readers in other cultures, a universal audience, in addition to her Hebraic culture? She herself would have read original or translated sources, Sumerian and Egyptian and Canaanite, all of which represented cultures quite different than her own, so however weird the ancient Israeli may have seemed at the time of writing—with its Hebraic cosmic theater of a singular God—they still may have found it interestingly exotic in proto-Phoenicia. I'd venture that J was more future-oriented then writers today, not having to depend on earning royalties or fellowships. Yet she would have been accountable to some kind of patronage, one that sponsored her contemporary audience, and I'm on the verge of telling mom that my own American cultural source of royalties, namely commercial publishers counting on earning back their advances, are largely cosmopolitan corporative atheists whose mother tongue is German or French. Who knows what they care about besides the bottom line? When I get a trashy review in a marginal Jewish weekly, my publishers may be sophisticated enough to know that all that matters is that my name and their name is spelled correctly, as long as a link is provided to amazon.com.

Then there's the question that often arises among the intimate audience at Passover seder meals, Did this really happen?—i.e. were Israelis slaves in Egypt and were they freed and did they make it to the Promised Land? This question requires no God; it's assumed we're getting real ancient history in story form. The drama of the text, the Haggadah, is constantly reinforced by the clapping of the audience, though clapping is replaced by little table rituals like eating symbolic things and drinking symbolic wine and saying or singing symbolic blessings/songs. Mostly, however, it's reading from the text, a collage of snippets from Jewish historical works spanning fifteen centuries, centered around supremely self-conscious questions (displaced onto the children present). What are we doing here and why are we clapping for this text? are the underlying questions—or, what kind of audience are we? I've not yet heard of a seder in which these questions are answered in adult form, other than emphasizing we are present at a drama before which we suspend disbelief, just as if Elijah were Hamlet's father's ghost. Yet Shakespeare's play is so much easier to ground historically—we know when and where it was written, and by whom. These facts, and the questions that might yield them are, however, missing from the seder's audience, starting with the oldest snippet of the collage of close to fifty snippets from different centuries of Jewish creative composition, namely the Torah's Book of Exodus. We know, more or less, that it was written many centuries after the reported events, the writers safely ensconced in Jerusalem and within their renaissance of Hebrew literature. So how did these two or three Hebraic authors know what God said to Moses? Good question.

But a better question would be to ask, What is a collage and how do you respond to one as a great work of art? It's not enough to recognize the sources of the snippets, though that helps; the work of art asks for a new focus to one's gaze. The same holds true for the Haggadah, only it's a more historical focus, one that acknowledges the huge shifts in time, idiom, rhetoric and pov over a far greater span than the single lifetime we bring to Picasso's late sculptural collage of a small gorilla, whose facial muzzle is composed of two toy Volkswagens, one clamped to the other's underside, mirror-imaged, their rounded fronts painted over. We don't need historical notes to readjust our focus on it, because we all know what a Volkswagen is, once we look deeper into the gorilla as a collage, but when it comes to the gorilla of the Haggadah, we can't be expected to tell the centuries apart between a biblical Psalmist and Rabbi Gamaliel, so our response, our focus has to be on questions. Who were these writers, imaginatively speaking, in the context of their day? What refocusing do we need to respond to the collage? (Answer: see it all as a journey through time.) I can hear the complaints already: the seder is long enough as it is without more questions! But I'd say, skip the text this one year (you already know it from previous years) and ask these questions; then next year, you can move on. The focus, ultimately, is beyond the original journey of the Israelis out of bondage to freedom. Instead, it's on the origins of writers *writing* in freedom. And a few centuries later, in ancient Jerusalem, with a Hebraic culture that is burgeoning in the arts. As for God, he has his own story to tell, as if he's the parental head of the seder and we are all children. He says, you ask why the sky is blue and I tell you, wait until you are grown up, and you can count the stars, and then you can ask, Why are we here? And I will answer you: it is to pay attention to your history of asking questions—it's the journey of questions that must continue, and will, but only if you remember how miraculous your being here is.

But the Haggadah begins further back than the Exodus/Moses history, back with Abraham, mistakenly described as a "wandering Aramean". He was actually a near-Sumerian, we know only now, thanks to archaeologists and linguists in the 20th century. At the time J was writing in ancient Jerusalem, Sumer was already thought to be ancient, long gone. Of course, so were dinosaurs, but if such a fossil turned up—say of an extinct cycad plant that dinosaurs ate—the interpretive power required to "read" it would have been unlikely without an evolutionary history. You look at a fossil and see scratchings perhaps, lines and circles; you can't know it's an animal or plant's skeletal imprint. It's not dissimilar to reading the Torah, you can read the words—the scratchings—and understand the Hebrew like yesterday's newspaper, except the flesh-and-blood of the authors is gone. We can reimagine them, however, just as they paint pictures of the Brontosaurus browsing on treetops.

There's a reason that even celebrated contemporary writers like Rebecca Newberger Goldstein and Jonathan Safran Foer, who have recently written commentary on the Haggadah, never confront its authorship, especially the biblical writers of Exodus. It's not just because the scholars they've read are arts-deficient. I know just how hard it would have been myself to imagine real authors, had I not been immersed for a time in spoken Hebrew and contemporary Hebrew literature, which allowed me to hold in mind both a new country that a previous American generation had little access to, and a similarly small country of Israel almost three thousand years ago, having a parallel cadre of Hebrew writers. It may be true that current Israeli writers still fail to imagine their ancient counterparts, considering themselves post-religious or ideologically opposed to a deep reading of what they consider a religious or primitive text. Jerusalem poet Yehuda Amichai once told me it was as if great writers had written the Hebrew Bible while they were still children, and then had stubbornly refused to change a word once they became adults. Most writers in Western languages think that way; it's more natural that they read the Bible literally, humorously, politically—as if J was not *herself* ironic when she created her history of the ziggurat/tower of Babel. And perhaps some writers today read the Bible privately as a sacred text, one too pure to require authors like themselves; or maybe they view it like a movie written by Hollywood hacks, "full of sound and fury, [though] signifying nothing," unaware that this quote from Shakespeare has deeper, biblical origins.

Now what about J's audience back in ancient Jerusalem. The question is starting to be asked in "reception theory," yet even there we're still faced with an audience whose text is bereft of its writers. The latest fashionable formulation, extracted from Jacob L. Wright's *David, King of Israel, and Caleb in Biblical Memory* (2014), goes like this: "a text's production and reception are not independent of each other, and there is no pure text independent of its production and reception." Too true, yet it's still a text with a "production" instead of an author. In the golden age of cinema, the picture's producer was more prominent than the title itself, as in "David O. Selznick Presents 'Gone with the Wind'". The script writers don't even appear in the rolling credits. That's the way it is in biblical scholarship today, still no flesh-and-blood writers; if J is mentioned, she's just a "strand". It was half a century ago that Susan Sontag called for "erotic interpretation" to invade conventional hermeneutics—and still no takers. Let's start, in other words, with a sexualized author, Ms. Sontag might have said, though actually she was in the "signifying nothing" mode toward the Hebrew Bible; but let's assume she could have faced it square, so that she wouldn't mean that the text is sexualized, but rather that the metaphors are (or are not), along with other rhetorical strategies. So even the simplest, as in "My God is king of the universe," asks for a flesh-and-blood king and not merely the concept of kingship. Imagine the difference had it read "My God is queen of the universe" instead—we may assume Sontag could have gone that far, but not so far to imagine the simple exchange for "book", as in "My God is the book of the universe." In the latter, it's an eroticized book not in the sense of only the book's sexuality but in terms of *our bond* with such an exalted object. A book of the universe entails the impossibility of physically holding it, as we do most books we read, including devices, as well as the impossibility of taking it all in, in the way that we suck in knowledge and experience from an ordinary book. However beyond our reach, our bond with the universe is erotically charged, thanks to a simile of a book—and its metaphorical suggestion that the book we hold in our hands, however unknowable a universe, cares about its audience.

To the extent that you, my readers, comprise an audience, I ask you to pull together your partial knowledges of culture, history, evolution, psychology, religion and art, into a little tapestry not too precious to sit on, like a yoga mat. Perhaps I'm asking you to do a kind of artistic yoga, with Balaam's ass in the Bible taking the place of downward-facing dog. If you don't know the story of that biblical talking ass, just google Balaam; and if you don't know the yoga pose I just referred to, you can google that too. And because you can google anything you might wish, without the distraction of notes for everything, you're a new kind of audience, beyond even the high-low amalgam of the postmodern. To call you "intellectual" would sound demeaning, perhaps as much as calling you Ted-talk-minded or artsy-fartsy or stuffed-shirt conformist-readers of *New York Times* or *Huffington Post* cultural reportage—or any cultural media, for that matter. You are all independent thinkers, is what I'd say, ready to change your notions in a heartbeat, if you could only find a heartbeat that didn't feel programmed. Think of the aforementioned tapestry, then, like a movie poster from the golden age of cinema, with a slick black roadster speeding behind the head of Anne Baxter, its upwind causing Anne's tight-fitting skirt to lift nonetheless, and as your gaze travels upwards you find the gun smoking in her hand, pointing you back down to a dead professor on the floor, some obviously intellectual actor like Orson Welles in *The Lady from Shanghai*, in which case Anne would actually be Rita Hayworth. Why must the intellectual always die? you might ask. (Ask Shakespeare that, about Hamlet.) The trouble with intellectuals is they want to erase procreation from the root cause of sexuality; they would rather have ideas than babies. And if no ideas come out of sleeping with Rita Hayworth, then you're only a pseudo-intellectual, a fellow traveler. But if the sex is that hot and spontaneous that no thought of even a condom intervenes, then who's going to raise the baby? My answer: you are, my audience, for you get it—the necessary collage of an invisible baby, as in your memory, with Rita's cleavage. You fill in the protruding baby carriage behind Rita's behind in the vintage movie poster I've described, you want a cosmos with biblical range.

They don't make posters like that anymore. Instead, you get noisy trailers and selfie book reviews and pretentious university courses—all of them too literally invested in the recent past and almost totally blind to the distant past when the future was more generously, more cosmically envisioned. Not to mention the pre-historical, or as Freud tried to help us with an understanding of it, the unconscious. So how are we going to de-grandiose the recent past, which appears just as dystopian (not counting the hippie summer of love) as does the near future, according to even our avant-garde poets, who are busily posing a language-in-crisis? Or, *language as crisis*, which at least echoes back to the prehistoric Homo sapiens acquisition of language, a species-conscious moment of both moving forward but also losing the relative innocence of our prelinguistic dependence on the natural ecosystem in which we evolved. I think there's a way, just as I once thought two late, great poets I'm about to mention, both biblically conscious, neither of them flinching before language-as-crisis, could help us. Today, I'd say we also need the millennia-long overlooked writers of the Hebrew Bible, or at least the greatest of them, in order to refocus—to see where we are going on this spaceship of Earth—by virtue of their writing into the universe and imagining an audience there, even if it's in the singular, like our inner voices.

Permit me now to stand aside for a moment and allow an earlier though recent self to speak from a brief bio for the Guggenheim Foundation website:

> "My family's escape before the Holocaust (the half that made it) shaped my desire to both measure civilization's shadow and to somehow escape the grandiosity in doing so (as my father did, establishing the short-lived American Popcorn Company—in Detroit, where I was born). In my twenties, when I taught contemporary poetry at Toronto's York University, I once brought bags of popcorn and flashlights for a darkened classroom, to help refocus the solemnity of reading. The texts that day were by Sylvia Plath and bpNichol."

If you must ask, Who was bpNichol?, you are permitted to google, but even so, you may not discover that the great poem of our era, the nine slim books that comprise his *The Martyrology*, are only available in limited editions from a small press in Toronto, not yet collected in a single volume (they just tried e-books, but those are atrociously edited, full of mistakes graphical and syntactical). Over two decades ago, colleague and poetry critic Harold Bloom asked me who Nichol was, and upon learning he was a Canadian, already dead, he exaggerated a tight-lipped grimace. "No, my boy, it all sounds too cold and dead for me, and too wordy." Barrie (bpNichol) had already deconstructed that last word, as in "w or d"—take your pick of the letter, for even one word is too wordy, he might suggest, if it's not heard with open mouth, open mind.

But that last sentence is me, not Barrie, who never sounded defensive. I'm the one who's over-earnest, still upset with both his early death and his lack of American mourners. A mourning audience—that's the best kind, I think. Readers who are conscious their response is enlivening, as when the eulogist tells secret jokes about the now tight-lipped author, and there's the sound of an audience laughing or crying, you can't tell which. The reader him or herself isn't sure; only that she is present in life as if within a poem, and the words spoken around us "set a table before me," as in the poem of Psalm 23, which ends (my trans) addressing the universe: "in your house/ in my life."

The Poem of Bloom

Cousin Harold,

Thankful I didn't have to root around in the back room for a winter coat and trek up to chilly Yale in order to catch your perhaps inimitable valedictorian lecture on 'Literary Knowledge.' Instead, I watch it sans distraction on Smart TV YouTube, in black bathing suit and Mackies of Port Stanley, Ontario orange t-shirt. But when, my old friend, back in the winters of the late '80s, I trudged through the West Broadway slush (they only cleared Broadway) to your campus apartment, where we traded private jokes on the complexities of the biblical text we were preparing a joint book upon, the thought that either of us would be one day peppering a public lecture with agonistic rebukes of the Judeo-Christian God was beyond our ken.

However, as a charming excuse for this night's borderline drollery, you claim, emphatically, to have arrived at the potentially enfeebling age of 81, though at the same time I assume this lecture was intended as a summa to the class of septuagenarians from which you have graduated, and thus it may be your last—although it's not impossible to imagine you thrusting your will forward, Falstaff-like, at 91, two canes in hand, with a valedictorian to the octogenarians, such as 91-year-old President Shimon Peres recently delivered to the Conference of American Jews. There in Jerusalem, Peres dramatized his own Falstaff in the form of David Ben-Gurion, to whom he served as prince-in-waiting, though at 24 he arrived straight from the cow-pen on the kibbutz, owning in the entire world but two shirts (one short and one long), two pants (one short and one long), and two pairs of shoes (one of them sandals). Ben-Gurion hardly owned more, though his oratory, unlike Peres's or yours, was fueled by a self-impersonation completely beyond both irony and self. Just as you say of Falstaff, Ben-Gurion embodied life itself (or at least it seemed so in '47 to the surviving Jews). Perhaps English literature might not have known what it lacked without a Falstaff, but it's still your project, at this very late date, to hand them the text—in the form of yourself, an aged Jew, waving off Yahweh, king of the universe, "a character I have never liked, wished to have gone away, yet He will not." For without memory of their kings, their Richards and Harrys, Elizabeths and Victorias, Lears and Claudiuses, what chance would there be for a Shakespeare, divine or otherwise? And as we plumbed the question together in the late 1980s, what chance of a Yahwist, a J, without Israel's God?

Or consider Lear, as you do tonight, refusing to identify with him—one of several refusals that characterize your lecture as well as your life, at least during those years when we were close.

Doth any here know me? This is not Lear:
Doth Lear walk thus? speak thus? Where are his eyes?

But that refusal to see yourself there, complicitous, as sweet Stanley Cavell of Harvard has it, is to miss the exposure required of tragedy. You emphasize, in contrast, self-sufficiency, a potential being sealed off from tragedy in the study of great books, for instance. Not that you'd lose yourself in the philosophical thought of Socrates—who himself is something other than a tragic figure; in fact anti-tragic, as Nietzsche suggested. That can't be you, can it? However, when Lear asks, "Who is it that can tell me who I am?" you do have an answer tonight, in the guise of Lear's fool: "Lear's shadow." It's an answer to Lear all right, but if the question be put to *you*—and perhaps you've answered this evening by inhabiting Hamlet in the form of your reading of him—where is the Fool's answer to you? Are you proudly Hamlet's shadow? Or, Bloom's?

I worry, too, that your theory-enhancing replacement of God's answer in Exodus with "I will be what I will be" instead of "I am that I am," dares losing the uncanny irony of the latter by an over-determination of meaning (were you to be a translator). Thank heaven you didn't challenge me when I was translating the Bible's J writer. Nevertheless, there are some peak comedic moments in your valedictorian lecture tonight, and yet I'm uneasy that it was not funny enough. Breathtaking, yes, even as you attempt to characterize it with dashing speed, with a lightning thrust of the mind, and with a self-admitted failure to catch up to the otherworldly discharge of Hamlet's consciousness—its many Hamlets enfolded into the one. I recall a time when you lectured a conference of New York psychoanalysts on the many impersonations Freud suggested for the ego—much to their puzzlement—but now, among your several iterations of Hamlet, you posit that his "I"s are infinite, by which you mean unknowable, and that human consciousness is as well, in line with the contemporary fashion in high-end poetry. Do you remember how we came to my literary agent at the time, Lynn Nesbit, with the proposal for our collaboration on *The Book of J*? You were quaking with guilt, wondering if you'd be able to postpone the contract you were already under with Viking for a life of Freud.

"Let's just cancel it," she said. Afterward, you were so relieved to not have to write that book that you kissed me. It was some time later you told me you had similarly "cancelled" your psychoanalyst, who dared admonish you (so it seemed to you) to leave out lengthy literary quotations from your free-association during sessions.

As I've posed in my own recent works, consciousness has become the be-all and end-all of contemporary literary knowledge, even though the father of it all, Freud, was skeptical of marginalizing the unconscious. Today, consciousness has appropriated the unconscious within itself, along with a totalizing skepticism; consciousness is so enshrined, so honorable in theory of mind or art, that only the counter-skepticism of a neuroscientist—whose unconscious is out-of-sight, out-of-mind—worries it, albeit slightly. Clearly you have struggled to outflank any doubt about the supremacy of consciousness by creating a character of yourself, dramatized by your self-possessed self-consciousness, and you brilliantly displayed it in your lecture tonight when you faux-apologized for the ambiguity in a sentence you'd just delivered from your lecture's manuscript: "I've looked at it many times, to see if I could clarify it further, but I've failed. So let me repeat it." If it had been a joke, the repetition would have killed it, but in this case (it really *was* a joke in disguise), by repeating it, it came to sound strangely indelible, as if it belonged in the Bible's *Book of Proverbs*.

The problem presents itself thusly: as a character-in-progress, there is no end to revelation, yet your own self-characterization is one of a writer, possibly even a poet, so on what stage are you truly situated? If it's all a performance, then your lecture is soliloquy, for those in public and those in classrooms, but if you are mensch enough to embody the writer of your own character, a Creator of creatures from which your own might dissent, then why do you fail to help us contemplate the scene of writing in historical context? Especially the table at which the godly Shakespeare would have scribed (nothing so two-dimensional and throw-away as the otherwise poignant film *Shakespeare in Love* had it). More than any occasion in the past, tonight you give us Marlowe for a foil, though he is hardly a wife or a teacher, and perhaps not as firm as Shakespeare's writing table for context.

Indubitably, so it seemed, you made Yahweh resemble a Shakespearean literary character in *The Book of J*, and primarily a comic one (or tragicomic, in the classical Greek sense), whereas, more lately, you've come to despise Him, to find Him unlikeable, let alone unloveable, so that tonight you tossed out all the wonderful complications we found in Him in the '80s. Finally, we agreed to

disagree on this, through almost 3 years of meeting several times
a week in NYC (where you lived in large but sparsely furnished
NYU quarters, like a symbolic grad student, buzzing me in as "Dr.
J"). Yet the generosity of your good humor seems to have soured.
The exuberant *épater les juifs* must have evaporated when you found
our book most often derided by Jewish critics, and even though
these criticisms were surprisingly shallow, I think you were hurt
more deeply than you showed. Paradoxically, in defense of your
idealized Yiddish-speaking mama, whose ears would brook no
ill word of her prodigy-like scholar-son, you became thoroughly
embittered with the Jewish world's across-the-board image of
a loving, nurturing, tenderly parental God—whose love could
nevertheless be bittersweetly complicated by the condition of the
Covenant. You decried the rabbis, calling them fossils of the council
at ancient Yavneh, where the loss of the Creator's physical, or rather
metaphysical presence on earth—the Temple and the culture it
nurtured or provoked for a millennium—was skillfully sublimated.
True, you always had trouble reconciling this overly sentimental (to
you) fact, of Judaism's re-founding, with the angry Prophets, but you
refused knowing—and I could not correct you—how the presiding
emotion in each epoch was not anger but grief. Isaiah, Jeremiah,
and all the rest down the centuries to the post-Roman remnant at
Yavneh, were grief-stricken at the worldly card table of their nation's
geopolitical losing hand and its dispiriting effect upon the culture.
When they railed, it was largely against avoidance, the head-in-the-
sand, and the appeasement mentality. They hoped to wake their
fellow citizens to the dangers, physical and spiritual, and not to
dissociate themselves from Judaism. They did not look down upon
Israel's God, but rather embraced Him as the metaphysical father
unhappily forced to become the disciplinarian. You seem to have
missed all that and turned your anger at our *Book of J*'s middling
Jewish literary critics upon Yahweh, as if He was responsible for
their self-righteous head-scratchings, and as if he was leading his
People astray by continuing to cultivate their love of Him. From
the Orthodox to the ultra-Reform, love of Israel's God, our singular
Creator, runs deep; when the great cantors of your childhood sang
to Him, they could cry a river of tears, imploring His affection; and
when the common folk welcomed His spirit into their homes every
Friday eve, for Shabbat, we sang 'Lechah Dodi,' verses from the
biblical *Song of Songs*, "My Beloved is mine, and I am His". Post-
Holocaust or not, the Jewish arguing with our Creator continued,
but again, it's not dismissive for the most part, not hateful, however
fathomless runs the grief.

You did not want to hear this defense of Jewish continuity (of your mama and tata, really, but in your mind they were immaculate, beyond need of defense), and since you were so terribly sensitive to criticism from anyone who came close to you, I dared not pursue it. You especially did not want to reconsider your belittling of many canonical biblical books. The disparaging of the *Book of Psalms,* for instance, by treating it *au fond* as a bunch of "praises", becomes today, in your valedictory lecture at Yale, the ultimate put-down, since you've built the case for a God unworthy of any praise at all. The majority of the psalms, however, use praise primarily as a refrain, a type of Greek chorus, behind the deeper structure of great ancient poems of argument. Not angry argument for the most part, but sometimes self-pitying and accusatory, within the confines of human frailty (the original "invention of the human") and parental love. They can resemble Blues songs, which you seem never to have understood. The closest you came was Louis Armstrong, enjoying his mugging and exaggerated stance, his outsized character, but did you comprehend his deadpan? I never saw such evidence, though I listened with you to your CDs often, as we lay back in matching LazyBoys, considering passages of J that I'd extracted. But even with Louie, much less the biblical Psalms or Lamentations, you did not want to grasp the deeper necessity of impersonating humiliation in order to exorcise it—in other words, Armstrong's embodiment of the Blues, that deadpan "praise" of loss, sorrow, grief—and sometimes, uncannily, true praise and joy of being. It is the same in the great poetry of the Prophets, a similarly deadpan humiliation there in the form of adultery, lechery, gluttony, thievery, and downright venality, yet the structure of the poem reveals the harmonics of an audacious listener—the poet-Prophet himself—rapt with attention, swaying with the rhythms, turning himself inside-out to mirror the visions. In short, a spiritual Blues, from which the more recent Blues of African-Americans derives. Lost to you even tonight, I'm afraid, and though you continue to gird yourself in academe, it will not sing to you when you're drowning, much less save you as a parent would.

Let me be generous and call it an innocence of the Blues (though I doubt that your totem this evening, Falstaff, would have been thus sorely innocent, for the drinking of "sack" can be an aid if well-used). Still, it's not hard to imagine why you've slid further in the direction of Christians and atheists—by far the larger crowd in which our personal literary books are read and appreciated—when they promote the anti-Jewish stereotypes of an "Old Testament" God of Wrath, a primitive God of Revenge. To you, there had to be something weird about the Jewish obeisance before such a crude

God, and so it might still seem among large swaths of academe innocent of the Hebrew Bible and for whom "weird" has become a gleeful subversion, as it long has been for you. Even though Picasso and his historical colleagues (including us) gave the word primitive a high-toned identity, its application to the misnamed "Old Testament" as a term of pity is still applied with a broad brush. And like the Blues, the determined slowness and repetition of the psalms can seem primitive to the "modern man" whose grandiosity encompasses membership in a high-minded aristocracy now faded away. Not you, of course; I've seen your enthusiastic embrace of modern artists when accompanying you to SoHo and Chelsea galleries, though curiously not of musicians, music perhaps a canon too far. Nor to animals! You were startled when faced with my golden cat, Ari, upon visiting my apartment in Tribeca, and then you did your best to ignore him. And not once did I hear you take an interest in an animal of any sort, real or imaginary; was it that the prospect of their having alien minds scared you or did you just look down upon them? Ditto Charles Darwin, scarcely a mention. I remember you were confronted with a dog in the street, whose owner, an old student of yours, stopped briefly to chat. While you ignored him, the dog gazed up at you curiously, as if he were the inquisitive critic, not you. And though certainly your mind was unknowable to him (her?) his curiosity never waned, seeming to strain on his leash toward you when we walked away.

Of course, a dog knows nothing of algebra or Cleopatra, is incapable of it, just as we are incapable of knowing the mind of God—though über-physicist Stephen Hawking, in love with the term, seems to think we can. You, on the other hand, are disinterested in such a mind, the *Zohar* notwithstanding, unless the Creator's mind might serve as a metaphor for Shakespeare. Of what possible use can the unknowable be to knowing ourselves in relation?— your obsessive theme. It's the relationship to gods and God that dispirits you, except for those like-minded master-obsessives, the weirder Kabbalists and Gnostics. The exuberance of the latter in their relation to catastrophe, also known as chaos, continues to fascinate you, probably because of their audacity in conceptualizing it, rather than in facing the Creator's unknowability. By imagining Him a demiurge, indifferent or hostile, you were able to illustrate Him tonight in your lecture as a figure worthy of your thinking-in-relation-to. But if we cast the Creator of the universe as unknowable, which is the impetus behind all characterizing of Him in cultures and religions—putting a face on him merely a work of art, a mask— then you prefer to engage the all-to-human mask rather than the fact of our limited Homo sapiens brain. You might ask: What is there to know of the mind of a dog, equally unknowable, except to the particular dog in her particular life circumstances? It is a non-literary mind, just as is the Creator's.

Whenever I thought of objecting to your disinterest in the non-literary, unknowable Creator, I caught myself, knowing how sensitive you were to criticism. Your way of brushing your critics aside was to consider them enemies, mere facts of nature, and certainly I couldn't go on enjoying your company as a potential enemy. You deflected that "potential" by calling me "son," and it scared me once, when I ironically corrected you and said "cousin," and I saw the fierceness in your eye as you replied: "no cousins, please." Perhaps you were thinking of the treachery of Hamlet's cousins or Macbeth toward his. But I was thinking benignly of mine, in the form of my poet-colleagues, and how to help find favor in your eyes toward them. Recommending a poet to you, however, one who was off your radar, was tortuous. I had to make the case to you for reading James Schuyler by insisting that his influence upon Ashbery was powerfully finespun. You did me the honor that time of reading Schuyler's *Hymn to Life*, but you still dismissed him by saying that *his* Nature was too sentimental for you, even too "uncomplicated." I couldn't go any further, though I'd have argued that those might be ironic visions of nature in Schuyler's deeply subtle sensibility. The word sensibility itself was somewhat foreign to you, as it is to most critics; it's more likely other poets who are alert to it in their poet-colleagues. You didn't mention the word once tonight, in all the great range of probes you directed at the poet Shakespeare, even though it was what could be surmised from your statement that it seemed impossible to encompass the depth of his humanity, his consciousness, his invention of the human. You became irritable when I mentioned poets you'd ignored, especially Jewish poets such as Reznikoff or Sutzkever, the latter of whom you could have read in the original Yiddish; you dismissed them as "weak," too "wounded" by the Holocaust. Not that you yourself weren't wounded by it, yet you had the strength to *resist* writing about the "incommensurate" (and thereby marked off as unknowable) Holocaust, or rebirth of Israel. That is, since you could put no face on it, the faces of each of its millions of victims were as if too saintly to contemplate.

Although you subscribe to the modern insight that biography is the only history left to us, and that Freud was the great tutor of it, you shied away. Your theory of influence entailed the biography of the literary works of writers, not their non-literary lives. I remember the almost hour's conversation we had with Philip Roth and Claire

Bloom in the Green Room, while the four of us waited to take the upper Broadway stage for 'An Evening with *The Book of J.*' Roth excepted, of course; he was there as Claire's chaperone. At one point he joked that you were a modern Moses; you didn't smash the Tablets, however, you simply forgot them on the mountain, distracted by thinking about their text on the way down. "Ah yes, my dears, perhaps that would have been too soulful an occasion even for old Bloom." In those days, barely 60, you still used the term "old" with irony—unlike tonight, when old meant old, as it did for Lear locked out of his daughter's castle. And then, wandering the heath like a Jew, the old king stripped to his soul (in the form of his Fool).

Souls have no biography, of course, no affect of their own. In this way, they too are unknowable, existing outside space and time. The word soul is used metaphorically, but nothing of it—like the word heart outside of a medical context—accrues to its understanding. Unknowable means just that. Yet when two people describe each other as soul-mates in the deepest sense, they may mean that each mutually believes in both soul and the soul's unknowability, so that finding such another believer proves uncanny to them. Regardless, souls have no face, no affect. They travel with us while we are alive, but they have neither been born nor pass away, being outside space and time. So what is the point in thinking of them? Thank you, that is the right question. The point is they allow us to think again about our mental limitations (the biological ones are too obvious to think about) and how we travel two journeys in life, one known, the other unknowable, which civilization has called the soul, in one context or another, for millennia. Your description of Hamlet tonight, Harold, is of a character resembling this unknowable state, seemingly lacking affect, loving no one, including himself, yet at the same time seeming to be one of us. In this sense, we might agree that he is the most soulful human ever represented in the most cosmic play. But I would go further, characterizing the history of religion as a cosmic theater in which myriad plays about the meaning of a human life have been tested—against what is unknowable and merely posed to us as supernatural. In that sense, I'd ask you to consider that the Bible is our Shakespeare, our best literary knowledge of the unknowable, and that its function within religion is simply not our domain; that we must be humble enough to let that go, and to return to our seats, whether we be readers, or astronauts in some distant future.

Finally, my old friend, I ask myself to consider the poem of Harold Bloom. It has a public narrative and a private one, and this evening you melded the two together into the reader of a poem about Shakespeare's works: how they encompass the limits of human knowledge, creating personages in the image of unknowable art. Hamlet, Falstaff, Cleopatra were your prime examples tonight, representing the ultimate words of the old man, as you self-identified, Harold Bloom. Now I ask myself: Who wrote this poem of Harold Bloom? To you, it may be a matter of disinterest, but to me the historical context for the question is not the Western Canon. It's a canon that includes the dog, the cat, the stone tablet, and the mountain (conscious or not).

Anyway, tonight I say: thanks for the memory. It was fun to see you in public, all dolled up like a regular person, even at 81. It occasioned this missive. I thought it was going to be a personal postscript about the modern faddishness of consciousness, as well as how the unknowable outside of it is too rarely with us. I thought it couldn't help but be funny, like a future biologist discovering one day that dogs actually do a silent algebra in their heads. Probably, it's not that funny. Probably, this letter is just a marker on a historical trail that only the two of us know the poem of. Poem, that is, as being in relation to; a map of closeness. This one, the trail between only us, perhaps too heady to read, still too private, not ready for the prying world. Unlike the poem of Harold Bloom you continue to declaim, as if the author was a lonely child prodigy, albeit doted upon by a parental audience: a public only dimly comprehending that it has inherited an American Yiddish, as enlivened tonight, but that it's a dying language. Not Hebrew, of course, which is so solidly reborn, and whose ancient roots undergirded our biblical intimacy.

Now, a late swim in the coolish Florida pool and to bed.

love,

David

Close to thirty years ago, I visited Miami in the role of Isaac Bashevis Singer's editor, finalizing a Yiddish text for the story 'Gifts,' to be published within a limited edition by the Jewish Publication Society. The story existed in English, not so much translated as improvised by Isaac from a much shorter Yiddish original. Now I'd assigned David Roskies to work up the Yiddish so that it could be printed with the English *en face*. It would be the first time one could read Singer in both languages simultaneously. Isaac was fidgety about the project. "Let's walk over to Sheldon's and have a coffee, then I'll look at it." There wouldn't be proper room at the drugstore to lay out the texts, which was fine with Isaac; he didn't really want to do this. His inclination was always to write or re-write, not to translate. If I wasn't careful, he'd have produced yet a third rendition of the story, either in Yiddish or English, and insisted we publish that one. I would have loved that, of course, and it might have been a greater literary coup, but it would have imperiled the JPS publication altogether, as the English was already set in type. Nor could we count on the Yiddish typesetter's patience: he was 88 years old; older and possibly crankier than Isaac at the time.

Besides, Singer's book was to be a twin publication with Harold Brodkey's *Women and Angels*, both books designed and on press at the same time, hopefully to be reviewed together as the start of a unique literary series. Brodkey was quite excited about this prospect. He took me to the ballet one evening, Paul Taylor's company at City Center, pumping me for details on the New Yorker magazine Jewish author held in greater esteem there than he was. His JPS book was to be Harold's coming out as a Jewish writer, at least in his eyes. "I'm so envious that you know Isaac intimately," he said. That was typical Brodkey exaggeration, inflated further by my own reticence. "You have to write about it," he said. "It's the most important thing you can do. We'll publish it in *The New Yorker*." But I had no ambition to publish in The New Yorker, a publication I derided to friends and colleagues, nor was writing about Isaac in my plans for that decade. I needed some time to separate myself from the influence of his prose, which pulled me in different directions within each and every sentence: I wanted each one, no matter how short, to be both ironic and grave, a possibility I wouldn't find the courage to embrace until faced with translating the J writer of the Bible, some years later.

While *The Book of J* was being copy-edited, Harold Bloom and I contracted for a new collaboration, *The Book of Kabbalah*. For the next year or so, we talked this book out while I pieced together texts and re-taught myself Zoharic Judeo-Aramaic, a truly dead language. Solo, without a Roskies, I planned to eventually place the text when finished in front of Harold, for his written commentary—just as I had finally accomplished with Singer and his Yiddish text. Hopefully with a different result. Isaac had started to read, then skim, then flip through the pages, then suddenly tossed the manuscript down. "I suppose I could have written it," he said. "But I have no patience any more for reading."

One day, I get a call from Harold Bloom's new agent, a former student of his and part of a cagey husband-and-wife team who had already snagged one bestselling author and who had now convinced Harold he was too hot a commodity to be doing any more collaborations. Forgetting it was I who had innocently brought them to Harold on a trip to New Haven, Glen said, "Harold wants to cancel the Kabbalah." But we already took half the six-figure advance, I replied in so many words and in a whining tone that shocked even myself. "And I've completed over a year's work on it." Comes the cool reply, not skipping a beat—"They'll allow you time to return the advance"—cutting off any questions about whether the publisher would consider my finishing the manuscript on my own. Harold assured me the next week that we'd continue with the Kabbalah book, but not long after I hear that his new agent had sold a different solo proposal of his for close to a million dollars. Since Harold hadn't invited me to the celebration, I didn't expect to hear anything more about how "this book of ours will be for Uncle Scholem, in loving memory." Besides, the Kabbalah had already waited many centuries to go mainstream—the original Kabbalah, that is, and not the Madonna version—so it could wait a bit longer.

Meanwhile, *The Book of J*, which had spent 7 weeks near the top of the *New York Times* Bestseller list, achieved a record paperback sale, thanks to my agent Lynn N, with whom I'd continue on for another two books but who was powerless to do anything about the Kabbalah, even though she'd been a religion major at Vassar or Smith, or so she joked. Losing Harold meant little to her; she already had Michael Crichton, author of half a dozen mega-sellers, along with many more bestselling authors. "I should have warned you about Bloom," she said. "He's trouble."

Well, perhaps I knew that. But so was my own dear, loving mother, an insight I had into her emotional life when I was eight or ten. What could I do about it? She was still the best mother I knew, and Bloom the best pseudo-father. My first inkling anxiety lay ahead came during another visit to New Haven, just before J hit the stands and we were still anticipating a tough sell in the marketplace. I'd scheduled an afternoon with Geoffrey Hartman to sample the Yale Video Archive of Holocaust Survivor Testimony he directed. Geoffrey was almost Bloom's equal in literary renown at that time; not long before, he was showcased on the front cover of the *Sunday Times Magazine*, touted as leader of the American wing of newly-fashionable deconstructionist literary theory. You'd think I'd have known a rivalry with Bloom had to have existed, but I didn't want to know; I took the respectful words each offered for the other at face value. And in the same way, I became immersed in the deeply emotional yet fluent and dramatically composed monologues the Holocaust survivors told on the tapes I was shown, skillfully prompted by psychologically trained interviewers, whose visual presences were edited out of the film.

Over dinner with Geoffrey and his wife, Renee (excusing herself after the soup), he asked about my luncheon meeting with Bloom and if I found him difficult. I hadn't thought of Harold this way; most of the significant people in my life were difficult and I seemed used to tolerating that, as I've said. However, Geoffrey was more naturally parental than a Bloom, and even in that single inquiry he showed a concern for my well-being that I brushed aside. Thinking about it later on the train back to NYC, I reminded myself how I instinctively refused most aid and comfort. Had I been interviewed as a Holocaust survivor, I too would have overlooked the questions and promptings—to the point that, on reviewing the edited tape, I'd have forgotten the interviewer's presence. That's how compelled I was to view my life as testimony to an original wound—one that I could not identify. I'd learned from my survivor relatives in childhood that there were no words for existential suffering—the kind where you could think you'd be better off dead; that just a notation of the events was hell enough. But what did I know of hell? On the road to becoming a poet, I was sure it was enough to create the context—not necessarily the words—for any experience, so that most of my early poems were scenes of being stunned beyond speech, as if a toddler before his first word. Mine had been *dorten*, *there*, let's go *there*, let's explore *there*, not here, where nothing could be said. If he is reading this, Geoffrey Hartman will understand that my "here" signifies a deconstruction of "there." It may be impossible to find the words to get back there.

One can pun, which is what deconstruction theory, like poetry, allows. It is essentially comic, not tragic, implies Derrida—or like midrash, implies Hartman. It's warm, not cold logic; it intervenes when rigidity threatens its subject. Presented with a rigid corpse, however, how to comically mediate, how to cut in? *Finnegans Wake* does it, the corpse at its core, but that was before the Holocaust, before such a word was spoken, and before it became the first tragic pun—on a burnt offering, in loving offer to the Creator. The first tragic pun, then, renders us speechless. "A toddler before his first word." Or, a number in Auschwitz, not a name; a nightmare repressed, daily, and not a Holocaust video testimony at Yale; the unspeakable "there" of the crematorium chimney, not a marked grave.

All this came up at dinner with Geoffrey, though not in so many words. It was enough to discuss midrash hermeneutics a bit, which he was planning to edit an anthology of academic writers upon, and to offer my response to the Holocaust video testimonies: "It was like a contest to see who would cry first, the Holocaust survivor or myself." Silent crying, the kind without tears or any other signifier. Yet with Bloom earlier that day, it had been no to *Finnegans Wake* and its endless punning, but yes to Joyce's *Ulysses*, where you could be clear on the characters, especially the one named Bloom. It was the strangest thing about Harold, especially as I reflect on it now, that he was almost incapable of punning, especially in informal conversation. He might quote one, from Shakespeare for instance, but for himself he seemed always to shy away, as if a pun were a kind of poem and that it would imperil his credentials as a critic to be revealed as a poet—or anything less than a major poet. Too bad he couldn't have become a critic in Yiddish, as if there'd been no Holocaust and the great Jewish language of his and my youth had continued to exfoliate. There his punning would have bloomed, beyond the highly literary sort disguised as irony. He might have merited a Nobel, like Isaac, had he become the great Jewish critic.

So Harold was no deconstructionist, and that viewpoint's wealth of puns; its insistence on punning, as in the poetry of David Shapiro, scared him. He wouldn't admit to being upset in this way, but rather dismissed Shapiro as not up to the standard of his mentor, Ashbery. To call David a deconstructionist in poetry might be an understatement; his every line recomposed the previous, fearless to employ any pun at any moment. Because he was a close friend of mine, I tried whenever possible to strengthen his case with Harold, insinuating how he was a beloved presence in the "Second Generation" of New York School poets. I was insensitive, however, to how the mere existence of that school—so at home with the pun and with the French modernists who had deeply domesticated it—was in itself the bane of Harold's role as critic of the latest in contemporary poetry. As I've said before, I could not get him to read the New York School masters, O'Hara, Schuyler, and especially Kenneth Koch, whose ingenious punning disturbed him and whose Ivy League position at Columbia enervated him (until, worn down at last, he wrote sympathetically of Koch in the late '90s). Although Ashbery was also of this school, Harold separated him out as a poet akin to himself, full of strange ironies more grandiose than the lowly pun. Before I'd fully realized this I did Shapiro no little harm in Bloom's eyes by pointing out Koch as his true mentor. However, I was alert enough not to refer to my own coming to maturity among second generation New York School poets, nor to my having been a student of Koch's before that. It was better for both of us that Harold thought of me as sui generis, a kind of "the last Yiddish poet," even though Hebrew was overwhelmingly my environment. Reading a manuscript of my most outrageous (a term of highest esteem for Harold) poems—a text that I have not published—he said that it reminded him of Kafka's sweeping ironies. Since Franz Kafka neither wrote poetry nor in Yiddish, I was unsure of how to take this compliment, one that he offered as a blurb should I require it. Perhaps it was meant to be outrageous (a high compliment rather than a low pun).

The outrageous, as normalized by the *New York Times*: "This is a story we've read before, in a stack of books that, laid end to end, would wrap 88 times around the outskirts of Tel Aviv." This poor substitute for a pun is offered up in a favorable review of a book in 2013 that retails the tale of Israel's founding. Certainly the reviewer has not read such a stack of books, perhaps not even two; nor would he expect that most of us had. There's something off here, something terribly wrong with this self-conscious exaggeration of exhaustion; it's a parallel to feigned Holocaust exhaustion. Too many books on the Holocaust, enough with the victimhood; it's always the same story, the train without brakes hurtling downhill. Do we need yet another gloomy book on it? Let's get back to real life, to our sensible present. Sensible to some, perhaps, but outrageous to me, for it's exactly what we do need: another book, another poem, another film, anything to show that sense is possible. Is there a book about the Holocaust on the bestseller list this week? No, not even one out of twenty-five.

Why do stories of Israel's founding have to remind us of the Holocaust? Was it only sympathy for its having to fight off five Arab armies that refused partition—was that what moved the UN to accept Israel? No Holocaust, no acceptance? So how could resentment against it have been avoided when it appears statehood was granted as compensation for the Holocaust? We can understand how Israel's enemies, losers of every war they raised against it, would want the world to resent the victor as an imperialist Goliath. The Israeli author of the book under question is himself ready to admit as much, that Israel is in denial about the unnecessary bullying at its founding. Wait—the author goes on to state that it was in fact necessary, if odious. Yet he too, at one with his praising reviewer, wishes to share this ambivalence with contemporary Palestinians, as if that would move them. But is the testimony of Holocaust survivors not also a kind of bullying, forcing us to consider the unconsiderable, rendering us ambivalent about the necessity to place yet one more testimony on top of the mound of testimonies? Our NYT review ends: "The more you know, this book suggests, the closer the shadows creep." He means the shadow of the bully, overshadowing the earlier sunny reports we heard about Israel's rebirth out of the Holocaust. Did I say "sunny?"

The same week, however, we do have a kind of Holocaust discussion in the *Times Book Review*, concerning the fiftieth anniversary of *Eichmann in Jerusalem*. "Indeed, the whole idea of the 'banality of evil' is at bottom a way of denying Nazism any glamour or substance." But it had already been destroyed, there was no recrudescence of Nazism in the 1960s that needed to be denied. In fact, its glamour had been undercut in the free world before the war even began, as in Charlie Chaplin's film, *The Great Dictator*. Chaplin was known to be a Hitler favorite, so it might have annoyed Der Führer to no end. No, it's not Nazism that needs de-glamorizing, not then and not now, but the context in which it was allowed to thrive, German culture in particular and Western culture in general—might it not deserve our attention? Not the problems of ideology, fascism vs communism etc., but precisely the history of a culture, German culture, in which a Hannah Arendt could grow and progress, as ineluctably as sheep to the slaughter. Precisely the subject Arendt seeks to avoid.

In an interview with Joachim Fest a few years after her book was published, he praises it like this: "You referred to the way that the Eichmann trial laid bare the total nature of the moral collapse at the heart of Europe, among the persecutors and the persecuted alike, in every country." One wonders about that moral collapse among the persecuted, especially since Arendt did not deny it, either in the interview or in her book. We've seen it represented in films, such as the classic *I was a fugitive from a chain gang*, where the persecuted hero is reduced to becoming a common thief, though even then his moral collapse is not commensurate with the evils of the chain gang and the corrupt court, for which the film's viewer is expected to have utter contempt. Of course, Arendt did have contempt for Eichmann, as a *New York Times Book Review* columnist explains, and the columnist does raise a question about blaming the victim: "For Eichmann, on the other hand, she had only contempt, refusing even to dignify him with hatred: He appears in the book only as a bumbling mediocrity.... But it's also easy to understand how this tactic could appear, to readers still traumatized by the Holocaust, as an arrogant inversion placing blame on the victim while minimizing the criminality of the criminal."

Yet another question, just as troubling, emerges here, concerning "readers still traumatized by the Holocaust." Am I among those readers? I hope so, because those who have gotten past any literary trauma and who reference the Holocaust as another historical event (albeit terrible) of the past rather than feeling it as a wound to their own humanity—it is perhaps these readers who will recognize themselves in that part of Arendt who is a grandiose thinker and not an emotional creature. Arendt wrote of Eichmann: "'I will jump into my grave laughing,' because having the deaths of millions of Jews on his conscience gives him 'extraordinary satisfaction'; he seems to do so mostly to cut what in his mind is an impressive figure." But how to know his mind? Yes, we all want to cut an impressive figure, at least some of the time. So the real question should be: what is the context for such a society, in which such a figure can be cut? Do the boundaries of Being coincide with the dimensions of Nature's slaughterhouse?

I don't think it's just me that's bringing up the Holocaust, it's the culture; for instance, the wide interest in the 50th anniversary of the Eichmann trial. The shock is not so much in how the German psyche is revealed in Eichmann but that half a century has passed and we still don't know how or what to consider evil, if anything. The Holocaust has been enfolded with other genocides to erode uniqueness, and if we can take for granted that evil tides arise in humanity as do natural tsunamis, in Rwanda, Cambodia, Serbia or Syria, then Eichmann was an instance of something larger and more impersonal. Yet unlike the others, the impending Holocaust was coddled and accepted for a decade before the Final Solution was crafted. Not spontaneous, but crafted, like a horrible Germanic epic, inscribed within the putative height of Western culture. As late as '38, England was happy to appease it. Heidegger, the cream of German philosophical tradition, subscribed to this epic, and we can track back to Wagner his deep roots in, and lifelong enchantment with slaughterhouse-transcendent poetry. So let's see, what were his thoughts about evil...

"Heidegger is the antithesis of the sort of philosopher (John Stuart Mill, William James, Isaiah Berlin) who assumes that nothing ultimately matters except human happiness. For him, human suffering is irrelevant: philosophy is far above such banalities. He saw the history of the West not in terms of increasing freedom or of decreasing misery, but as a poem. 'Being's poem,' he once wrote, 'just begun, is man.'"

Bloom was no lover of Heidegger, though he was swayed by the Heideggerian love for Nietzsche and the primacy of poetry. Harold found his antidote, however, in Shakespeare, several years after *The Book of J.* When J first hit the bestseller list and we were congratulating each other, I said, "It's the best book on Shakespeare yet." I wasn't all that witty; I was just referring to the Shakespearean character that Bloom had made of Yahweh. Not many years later, Harold had determined that it was Shakespeare who had "invented the human," in a manner of eclipsing both God and Heidegger. Shakespeare was one for whom human happiness mattered, as did the suffering of Hamlet, and from pretty much post-*Book of J* onward, Harold was consumed with writing books that, unlike his earlier probings of the literary-philosophical-psychological underpinnings of poetry, had become manuals in the joys and necessities of reading. Reading, in other words, was the form of transcendence that could allow for our ambivalence toward the Holocaust. But at least it wasn't quite German transcendence; it was more Yiddish-inflected.

Richard Rorty, an American critic of philosophy, observed this ambivalency in '98, already 40 years after Hannah Arendt decried the *trial* of Eichmann as almost as banal for its dramatic emphasis on survivors' (and non-survivors) *suffering* as the banality of Eichmann. "Suffering is not the point... as she might have echoed her mentor and lover, Heidegger." Anyway, she was a torn woman, wonderfully tragicomic in her way. When I caught sight of her in the New School halls, the grossly weathered features of her last years resembled those of Auden, both of them presenting as tragic clowns, albeit noble ones.

"Aristotle is our teacher, Heidegger argues, in learning to hold on to the wonder of the dimension of Being, and, thus, to hold on to the wonder that lack, loss, and absence is." (Richard Capobianco, another U.S. critic of philosophy). Ah yes, the wonder of all that loss and absence that is the Holocaust. Comparable to the endless wonders of nature—endless, that is, if the universe is truly expanding, and if our winding up as stranded in darkness remains a wonder.

But let's keep to the infinite wonders that still exist on earth. I'm reading a feature on the Hula wetlands in northern Israel, on the Times of Israel website, written by the daughter of an old friend. She focuses upon the birds, in particular the migrating species of geese. "What are they talking about?" she asks. "It's impossible to know. Perhaps they are debating where's a good place to land." Often I work in my writing hut tucked into a remnant of the Everglades, the great wetlands of North America. Nearby, every day, a flock of over fifty ibis stand in shallow water, chatting in random conversation. Just before dusk, they begin talking all at once that at first sounds like the improvisation of the Sun Ra Arkestra of the '60s. Then a flapping of white wings becomes noticeable, a testing out of them, like dancers at a barre. Suddenly they all take flight at the same moment, just the whoosh of the wings left as a brief coda. They always go in the same direction, flying into the bay and then a sharp left toward the ocean. Long ago I stopped asking what they were talking about; at first, I listened as if to a Bach cantata, my German too rudimentary to parse the texts. Well actually, I do understand the Bach works, having studied them over many years, but I need this analogy for a different reason. The ibis language, I've come to understand, is one of song, and the work they finally accomplish before take-off is the great ibis poem. When the poem is accomplished, they are ready to fly, as if each ibis has been swept away by the art, swept into the sky. The poem is not descriptive; it doesn't say we'll go this way at such and such a time. They all know what time it is by the failing light, and they all know where they're going; the leading bird is more like a musical conductor than a pathfinder. I too know exactly when to raise my head from the computer screen and catch the gorgeous take-off: a poem to me as well; its tapping of inner wells, of harmony with the vaporous realms of sea and sky, override any need for instruction.

It's the same with the poem that humans make, pretty much defined for all time by Aristotle and Plato. What do we learn from a poem? It's a time capsule. The poem of the white ibis reaches deep into time, when the species evolved, and even further, suggesting its original ecosystem. Science can probe it, but for the artist the original scene of writing, the time of evolving, resonates with his own, which is why what we want most from a critic of Bach or Shakespeare is a glimpse of the scene of writing, the ground at which the poem takes flight. I don't mean the desk at which Emily Dickinson wrote her great oeuvre, but rather the mind alive, testing the limits of its New England environment. The desk helps set the scene; we need to see it's a Puritan desk. In the Bach biography, the situation of the Thirty Years War backlights his table; in Shakespeare's, it's the daylight and candlelight of Elizabethan London. Superfluous to me is Shakespeare or Plato walking around in the U.S. today, though that's what most interpretation gives us, including today's museum-like idea of the past.

You won't find a time capsule in a museum because when you open it, the smell of life hits you. It's not Emily's or William's writing table that matters, even as it evokes the great writings. It's not even the great writings that matter, and a risk I take in stating that startles me. It's simply the life of the creature Shakespeare in itself, a creature of life. I doubt any writer would commit suicide by rushing into a burning house to save his manuscripts. Not even Sylvia Plath; not if she hadn't first saved her children. It's the living breath that's precious.

Shakespeare was a man first, a writer second, and the same is true of the J writer of the Bible—except that she was more likely a woman. Even today there are dyspeptic critics who say there is no evidence for that, but what better testimony than the literary text, a far more articulate fossil than Australopithecus footprints. From the latter we can deduce male or female, but as the *Book of J* testifies, J's pov is in direct contrast to the putative males who wrote the rest of the Torah. If she was not a woman, at least the burden of proof confirms that she or he had a sexuality. Once you give this great Jewish writer his or her life back, her *breath*, the Hebraic culture around her also comes to life: we can imaginatively walk the streets of her Jerusalem, visit the palace archives, look over her shoulder as she works at her table. Would we trade her Genesis and Exodus for her life? There's the true biblical question, a parallel to the question of whether Abraham could sacrifice his son (or instead had dreamed it, a nightmare, in the dreamlike ancient style of the E writer). No, I would have saved her first from the burning house, at the risk of losing Genesis. Because there would have been another Genesis, possibly even the E writer's in Samaria, but it might have been a tragically (for us contemporary humanists) inferior one.

However, let me state the case a bit more popularly, in terms of movies. Last night we watched part of *The Leopard*, the full 3½-hour Italian original, lately re-released and now ensconced on our DVR (the original 1960s art-house release chopped it down to a dubbed and incomprehensible 1½ hours) and also part of *Bundle of Joy*, a 1956 inferior Hollywood remake of the Ginger Rogers version, live on TCM. As time-capsules they were equal, though I'd say *Bundle* has the edge. Debbie Reynolds is a superior actress to Claudia Cardinale, but that's only part of the reason. *Leopard* draws you in, perhaps the peak of its great director Luchino Visconti's oeuvre, and *holds you* there, in its setting of the 19th century Risorgimento, hypnotized by the complex layering of plot and scene (based on Lampedusa's major novel of the same name). Burt Lancaster speaking perfect Italian, and aging before our eyes, is startling as the prince, aided by his Fool of a constant companion—a foil of a priest as compelling as King Lear's. You get a time-capsule of history here on many levels, but they are mainly within the film itself, while in *Bundle of Joy* the historical context surrounds the film like a huge, deeply-textured frame, the cultural dimensions mostly outside the movie. What this bauble preserves in its time capsule are the tragicomic dimensions of the postwar baby boom, the idealization of marriage and family, job and title, at the expense of social conscience. Debbie is swaddled in mink, while I ask: How many animals had to die for it? Eddie dresses her in expensive clothes and jewels, seeming to pity Debbie for the fantasy of a brute husband who left her with child, yet I ask: How come we see only white people inside and outside the department store he owns? Meanwhile, I'm feeling pangs of loss at the gorgeously designed and colored cars of the

'50s, especially the cheap Plymouths, Fords and Chevys, and the mobs of Checker cabs on the NYC avenues. It's not so much a period that's invoked, as the horse-drawn carriages do in *Leopard*, but a cultural conflict that in its way is more subtle than most art-house films. It's the conflict between conscience and consciousness, for underneath the unconscious trappings of the postwar boom in capital and babies, the characters of Debbie and Eddie are in fact rebellious, cultural revolutionaries with great moral consciousness—we could only hope that the youth revolution to follow in the '60s would be half so heroic and unassuming about it. It's the infant in swaddling clothes, the "John Doe" of the movie, who is treasured over all the trappings; the scoldings of adultery, illegitimacy, and social status are tossed out the window like torn diapers, so that you feel it would make no difference at all if the baby was black, the mother was gay, or Eddie was a communist—a far more radical anarchy than the historical strictures laid bare in Lampedusa's novel. Probably the intense freedom of the *Bundle* characters went unnoticed in the '50s, with Hollywood assuming it was making a toned-down version of the 1939 original, entitled *Bachelor Mother*, which itself was a domesticated version of '30s screwball comedy. But it doesn't matter now; what we are viewing in the '50s movie today, in terms of historical context, is a huge battle between public norms and private behavior. (Also, not-so-private, when we recall the dumping of wife Debbie and baby in the real-life Eddie Fisher-Liz Taylor affair).

In the *Wall Street Journal* last week, I read that "by the time the freshmen boomers were in college, feminism was an essay topic for the 'Reading Shakespeare in Cultural Context' course." Lady Macbeth, Cordelia, Cleopatra, Rosalind, *et. al.* But not the context of Shakespeare at his table—his body, the human creature in time, over and above his timeless mind. True, it would be speculative, but imaginative rediscovery is what's needed. Or so I've pleaded. I'm sometimes brushed off as a mere speculator, especially in the years since *The Book of J* was published, in the four books that explored how the scenes of writing behind the Hebrew Bible are the most hidden and most revelatory of what a writer and a culture can accomplish. And not the Bible's obvious success as the all-time bestseller but as progenitor of all the possibilities open to a writer. Of these, the most atrophied today may be the visionary, the mythic, the lament, and the deadpan epigram.

Seeing even a contemporary literary work as a time-capsule can achieve the same deep dimensionality of the biblical, read millennia later, or *Bundle of Joy*, viewed half a century afterward. Perhaps only a Stanley Cavell, with his potent books on Hollywood film remarriages and Shakespeare, could have understood *Bundle* in 1956 as a subversive time-capsule; similarly, only a few strong minds (or poet colleagues) might be capable of reading a new poem as a time-capsule, just after it's written. Or even the moment it is written, if one can look at creaturely life as a process of dying, one that begins in us soon after adolescence. Once we recognize it—that all poems are time-capsules in harmony with a species consciousness of mortality—we can feel time as it passes through us, a flashlight scanning the walls and the environments that we share with those of our fellow humans, the poets who are writing today's time-capsules. In this view, our own moment of reading is historical also. These scenes of writing and reading are very complex, almost impossible to bring back into focus, except with great interpretative strength. Watching *Bundle of Joy* today appears easier because its throw-away quality as art allowed me to focus on its historical frame. So in that case it's my historical scene of watching—and writing about it—that facilitates interpretation. *My* scene of writing becomes the significant one, over and above the scene in Hollywood of the making of *Bundle of Joy.* In a great, or even good poem, however, we need the imagined scene of writing behind it, in which the poet composes, in order to feel how alive we can be, or might become. Even though biography may be the only history left to us moderns, as Freud's theory of psychoanalysis implied before the war, the irony of that insight darkened after the Holocaust, when such an incomprehensible mass of human biographies was lost, obliterated.

So that's how I came to consider the poem of Harold Bloom: first as a character in the artless film of daily life, akin to *Bundle of Joy,* in which I visited with him intensely during some three years. It helped me to see that the poem he strove to create with his critical powers was a poem of great loss, of attempting to reach deep into the past and bring an ancient fish to the surface, still struggling for breath. This could be true even if it only *seemed like* an ancient fish-poem yet was actually a contemporary one. But why did he require so grandiose a reach? I think it was his knowing that the context of the Holocaust in his lifetime was the crucial one, yielding a struggle to avoid and get past it. A loss of confidence in humanity is what such a struggle should entail, yet that loss is marginalized; after all, the absurdity of life was already worked through in the arts even before the war, so what's left?

"The novel helped him reconstitute things he'd lost," the son of Lampedusa said at NYU in 2010. Like Thomas Mann, he said, Lampedusa had been born into "the full flowering of European civilization," only to see it eclipsed. "They became prophets of the Europe that thought of itself as the hegemony and then was superseded by the United States." But where in this statement is recognition of a greater loss than "hegemony?" Where is the prophecy—or at least the recording—of evil, of the Italian fascist compact with Nazi evil?

Although Bloom did hold such radical loss of humanity in mind, he didn't quite know what to do with it; he saw it, perhaps, as the evil side to the lost world of his pious parents, their goodness in his eyes exposing the evil at the heart of European civilization. Kafka and Freud, Harold's champions, knew it in their bones, but Bloom himself remained stuck in a prodigy's pushing ahead for more life in which to embody his talented insight into the Western Canon—an acknowledged Talmudist of it. The Talmud preserves the Hebrew estimation of the world, as the Western Canon does the Greek; Harold reconstituted the latter by adding additional Hebrew literary weight to it, from J to Moshe de Leon, primary author of the medieval *Zohar* (though I couldn't get him to reread the faux Judeo-Aramaic of it: "I trust, my boy, you'll find a way to translate its innovation.") Had Bloom's Yiddish-speaking parents stayed on, unmurdered, in Eastern Europe and he grown up in the Soviet empire like the Jewish writers executed by Stalin, likewise unmurdered, we might have had a Yiddish Kafka to compliment the Yiddish Dostoevsky (combined with the Yiddish Appelfeld) of Bashevis Singer.

"You call me a Holocaust writer," Singer said to me the year I was trying to persuade him to contribute to my anthology, *Testimony,* "but you're the only one who does." I had written that he was best understood as uprooted by the Holocaust, that "uprootedness is the prime condition of his insight." Strangely enough, I recall Harold's envy of Singer (this, before Harold became a part-time NYU professor) for living in NYC and thus being lionized by the *New Yorker* magazine crowd and Dick Cavett TV interviews. Singer had access to American media, from Hollywood's Barbra Streisand to what was left of the Partisan Review clique, all of it leading to a Nobel, while Bloom was stuck in New Haven, which he considered a small college enclave wrapped in the shell of "a hick town." Poems can get written anywhere, including Emily Dickinson's bedroom, but the poem of Harold Bloom wanted to be as cosmopolitan as Falstaff. Falstaff cosmopolitan? For his access to the highest in Prince Hal as well as the bawdy house lowest, yes. NYC did get Harold media access, but not quite the reach of Falstaff or, in lifelong terms, of Singer.

The Poem of the Jewish Writer

Several of my uncles were involved in the shmata business. Shmatas, Yiddish for rags, was typical mordant irony among them, including the names of their stores: Jack's Fifth Avenue, for uncle Jack, Varsity Mens Shoppes, for uncle Louis; I worked on weekends at Varsity during high school years, pointing out the genuine shmata lining in the cheap sports jackets to the clientele in Hamtramck, a Polish gentile enclave. Sometimes too, I risked admiring the genuine Dreck (shitty) from Hollywood styling, though this mainly with customers my own age. Among these uncles a bit later, especially after I won the university's Hopwood Prize at Ann Arbor, I was known as the scribbler. "How's the scribbler doing?" they asked their sister, my mom, when I was pursuing a Ph.D in England. It was as a fan of the UK Colchester side while at University of Essex that I was initiated into soccer and that I now in 2014 watch the US goal unfold in the final minutes of the World Cup match against Belgium in Brazil. It's a wholly unexpected thing of beauty, created by a 19-year-old in his first big match, but the manner in which it unfolded was occluded by the eventual US loss, 2-1. That is, the creativity required for that goal to unfold was so unexpected it went unremarked, thanks to the character of US play during the preceding 115 minutes, which was entirely conservative, defensive, with our goalie designated the star of the game.

So it's not surprising, as I look back, that what seems the biggest goal I scored in life was as a Jewish scribbler/editor in Israel, c.1983, a goal it took me more than a year to create, and in which my teammates had little belief. It was the creation of the first stand-alone issue of *Forthcoming: Jewish Imaginative Writing* (previously an insert in *Moment* magazine of Boston). Then as now, US secular Jewish culture was largely a defensive effort, accomplishing just enough to keep the worriers about total assimilation at bay. For them, there may always be a candidate for the next Philip Roth, if not Saul Bellow or Cynthia Ozick, yet this sentiment is built on the assumption that Roth was a goalie: he was so like a worldly un-Jewish writer that you couldn't score any anti-Jewish goals against him. Roth made a show of trying to score those goals upon himself, which were always deflected by the fact he didn't deny being Jewish and that he used his experience of growing up among Jews to startling effect. When the Jews came off poorly in Roth's books, even scandalously so, it showed how mature we readers were—so went the line on cultural pride. Never mind that Roth had little interest in Jewish languages and historical literature, the main thing was that you could still identify with his Jewish shtick, as many tortuous academic articles and reviews contrived to show. Far be it for me to complain, since as a goalie Roth held up his part to the end, through a messy duel of memoirish books between himself and his former wife, the actor Claire Bloom, and through a bunch of late awards for his late books, including one by the Jewish Theological Seminary, in which he was required to stand on stage among rabbis, in a kippah, though not asked to utter a word. You had to love the goalie in such circumstances, but meanwhile I was trying to score an offensive goal against all odds. Few Jews in America were looking for a journal that exclusively published Jewish fiction/poetry and attempted to build a bridge between American and Israeli writers. The project was tenuous enough that it had to be called *Forthcoming* even after it began to appear. It even had enemies, mainly literary critics who decried their exclusion: Jewish culture needed to be a scholarly endeavor, they huffed, refusing to take notice of the venture to this day.

Up to the last minute, I was uncertain an offensive goal could be scored. Outside of the personal support of an editor in New York, Nessa Rapoport, the American facilitators at *Moment* magazine and the National Foundation for Jewish Culture were dubious and cried penury whenever a small subsidy was needed. Maybe that isn't quite fair; the Jewish culture leaders claimed their mandate was to support scholarship and, mainly as a sideline, the "performing" arts, while *Moment*'s politically motivated editor worried that too much fiction was a cop-out from left-wing causes. How I managed to keep these reluctant backers in the game is beyond me; I think I insisted to them that the Israeli supporters would take responsibility for any problems, and I told the same to the Israelis about the American affiliation. No one wanted any responsibility because none of them believed there was an audience, or even enough writers and translators to publish. While Nessa stood in for me in the US, I was as if underground, commuting between my Jerusalem apartment and Tel Aviv demi-office, shared with tough-minded, angelic Nili Cohen, to produce *The New Yorker* look-alike extravaganza, right down to the metal plates from which the issues were to be run off in Boston—Moment had to be kept under the impression that the Israelis were so gung-ho that they footed the entire printing bill. This was not the case. It was I who was the only putative Israeli responsible, persuading the contributors that a parochial publication would further their worldly ambitions; so I performed all the editing and printing services myself, including paste-up at the printer's empty factory on several Shabbat weekends, coercing Israeli artists to contribute illustrations and to pay for the negatives, etc. All of this on a strict deadline for *Moment*'s publication date, that could only be accomplished by sweet-talking Israel's foreign ministry into allowing use of the diplomatic pouch to get the printer-ready issue stateside. I could not have afforded the hundreds of dollars it cost to send it express, and even then risking delays, diversions, even loss.

So after months of preparation, I was sitting in a Tel Aviv cafe with my graphic artist Eli Gilad, an idealistic kibbutznik who asked for no compensation, going over the final paste-up. It was Shabbat and I'd have to catch a gypsy sherut-taxi to get to Jerusalem around midnight, carrying about 20+ lbs of one-of-a-kind plates, manuscripts, and original artwork. I would then stay up until 6 AM, getting the work to the Foreign Ministry in time to arrive in Boston on Monday. And then, leaving the FM office, I'd have no idea if the shot had made it into the net until I actually saw the printed copies a month later. My haberdasher uncles, who played Maccabi soccer in their Lithuanian youths, might have been proud I'd acquired some tricky salesmanship back in Detroit, even if the end result was no profit.

How does this describe if not profit a Jewish writer? For one thing, it allowed me to establish intimacy with I.B. Singer, as I've described elsewhere; we joked about turning out Jewish lit like dressmaking: to your readers you had to appear in casual clothes but to your editors you had to be formally dressed. Since you could only afford one set of clothes, you had to turn them inside out, the beginning of the reversible trend that I met in the '50s at uncle Jack's Fifth Avenue. Casual on the inside, formal on the outside, and reversible. So it is with many Jewish sources: Jewish on the inside, if not always the outside, such as even the New Testament, but more often the reverse. Any diaspora Jew should know this. My outward context in Western culture inherits Christian humanism, and up until the age of thirty I could feel inwardly beholden to the Puritans—to struggling with or against them—as were Emily Dickinson or T.S. Eliot. Yet inside, as the child of near-Holocaust survivors, I was more Jewish than they were, sensing from my observant maternal grandparents that something precious had been lost—possibly more precious than the modern culture gained. Feeling that made me a kind of natural avant-gardist, for early Modernism had deeply conflicted feelings about modern life, especially the hubris of progressivism that smashed up in the First World War. The carnage was bad enough, but it also exposed hidden layers of loathing that quickly devolved into World War 2, the Holocaust, and the Cold War with totalitarian communism whose Nassarite and Maoist embers still threaten—though the real inheritors appear to be a darker mirror-image of progressivism gone wrong, Islamists. In literature, the avant-garde's increasing focus on deconstructing language and meaning helps it resist cruel ideas—but that's on the outside. On the inside, Jewish thinking, so richly latent in Freud and Einstein, remained the original avant-garde, testing Christian and atheist grandiosity, yet how was I to access it as a postmodernist? A reversible jacket was my answer; modern on the outside, ancient on the inside.

Today, after Charles Reznikoff, there are few major English-language writers who can be said to love the Hebrew Bible, although you could say that it was also a source for Ezra Pound, in that he reacted violently against it. As a positive source for modern poets, the Hebrew Bible comes in far down the list of Homer, Sappho, Sophocles, Aeschylus, Confucius, Gilgamesh, and various primitive and Indus Valley epics. I wouldn't say writing your own "psalm" without reading Hebrew counts as a source, anymore than writing your own sonnet while ignorant that Petrarch and Shakespeare wrote. Not that I'm saying anything new, except that if your sources are the inside of a reversible jacket, then they have to stand up to the weather on the outside too. The Hebraic flood story of Noah in Genesis is superior literature to the Sumerian flood story in the sources that have come down to us, but the Sumerian is still strong enough to float on its own, for it was already a classical literary source for the J writer in Genesis. A recent episode of Neil de Grasse Tyson's probing post-Carl Sagan doc on mainstream network TV, *Cosmos*, describes a Sumerian flood story predating the one in Genesis by more than a thousand years. Yet if scholarship-challenged viewers are surprised by this offhand remark, indicating that the Bible's hundreds of writers had sources, what are they to make of a modern Jewish writer's sources?

For the Bible's Hebraic authors, Sumerian literature consisted of millennia-old literary classics, and if not all of ancient Israel's formative writers could read the original cuneiform script, then there surely were a few translators at that time and of Solomonic culture who could. Why would we expect a Jewish writer to exist in a Jewish vacuum, when Jewish culture itself never has? Perhaps it all comes down to the misconstrued figure of Moses as writer: If he's taking dictation from God, as it were, then why would he be in need of worldly sources? Yet the Creator himself has partaken of the all-too-human Hebrew language for a source, not to mention his frequent reference to historical events, and the sources of ancient Hebrew are as varied as those of English. Still, that leaves Shakespeare or Joyce as solidly English or Irish authors—but what if they had written in Chinese, their British Isle parents having emigrated to Shanghai? That is the problem with the Jewish writer in a non-Jewish language and history; not just the issue of his or her sources but the larger question of her influences.

I tried to solve this problem for myself by intertextually translating a few Hebrew psalms, and quickly discovered the depth of my ignorance about the Bible's sources. It's not hard to get up to speed on the nature of "source criticism," but more insight is required to discern a historical Jewish sensibility. It could take decades of study, as it took for ancient translators invested in acquiring the scholarly equivalent of cuneiform literacy. Did I have that much time to divert from my imaginative writing practice? A decade after I decided I would have to—a decision whose implications I'd be grappling with the rest of my life—I faced a similar question about taking on a few years of psychoanalytic therapy. Might it not inhibit my creative writing and the mysterious (to me, anyway) sources of my inspiration? Not to mention putting a dent in my finances and possibly my resumé? What I found is that in psychoanalysis, you become a witness to dangers your life has survived, and in ancient Jewish texts, you become a witness to the danger of missing what the writers were up against in a world ambivalent about truth-testing. So, being a Jewish writer today might mean something special if one's contemporary testimony to the non-Jewish world is echoed by Jewish sources. And the reverse.

In 1985, I asked my old movie-going companion, independent filmmaker/photographer Rudy Burckhardt, to accompany me uptown to a full day's showing of Claude Lanzmann's *Shoah*. To my surprise, 80-something Rudy stayed alert for the entire eight hours, though he'd told me in advance he was limited to just 2 hours a day of serious concentration. I was worried I could be "laying a trip" on non-Jewish Rudy (an expression from the '60s that hung on among downtown artists) but he buoyed my better instincts, reminding me afterwards, as we walked downtown from the upper west side, that becoming a witness was what art-making is all about. And in his review that year, Roger Ebert described a further complexity:

There was an even deeper message as well, and it is contained in the testimony of Filip Muller, the Jew who stood at the door of a crematorium and watched as the victims walked in to die. One day some of the victims, Czech Jews, began to sing. They sang two songs: 'The Hatikvah' and the Czech national anthem. They affirmed that they were Jews and that they were Czechs. They denied Hitler, who would have them be one but not the other. Muller speaks:

> That was happening to my countrymen, and I realized that my life had become meaningless. (His eyes fill with tears.) Why go on living? For what? So I went into the gas chamber with them, resolved to die. With them. Suddenly, some who recognized me came up to me. ... A small group of women approached. They looked at me and said, right there in the gas chamber...
>
> Q. You were inside the gas chamber?
>
> A. Yes. One of them said: "So you want to die. But that's senseless. Your death won't give us back our lives. That's no way. You must get out of here alive, you must bear witness to our suffering and to the injustice done to us."

Ebert continues:

And that is the final message of this extraordinary film. It is not so much a documentary, not journalism, not propaganda, not political, as an act of witness. In it, Claude Lanzmann celebrates the priceless gift that sets man apart from animals and makes us human, and gives us hope: the ability for one generation to tell the next what it has learned.

Roger Ebert was neither rabbi nor Jewish, but his last phrase here echoes "every generation must teach the next what it has seen," prescribed in the Torah about the revelation at Mt. Sinai. Although we've progressed in our styles of interpretation, it's all in the service of the original event, since we're still a long way from enacting even the short list of the Ten Commandments. Just accepting them is hard enough, as former VP candidate Joe Lieberman wrote in a *Wall Street Journal* op-ed, compelled to explain his Jewish identity: "...accepting the Ten Commandments at Sinai endowed the world with a sense of purpose and destiny." Warm but fuzzy. To fully understand what that particular "purpose and destiny" means—there certainly was purpose before that, as there is for every living species—I had to go back to Sinai and read from there on up through the centuries to ancient Jerusalem where the early Bible was written. For others, it's enough to follow after the writing, down more than two millennia of commentary. Does this seem to be making too much of the past? Probably so, to those who believe in the "future" and the one-way arrow of human progress. Let's imagine that the latter represent "what the world thinks," at least as determined by the UN and the all-inclusive universalist ideologies, and that Judaism stands in its tiny peoplehood stubbornly against it. If so, it's a parallel to when the Bible was being written and its Jewish authors established the revelation at Sinai as the ultimate vision of Homo sapiens destiny, forever to remain behind us in the past, just like anyone's parents and family drama must.

Even the messianic interpretation of the later Prophets couldn't envision a greater destiny, which is why the biblical writers behind them needed to constantly warn of the human desire to cover over the past. Or to repress it, in Freud's modern terminology. This desire to ignore the difficult confusions of the human psyche, its own buried conflicts between good and evil, can hardly be separated from the desire to be clear of it and make a fresh start. Perhaps the human colonists on a terraformed Mars will think of themselves that way, like the old Plymouth Colony of the New World—except that the latter were Puritans invested in the past, colonists who thought it was a New Israel they were creating, like so many other New Israels. The old Israel, however, is historical, and it isn't until our time that an Israel has been established as a restoration of the old. It's no longer a pushing of ancient Israel further back into the mists of time, a messianic Christian division of "old" history versus the new—as if we'd cured the division between repression and neurosis, so that we can say to ourselves, "now we are healthy," like the Third Reich and the Communist revolution said to themselves. Yet as every "cured" alcoholic knows, one drink and the slippery slope returns. And even the simplest reading of the Torah, as in the Book of Exodus, shows how quickly the light of Mt. Sinai devolved into the golden calf (or "Heavenly Cow," as a deep reading of ancient Egyptian literature suggests). It's a struggle to keep the path back to the Ten Commandments clear, no doubt a greater struggle than to land on a foreign planet. Were we to colonize Mars in the pride of our intellectual accomplishments, we'd still be left with the same misapprehension of our Homo sapiens psychic history as the one that split the consciousness of the spiritual visionary, Martin Luther: his idea of democratic biblical rights was counter-balanced by dark anti-Semitism.

Rhonda tells me that *our* only significant conflict, going back more than two decades to our courtship, continues today: it stems from her desire to react to provocation in the news, including articles and letters to the editor. "But where will you publish it?" I ask. My side is not to react but to wait; wait for a context or stage upon which I'd be heard with some authority. Of course, one can die any day, especially at my age, and RR reminds us of the seventeen years between us, that she'd be left with. No essays and books she would write then could bridge our conflict, because how should she know it would have been better to wait, as I would have, for the right moment in which she could be fully revealed, rather than as yet another writer to be respectfully acknowledged and little more? But I, being dead, can no longer hold up my side of the conflict, since waiting is meaningless when you've been fired from humanity. That's just an argument for the moment, I'm still here, and RR uses it to insist on making her mark on the world now, before the West burns, its intellectuals content to be an over-articulate mob of fiddlers. They are neither waiting for a saving idea nor readying the hoses.

We're both half-right and it goes deep into our psyches. She can feel trapped by events, boxed in, a condition that goes back to primal Homo sapiens origins, complimenting her specific personal history. On a more literal level, it takes the form for her of the great waiting-mistake of the 1930s, refusing to take sides when Germany's rearmament violated the Versailles Treaty. I agree, yet want it to be even more clear-cut before reacting: if it's a mass psychosis knocking at the gates, you can't engage such hatred rationally; it's going to take a violent response to break the spell, though first you have to develop convincing proof. "But these people look at the images on their TV's and they're going to believe whatever they see— 'seeing is believing'—they're not going to wait for you and your interpretive proof," counters Rhonda. "However, they can see all kinds of violent imagery and yet a call to react still leaves them fuming on their couches, waiting for a Pearl Harbor." There's acting-out and there's withdrawal— that's probably the basis for many a conflict. Still, "something happened," as the TV presents, that's agreed, unless we argue over interpreting the fact, however mundane. "You forgot to pay the Comcast bill"—after the internet goes out. "No, I didn't. It was just a day late…" Or, why can't you just answer the basic question, instead of prevaricating: Do you or don't you believe in God? Did something happen—a world created or a revelation of divine intimacy—or is it all just what happens next?

Seriously, if we go back to Sinai in the Hebrew Bible, something happened, which leads to the Jewish writers down the centuries interpreting it. Is it an agreed-upon fact? If so, it's enfolded into an interpretive story from the beginning: the ur-writer, Moses, smashes his tablets, yet then there's a second draft, and its encased in a traveling sanctuary for more than forty years, during which time Moses is constrained to write up the interpretive stories of Exodus through to the Book of Deuteronomy. Seem far-fetched? But in our own time, it seemed like forty years that James Joyce was writing *Finnegans Wake*, where a single corpse engenders all that follows. Perhaps it was common knowledge among scholars in ancient Jerusalem that the poet who wrote up the late Akkadian version of the *Gilgamesh* epic spent his life on it, a putative forty years. Anyway, after recognizing the primal conflict behind any argument over "facts," Rhonda and I generally revert to a passionate "kiss-and-make-up." And what counts in the Torah are the levels of poetry—"truth-testing"—that sink down into time, into the inner understanding that "something happened," be it the revelation at Mt. Sinai or the catastrophic expulsion from Eden.

A conflict of faith about one's own time, as Moses had when he smashed the tablets, happens to almost every Jewish writer. "That Singer was turning himself into a Jewish writer… while under [apostate] Wein- inger's spell is a good indication of the contradictions he thrived on," writes Jonathan Rosen in a clear and sharp investigation of Isaac Bashevis Singer's oeuvre in *The New Yorker*. "[As] a vocal advocate of the Yiddish avant- garde, he sought inspiration in the Jewish past." Singer's reversible jacket was as natural to him as my own. Yet I'd elaborate further: it's precisely the situation of the Jewish writer to be running forward to ancient Sinai, as was the original J writer of the Torah's earliest strand, in ancient Jerusalem, several centuries after the recounted events.

"Warsaw, Poland, the Writers' Club, my mother, my brother Moishe, and the women who were near to me had all passed over into the sphere of memory. The fact is that they had been ghosts even while I was still with them". Quoted from Singer's memoir, *Love and Exile*, I could have said the same for the ghost of Ezra Pound, still alive when I was writing about him in college. Although I had just absorbed the devastating postwar

Jewish book, *The Destruction of the European Jews* by Raul Hilberg, I was also the undergrad student of poet Donald Hall in Ann Arbor at that moment, who had awarded the Bollingen Prize to Pound's *Pisan Cantos* by allowing Pound and his anti-Semitism a poetic license to be mad. I bought into that, though it was clear that Hall and every other poet I knew had not read Hilberg. If they had, perhaps they would have more severely questioned the method behind Pound's madness. Barely 20, I wasn't able to even articulate the question. Half a century later, I'm still shocked by this passage from historian Alon Confino's *A World Without Jews* (2014), in which he traces the European obsession with Jew-baiting back to the Hebrew Bible:

> The Holocaust offered "a solution to the problem of historical evil." The solution took the form of what psychoanalysis calls splitting. In order that Germany could become pure, Hitler fabricated an enemy onto whom he projected everything bad and corrupt. This included the Hebrew Bible: As the fascist sympathizer Ezra Pound evocatively put it, "all the Jew part of the Bible is black evil."

Back in the 1960s, I might have let this slide, still under the black anesthesia in which the Hebrew Bible was dismissed by most modernists. You could substitute "Hebrew Bible" for "Leviathan"—and that creature's association with the Devil—in a superficial reading of the Book of Job. Yet the Joban poet raises to awareness that utterly other manner of being that is no less perfect than we are: the Leviathan that Job hears God describe to him in intimate detail as the Nile crocodile. It is a created creature that only God could love—until now, that is, with the advent of species consciousness. Even today, few of us are reading the Book of Job as the poem of a life it is, with its unfamiliar (to us) cosmic dimensions. Satan's truth-testing of God, in its ultimate failure, reveals the Jewish writer in the Joban poet. After intertextually translating Job in the '70s, I went on to the books of Isaiah and Kohelet (Ecclesiastes), rediscovering how they too were poems of a life struggling to devote itself to truth-testing. To the extent that they fail or succeed, they confide a new bedrock for poetry, the Jewish writer's existential quest for meaning.

Today that takes the form of what Paul Celan described as "the reconstruction of the possibility of poetry—which is very different than poetry (not possibility but its doubt). It is one response to the traumatic [dark] enlightenment [of Auschwitz]." Before I thought of myself as a Jewish writer, I was of the doubting school of poetry; that is, we wrote established avant-garde poems in an already 150-year-old tradition going back to Baudelaire, even as we doubted that poetry could recover from the wound to humanism inflicted by the First World War, if not the death of

God in the nineteenth century. Celan means that now, post-Holocaust, no new poetry can be taken for granted, so that the very possibility for writing a poem or having an audience for it needs to be implicit in the poem itself. Of course he means a significant poem and not your average or academic poem that fills the need for talent or high-flown sentiments, such as feeling good about yourself after civilization has been sorely eclipsed by the European Holocaust.

But what happened to me, as a former Pound scholar while at Syracuse University, and with the avant-garde periodical I edited entitled *The Ant's Forefoot*, taken from a line in Pound's *Cantos*, is that I kept the association with Pound going by reacting blackly: to make the Hebrew Bible central to my life's poetry/translation project. Irony persists, however, in Pound's devotion to innovative translation, so that I was still in his debt when I began to "make it new," i.e. to engage the Hebrew Bible in poetry. If it meant facing down the Poundian tradition that continues to this day, I was going to go him one better: neither the dubious depth of his Chinese scholarship nor his failure to visit China—in regard to his Chinese translations—was going to influence me against becoming immersed in Hebrew in Israel and in decades of Hebrew Bible scholarship.

One summer in the mid-'80s I lived in the guest house downhill from Chaim Gross, the sculptor, in Provincetown, Mass. I was invited up to dinner with Raphael Soyer, who I considered a representative Jewish Painter, meaning his style vied with his subject for Jewish historical resonance. (If you could say the same for Barnett Newman or Mark Rothko, your judgment would have to be far more subjective). I was at a bit of a loss for not knowing any American writing peers at the time as steeped in Judaism as these aging artists, except for Singer, who was hardly a peer. I offered him as my intellectual chaperone nonetheless, thereby turning the conversation over to Soyer, who had famously illustrated him. "'How come you never write about painters?' I once asked Bashevis [Singer]. 'Maybe they can't sit still long enough,' he quipped, meaning for a word portrait." This was more biting in Soyer's Yiddish—not about Singer, whom he adored, nor about fellow painters of New York's "The Ashcan School," but about the dead left behind in the Holocaust. Too blackly ironic for me to fully catch at the time. My friend, Gross's daughter Mimi, herself an artist of renown, provided the guest house key. She also offered the phone number of Mira Schor, who was visiting her mother nearby, and who had just begun, with Susan Bee Bernstein, a long-running journal of artists' writings, theory, and criticism, *M/E/A/N/I/N/G*. A blind-date dinner ensued; however awkward it might prove, as most blind dates do, I thought the conversation would be scintillating. When I called for Mira I was introduced to her mother, sensing instantly the intensity of the bond between the two, and later wondering if that was what underlay Mira's friendly but distant manner.

I do remember she was happy to discuss how the title of the journal came about, which worried me; I already "read" contemporary painting like music, as a language beyond meaning, and the art criticism I preferred and sometimes wrote was ironic and overheated, though less with theory and more with metaphor, as in the reviews of Ashbery, Schuyler and Schjeldahl. Mira had much bigger ideas of what art writing could encompass and mean, though it included resistance to meaning, so that she was ready to make meaning purely out of that resistance itself. By the time we were walking home the length of the town, I seemed to be laughing while she was serious, and vice versa, so that further dates might be called for, at least to iron out the disjunctions.

That didn't happen, and it wasn't long before I was dealing with similar issues in psychotherapy. "Tell me about your anxiety…" said my analyst, and in the telling—"It feels like there's a child inside I'm supposed to be taking care of, yet I keep forgetting him"—I make meaning out of the feeling. On the same day, later in the evening, I'm working to get behind the meaning of biblical text to reanimate the feeling of the writers.

Decades later, his new bio simmering on my poolside work table in the Florida heat, I turn again to my translation seminar colleague, analyst Adam Phillips, as he deflects meaning from Freud's life by suggesting that psychoanalysis is a contextualizing of mental symptoms, of human anxiety and our desire to curate everything, to present a show of coherence— behind which quantum feelings are bouncing around at speeds approaching the speed of light. Freud saw himself as a quantum scientist, I might agree, though in his day the main opposition came not only from scientists but from a free-floating anti-Semitism pervasive in Europe, a veritable congregation of anti-meaning turned into a political religion. This turn of events could have been predicted in Freud's 'Civilization and its Discontents,' except that "civilization" is used here in its universal and non-Germanic aspect, applying to any culture (as would later prove the case in Cambodia, Rwanda, Sudan, Bosnia) where resentment topples the psychic economy of counter-balancing restraints. Like an analyst with a psychopathic patient, Freud hoped the Germanic resentment of his being a Jew, as he'd known it throughout his life, would be forced into a self-aware paralysis by the democratic West. A vain hope, of course, as he reluctantly escaped Vienna by the skin of his teeth; or rather, not so vain a hope, since the democracies eventually did overwhelm the Germanic psychosis by strength of arms, though not without the help of the Stalinist psychosis of the Soviet Union.

Part 2

Psychotic Holocaust inversion—the claim that Israelis are the new Nazis and Palestinians the new Jews—makes meaning out of silence, against critic George Steiner's conclusion that the only possible response to the unspeakable horrors of the Third Reich was silence. So much for silence, which apparently had not even occurred to Isaiah and Jeremiah in the catastrophic captivity of Babylon. If there is no *new* poetry after Auschwitz, according to the oft-misunderstood Adorno, it's because the wound to civilization represented by the Holocaust has not been internalized. That it can't even be repressed is made evident by Holocaust inversion: Israel seen—if not spoken—as the new German state (as if Merkel's Germany is post-German). However, in his first press conference after the cease-fire, Gaza's Hamas leader Mashaal asserts: "The leaders of the enemy perpetrated a Holocaust, twice the Holocaust of Hitler's". But how to internalize such a wound to humanity as the Holocaust? That too is at the core of the Bible. The ancient Israelis, subject to pulverizing centuries of slavery in Egypt and isolated in the Sinai wasteland, internalized their wounded humanity (for Egypt was civilization's standard-bearer at the time) as the revelation of an awakened Creator commanding an ideal morality that is almost Edenic in its dream of an internal moral law. Only a wounded-in-behalf-of-humanity Creator would be in need of a Covenant with a society of his creatures, and vice versa. A covenant or contract, that is, in need of deep interpretation down through the generations, elaborated foremost in the centuries of writing what became the Hebrew Bible. In order to confront this deep defect in civilization, there's no starting over, no "new" poetry that is not a restoration of the oldest wound. The poetry (he called it a novel) of Freud's last book, *Moses and Monotheism*, is a probing of that wound; and probably the most significant postwar Jewish writer, I.B. Singer, dug deeply into the lost world of the Holocaust to reveal its battered ghosts, still dreaming the Edenic dream, if not confused by it.

The poet of my time who I was lucky to know and who best lived that postwar wound was Barrie Nichol, the pseudonymous "bpNichol". Canadian North American, and thus not well known in a chauvinist American literary context, his powerful lifelong poem, *The Martyrology*, bears the wound of an adolescent psychosis in which a gaggle of fantasized saints are lost on Earth. Into a mature adulthood, language itself comes to stand for the dilemma of Homo sapiens lostness, our having lost touch with origins. Like a postmodern biblical poet, Nichol finds those origins in an English language so wounded that it can no longer deal with the past and with the buried sources at its root. Nichol was not Jewish, but unlike many of his post-Judeo-Christian cohorts, he looked back in time—both historical and personal—to the catastrophe within modern poetry. When he wrote "poetry is dead, dead, dead" in an early book of *The Martyrology* he wasn't kidding; like Adorno, he understood that only a restoration of the oldest understanding of a wounded civilization could restore the poem. At the origins of humanity he found the biblical apprehension of language (as conduit and interpreter of the catastrophe in Eden) to need re-encountering—if, and only if, it could recognize its own grandiose wish for progress and disinter its original need for some "outside help." Facing his own disinterment of the family drama in his day job as a lay Freudian analyst, he was able to keep it in mind throughout *The Martyrology*, and to lay bare similar wounds in our forgetfulness of Homo sapiens history, our near-destruction in the Ice Age, if not a primeval Flood. Homo sapiens origins also were in need of reanimation: our physical body was central to imagining a cosmic-centered language. Both Barrie and I, ephebes of Ezra Pound's hatred of the Bible (though we didn't know it), reacted against Pound nonetheless, Barrie finding his way through historical iterations of creation myths a decade before I bumped dangerously once again into the Hebrew Bible. I found no way around it, just as my avant-garde mentor Pound, whose answer, unlike mine, was to hate it.

When Bible-bashing erupts today, it's often from a literal-minded and even progressive reading of the history it contains, blaming ancient Israel's writers for their realism about war and existential threat. In contrast, a history of the U.S., less than three centuries old compared to ancient Israel's ten, would, if its honesty matched the Bible's, include such horrors as our incinerating nearly a quarter million "innocents", mostly women, children and the old, in ten days over Hiroshima and Nagasaki, and double that in the firebombing of Tokyo, etc.; then there's Dresden, etc. on up to carpet and napalm bombing in SE Asia. Also the horrors of a hundred years of slavery, in quantity and quality beyond anything in the Hebrew Bible. Yet with the intelligence of a *New York Times*-level anonymous article-commenter online, atheist guru Sam Harris writes (in a link to a rave NYT review of his latest book): "Let me remind you that parts of the Hebrew Bible—books like Leviticus and Exodus and Deuteronomy— are the most repellent, the most sickeningly unethical documents to be found in any religion. They're worse than the Koran. They're worse than any part of the New Testament." Harris is referring to ancient historical accounts by the Jewish writers of the Hebrew Bible who refused to paper it over: it's doubtful, however, that Harris would risk his own audience by condemning the ferocity of our war against Japan and Germany. In most recent histories, the work of our bombers is condoned for strategic reasons, just as the "unethical" and far less "repellent" events in the much longer view of history that exists in the Hebrew Bible (not including the "sickening" catastrophes that befall the ancient Israelis themselves over a millennium). What is more, I doubt Harris has read the Quran closely;

its historical context is a small fraction of the years covered in the Hebrew Bible. Even less time passes in the New Testament, hardly more than a century, though what can be more hateful than the crucifixion of thousands of Jews by the Romans, resulting in a tarring of the Jews for one of them, pursued through two millenniums as a Deicide?

History can also collapse in an inadvertent moment. I was looking up the email address of old colleague Andrew Crozier in UK to discover an '08 obit in *The Independent*. Brain tumor at 65. I last corresponded with the against-the-grain poet a couple years before that, when he told me of the prolonged illness of his wife, Jeanne, from cancer. In the second paragraph of *The Independent*'s obit, it says Crozier was the founder and editor of *The Ant's Forefoot* while living in Cambridge. I did send him a hundred copies to distribute of some issues, and he did contribute some poems, but otherwise there's no connection to *The Ant's Forefoot*. How quickly one's history can devolve when you're not looking.

A professor at Princeton, specializing in the avant-garde, said "I didn't know you were *that* DR," of *The Ant's Forefoot*; he knew me as Bible-translating teacher of translation workshops. On stepping into my office across the hall, colleague Joyce Carol Oates notes a copy of my anthology, *The Movie that Changed My Life*, to which she had contributed an essay on Dracula some two decades previous, now commenting, "I didn't know you were *that* DR, I thought you were a Hollywood writer." What mattered to me was how I could have been *that* DR, a grad student at Syracuse, writing studies of—and identifying with—Ezra Pound, several years before I, upon closer reading of *The Cantos*, would face his hatred for the Hebrew Bible. After, that is, I founded/edited TAF ("when the mind swings by a grass blade/ an ant's forefoot shall save you"—*Pisan Cantos*) in Toronto, London, Paris, New York, 1967-74. By '73, however, I'd also found myself translating—with my own presence on the line, as Pound taught—from Psalm 30:

> I thought I was experienced
> nothing was going to shake me
> I was serious as a mountain
>
> Lord, you were with me and then
> you were gone
> I looked for your face in terror
>
> my body was made of clay
> My Lord, it is now
> I call you

what good is my blood my tears
sinking in the mud
is mere dust singing

can it speak
these words on my tongue...

Here was a Lord I knew well from Blues heard in my inner city Detroit street education, unchurched, unsynagogued, yet He was a provocation to Pound and his poetics, especially Pound's famous ear, which echoed Blues and Bible diction without really hearing it himself.

Of course, everyone has their earlier selves, yet even if the youthful ones are outgrown, the original family drama stubbornly remains through a lifetime. Mine was more than the child of near-Holocaust survivors; it was a transformation of rejection into tolerance, so that I was a natural-born über-liberal and thus a Hippie-identifying professor at 23. The latter stance, however, incorporated its own rebellion; although my parents saw themselves as breaking with centuries-old traditional Jewish culture, I returned to it in the form of a passion for origins—not recent historical roots, not traditional origins, but the über-lost one, the original writers behind the Book of Books. Nobody wanted these great Hebraic writers to be identified as individuals, since that might privilege a Jewish *culture* over the religion. So the Hebrew Bible as later pieced together seems to reflect a communal enterprise in which writers submitted to a code of anonymity in the belief that a supernatural destiny required the earthly one to be in its service. The text to my poet's eyes and ears, however, found its truth-testing to be earthly, and when a covenant is required with Israel's God it comes down to retelling the Earth's history, as in Genesis; the people's history as in Exodus; and the nation's historical and cultural identity, as in most of the rest of the Bible. All of this history was embodied in ways that only a writer empowered as an individual could express so dramatically, just as merely a priestly community of ancient Greek religion could *not* have written the Iliad and Odyssey. So was the citizen writer of ancient Greek or Hebrew, no doubt of the highly educated class, anything but a flawed individual? To my mind, that was also my over-ambitious self, taking ownership, with only a shred of entitlement, of the Blues, the Bible, and Whitman/ Dickinson (my youthful idea of American poetic patrimony).

So here's the problem of the Jewish writer throughout history in a word, whether faced with a Luther, Heidegger or Pound: authorship. The owning up to it. The flawed man behind the writing Prophet requires the context of his struggles: How did he or she, and their hundreds of Jewish colleagues down the centuries, manage to create such startling poetry and lambent prose? For this contemporary Jewish writer, I also ask myself how my eidolon, poet William Carlos Williams, failed to at least politically correct his anti-Semitic comments after the Holocaust. Like any tainted racist, he could have pointed out that "some of my best friends are Jews"— Jewish poets like Reznikoff, Zukofsky, Rukeyser, Ginsberg—yet that didn't stop him from announcing over a mainstream radio program in the '50s that Jews are destabilizers of society, control the media, etc. How can I refuse to paper this over, but still give it the context of a flawed individual? Henry Roth does it in *Mercy of a Rude Stream*—to himself. His old communist sympathies transmogrify into Zionist ones over the decades, while he performs the self-abasing chores of duck farming (not altogether dissimilar to life on a struggling kibbutz). It would mean little if Roth did not remain true, deep down, to his calling as a writer, and so it was for the biblical writers behind Israel's history, whether a "court historian," a prophet, a psalmist, or a worldly "preacher," as in Ecclesiastes, who has earned his bona fides through hard experience.

Ultimately, the poem of the Jewish writer was written on Mt. Sinai: The Ten Cs. It has required fertile interpretation ever since: not kill = not murder, but then there is self-defense, there are accidents, there is "temporarily insane," and there are endless wars and conquests, etc. What animals can you or can you not kill, etc. What constitutes suicide, etc. I said "fertile interpretation" because all the questions raised by The Ten Cs are existential, concerning life and death—setting the bar for all poems to come. It's the poem of Moses and God, who eclipses the Muses, putative and otherwise. There are historical sources in Mesopotamia and probably earlier, but it becomes a Jewish poem in its fraught relation to authorship, to Moses' need—or God's mutual need—for an understanding, a covenant, between "writer" and "reader," between cosmos and creature. An understanding about what death or life can mean, and where the boundary between them lies.

And it's a cosmic poem, a confrontation with the cosmos and its origins or originator. The Ten Cs are a lyric that opens into an epic, a journey through the wasteland of Sinai to "a new/old land," and it exfoliates down the centuries of ancient Israel, becoming the Hebrew Bible. During the centuries that follow, it continues as intertextual commentary and poetry, through to leading exemplar of the Jewish writer, Moses de Leon and his *Zohar* as well as to the Platonic/Aristotelian reversible jackets of Maimonides' and Karo's codes, to the ambivalent intertextuality of Spinoza and Amichai. It's a nugget unfurled into an epic that suggests more than a human reader of Homer's cosmic poems, more than an aesthetic of journey and home; it suggests a cosmic reader, one who is continually testing the cosmos and his or her relation to it, as a creature.

And the original nut of The Ten Cs is a terribly modern poem. In Leopardi's critical terms, it's mystically vague and childishly oracular.

Baudelaire's and Benjamin's *flâneur* looks in the shop window of the universe and is transfixed—if only for a moment, the fundamental moment of the poem. And then they pass by, to recollect the experience as a species of loss. As in losing one's place in the text of the cosmos, and filling the missing place with poems lamenting it, or praising it for the freedom it allows— that loss allows—to fill its emptiness, again and again. But that's not the poem of the Jewish writer, who must always search out a way back to that original place that is not missing. It's there, encoded in the Covenant and a promised place that has to be struggled for and with, that is existential, and that sits over a meaning in the form of a dream: a cosmic garden for the poet and his or her failing muse, his or her "partner" in Eden, fellow creature, and collaborating adversary God.

Yet it all comes down to the value of interpretation. The Ten Cs are at the heart of a culture and religion that privileges interpretation, because all that comes after, starting with the Hebrew Bible, has been provoked in some way to interpret that short visionary poem. I'm provoked even at this minute, after a colleague, also a poet and critic, who's read an early draft of this and other chapters, asks how The Ten Cs could square with what I described as "edenic" (or as the "Gan Eden" my grandfather believed might await us after death) as if it were "a paradisiacal Earth to which we could return—I don't see that at all—is paradise a materialistic selfishly patriarchal society? One in which women are listed as parallel to other property, children shamed into agreeing with and supporting their father for all his life, in which propertied males build metaphoric gated communities around their accumulations of cattle & other 'stuff' by prohibiting coveting and stealing? This is a society that hasn't yet considered the equitable distribution of its resources or realized that women are 'persons'."

Here's why it's edenic, I tried to answer: If there's no killing, no coveting (implied on all levels), no idolatry including mental, and if you're reading this *sui generis* poem as cosmic, i.e. the words of the Creator, then it leads toward Isaiah's visionary wolf lying down with the lamb. It's post-historical, as any great poem is—we don't want to limit the classics because Greco-Roman slavery was normative, do we? It's no different in our own timebound context, when our various ignorances about what constitutes a just world are invisible to us. We don't know all the physical laws that underlie the universe but we continue to act as if they exist and may be knowable, so it's the same for the moral laws: we don't yet know what an ideal society that internalized the Ten C's would do to our human psychology, as if we'd become post-human like Isaiah's wolf and lamb become post-wolf and post-lamb—or, that such knowledge would make us fully human, like Moses may have been on top of Sinai, or Adam and Eve in the Garden. Or let's just say they were poetically represented so, as The Ten Cs are later elaborated into messianism, the end of history. For the Jewish poet, however, it's not a messiah that's necessary but rather the awareness of its absence—especially acute if the threads back to Sinai and Eden are grasped. For other poets, the concept of absence reduces such a cosmic stretch to the pastoral, in consequence raising absence to something like a god, a truth-telling trickster, ironic as hell, unless one's conceptual intensity can reanimate Shakespeare's cosmic "heaven's gate" in his Sonnet 29:"

> Yet in these thoughts myself almost despising,
> Haply I think on thee, and then my state,
> (Like to the lark at break of day arising
> From sullen earth) sings hymns at heaven's gate."

But change "state" to "soul" and capitalize "Thee"—and you have a Hebrew psalm for your hymn.

Meanwhile, back home in the second decade of the twenty-first century, the conceptual poet Laynie Browne of Philadelphia follows the Jewish poet's path, however reductive. Her project "To find and underline alms in psalms: To write one's own psalms," entails a poetic process that typically suppresses meaning in avant-garde manner. We get the linguistic *how*— about doing, moving on—but not so much the *why* and its questioning as to why the Hebrew psalms must engage us. That "why" is not hard to discern: we've lost the original, even in the de-historicized Hebrew, so that the best translations and interpretations reflect that loss of the original. It's a matter of both Jewish history and personal history to the Jewish writer whose task is loss and restoration, a blues, rather than a poetics of absence for one's resumé and making your place in the Diaspora culture.

On the other hand, the Buddhist skeletal bonhomie of Zen poet Norman Fischer wants his translated psalms to suggest prayers, as if they hadn't been poems in the first place, in their origins. If they're not original and even great poems, then they don't require Fischer to think of the Hebraic poets who wrote them. Which, of course, he doesn't, much like religious translators. And like most English-language Jewish-tinged poets today, Fischer has not thought it worth the time to take a summer out of his busy career so as to vacation in Israel, where he could take at least a beginner's course in spoken Hebrew. Actually, he could do this for free in New York City, as I once did at the Herzl Institute on Park Ave., or for a modest fee at various college campuses around the country. Israeli poets are at an advantage here, and among those whose mother tongue is English, they come the closest to what a Jewish poet might mean today: Harold Schimmel, Gabriel Levin, Linda Zisquit write in a manner that interacts with Hebrew texts or history, at the same time as they remain *au currant* with the postmodern post-Avant. Part-time Israeli residents as I once was and Peter Cole still is, can seem more invested in ancient Hebrew texts than are Israeli poets, though with several obvious exceptions that include Michal Govrin, Rivka Miriam, Haviva Pedaya, and Maya Bejerano. While several American poets engage their knowledge of Yiddish, such as Jerome Rothenberg and Kathryn Hellerstein, and many more recruit Jewish topics, they're unlikely to identity as Jewish poets except in ethnic anthologies. Some American poets, like Marcia Falk, who know and improvise on Hebrew, can also weight toward an overdetermination of meaning.

I'm naming poets who are living and who I've known; far more have passed on who could fit in these categories, especially some I knew while still alive, Charles Reznikoff and Harvey Shapiro among Americans. Many can be found in the unfortunately watered-down Norton anthology of *Jewish American Literature* (as if this mirrored an anthology of "Christian American Literature") though my indigestion warrants full disclosure: my own intertextual translations from the Hebrew Bible are not included because, as was baldly explained to me by one of the non-Hebrew speaking editors, they are "too close to the Hebrew." At least he didn't say "too Jewish," yet if he had I could have felt better for the irony. As it turns out, American poets and critics who have commented on my Jewish work have mostly been non-Jewish, bypassing Hebrew or Jewish issues in favor of the authority of American poetry. Shouldn't I be proud of that? At least someone's reading the too-Jewish poetry of the Bible, though to them it's possibly post-Jewish, thanks to the NT. How strange nevertheless that the Jewish Norton editors think their very assimilation into American academe and their lack of Hebrew has made them *more* authoritative about Jewish inspiration.

I've described how I met the poet Maya Bejerano in earlier pages. Last night I read selections from her book, *The Hymns of Job* (2008), translated by Tsipi Keller. She is looking back at herself from a negative future, from death; death not simply as a future historical event but as a state of mind. Maya, writing in the language of the three-thousand-year-old biblical poets, has so pressing a weight of meaning against her that there's no avoiding it, no pushing it off or subverting it. She has to engage it and subdue it, like Jacob wrestling the angel, but unlike Jacob she wins by losing. As if she's dead, the ultimate loss of meaning, Maya continues to struggle and finish her poem, so that no meaning remains but the fight for survival itself.

> "…the knowledge of otherness
> is divinity from its primal beginning to its end;
> in a black bodysuit in a stain of light he waited for me
> in his hand a pistol with a tiny muzzle ravenous as a child's,
> very near me near me in the shade
> at dusk he calls my name in hushed tenderness:

M M M and when I say: Yes yes here I am
he'll shoot once and vanish, I'll vanish with him
in a black bodysuit
into the void."

When I met Maya for a date, picking her up at the Tel Aviv main library where she worked, I asked how that profession helped her. "I grew up on a kibbutz," she said, "but groups made me anxious, I was an impossible loner in a collective endeavor. The library calms me, especially because I'm a solo audience to all these dead voices of the past, lying on their shelf-beds, asking only to be given the meaning of a bed in the house of knowledge, an address, a number."

That didn't sound so calming to me, and I remember my formidable colleague, the poet bpNichol, also worked for a year in the University of Toronto library, barely in his twenties, and contemplating in the stacks that however many books he produced in a lifetime, they would be only an infinitesimal contribution to the library, so why even start. It was that year he wrote the fragment that would soon appear in his epic *The Martyrology*: "Poetry is dead. Dead, dead, dead…" Now that might seem a pathetic line, undestined for immortality, but Barrie worked it for many meanings, then pushed off from those meanings in an autobiographical verse resembling a many-yeared psychoanalysis, engaging events, tracing his origins, digging deep into language, talmudic, "processual". Keep in mind that among poets after Olson's *Maximus*, Ginsberg's *Kaddish*, and the confessional school at mid-century, autobiography became ostracized (too much boring meaning there) and psychoanalysis itself was pushed away except as theory—especially Lacanian, in itself a strategy for subverting biography.

Maya went further, turning any strategy into a void, toward the final subversion of the exotic image, "a black bodysuit"—just as she had negated "divinity". But *that* Creator has a text, the Hebrew Bible, which can't be avoided in Maya's Hebrew, and like Adam in Eden and the poet writing in the name of Isaiah, you can't hide from the language, its call for a witness. "Here I am"—but Maya is a post-Holocaust poet and when the Jew is called, as to an assembly in the European town square, one is already as if dead; your audience exists only in the future, a putative cosmic Creator who finally answers Job when his questioner turns silent.

Rosenberg Estate discourse, during walk this evening on the bay with Rhonda. "Did you see the article in today's *Times* about the Earth-like exoplanet that has just been vetted by astronomers as more Earth-like than the previous ones discovered?" "No, I didn't have time to read the *Times* website today. How far?" "500 light years, i.e. 5 million of our years to get there at present space speeds." "But if life is there, what does that mean for Mt. Sinai, the Torah?" "It means they have their own Mt. Sinai, perhaps one they haven't yet arrived at, or one going further back in time than ours." "That means they'll appreciate your interpreting power, one way or another, and they'll be asking for the Rosenberg version." "True, they won't be asking for the Ashbery version." "So what should we do to let them know it's available?" "You can't give anything to anybody unless they ask for it—they have to ask a question to get an answer." "But we didn't ask for it at Mt. Sinai, did we?—it was just given." "Maybe that's the problem, maybe we still have to figure out what was the question we didn't consciously ask…" And so it goes every night during post-op recovery time, for two laps around the atoll.

That question might be (in two parts): How to live? How to go on living (knowing we can't go back to Egypt, back in time)? If that were the question, the Ten Commandments was an impossible answer. It's impossible not to kill, impossible even not to covet, such as thy neighbor's wife. Yet all the commandments constitute the basis for civilization, so that if you didn't try to repress your urges and resentments—or if you resisted the repression—wars would result, in which all the possibilities are open again: murder, rape, torture, pillage, hopeless prayer in the trenches and the cockpits, etc. The modern version of an answer is contained simply in its title: "Civilization and its Discontents," by Sigmund Freud. "Discontent" is rather an ironic term, as if we're a bunch of grumpy art-lovers complaining about the admission price to the Metropolitan Museum of Art.

Anyway, it's impossible to keep the Ten Commandments—but was that the intention? Everyone in or coming from Egypt already knew it was wrong to kill, rob or commit adultery, but that it happened anyway, if only in one's mind: "I wish he were dead," or "That woman should be mine." (Substitute iPhone for woman). So the intention of the commandments (which I once translated as "desires") must have been to give gravity to interpretation, inasmuch as the rest of the Bible is in one way or another further interpretation in terms of human drama, human thought, human philosophy and poetry, followed by centuries of it. Even last night, on the latest episode of Neil de Grasse Tyson's *Cosmos*, Tyson says: "Of course, the 'days of creation' in Genesis were not actual days…"—so he wants us to interpret the Bible in a literary way, in terms of metaphor. At the same time, however, his intention is to debunk any literal reading of a text he considers pre-scientific—so right there I am already interpreting *him* on the Bible. In other words, the Ten Commandments are the bedrock of our ongoing need for interpretation, just as much if not more so than that powerful metaphorical tablet, the Oedipus Complex.

It's hard to say, after the worst century in civilized history, that we've learned anything about war. One of the best US documentaries of the twentieth century, Ken Burns' *The War*, makes me ask why didn't mom and dad talk about it; why didn't mom, for instance, tell me about the day that's so riveting in the film, D-day, the news that hit the radio and papers that the Invasion had begun with dad in it, let alone V-E and V-J day. But of course, already when I was seven, it was the war in Korea, later in Vietnam. We can't even remember the last one. Was anyone during WWII asking about memories of WWI or even the Civil War? The Passover Haggadah's dictum: bechol dor va'dor chayav adam lirot et atzmo... "In every generation we must tell the story as if it happened to us." That is, the original creation story of our cultural consciousness: to imagine we are no different than thousands of years ago, when we survived slavery and had the revelation at Sinai of how hard it is to stay civilized. The death slavery of the twentieth century Shoah is even more to the point than wars.

An article today about "Jewish Culture" in Miami Beach finds the *Herald* journalist joining a tour organized by Miami's Jewish Historical Museum: "There is even a resurgence of young people looking to learn about Jewish culture," said Arnowitz, pointing to a group of college students registering for the tour. "I really wanted people to get a sense of history for the area and the Jewish presence. A lot of Jews came to this country to escape persecution, and they brought their culture with them," Arnowitz continued. "We make a positive difference by showing diversity." And, she stressed, food is a way of keeping the culture alive. "The idea is to pass on information from one generation to the next," she said. "There's a feeling of comfort being in your own culture, and people should feel that."

Yes, we tend to feel more "comfort" after we've eaten than before our first bite. Is a culture, however, about such comfortable accessibility? So here we are, with an impoverished notion of Jewish culture, grossly amplified by self-satisfaction, as if a tour of Jewish restaurants of the past tells us anything more than nostalgia can. Yet when, in notes to my biblical translations and in my biography of Abraham and his authors, I imagine the Jerusalem teahouses beside the royal campus, in which biblical writers compared notes, I'm not only nostalgic for ancient tea or Hebraic beer, but rather hungering for context. Not layers of nuance that puff up the text, but its very historicity as a document written by individuals and not committees or editorial redactors. If the complexity of the biblical text has been put on a modern pedestal in a mishmash of context, I want to simplify it by turning back to a sense of the original writers. I don't think so, but it's possible I could be wrong about the nature of those original poet-historians, but so were the great historical commentators who took it for granted that the writers were Moses, David, and Solomon *et. al.* At least they got it half-right, while theories of redaction, which may have something to do with religion and history, have little to do with the creative inspiration of the writing. The latter is a product of culture in which the prevailing hunger is not for pastrami on rye but for art, and for translation of the art within recent cultures as well as those of the distant, classical past. The architecture and the sculpture or friezes in the Temple and the royal campus were not so much translations of forms found in what today we call Lebanon but creative variations in many cases. The same holds true for the forms biblical writers adapted. It's hard for archaeologists to prove this, without more samples from ancient Israel, but there is enough for them to reimagine the art of Hebraic culture, if our modern culture's explorers of the past had the imagination to do so. The same holds true for the biblical writers—but please, no further dissection of the text with linguistic scalpel, we have enough on our plate already. Imagine the writers instead, because more than corned beef sandwiches the intuition of their presence tells us more about Hebraic culture than the brand of beer they imported from Assyria.

When it comes to modern writing, the scientific creation story is neatly limned by astronomer Tyson, from Big Bang to our looking up at the sun moving across the sky, to our moving into the solar system toward Mars. If it were coupled with the internal creation story of civilization and the psyche by Dr. Freud, it might rival Genesis in beauty and depth. Our scientific story, however, is "unmoral," to use a term of the contemporary Norwegian novelist Knausgaard, and hence its beauty unmediated by civilized thought. Genesis also tells such a wild story, but in the form of a struggle with the imprint of moral necessity; its original Hebraic writers overlay rough historical sources with a struggle for cosmic meaning.

Jewish writers ever since the first biblical ones have followed their lead, from the Prophets to the Talmud's Gemara to the Midrash, and on to Moshe de Leon of the Kabbalah's *Zohar*, to Proust and Kafka, Freud and Stein, Bialik and Agnon, Singer and Bellow, Sutzkever and Appelfeld. They are basically unmoral on the surface, moral underneath. The sun for some of them is the revelation at Sinai and the mirror of the Decalogue. It may seem that the modern Jewish writer is quick to demur from the Ten Commandments, implying "this is the best I, or we, can do," profoundly imperfect. Yet this was the case from the beginning, in the Golden Calf story. It has an Egyptian source, in the literature of the Golden Cow, but here it's not simply a case of Egypt-backsliding getting its comeuppance; Aaron too is implicated in a more nuanced chastening, and the stylishly grim proceedings reflect back to modern iterations of debauchery. On the other hand, the memorial for the Pentagon 9/11 attack, designed by Jewish architect Michael Arad, elides such moral complexity: the 184 dead are enumerated by victim's birth years, as if the lesson was their diversity rather than the perverse attack, even more debased by the killers' religious motivation.

The historian Simon Schama, however, noted that "Jews are having to do the work of explaining to non-Jews all over again. And we have to do it. We have to support Israel but we have to do it outside of our own tent as well or we really are in trouble. We have to find ways of doing this. It is fallen to Jews over the centuries to do this". Still, I'd be hard pressed to think of Schama as a Jewish writer, whose BBC history of the Jews is all too often a series of cultural moments, good and bad, as if these events had personalities and reflected back upon each other in the tale of the Jews—but echo no larger moral or cosmic dimension to us. The Torah, a beloved totem but not a revolutionary culture in this view, is deprived of the history of our bedrock Jewish writers.

So I'd call those overlooked dimensions Israel's original testimony to our human resentment of deep history and origins. It's as if we can assimilate our species lineage back to a little mouse, the first mammal, but we can't identify with that hearty mouse's creaturely intelligence if we can't internalize that he or she was a creation of the same Creator as we are. Okay, we can substitute Nature and say she unites us as her accidents, and we may love Her and her poetics of chance for it, but we're not going to internalize kinship with the mouse. As for the later monotheistic and posttheistic religions, their Creators or avatars are weighted so supernaturally (or heroically) that deep history—and the moral revelation at Mt. Sinai that warned us of our grandiosity—is occluded. All this may sound like the Jewish Writer's excessive pride, but in its unique form it is also an acknowledgment of loss: lost history, lost Hebraic culture, and in my own terms, lost authorship and lost lives: the original writers themselves. Even modernist and postmodernist culture wants to inhibit me from engaging it as loss, as if it would be Orpheus looking back at Eurydice; it prefers an Orpheus looking forward exclusively, progressively, freed from the original myth of grief, playing only an upbeat Kansas City Blues, bereft of Mississippi Delta origins.

I'm listening to doowop channel online, in bathing suit beside pool, drying off, iPad with keyboard on the old tiny black dining table from tiny apartment in Tribeca days. All the words are straightforward and prayer-like: "Please, baby, gimme one more chance." Similar but more optimistic than the Blues, where baby's never coming back. Although just the singing itself expresses some kind of optimism about living. So when I read the Oz duo writing "there's not a religious bone in our bodies" I also hear that they have no understanding of the Blues and its sources in the biblical prayer-poems of Psalms, Lamentations, the Prophets, and ultimately, the Torah. Because the God addressed there is not simply a metaphor for a creative writer, as the Ozes refer to him, but the veritable "baby" of the Blues: Can you imagine that the Blues singer made her up—or him, if Bessie Smith is singing? God is that baby that we all once were, a helpless but singular object of affection. Helplessly in love, as the Blues or Psalms singer has it. Helplessly locked in war, as the Prophets have it; helplessly in struggle for Israel's existence or in exile from it, as the Torah has it.

So the Torah's revelation at Sinai, as boiled down in the Ten Commandments, is God's worldly equivalent to the Garden of Eden, a paradisiacal

Earth to which we could return if only we could regain the innocence and moral bond with him we once had there. We were his baby then, as Adam or Eve, and he's our baby now, to whom we can sing or pray for one more chance. The Blues or the Torah tell its stories as history or vice versa, unembarrassed by speaking straight, without irony. And yet their histories of lost and found are mediated by singing itself, by poetry and the art of writing. Can we have just that, the art, without the baby baby baby-business? The Ozes (Amos Oz and Fania Oz-Salzberger, *Jews and Words*, 2012) believe so, and so did I, swinging back and forth from such belief to uncertainty of what kind of creature I was—until I rested, ultimately, on unknowable and in need of an unknowable mirror. The Ozes believe it all can be explained, pitting the fact of human authorship of the Torah against the hardened, to them, religious view that God wrote it and dictated to secretary Moses. Not so fast. Moses has traditionally been viewed as a writer, we can literally see him in his tent writing (in Deuteronomy), just as David, Solomon, Asaf and Baruch were writers. If we may now consider some of them as stand-ins for the original writers in Jerusalem, the actual and lost Hebraic poets and prose writers were still writing the Blues, Soul, Prophecy (lyric geopolitical analysis) and literary epic in which the Creator listened to his children.

Mostly I live in the secular literary world, having coffee and catching up with novelist and half renegade Catholic/half Jewish Mary Gordon before a dual reading of our recent Bible-referencing books. (Mary says she identifies with the New Testament social justice concerns, while Jews are "too New Yorkish," by which she means conflicted, I presume. Of course, she's thinking liberal Catholics and liberal Jews, and she's not sure about me and my biblical scholarship—am I religious with a postmodern veneer or postmodern over a religious sympathy?) Mary asks if I really thought a woman wrote the early strand of the Bible and I answered by moving the question, as I had so often done before, to more contextual ground. It's not about my opinion, I try to answer, but about what we can or need to know about biblical authorship, beyond the *fait accompli* that humans wrote it. Not "humans," I added, which fudges the issue, but *Jewish literary writers who drank ancient beer*, to more accurately enliven some of them, whose sources and art still need to be confronted, or reimagined. If they were more human to us, not religious officials but poet-historians, their literary art becomes more unique. If I asked you who wrote "The Book of Love," I pose to Mary, what would you answer? God, Mother Earth, Darwin? Blind chance, we both might agree; it's the blindness that makes it precious. Exactly, I respond, and that's the reason blindness is preferred concerning who wrote "The Book of God," so that it can be precious enough to be sacred. Now, however, we have larger historical, cultural and artistic contexts to explore for biblical authorship, whereas "The Book of

Love" has a ways to go: it's first referenced, as far as I can tell, in a doowop
song of the 1950s, written by African-American lyricists in Detroit, behind
the group, The Monotones. (Like a rigid fundamentalist, I don't want to
know where they got the source or the inspiration—that song, whenever I
hear it, is too precious, as is the uncanny name of the musical group. Not
so, the recent version by The Magnetic Fields of the Peter Gabriel "Book of
Love," which is only canny, at best, and pretends, like Peter Gabriel, not to
know of The Monotones).

Soon, over-caffeinated on free cappuccinos (the venue covered
the tab) the duet of Mary and I began singing "Who (who, who, who)
Wrote the Book of Love?" It went back to our parallel early teenageships,
when romantic love trumped history, family, what-have-you. And yet, we
confided, we both were already writing stuff and contemplating authorship
at fifteen. Now, however, we were helping each other test our senior
memories by recalling additional stanzas...

"Tell me, tell me, tell me
Oh, who wrote the Book of Love
I've got to know the answer
Was it someone from above

Baby, baby, baby
I love you, yes I do
Well it says so in this Book of Love
Ours is the one that's true"

There it is, I said to Mary, we've got to know the answer to who wrote it.
That's the answer to your question, that's what's behind my work. There's
a "baby," a true love, and there's "someone from above"—and they're
both the same, so that "we were made for each other," in the case of the
Creator, and "meant for each other" in the case of human-made meaning.
Except—"meaning" preceded us, because the singer is reading a book. So
who is he asking, author "above" or baby-reader below, about the question
of authorship? It's enough he or she's asking the question.

One morning I get an email from another writer, Canadian poet-critic
Frank Davey.

Hi David,
I was looking today at the discussion of the word 'diaspora' on
Wikipedia, which assumes it to be the Greek word into which
certain biblical words were translated. So that the word itself begins
in Greek history, rather than in that of Israel 740-722 BC—an
understanding which de-links the word from Jewish history and

enables its promiscuous use by almost any group today.

I guess this comes about because English borrowed the Greek word rather than the Hebrew one in Deuteronomy 28:25—would that be a reasonable assumption?

These thoughts occasioned by reading an essay by Canadian First Nations novelist/activist Lee Maracle in which she names all non-indigenous North American residents as "Diasporic" "dominators"—her capitalization.

Hi Frank,

A Hebrew word for it is "galut," meaning more like exile. Not expat exile but exile in its variously onerous depths of connotation. Contrary to the exoticism of "exile" among 20th cent writers, it suggests the opposite: the exoticism of home (since that home in itself, ancient Israel, was lost).

As well, the Jewish writers of the ancient Diaspora, such as those at Alexandria, are mostly lost in name, along with those in pre-Maccabean Israel. An exception, what made Philo typically Jewish was not so much a desire to explain the Jews—and especially the Hebrew Bible—to the Gentiles, but to make a new kind of Jewish art out of it, in his case a biography of Moses. You'd have to say the opposite about Bellow and Roth, in that their fictive Jews are just that, not explanations; as the authors themselves avow, it's their *American* art that matters. Imagine Philo saying, "It's my Egyptian art that matters." Not very likely. His cosmopolitan Alexandria was still a satellite of Israel, but can you imagine a North American writer claiming that? Perhaps it's because America is the "New Israel," once consciously but now, of course, subconsciously. Yet the parallel is there in the form of the US being self-consciously exceptional. So who can imagine exceptional American writers wanting to downgrade their status to "suburban"—as if in a continental suburb of a tiny old/new country in the Middle East? On a starker level, they might rather be "new" American, than old. Ever since the invention of the Morse code, or at least the telephone, nobody wants to be identified with the old, with its connotation of village life and village idiots...

Of course, ancient Solomonic Jerusalem was no village, and even a thousand years later, before Jesus was born, Herod's Jerusalem was a city plus suburbs of a million. North American Jewish writers, however, think back only to the shtetls of Eastern Europe, having lost the connection to ancient Israel with their loss of Hebrew. I was in that same boat once, having neglected my childhood and Hebrew School Hebrew, along with my childhood Yiddish, but in

1969, at 25, on a visit to Israel I rediscovered Hebrew as a cultural rather than religious language, with contemporary poets as peers. That wasn't likely for the preceding generation; when Bellow was that age it wasn't so simple as to take a cheap student charter flight from New York; for him, it would have meant an ocean voyage to a just-born country where he would most likely have spoken Yiddish with his own peers born in Europe and Russia.

When I translated pages from 2nd Maccabees, in 1978, I began to internalize the ancient Jewish Diaspora, so that I could hardly wait to board a bus in Tel Aviv after the Egypt-Israel peace treaty that year and visit Alexandria—a far cry from listening to the Rolling Stones' "Exile on Main Street." Of course I could identify with an alienated, inner exile, but I could also turn it inside out by pulling on a thread to ancient history, from Maimonides ("Laws of Repentance"): "Among the paths of repentance is for the penitent… to travel in exile from his home. Exile atones for sin because it causes a person to be submissive, humble, and meek of spirit."

Tell that to The Rolling Stones, and to my early writing self, the one who identified with exiles Joyce and Stein.

A couple years ago, before Holocaust inversion was a thought an ordinary Englishman might have, RR and I were visiting with novelist and critic Jonathan Rosen (fellow inner exile) over drinks in midtown, training in from Princeton to see a rare (these days) all-Balanchine at NY City Ballet. We got going on "what happened to (not *in*) the Holocaust." It was still brought up in all seriousness here and there, but the Holocaust's hold on the psyche of humanity had dissipated. Nobody felt it had special relevance, as it did until the Clinton years, whenever art, politics, philosophy, psychology or religion was the topic. With a less sanguine civic religion back in power in '92, intellectual energy shifted to a future optimism in cyberspace and "the global village". The Holocaust got lumped in with the Cambodian and Rwandan genocides, while the consideration of genocide itself became a conscious UN endeavor, lifting the burden from the individual psyche and projecting it onto a public agenda that dissolved into more mundane issues such as memorials. What happened to that devastating psychic wound to civilization that revealed our darkest interiors and origins—not because the Holocaust showed a capability for genocide but because it was built upon a psychic disease going back millennia, anti-Semitism? And what happened to the unlikelihood of talking about the arts without posing the Holocaust as a dark mirror? Today, as far as mirrors go, it's been passed down like a small, out-of-date telescope to a state university observatory, while our attention is diverted by small wars, "fights" against terrorism, the nuances of diplomacy, and the worldwide sort of mirror that is the Internet. Lest we forget, Jonathan interjected, there's global warming and asteroid-crash avoidance, added to nuclear holocaust, to take the Holocaust's place.

"Those are typical species worries, like the great flood, the endless drought, etc. They aren't changing us that much, if Noah's flood ever did," I said. But RR had listened to us creative writers enough and silenced us with her Public Health research scientist's take. "It's like our brains were cracked by facing the enormity of the Holocaust and have healed up imperfectly. Maybe badly. We think we're fine again, having survived great wars, great evil. It's the way Public Health felt after cigarette smoking was linked to lung cancer, that we're finally going to beat cancer. But cancer still remains one of every person's eventual dreads, just as the Holocaust remains an obsession of those who resent the modern world, not least in the current 'wipe them out' wet dream of Iran's supreme leader."

There was hardly another subject that Rhonda would use a sexual parallel like wet dream in. It might sound hyperbolic and she was usually careful to build a case from understatement. RR also preferred a less stimulating tea to the double cappuccinos Jonathan and I were drinking, but when it came to the subjects of Holocaust and Israel-bashing, her usual caution could drink a hundred espressos. For Jonathan and myself, the occultation, scientifically speaking, of the Holocaust, however emotional, was a problem to be wrestled with, but for RR it was a matter of eternal vigilance: she couldn't allow it to be confined in something so normalized as "an argument". It had to be made present as a corollary to every "good" thought; it reminded us that human evil had to be actively pushed away, at every juncture, and never assumed to be marginalized. Nothing supernatural or superstitious about it, but more like disease to a scientist: whatever cures are found, there will be no end to invisible attacks upon the human body. In addition, the Holocaust had been visible and inexorable, yet we were impotent. It was an eruption of the extinction of the human species, made present in the form of human skeletons staggering out of the death camps toward us, the "survivors"—we could not turn away, although it was already too late. We shook our heads slowly, in agreement with Dr. Rhonda; we vowed that at least we would never cease to speak up. But it wouldn't be long before we were holding our tongues in polite conversation of a political or aesthetic nature, for interjecting the Holocaust at this late date (even though elderly survivors are still among us) might constitute an interruption that would marginalize us as old-fashioned, if not special-pleaders.

Neither could I bring myself to risk cutting off our relationship with Adam Phillips when he writes in the intro to his new biography of Freud, in the Yale "Jewish Lives" series, that Freud's "older Vienna sisters died in the concentration camps." *All* his sisters were murdered in Auschwitz, not just the "Vienna" ones, and Freud had to have anticipated it when he escaped Vienna by the skin of his teeth. But why did Adam feel consciously compelled to write "died" in place of murdered, "concentration camps" instead of death camp Treblinka? He is the most conscious of writers and psychoanalysts, so it was done on purpose: we all die, he might have averred, and however sugar-coated, it's a miserable death for all of us. In his brief intro, the words "horror" and "terror" appear many times, although primarily to shock us generally awake to the business of being animals who've developed defensive strategies.

We had a goodbye haute sushi dinner with Adam in Urbana, following the panel we shared on the nature of literary translation (with RR as respondent from a scientist's perspective). I describe the inebriated dinner elsewhere, but now I'm remembering that evening's conversation about the superego's "never forgetting" and how both Rhonda and myself failed to bring up the Holocaust, which we complained to each other about later, safely ensconced in our hotel room. Perhaps it was because we were conscious that Adam was Jewish and that it was a subject never very far from his mind, or so we told ourselves.

If Phillips and Freud can be considered Jewish writers, it would entail their focus on boundaries, particularly the tension between history and story. It all started with J in the Torah and her primary source in the Covenant with Israel's God, a struggle between boundaries of known and unknowable (His insight (or understanding) are completely beyond us). The moral boundaries, however, were about to become knowable at Mt. Sinai. You could call the Ten Cs the deity's defense against his creatures' wish for cosmopolitan Egypt ("no other gods before me") or worse, backsliding to Babylon. What else at the core of Phillips' and Freud's work but defenses against terror or horror, the symptoms of breakdown. The work requires an extreme of listening for dangerously unnecessary defenses, erected as baleful boundaries; the writing also probes these and the unsettled boundaries between enslaving neuroses and social life—yet the Jewish writer proceeds only by alertness to the ironies produced, with the primary irony of wishing to return to Egypt, the source of Jewish slavery, a basic insight of our earliest writer.

Not long before, in my creative writing class at Princeton devoted to translation, I'd assigned the new version of Flaubert's *Madame Bovary* by Lydia Davis. The kids had some questions about it and I said I'd see what Lydia had to say. We met for drinks at the Algonquin Hotel in Manhattan and I asked a student's question about whether she identified with Madame Bovary, tongue in cheek. "Psychologically yes; as a divorcee, no," answered Lydia, who had been the first wife of fellow writer Paul Auster. Then we compared notes as translators: she was meticulous with respect to language, I was meticulous with respect to original writer's meaning—a huge gap. "When you're translating Flaubert or Proust, you can identify with them as writers, but when I'm working with the Hebrew Bible I have to reimagine the writers altogether."

When I reread the Hebrew Bible as a mature writer, I was like an alien from another solar system, entranced. It resonated with my own typically modern alienation: here were ancient writers often alienated from their society, yet comfortable—or at least not speechless—speaking into the universe or listening to its Creator. My generation too wished to address the universe but had no language or creative context for it; at best, we could report from the universe's pov in various shades of irony. Not only the creator was ironic but we ourselves looked upon our creatureliness as ranging from weird accident to giddy high accident.

I was telling something like this to Lydia but it didn't make an impression. So I strained for hyperbole. "Some astronomers at Berkeley predict that we'll have contact with an exoplanet's superior civilization within twenty years," I said. "Surely they'll want to look into our books, just as if we found books written by an inferior civilization, say a Neanderthal one, we'd certainly be interested. But of all human literature, I think they'd come to focus on the Hebrew Bible, where humans speak with some confidence to the Creator of the universe. It doesn't matter if they believe in a singular Creator. To them what matters is the Bible's cosmic theater, in which there's constant tension between human and unknowable, in the effort to nail down a contract, a covenant, with compromises implying unhappiness and caveats on both sides."

Speaking of cosmic tension, Rhonda and I were watching a Henry Jaglom film from the '80s, *Someone to Love*, in which Orson Welles, in his last year alive, is asked if he ever feels alone. "Always," says Orson. "We're born alone and we die alone. We're made to be alone." We'd like to ask him if he's thought about why, in what kind of cosmic theater this would be fruitful, since we're talking about a supreme showman of the 20th century, but the film doesn't go there. In late interviews, Ingmar Bergman talked in this existentialist manner, but not with Orson's grand ability to break out laughing at himself, if not the human predicament. The star of the movie is Andrea Marcovicci, the director's lover at the time, who we are quite

aware sang deliciously for decades at the Algonquin Hotel. She was singing
the night Lydia Davis and I met for drinks there, Marcovicci's 25th and
last year at the Oak Room of the Algonquin, but since Lydia and I were
there simply to converse in the lounge, we heard the singer's torch-pure but
fading voice only intermittently, when the doors to the Oak Room opened,
letting people in or out.

When Paul Auster became conscious of being Jewish in early youth,
it was a source of anxiety: "To be a Jew was to be different from everyone
else, to stand apart, to be looked upon as an outsider... that even in the
place you called home, you were not fully at home." Yet all he can make of
this later, in his 2014 *Report from the Interior*, is pretty much that anxiety is
necessary to a writer. He seems incurious as to why Jews "stand apart," or to
Jewish history beyond the European shtetls in which his parents and their
generation were born. Strangely enough for a writer, he shows little interest
in Jewish texts, especially the Bible. And what American exceptionalism
he imbibed as a child he ironizes. Once he's made it to the Ivy League,
and although he would have been the type of Jewish cosmopolitan resented
between the wars in Europe, he identifies more readily with France and
French writers than Jewish writers like Kafka or Babel. Or rather, that holds
true until his own work is compared to Kafka. By that point in the '60s,
"alienation" has become exotic and it doesn't have to be a *Jewish* Proust to
consider in Auster's literary-historical company, yet why is it that alienation
and the alien ancient nation he was saddled with as a child fail to connect
in his mind? Is it because, as Adam Phillips might say, Auster writes as if in
some *exotic* exile—yet exile from what? Whereas the interior exile, starting in
childhood, is richly limned, the external reality is barely explored, especially
in terms of a Jewish literary origin, as if it might taint the American author.

The historian James Loeffler, considering the modern Jewish writers,
says "It is a commonplace to note that, in reading the works of I. L. Peretz,
or S. Ansky, or Franz Kafka, one comes away with a sense of impending
doom—almost as if they knew the Holocaust was coming. Of course, they
did not. What they did know was that, already by World War I, European
civilization had entered a perilous phase of catastrophe, with massive
historical consequences for Jews everywhere. They also knew, or at least they
hoped, that their ideas and their art might yet turn crisis into opportunity."
I'd say their hopes for art were no doubt doomed as well, accounting for the
black irony, which is hardly a harbinger of "opportunity," anymore than my
extolling the genuine shmata styling and dreck lining of my uncle's wares
was going to lead me toward a great career in haberdashery.

"More than we realize," Loeffler continues, "we are still living in their
world. For all that the earthquakes of the Holocaust and the existence of the
state of Israel have altered the terrain of Jewish history, we share a dilemma
with the artists and intellectuals of a century ago. And so we would do well

to heed their message." Message, as in "Kafka's message?" But that would not even amount to Holocaust-surviving Paul Celan's "message," if he admitted to one, and if his suicide italicized it. Perhaps we could make something of Celan's bitter deconstruction of the German language, in the hope that a "new language" could emerge. But a new tragicomic language would need a larger mythology in which to breathe, because if it lived only on the same air as wafted through Auschwitz, it would be ironic air, if not flirting with dead air. Celan did not have the Hebrew to fall back on the historical myth and prophetic history of his ancient Jewish colleagues who wrote the Bible, or else he might have been in tune with I.L. Peretz, his precursor Jewish writer in another deconstructed German language, Yiddish. For both, then, language was not enough in itself to animate a Homo sapiens creature. How blackly Peretz intended the following depends on your hopefulness, but I'd say that at least a flirtation with the Torah's writers might have eventually buoyed a Kafka and Celan, had they lived a full lifespan, and as it may yet romance an Auster. I, after years of truth-testing living in the moment, and thus alienated from a brutal century, fell into the embrace of ancient Jewish writers who willed themselves out of alienation from history.

"If you have no God, then you look for idols; but they give no Torah. Then you can't write, you only write about things. To write, to create, you need religion. Without it, you have no world-concept.... And if you have no world-concept you have no world, only detached scattered facts, unrelated manifestations and phenomena. You play with sand. That is child's play. You have nothing with which to link the ages—today doesn't emerge from yesterday, or tomorrow from today.... If you serve only yourself, you measure and weigh everything against yourself—there is nothing for you to strive toward. You have moods, but no character, desires but no will—no great love, no great hate; you flirt with life".

Peretz's God provides purpose because it's not so much literal as a cosmic mirror to our lives, so that we can at least *imagine* having a meaning. Let's say it's an imagination with a purpose grander than making ourselves comfortable on the train to nowhere. "Grand" in the sense it's not about us, as ideology is, but about what we can't know, like the origin of time. Although we can represent time's flow as history, we can also imagine its creation, its origin, as containing a moral universe. Granted, it's a huge stretch to see anything moral in a black hole—so that's it, the stretch itself.

If I was going to be original as a writer, I had to have a true original in the past, a cosmic literary theater. Joyce and the Euro tradition back to the Romans had it in the classics of ancient Greece. Still, the modern avant-garde tradition allows for a *flâneur* approach to history though it revels in the break with the past, not the absence of disruption. There is no continuity from the Greek mythic cosmos to today, no Athenian covenant that you can study in Athens today, not even the modern Greek language connects. I saw the grandeur of the ruins there, made grander in the moment by sharing a hash pipe; next day, I could think about the loss, about the impossible stretch to retrieve Sophocles' living sources. And then, after a journey through the islands, past Crete and Rhodes, I stepped off the boat in Haifa, where the Hebrew spoken was good enough to read the ancient biblical text and thus to hold two worlds in mind at the same time, natural and supernatural. Holding those two made a third, a poem waiting to be written. That's what a cosmic poem is, the stretch between inside and outside jacket, reversible. For the contemporary writer, you need a modern imitation, like Eliot's *The Waste Land,* or a "personal bible" as H.D. called her reconstruction of Greek, Egyptian, and biblical sources, *Trilogy.* But for a Jewish writer today, the original threads are still there. I thought I could engage the actual Bible personally, writer to ancient writer, a talmudic dialectic, a reversible jacket.

The Poem of the Bad Hand

When I lived on St. Mark's Place (1971-1980) the poetry scene centered around St. Marks Church included a hundred published poets within walking distance. Outside of writing and small press publishing, which entailed much party-going after weekly readings or for book and magazine launches, my connection to the community was, in a manner of speaking, sports- and poker-driven. During a couple of summers, Ron Padgett and I walked over in our tennis shorts to the public courts by the East River, near the Williamsburg Bridge. It was a long walk and a bit tiring, yet since we'd have to wait an hour for a court to open up we caught our breath on the benches and discussed the current state of poetry. Such a discussion privileged the aesthetic aspects by their absence; that is, resisting pretense, we went over the local gossip and daily foibles of poets we knew, right down to the most mundane details. In fact, the more mundane the more profound, in our eyes—"no ideas but in things"—or at least in those moments of waiting, and not just for a court to open but, on other occasions, for a poetry reading to start, a party to end, or on the subway to a gallery opening. Once, on the long subway ride to Yankee Stadium, I was made especially conscious of barely a minute spent discussing baseball, after agreeing that the Yankees in those years, before Steinbrenner came on board, stunk. Instead I heard what a fellow poet's (Maureen Owen's) estranged husband might be up to, vis a vis the kids. I might have said I saw poet Dick Gallup at Gem Spa, who said wife Carol had just thrown him out of the apartment. I might have added a tale about Dick's temporary ambition as a chronicler when we sat together with poet Phil Lopate in the slightly renovated Cedar Tavern of '71, after the book launch at NYU for O'Hara's posthumous *Collected Poems*, built upon John Ashbery reading his intro to the volume and a poem or two of Frank's. That's how we talked about him, always as Frank, as if we had more than a passing acquaintance with him; if you'd just arrived on the scene, you might never have heard the patronymic, O'Hara. Anyway, Dick, who had actually conversed with Frank, unlike Phillip and I, told us we still had some catching up to do, since we missed out on the formation of the scene. Phil had just returned from a year in Spain, I think, and I from five years in Canada plus *Paris & London* (a book title of mine from '71 I was disappointed to hear Dick and Phillip had not read). Telling the latter snippet to Ron while we waited on the bench for a court, he at least apologized for not having read it either, it was still waiting on the stack of his bedside table, though even that form of communal validation changed once the games commenced.

In a couple of sets, I was lucky to win two or three games. Ron's superior strokes allowed for no mercy, every ball slammed home even when I'd fallen while lunging for the previous shot. Afterward, not a word of consolation, as if I were no more than a ball machine, yet I was full of sympathy for Ron's plight, his having to put up with my miserable challenge. On the other hand, in the '80s, I sometimes played with the ambitious yet awkward Lopate, now by the other river, the Hudson, on the Tribeca court across from my apartment. It didn't seem to bother Phil at all that he was losing and I often gave up on a point for his benefit, something he never seemed to notice. Catching our breath on the bench between games, we discussed girlfriends, past and present, as if they were poems: gave up on this one after a weekend, that one refused to let me get closer, and that one I thought my best ever until what's-her-name came along.

All this was as nothing when playing the poet Kenward Elmslie up near his place in Vermont. Forget about games, I was lucky to get one or two points in a set. It didn't occur to me he might enjoy his mastery over me; I thought he just was glad to get out on the tennis court at all, since none of the other guests—Joe Brainard, James Schuyler, John Ashbery—were players. Besides, I was the lone straight guy whose manly feelings should have been strong enough to take a friendly beating. Again, I apologized profusely while Kenward offered stern fatherly advice: you could use some practice. He may have meant tennis practice but I took it as learning how to deflect humiliation with good humor. Some years later, after John Ashbery's *Self-Portrait in a Convex Mirror* won all the poetry prizes of 1988, a book of critical essays about that major poem was being put together and I planned to contribute, banking on a true dinner conversation about Marilyn Monroe from that aforementioned week in Vermont when I fumbled at playing tennis, hardly 12 years since high school varsity stalwart.

Among all the poets and writers we knew, who, male or female, walked the most like Marilyn? That was the uproarious conversational gambit. I was somewhat relieved that my name hadn't come up, but anyway I withheld my later essay, wary that its humor would be rejected (and judging from the volume's über sobriety, I was right). Yet I didn't plan on humor, but rather appropriated Ashbery's spirit as found in many of his art reviews, which were not exactly circumspect about occasionally going over the top. It was rarely employed as satire; in fact, it was a brand of avant-garde gravitas that matched the art under discussion with a poetic flourish. I did send it to John, however, who responded that my dates were more than a month off, but I took this complaint as tentative approval of my poker face. Not that poker was ever played at Kenward's; everyone was a bit too stoned at night for that. Instead of a card hand, we each sat around the kitchen table with an old issue of "Vermont Sewing Circle" in hand, reading off deadpan sentences, in turn, that more often than not collaged well with the previous selection.

Eventually in '80s Manhattan one turned to the game of squash, which could be played year round indoors at interesting clubs. The basic one around the corner from me in Tribeca was geared to young Wall Street assistants who were still making peanuts. In addition to tournaments when I played them, my regular partner was the poet Michael Andre, who lived down the street. I was in the Ron Padgett position to him but I enjoyed letting him win occasionally because he was capable of brief runs when his whacks three-walled in—that is, if his confidence was up due to winning a previous point. I guess this sounds like another form of manipulation; perhaps Ron had enjoyed an aspect of my tennis game of which I was unaware. Meanwhile, back at the squash club, I'd run into artist and neighbor Alex Katz, who knew me from readings and show openings and suggested we play sometime. I'd seen him on the squash court, however, and knew I stood no chance of winning, so put off a potential match. I didn't want another drama of apologetics in place of acknowledgment of one's equality on the scene. One had that merely by occupying a chair back on St. Marks Place, for the premier sport of my community was a sit-down one, poker, that nevertheless required great reserves of stamina and concentration.

In order to maintain one's chair in the weekly Friday night game of eight hands, one had to play until the end, until after dawn, a solid eight hours, often more, that began the night before around 10 p.m. The venue was the top floor of my building, the artist George Schneeman's residence, and usually included one or more female players, Katie Schneeman and the artist Jackie Ferrara most often. But the seriousness of the stakes (your month's rent could be wiped out in a night) kept many away, along with the question of stamina; either you'd just worked a hard week or you smoked too much dope. Not that there wasn't a temptation to drink or smoke during the game, even as each player knew this was no friendly eve of relaxation but possibly the most deadly serious event of the week, rivaling poetry readings and even poem or art making. Of course, the evening flowed like one epic poem, with its themes flowing from cards to chips, from hands to heads calculating risk and maintaining poker faces, each new card like the line of a poem whose end had not yet been determined and could end in a feeling of well-being or depression. Yet none of those feelings could be held onto, since the next game was still to be decided. You could be "on a roll" and win several hands in a row, only to become destitute an hour later. Several players like myself tried to hold steady; I rarely won or lost very much, though that could still amount to thirty or forty dollars, no mean sum in the 1970s. Other players could swing more wildly, usually in the losing category. Dick Gallup, Mike Brownstein and

Peter Schjeldahl were in the latter category, often falling victim to one joint or beer too many. George Schneeman and Ron Padgett were among the more often winning of the steady players; me and Ted Greenwald among the middling steady ones.

Additional poets and artists would come by during the night to watch briefly but they could rarely resist joking around and were quickly shushed, encouraged to depart. Besides, they were intimidated by the intensity of the play—as I said, this was no lyric poem but an all-night epic with dangerous stakes. Ted Berrigan, Lewis Warsh, Larry Fagin and Anne Waldman were among the non-playing casual visitors who could affect an appearance of having better things to do in the night, though we all knew that if they sat down at the table for even an hour their innocence about the game meant their life savings might be gone. You had to keep on your toes just to keep up with the complexities of the games, which would slide from variations of high-low with differing wild cards to Texas hold-em and a unique variation called "New Jersey." More than one player lost track of which hand they were in. I don't think I ever did, but the effort to concentrate on it could also lead to missing cues that certain players might be bluffing, not to mention my questionable stamina after a Friday that began with rising before 6 a.m. and driving out to Westchester to serve as a high school poet-in-residence. Whatever the state of one's physical condition, holding the poker face was crucial: you couldn't allow it to be read and yet there was a constant banter meant to probe it, a simulation of casual talk among friends who otherwise knew each other. Since many of us were in the game every Friday night for years, the vigilance over one's personality could resemble a chapter from Proust.

On the day I'm writing this in 2014 it's Purim and pics of Israeli cousins in outlandish costume (one is a refrigerator) come via email. It's an incredibly joyous holiday, celebrating survival (by a hair) of an earlier, ancient Persian threat of genocide. But what is so happy about mere survival? Most cultures demand more of their commemorations; I doubt the Germans happily celebrate their survival of the last world war, though the victors do, albeit not as crazily joyous as Purim.

But then there's New Year's Eve and its focus on the survival of another year. Perhaps it's not the survival that's celebrated but the unconscious wish for immortality that a new year can represent. Anyway, there's no text for New Year's or for VE or VJ Day. Purim is centered on the great text of the *Book of Esther*. I've carved out the core of that book in my translation: a poem of near genocide averted thanks to the nerves of steel and poker face of Esther. She confronts her husband the Persian king not with pleading but with the icy resolve that says my hand is a full house. Of course, she knows she holds only a weak pair, namely the support of her cousin Mordecai. I don't know of a more inspiring poker face than Esther's in all of literature. Even Joan of Arc was counting on her connection to God, but Esther and Mordecai had only their wits.

Written in prose, why call the *Book of Esther* a poem rather than narrative? A poem shows us its poker face; it doesn't plead for our understanding. You either get it or you don't. Getting it doesn't mean, either, the specificity of plot but rather an existential ambiguity—it may or may not be a question about the meaning of life hanging in the balance. When you look at a story, you see a drama of life (beginning, middle and end) or consciousness (slice of life) but in a poem you get a poker face: it's up to you to risk the call and show your naked hand. Or, as in a psychoanalytic session, where Lacan describes the transference as poetry, since there's no meaning to nail down—just a relief and exhilaration at becoming aware one has shown one's secret hand and survived.

A specific poem or transference can be more than that, of course. Crucial to a poem, a metaphor is the scene of an accident, where two disparate images collide. A poem is then made up of a series of accidents that are resolved into a poignant (sometimes bitterly so) acceptance of survival: the poem's, the poet's, and the reader's survival conjoined, suggesting a renewed preparation to face the future. I refuse to give specific meaning to a poem, however, because the scene I've just described is so much bigger than that. You could say a poem gives more life, if it's great enough to inscribe its accidents so deeply into such a scene that it becomes unforgettable. As Lacan has hopefully intended, that scene resembles one between analyst and analysand: a transference (going both ways) that allows for internalizing the scene of the analysis. Within that scene, meanings may arise and be considered—the meanings themselves like *accidents of recognition*. So the analysand or reader of the poem comes to recognize within herself that there are memories buried and that proved too painful to accept: accidents whose pain we survive but without benefit of acknowledging. In a transference, for example, one may come to recognize that the analyst has served as mirror for a long ago mother who anxiously overvalued and unintentionally burdened a child psychically. Through the accident of transference, like the one of metaphor, the child's fear of the original accident, which resulted in repressing it, has been allowed to become unburied and cherished like a poem.

Another way to understand the accidents that make up a poem comes via evolutionary science, especially the recent advances in genome sequencing. New species—including our human one—result from "a type of variation that occurs over time when the genetic material is altered by mutation or imperfect copying." We could say "altered by accident," so that our very existence today is dependent on a series of accidents, like metaphors, that have been resolved into the specific creatures that we are. Even more specifically, we can say that the names we carry have resulted from accidents that make up the poem that we are. We might say we are great poems if we can recognize how resolved the history of the universe has become in our conscious minds. And since we can't know if the universe itself is an accident, our great ancient poems, like portions of the Bible, are ones that pose the metaphor of a Creator—or, in the attenuated modern sense, of a poet. As I myself am such an accident of a poet, you could say my life—as I write my memory of its historical accidents, physical and mental, and thereby attempt to resolve them into a coherent self—is a life in a poem.

Perhaps you could say too that survival, when your life seemed at risk, is always a *surprise* (as in surprise at surviving an accident). In that case, a poem can also be *about* surprise, as in many an O'Hara poem when the phone rings in the middle of it, or a Schuyler poem when a meditation on nature outside the window is washed out by a rain shower; or even about the lack of surprise, as when Ted Berrigan finds himself at Gem Spa contemplating a pack of cigarettes when the last late-nite bundle of the *Post* is flung off the truck through the open door, with a full-page headline reading "LBJ DECLARES WAR," and Ted comments, that should have been in an Allen Ginsberg poem. Yet one still has to sense, surprised or not, one has survived the poem in order to comprehend it. So that once again, one is ready for another chance to bring your secret mind to the table, deadpan—that dead or alive, every thought is a figment of the imagination—and survive it.

2.

In his Joycean novel, *The Second Scroll*, the late Canadian poet A.M. Klein visits the suddenly new/old state of Israel in 1949, on a mission to write about its unique poetry. But what he finds in Hebrew journals dissatisfies, including the avant-garde *Canaanites*. Never mind that Klein was looking in only the conventional places, for it serves his purpose to describe the really new poetry of "ordinary people" doing extraordinary things by reconnecting long-disconnected wires to the ancient land. It was a poetry of new streets named after prophets and Hebrew-numbered lanes between tents where the immigrants from Yemen, Tunisia and Morocco were then living. The modernist dream of re-energizing poetry with the idiom of daily life had blossomed here into a full-blown hologram. We might say the same for a Reznikoff-to-O'Hara Manhattan, except their writing is too self-aware, perhaps more intent on reinventing poetry than documenting the city. That gets broken down a bit in the poems of Second Generation New York School Ted Berrigan, so that what had already been assimilated in the 1930s as absurdist literature now steps beyond the absurdity of daily life and the weirdness of the human condition, and into a hyper-reality that casts the poem itself as absurd, albeit the tenderest form of communication. What emerges as authentic from that breakdown (and it does resemble a much-needed literary nervous breakdown) is the poet at his writing table, anchored at the scene of writing, more human than ever. He writes in 'Wishes': Wish I were walking around in Chelsea (NY) & it was 5:15 a.m., the sun coming up, alone, you asleep at home... At home during the scene of writing the poem, Berrigan is not "walking around," except in his mind. *That* Berrigan, the one walking the streets—who really embodies such *flâneur* behavior elsewhere in this and other poems—remains marginal compared to the writer at his desk (who really is at the page's margin, creature-wise, and is the truer subject of the poem). So what enriches this art is that it never settles for the poetic but rather assumes a poker face of playing for higher stakes.

Same goes for A.M. Klein, in the words of a review I've just read of how Alex Garland's 2015 film *Ex Machina* creates a robot character who exhibits "the essence of being human: unpredictable behavior, saying things that don't need saying, reaching absurd conclusions and experiencing joy as a consequence." That characterizes Klein's experience more than a half-century ago, in newly independent Israel, meeting unpredictable and seemingly absurd exuberance at every corner—and it fits Berrigan's '60s poems as well, where the character of Manhattan streets is internalized. The wall between life and art is so nearly broken down by Berrigan that it took a hard toll on him (as it did on Klein, who suffered a nervous breakdown). I've written about our conversations and Ted's influence upon me in critical essays, but here I see it was a kind of preparation for my living in Israel, where the price for joyous independence requires a hard vigilance toward one's enemies. Ted's enemies, however, were largely internal demons—and the toll of subduing them was accomplished with the blackest good humor. I remember an afternoon-long conversation with him almost forty years ago, sitting on the stoop of my St. Mark's Place tenement. "You're just like your 'uncle' Harold," Ted was saying, conjuring Harold Rosenberg, the art critic. "Everything you encounter is a question that has to be answered, instead of a thing wanting to be greeted affectionately." I wish he could have disarmed his demons and the conventional world that easily; instead, the war against them that his poetry fought was etched in his brow, a most Hebraic warrior of brows. At the same time, it was hidden from view in his art, like a Jew hidden from the Nazis while Ted was a child and I was just being born.

3.

"In the last two chapters of my book [*Hunt for the Jews*, about the responsibility of Polish peasants for the murder of many Jews during and after the Holocaust]," says Jan Grabowski, "I bring up the stories of Poles, who despite the negative image of Jews and the enormous pressure from their relatives took a huge risk in hiding them. It is undeniable that certain things have happened but you must understand the atmosphere in which it happened."

It's the word "atmosphere" that gets to me; it's what is meant by historical context. So it's the *atmosphere* around the writing of books of the Bible that we're missing if we're to envision the scene of writing. It was not just dangerous for a Christian Pole to hide a Jewish Pole—no doubt a German bullet in the head for both—it was existential. Friends, relatives, neighbors would pressure you to give the Jew up; your own mother might scream bloody suicide if you didn't. Even if you did, you'd be branded forever as a potential traitor, and your children too, including the ones born later. Hiding a Jew, then, is no normal bravery, and likewise, when a Jew sat down at a table in ancient Jerusalem to write a book of the Bible, a complex, existential atmosphere prevailed. Even more than life and death, there was the question of the afterlife. Not that of the individual; the biblical writers didn't seem to have any clear expectations in that direction, like many of us today. It was the afterlife of their culture, of the place their book would have in it, that held them spellbound to a truthful rendering of the past—or as truthful as one could be with their historical sources (lost to us now). Like great historians, truth was the beauty they were after; it must have been an atmosphere for writing that was fraught with the dangers of success or failure: How would you know that the Assyrians wouldn't arrive in all their might next day, or next year, or next century, to wipe out your culture, your archives and libraries? They certainly weren't going to be reading any Jewish books in ancient Nineveh, anymore than in Germanified Europe, had the Third Reich prevailed. Sensing that, we can sympathize with the writer and critical historian Walter Benjamin's suicide in 1941. Had he been one among many ancient Jewish writers of the Bible in Jerusalem, he might have been spared his European Jewish despair, but still, the existential atmosphere at the scene of writing must have been palpable. As Grabowski in his book pleads for engaging the historical context, the atmosphere, the scene—in which a courageous Pole hid and fed a Jew for days, months, years—we have to do the same for the historical writers of the Bible.

But you may wish to ask: Didn't they create scenes of their own to convey their historical context? Moses on top of the mountain for forty days and nights in an existential encounter with chisel and tablets, for instance—isn't that a scene of writing? Or even more acute was the scene where he returns with them, the written tablets, to find that his culture was no longer interested in his writing, that it preferred the rock 'n' roll dancing around a golden guitar. Moses smashing his tablets—there's the scene of writing, *par excellence*, followed by a return to his mountain, to work on a new draft. Perhaps that's what it might have felt like to be actually writing this historical record in Jerusalem, in a culture for whom that history would determine whether it could survive its eventual destruction by the powerful Assyrians, along with the dragging off into Babylon slavery of a portion of the elite among the Jews, the educated ones who could read and write. Who among them risked hiding in their donkey's saddlebags—if they were allowed donkeys—the Hebrew scrolls from an earlier century? In essence, those biblical scrolls had to be hidden like Jews in the Holocaust or like my New York colleague Ted Berrigan's demons: in order that the poetry survive. The stories might live on orally, but the power of the original writing only survives by stealth, in its refusal to compromise the art.

Today is the UN's International Holocaust Day, a good day for the AP to post results of two European polls showing that nothing has been learned in the 70 years since Auschwitz was "liberated." In the Bertelsmann poll, 60% of present-day Germans say the Holocaust should be consigned to the past as an "anomaly," having nothing to do with them. This is hardly different a result than in 1945, when a larger majority of Germans said they knew nothing of the Holocaust. But in 2015, more than a third of those polled said Israel followed the same Nazi policies as Hitler—complete with mass gas chambers and crematoria, and with those Arabs not yet exterminated forced to sew Islam's crescent or the Christian cross on their clothes. Of course, they didn't supply the aforementioned details, since they're also among those who believe the Holocaust is too much remembered. Are these people psychotic? Perhaps not, yet they live in the shadow of a mass psychosis, and they resent that fact, projecting their resentment onto the Jews of Israel. The majority of Germans in the first half of the twentieth century were not perpetrators but simply enablers of mass murder of their fellow citizens, as in many other European countries. Unfortunately, the dead Jewish-Germans were not allowed a say in their government's policies.

The other poll published today found that 84.4 percent of Palestinians believed that the attacks [on cartoonists and Jews in Paris a couple weeks ago] were "suspicious, and that Israel may be behind it." Is that also not psychotic? A rationale is offered that sounds suspiciously similar to classic anti-Semitism: a Palestinian interpreter of the poll writes that the Paris attacks [*vide* murders] "raise legitimate questions as to who is behind these crimes, if not the Israeli Intelligence, given that 'Netanyahu's Jewish State' was the only one to benefit from them." In Hitler's bestseller *Mein Kampf*, he uses similar reasoning to demonstrate that Jewish lawyers, doctors, and financiers benefited not only from World War I but from all wars, which is why the Jews themselves conspire to start those wars. Granted, there is a similarly psychotic strain in all nationalisms, including in Israel, but it is confined to the fringes. 84% of Palestinians, however, is not peripheral; let's say they're not actually in favor of murdering Jews, yet that still makes them enablers. What is an enabler of a psychosis? It's a poker face, but in this case it's the inverse of the image I've been elucidating: not deadpan but deadening. In contrast, the poker face I illustrate enables the freedom to break through a psychosis. You can take a stance of never compromising with the truth, for instance, yet behind your poker face you can compromise *for the sake of* the truth, which is why we are all ambivalent about lying. Lying about the Jews you are hiding in the root cellar to a representative of the Nazi psychosis—which would take quite a courageous poker face—is actually in service to breaking a psychosis.

Within A.M. Klein's *The Second Scroll*, he inserts his Holocaust poem, 'Elegy.' It's especially potent if you can imagine it as an English translation of a pre-war Yiddish elegy on a pogrom, by Bialik perhaps, but as itself in the late '40s it's a pre-modernist anachronism, albeit Joycean, because it takes poetry for granted. A successful modernist poem integrates a struggle to reinvent poetry, honoring the loss of poetical grandeur that was finally sunk like the Lusitania by a Baudelarian U-boat. Yet I have the sense Klein purposely antiquates his poem, although we won't know to what success for perhaps another century, when the Holocaust might reemerge as a monumental scar on the face of humanity (today that scar is more like a serious lump on the head, hidden beneath the hair), something you could only avoid by refusing to look in the mirror of Klein's poem—as it becomes a precious antique.

I come up against a similar tendency to avoid the heart of the matter, the implacability of the past, when Cole Porter's campy reinventions of the show tune seem to be sentimental chestnuts in the 1946 biopic, *Night and Day* (one can't always watch war docs, though I can recommend the recent French world war surveys, *Apocalypse*). Latter-day commentary says the film whitewashes Porter's homosexuality but I disagree. Cary Grant as Cole wears a perpetual poker face, and while he's constantly surrounded by shapely dancers and showgirls, this erotic undertone serves to reinforce his indifference to women (including his wife, whom he prefers to peck on the cheek) for some higher purpose. But mostly his wife's hidden away overseas, maddened by what appears to be Porter's workaholic addiction to sitting at the piano. The appearance of being a workaholic, however, is a wonderful metaphor for this closeted gay man—too busy for women, yet devoted to erotic song-and-dance. He's hardly the castrated Paul Newman that will appear a few years later in the film versions of Tennessee Williams' plays; instead, Grant's deadpan smirk suggests that real sex is in his songwriting pen/penis, which apparently accounts for all the doting females and convivial males, especially his best friend Monty Woolley, who's far more interested in Porter than any of the ladies he flirts with. Monty and his famous beard would seem to be a womanizer, full of witty bon mots, but he's Cole's pussy cat, while Porter himself is totally incapable of uttering a pun throughout the movie. In a way, that's a shrewd characterization of the artist, who puts all his creativity into his work, and what is a Cole Porter song if not a seductive critique of our otherwise impoverished, unwitty lives? We look in the deadpan mirror and see that we're hopelessly addicted to avoiding the past, whether it's 'My Heart Belongs to Daddy' and 'It's Awfully Hard When Mother's Not Along,' or, to insert some gravity here, it's the Holocaust in Klein's 'Elegy.' As with Klein's poem, we may one day look back at *Night and Day*, and allow it to come out of its time-bound closet, to become timeless. Yet it was the constraint of the closet (for Klein, a poetic closet) that forged their uncanniness. You've got to risk everything for the uncanny, including hiding your broken heart behind a poker face.

4.

"Lou Reed Never Compromised"—a headline from *The Atlantic* online, on his death day. Surely Lou, if not *The Atlantic*, would know how ironic that was. His was a deathless stance, compromised in this case by mortality. In his subtler art, we know that *ars longa* allows for a pretending to immortality, so we can say "no artistic compromises." But compromise with what? With immortal beauty, as Reed wants to say with too much certainty in a review he wrote of Kanye West's album, *New Slaves*. "Very often, he'll have this very monotonous section going and then, suddenly—"BAP! BAP! BAP! BAP!"—he disrupts the whole thing and we're on to something new that's absolutely incredible. That's architecture, that's structure—this guy is seriously smart. He keeps unbalancing you. He'll pile on all this sound and then suddenly pull it away, all the way to complete silence, and then there's a scream or a beautiful melody, right there in your face.

"Immortal beauty is unwavering, like our silence after death, but we humans can be reminded of our dangerous wish for any kind of immortality when we're thrown off balance, like the builders of the Tower of Babel—speaking of architecture. A wish is one thing, but how do we leave the realm of compromising with death and building smaller towers, while still striving to imagine uncompromising eternity? That's a question Lou didn't ask, but his mentor at Syracuse University, the poet Delmore Schwartz, did. He was my teacher too, for less than a semester, a year or two after Lou. At first, Schwartz read T.S. Eliot like I'd never heard or imagined, as if Prufrock's voice was the voice of the Oracle at Delphi. And then he started disappearing from class; we'd sit there for half an hour before deciding he wasn't going to make it. Once, not long after, I

saw him panhandling on East Genesee, pretending not to see him. Here
was Lou Reed's idol of no compromise—not with the academy, not with
his students, not with human society—he didn't need the money at that
point. It shocks me in retrospect that his friends and university colleagues
coddled him; they were too impressed with themselves for having him in
their company. Just to know he was there, that is, for the less they saw of
him the less they had to worry. They saw him only as the legendary writer,
not the man. He needed help, badly; he needed a New York psychoanalyst,
not an over-medicalized Syracuse psychiatrist. But the New York variety
would certainly have required some serious panhandling to support, and
he didn't have a friend or colleague close enough at that point to organize
it. Besides, the '50s literary hangover was still in effect, the one in which
poetry and madness were on good terms.

But at the end of that academic year, summer of '66, trying to finish my
incomplete papers and poetry thesis on the summer island of Vinalhaven,
Maine, came the *Times* obit. He'd made it down to NYC but his heart did
not make it out of a cheap hotel room. A couple months later, already up
in Toronto, I finished this poem:

> 'Delmore is dead, but this spider still lives'
> a line hanging from a dry summer
> a web unspun I was 'afraid to be alone,
> Each with his own death in the lonely room',
> stepped into the stall shower of my wife
> waiting by '66 like an old Rambler
> that almost talked it was so present
> on that island, something is always coming
> alive Delmore you just have to look
> to find yourself by the road someone
> is building, your half-beard (sign
> of travel) a constant revision
> to an unfresh concept of 'alone'
> that doesn't bounce back from a mirror
> even, even this dry thread
> in the working cement-mixer of memory
> becomes a highway
> cut thru the smothering luxury of the idea
> you spent your *life* unproving, that there's always
> a room to check our deathcoats in
> before we enter the poem.

Too late for my manuscript thesis, that poem would appear in *Disappearing
Horses* ('69) (the line 4 quote is from Schwartz), but I'd sent it on to my

committee anyway, one of whom wrote back that he thought it a regression from the talent I'd displayed for my MFA. Lou Reed might have liked it, or maybe not. It's too much stuck on immortality, perhaps, as something attainable, as if the nature in which the spider weaves also allows for a supernatural, a post-deathcoat. Or maybe I'm just over-reading it now, reading the tea-leaves in it of my discovery—seven years on—of how a Hebrew psalm works. I don't think on Vinalhaven I had a sense of talking to creation, or not as a psalmist does, via a Creator.

Lou Reed continues: "He's not just banging his head against the wall, but he acts as though he is. He doesn't want to seem precious, he wants to keep his cred... I've never heard anything like it—I've heard people try to do it but no way, it just comes out tacky. Kanye is there. It's like his video for 'Runaway,' with the ballet dancers—it was like, look out, this guy is making connections. You could bring one into the other—ballet into hip-hop—they're not actually contradictory, and he knew that, he could see it immediately. He obviously can hear that all styles are the same, somewhere deep in their heart, there's a connection."

Styles (species) of organisms, styles (cultures) of being—in this sense, we can imagine the Creator's vantage from beyond the physical world. Lou was close to this timeless vision of creation in his penultimate paragraph, quoted above, from a review of Kanye West's 2013 album, *Yeezus*, but I doubt if he smoked cigars, as in "close but no cigar." Close is not good enough, neither is it for West. "Kanye is there," he's made the connection for us that everything is or can be connected, but as we absorb this epiphany, what are we looking at? Are we looking over the shoulder of our soul and onto the personal page in front of us, or onto the metaphorical page of history, which would be impersonal? In either case, I can't make the page out. Perhaps the beauty gets in the way. Beauty—as if it's the brown hair that gets in our way as it falls over our eyes. Lou Reed takes his sense of Delmore far enough to make Schwartz's manic depression stand in for immortality—that is, eternity as heaven *and* hell, either one, what's the dif? But it wasn't good enough for Delmore, and not for Reed, for the dif is real, even if we're in back of the Creator and can't get past him to see. So although that's all where we can look—like Moses warned he could see only the Creator's back—we have a historical context for it, the biblical text that affirms an encounter with creation has happened (we're creatures), you can read it (you're *commanded* to read it). If you believe the poet was making this up, you also don't believe in brown hair, in the truth of reading a text, human or any other kind—in the sense that all creatures are texts. Reed continues further: "At first, West says 'I can hold my liquor' and then he says 'I can't hold my liquor.' This is classic—classic manic-depressive, going back and forth. Or as the great Delmore Schwartz said, 'Being a manic depressive is like having brown hair.' 'I'm great, I'm terrible, I'm great, I'm terrible.'

That's all over this record. And then that synthesized guitar solo on the last minute and a half of that song, he just lets it run, and it's devastating."

That's the devastation of being mentally unstable. If the artist isn't born or acculturated that way, his art still leads him to know the necessity of risking that instability, with Beauty to rescue him, in place of a Creator. Rescue, but not save. Both West and Reed seem to show us that not even fame and success can hinder their art; their access to dysfunction remains. It's the same access to the uncanny, which any poet needs to lift a poem, as if off the page. It's dangerous, but so is *falling*, as in falling in love. However, seeing the face of your Creator is risking your death, or so went the literary myth in biblical times. That's a bigger risk than any we pose for ourselves now. Although there's always exceptions, like the poem the great Osip Mandelstam wrote to spite the face of Stalin. He must have known that being brought before the real face of Stalin would mean certain death. Then again, there's no good side to Stalin for Mandelstam, unlike our uncanny Creator.

Perhaps last century's most popular representation of the dangers of art, no less than that of a descent into madness or criminality, was the great Lon Chaney in *The Phantom of the Opera* (1926). For my postwar generation it was already lost; it had become as silent as the era of silent movies, yet nothing subsequent to it captured the potential horrors behind the beauty of art as Lon Chaney's skeletal face. And there was beauty aplenty in the original release, with its shocking "technicolor" scenes of the masked *mardi gras*-like evening and the red ghost of the phantom. This mad artist played a heavenly organ in the gorgeous hell of his dungeon, and like most artists, his heart was pure, fastened upon the equally pure, not yet diva-tainted opera singer.

Now, in a 1994 restoration for video, instead of the cheesy verisimilitude of hearing the phantom seem to play his organ in the old piano score, we get the mellifluous, neo-classical score of Carl Davis conducting the Prague Philharmonic. In addition to Davis, you get something more, you get the sense of being there in historical context—so crystal-clear the print, so natural-sounding the art of the score—natural also to the Surround Sound of a contemporary flat screen with Blu-ray. It's the way that Olivier's Hamlet during World War II could be more devastating—re-echoed by the devastation of mid-war—than the original productions in Renaissance London, or the way reading the books of the Hebrew Bible during the centuries of exile, especially the century just after, could be more devastating than it was for the original audience a millennium earlier. At least for the Jews; and no doubt too for the early Christians, who transfigured despair, however innocently—or shall we say, artfully—into a supercessionist reading.

And as it was for the Jewish Christians, the desire to transcend art goes back to Sinai, the writing of Moses in the desert—the desert! But the historical context that is really missing is the scene of writing in ancient Jerusalem, the scene of writing in Shakespeare's study, the '24 scene of making the Phantom, the scene of being on the same street with Delmore Schwartz, he panhandling—as if re-enacting the Great Depression into which, as a teenager, he was born—as a poet, as an artist. It turned into a bad hand for Delmore, as it would seem for the ingenue diva-artist of Phantom, who is given this hard choice: Which will her hand turn, the golden scorpion or the golden grasshopper? It's in black and white, so we have to imagine the gold, but both lead to her own destruction—unless the greatest artist of the Phantom has missed something. And he has! That is, the theater could not save him, all the artistic machinery of the grand opera that he has transfigured into his underground palace of art and gold eventually fails him. But the heart of Moses was dedicated to the truth, or so his writers in ancient Jerusalem portrayed him. His second draft of the Ten Commandments transcends the art of his Jerusalem writers by teaching us the laws of human nature and thereby how beautiful was creation.

Do What You Want, Lady Gaga's new album, repeats Lou Reed's dictum. No boundaries. When I moved into my St. Mark's Place apartment in '71, Lou's Velvet Underground was still playing two doors down. I couldn't afford the cover charge (nor at Max's Kansas City a bit later, speaking of boundaries) but I also was wary of the hard drug boundary, the heroin-esque lives of Andy Warhol stars, or at least the amphetamine drive. Could I avoid it, yet still become as authentic as I understood Lou Reed might have been? True, he was rock and I was poetry, a more venerable, refined art, but that division had already been lost when Allen Ginsberg, who came as visiting instructor to Syracuse for a week in '65 while I was there, advised us all to "turn on" (aiding our poetry workshop with the biggest joint I'd ever seen). I'd had a foretaste as a New School student in '61 through '63, assistant to slightly mad Lowell, neighbor to addict Wieners, and impressed by gay O'Hara—was I going to have to be like one of them to write authentically—gay, addicted, or mad? Was it possible to be normal, to write with Freud's "ordinary unhappiness" yet amount to more than an academic poet?

Perhaps not, my reading of Raul Hilberg suggested, for the most ordinary of Europeans had been demonic just two decades ago. Hilberg's *Destruction of the European Jews* so absorbed me in '63 that I barely attended classes. Ordinary Europeans were doing what they wanted, namely mass murder. I suspected I'd need to learn where the boundaries were between normal and psychotic, with the help of the expanded consciousness of poets Lowell and Ashbery, Hughes and Plath, none of them with an ordinary life. But that was no longer enough; I needed a vision of my own limitations, of what I might want to but never could know. In the past, that cosmic vision employed the supernatural to represent what is unknowable to the human species. The little poem of the Tower of Babel, for instance, dramatizes how far from supernatural we are, how we're bounded by birth and death from a literal cosmic vantage but not a poetic one. It also contains a capsule history of the origin of languages and civilization, as if they are the price we pay for wanting too much literal power.

A price forgotten to be paid in the last century; no civilized language could ransom babe or grandma in Auschwitz or Hiroshima. Carl Andre was only half ironic when he called the 9/11 bombers, with their primitive language of destruction, our greatest performance artists. Still, sculptor of consciousness that he was, Andre was cut off from the dual vision embodied at Mt. Sinai: you can imagine the back of your Creator, see all the way to the back of the physical universe at the Big Bang, and yet it's meaningless unless anchored in a moral vision that bounds desire with the ten poems of civilization, the Decalogue. "Thou shalt not murder": a poem we can feel the justice of, that we can read and enact on any one day, but whose permanence, or eternal feeling, needs to be imagined.

Freud might have agreed, had he survived the Holocaust. He saw the back of desire all right, he saw what a bad hand we were holding in *Civilization and its Discontents*, but he may have thought the way to play it was to whistle past the graveyard and take a seat at the table. The supernatural he saw sitting across from him was a literalization—the wish for magic to be so real it's psychotic, a sign we're entitled to whatever we want. The supernatural contained by poetry, however, speaks to our imagination without subduing it; the poetic text removes it from the realm of unbounded grandiosity. So, reading the poem of the Bible you distinguish between an actual image/idol and a textual one, that I read as if scrubbed free of magic. Perhaps Freud or a disciple would not value that scrubbing, since text too could be—and was—taken out of our hands and appropriated by the psychotic nation: "Yes, 'you Jews' should not murder, as it says in your Bible, but it doesn't apply to me, a member of the master race, or the superior religion, etc." Anyway, Europe was a bad hand that stayed on the table for years, centuries; no way the Jews could play it successfully. Even Schoenberg and Einstein had to jump ship. Karl Marx turned himself inside out to bluff a gentile hand. As if he was holding three aces—workers, intellectuals, peasants— and drew to a pair (Bolshevik and Maoist). And he was in fact holding that full house; the bluff was a fist. Which is why the genocidal Khmer Rouge didn't know he was Jewish.

They got it in the end, those Red Cambodians. They had a poem of "off to work in the countryside" and "burn the evil metropolis down," to the tune of "We're off to see the Wizard." But that of course was an evil hand. Not the ambiguous hand of my cousin-in-law Yip Harburg's actual lyrics to "Somewhere Over the Rainbow": It was a wish, it was a dream—but a bad dream overall, Dorothy dealt a bad hand, thumped on the head by a prairie twister. Dorothy played that bad hand as well as Yip or author Frank Baum had, staying in for both, until witches and wizards were unmasked. They got somewhat rich of course, unlike her, but Dorothy's the poem. And in the same way, the Bible's the poem. But too many wish it was written and staged in the realm of the supernatural—and not the historical twister of Israel's fight for independence of mind and body. The supernatural is real all right, inasmuch as the unknowable is real to a limited primate species, Homo sapiens. But the twister and wherever it came from didn't create Dorothy; her concussion of a dream or nightmare was the metaphorical scene of writing, and it created her for us. As for us, her readers, as well as the Bible's readers, we need to play the hand we are dealt, even if it's a twister's bad hand We creatures sit at the existential table no human may have created.

History rolls over us so inexorably that all our efforts erecting artistic dikes and scholarly dams are at best mouse-holes. I don't really know what happens to the hole when the mouse dies; are they taken over by the next generation and do they last for eternity, as alligator holes seem to? The latter can become architectural wonders: later generations add new dimensions to these wetlands structures. The incredible articulation of the alligator paw strives toward a reptile art, primarily a female art, as the mother alligators elaborate a defense for their young in these alligator "holes." (The males are bellowers, singers). Like a modern artist, alligators—and all animals—hold a poker face to creation, as if we've all been bumped on the head by the trauma of birth. The world we find is natural, a poker table; putting table aside, who made the game? We don't have to know that, but why pretend chance invented a game of chance? It's more revelatory of our predicament to conjure a yellow brick road, a supernatural wizard—even one with a writer hidden behind the curtain. Finally we meet that writer of Oz, just as we're now on the road to encounter the biblical writers.

In 2013, Reza Aslan's *Zealot*, a book on Jesus, depended for its secular bestsellerdom on the passionate rejection of the supernatural. Readers wanted their doubts verified—yet those doubts were grandiose (as in, we're superior to all that) and grew gargantuan, along with the author, page after page. Jesus wasn't even born in Bethlehem; or, Nazareth was a backwater of illiterate day laborers like Jesus, with no synagogue. Never mind how that's disproven by recent sociological studies of ancient Judea, none of which appear in the bibliography. What does appear there and in the notes are a hodgepodge of outdated sources from Religion 101. But what hooks our latter-day readers is the author's debunking of the concept of unknowable. They are willing to believe that we have reached a superiority in intelligence that reduces the unknowable to the merely unknown: what's bound to become known to us eventually, if not soon. Meanwhile, the author and his readers are feasting on the knowable unknown—as no self-respecting alligator would. Instead, the alligator acknowledges the unknowable wisdom of her ecosystem. It places her, after all, as the keystone species in the Everglades near my Florida home, providing those deep, complex holes for a myriad of species to survive in, during the dry season.

What are *our* deep holes but our own eyes, in which the world rests during our brief lifetimes. When it departs from us, we look up from our reading beds with our last breath, knowing the world remains without us. *That's* the knowing that is numinous, because the world *without us* is unknowable. And the history of the passing-down through the generations of particular mouse-holes is a numinous unknowable as well; like us, the mice seem to know the world will go on without them, that the hole, though mouse-size, is bigger than they are.

5.

My agent might pretend to be snoring were I to offer the paragraphs above as answer to his question, "So what's it about?" He needs one or two sentences he can wake up an editor with. "But why should anyone be interested in you?" he might ask of a memoir, "and we already know from the failure of your last book that hardly anyone literary is interested in the Bible anymore. The Scene of Writing? Who would care about that, other than Christmas card salespersons? Regardless, we all know it's a game of chance, that it's just a matter of time when the book's on the sales table and the review radar passes by—picks it up or puts it down. What's going to intrigue them in that slippery moment? Just tell me what's your drama, what's it about?"

But my mind won't sit still for my hardheaded agent; I hang up the phone by saying I'll think about it some more. Yet will my thinking and my agent's needs coincide? I'm already thinking about his words, "matter of time" and "chance." He probably didn't choose them carefully, yet to me every word of my agent is like the anthem of a foreign country to a spy living in that country: know it by heart or die.

So first I have to work it out for myself: Can my life come down to a few catch-phrases? I go to sleep and wake up in the middle of the night with the answer tugging my fingers toward the iPad. It seems to me for a pre-dawn moment I may be able to think this through and delight my agent with a simple answer: it's about the game of life... When I look at this in daylight I'm laughing at myself for having an instant answer.

The real answer starts with having some time. Time's a result of various players of matter sitting at the table of the universe. Planetary matter, solar matter, galaxy matter, *et. al.* They all have different hands, i.e. they're moving at different speeds, but all together they're in the game.

Then there's the tiny little matter of you or me; we're in the game too, but our card table is just a metaphor for the universal one. So is the length of the game. We may play for hours, but the number of hands is unknown. Could be fifty, could be a hundred. You could make an educated guess in advance, but then there's something that's really unknowable: once again I ask, who made the table? Oh, it appears humans did, but who made the materials used—and finally, who made the humans? Chance seems to offer the best answer. You can't play poker without it. So: Who or what made chance? Poker has an answer to that: it's the poem of a bad hand. Chances are, you'll get one fairly often. If you just fold it and wait for a good one, odds are you'll get little return when you win. So you have to know how to play the bad hand too. Chance, therefore, is both in the cards and in the players. For both, it's a matter of time: how long you can play and how quickly you can win or lose. Are we into game theory? Old friend David Gelernter of Yale might say yes; but no, we're into who made the table.

That's how I came to think about "knowing belief" and the scene of writing, the two most crucial concepts for thinking about that table and all other tables, such as the one we all need a seat at in order to eat. Those who believe in the supernatural seem to have all bases covered—except for the nature of the human mind. And those who believe solely in science have forgotten the back door to the unknowable: all that our limited sensibility can never know, the way a dog can't know algebra. You can go through life simply "not knowing," or more precisely, not caring, but then what was the point? Knowing belief says the point is imagining who or what made the table—not the game, not the celestial or earthbound players, but the table. It's the table that makes the game—the drama—possible. We live in the drama of time: a fossil female mosquito was recently discovered with a bellyful of a blood meal; she'd been swept away in a wave, an instant of time 43 million years ago. You can say she played a bad hand. Had she folded and forsook that blood of a dinosaur-descendent, she might have lived to another day. But she played it and lost—though maybe not, for probably she's the only mosquito of her time who is still being read, albeit through a microscope.

"Knowing belief" requires the ability to read, even in its elemental sense of reading tracks, the way an ant can follow a chemical track, or a Neanderthal a woolly mammoth track. In the case of civilization, humans made the tracks of writing. It was human Jews in ancient Jerusalem who wrote the texts in which the unknowable is imagined as a singular writer of creation, the Creator. He's both like us and unlike us; in other words, we both believe in the unknowable but at the same time know that we imagined it. This doesn't simply mean we should read the Bible as a literary text like the *Odyssey*. It means we can read it as if we believe it, that we fully believe it as we read, knowing that humans imagined it in a work of art. If we can keep both things in mind at the same time, we can play bad hands as well as good ones, because to play a bad hand you have to believe in the game even more than the hand. I would say you also have to believe in the table—since no game can be played without it. That's a lot to hold in mind, but that's precisely what stretches the mind and allows one to play a bad hand.

Essentially, then, it's a bad hand that the writer plays at the scene of writing *anything*, especially cosmic works like books of the Bible. If it was a good hand, there'd be no serpent, no murder of brothers, no slavery, no exile. There'd be no need to argue with the Creator or His people, as the Prophets do so brilliantly. The good news they deliver is way outweighed by the bad. But you can play a bad hand and survive, and thus we have great books of the Bible along with the boring good parts (eg. the laws and the begats)—or rather, not so boring when taken as historical artifacts that serve as tables for the larger game. But you have to know the difference, which the good hand, which the bad, and the way to know that is to focus upon the scene of writing: the creature in his or her chair at his or her table, or possibly the library archive's table. Who is she, and what does *she* think she's doing? How did she get there, and again, what's the game and who made the table. You'll find an answer to these questions even in Emily Dickinson, for she too thinks about the table at which she braids each poem, after it's written, into a little booklet—a kind of present to creation. Anyone could do that, perhaps, but there's only one scene of writing that holds Dickinson, and when we can imagine ourselves there, it makes no difference if she's a recluse or a world explorer, a dreamer or a metaphysician, for any creature's art boils down to a scene of writing. We must follow the tracks to survive, like an ant, but also know that the creature at the table is likewise a made thing.

So I'm watching a webcast of the "ModPo" (modern poetry) class on *Coursera*, the global internet university, with thousands of students tuned in around the world. This one on Gertrude Stein (who a call-in student from Germany with a somewhat intelligent question pronounces "Jertrud Shtein"). The four professors at the UPenn avant-garde headquarters answer questions with a precise and complicated articulation that was foreign to Stein herself; her discourse was smoothly, teasingly erotic, and theirs, hesitantly analytical, with the hesitation meant to suggest, well, hesitation at presuming to elucidate Stein—a master elucidator of her own poetry, in their complimentary genres of biography, autobiography, history, and litcrit. Nevertheless, an A for effort all around, on this celebratory centenary of Stein's *Tender Buttons* (1914).

Almost half a century before this webcast, I was pursuing a doc thesis entitled 'Gertrude Stein's Pipe' in the American Studies program of the University of Essex, England. I'd taken a hint from Man Ray, who granted me a brief phone interview in Paris, shortly before his death. In answer to a question, he replied, "Oh, we all smoked opium in those days, also cocaine, and of course hashish. We didn't think of them as drugs, just work aids, even health aids! I don't think Stein cared for alcohol at all. We did, however, think Cocteau went a bit too far in his opium and cocaine obsession. As I said, we didn't think of ourselves as using drugs—or at least, we used them in moderation, like salt."

Suddenly, re-reading Stein's prose poetry, words like "snow" and "spoon" and "nose" jumped out at me. I tried opium—once was enough—to get the effect, ditto cocaine, and less researchingly, and somewhat more often, hashish in moderation. These aids opened a dimension to her work that I was hesitant about in the past, namely, the great whoosh of her steadfast, tenacious humor. It was as if just breathing was a thrill—the "joy of being" an antidote to her baleful regard of Heidegger—and in every breath, the picked wildflowers of words filled up every sense. The sense they made is another issue, and I attempted to describe it as a "come hither," by which I meant a seduction of the brain that leaves it gasping, not knowing how to respond, "at a loss for words." I realize now that this sounds like an evasion of critical thinking, and it's true in a way, for in my twenties I simply could not command the proper critical vocabulary. In fact, no one else could either; the few critics engaging Stein at that time leaned heavily on her biography, especially her love of painting.

I myself fell upon a biographical angle into Stein: her love of philosophy, from William James to Alfred North Whitehead. The poets of my time thought of themselves as the successors to philosophers: experimental poetry, especially, was a kind of irreducible, post-Wittgenstein crucible of thinking-as-breathing, or what Nietzsche might have called a blindly tragic music. Death was such a powerful presence that it was almost totally excluded from that poetry (less so from Stein's, whose *The Making of Americans* plays heavily with "becoming a dead one"). Yet along with the supreme effort at holding the door barred against it, death, a new music arose, as if Ezra Pound's enlivening of the medieval troubadours was transformed into a recitative of a new grace after meals—the meal in this case having been a feasting on the flesh and bone of language itself, including all the historical trimmings that etymology proposed. I'm reminded of it today by a *New York Times* feature article (not a review) of the latest book by poet Mary Oliver, *Dog Songs*, described as an instant bestseller: "as high as No. 2 on Amazon's poetry list (behind a 99-cent Kindle edition of Poe)."

If we change one word in its title, replacing 'Dog Songs' with 'Death Songs,' we begin to read, "Mary Oliver has spent most of her life with a mind ripe with poems—and with death by her side." It continues: "Ms. Oliver is the kind of old-fashioned poet who walks the woods most days, accompanied by death and notepad. 'Death is a perfect companion,' she said. 'It doesn't speak.'" And further: "Besides nature, Ms. Oliver's muses include the poets blank, blank, and blank, and, of course, death. And the book transcends death. It's also about love, impermanence, and the tears in things."

"But why write a book of death poems? When asked about those allergic to her work, one could almost hear Ms. Oliver shrug over the phone: 'It's a kind of eliteness among academics.'" Continuing, the California poet, blank, is quoted: "So many poets obscure the world. Mary Oliver clarifies it." And then Mary Oliver is allowed to speak for herself within the *Times'* journalist's piece: "In a sense, her poems, with their charity and lyric clarity, can provide the kind of solace that death gives. 'I think it's a companion in a way that people aren't. It'll lie next to you when you're sad. And it reminds us that we're animals.'" Finally, Oliver is allowed a measure of levity, to offset any impression that her own death is all that she thinks about: "One time a stranger came to the house and asked if I was Mary Oliver," she said, laughing. "And I said, 'No, I'm not Mary Oliver.'" Nevertheless, It sounded as if it was a perfectly rehearsed rejoinder, as if that "stranger" coming to her house was death itself. "No, I'm not Mary Oliver."

To clarify: I'm not poking fun at Oliver herself; dogs and death are each a feature of the natural world, which she lovingly evokes. No, it's the Times's breathlessness about the canine canniness of the subject that is funny, especially the bone their reporter "dug up": that the book wasn't Oliver's idea but rather one that her publisher and editor cajoled her into. Nor am I criticizing my colleagues at U.Penn or gently hinting they should put hashish on the curriculum. Rather, I may be implying that it can help to *imagine* the effects of opium, for instance, and upon oneself as reader, more than on Ms. Stein the writer, for she was no doubt a great imaginer. But I do regret the absence of death in the academies of poetry today—the evocation of death, that is—as if Heidegger and Jaspers had been buried in a Marxist flower garden tended by the trendier continental philosophers, Deleuze *et. al.* No Garden of Eden this, yet returning to the soil from whence thou were made is out of the picture; instead, although they have envisioned their own paradise of poetry and close reading (much like Talmudic scholars image a heaven where Torah continues to be studied) my contemporary colleagues in poetry exude the impression that they would sit up in their own coffins and criticize the service: "No psalms please, I specifically left instructions that O'Hara's *Meditations in an Emergency* was to be read."

It's funny to think of Frank O'Hara's *Meditations in an Emergency* as a "text", sans O'Hara. It's the character he created of himself that still tugs at us, and it's the same for Ezra Pound, the legendary "EP". When today's avant-gardist, Vanessa Place, seems to decry character ("No more superiority of the interiority of that unnatural trinity—you, me, we ") she is also in the process of creating a character of herself that shines through her poetry. And as a nail in the coffin of death, Place instructs, "No more death without dying—*immediately*," continuing Pound's century-old prescription against pre-Modern tropes of that "dim valley..." Out with the 23rd Psalm's "valley of the shadow of death" as well? I think not, and probably Pound, O'Hara and Place would agree, for even though nameless, the Hebrew Psalmist's unwavering attention to the context of his dialogue with a fully attentive Creator renders the poet alive."

The slightest loss of attention leads to death," writes Frank O'Hara in 1964—and that strict dictum holds true for the Bible, perhaps more than any other poetry. Of course, modern poets, especially, fail to read the poetry there, averse to accepting the omniscient attention of a Creator. It seems to me O'Hara in his way wishes the poet to fill that intense a creator-space. I don't know of any modern or postmodern poet, however, who elucidates this modern bind better than the legendary Canadian poet, bpNichol. Although he died tragically young, as did O'Hara, he had already encoded in his lifelong poem of twenty years, *The Martyrology*, his own death as a character, namely himself as a poet. For I become a character the minute I pun or invent (*Who is that making it?*)—it's just that today, as we continue to repress our great despair at being a creature without a maker, ModPo poets appear able to keep going by way of self-deprecation. Yet it's a faux deflation; character is created nonetheless. Shakespeare had his plays in which to work this out, but as a fledgling ModPo myself, I was lucky to read more biology than literary theory, and followed E.O. Wilson's advice to the young scientist: "Get thee to a field where nobody wants to go." He got himself to the lifelong study of ants; I got from *The Ant's Forefoot*, a poetry journal I edited in my twenties, to Hebrew poetry, biblical and modern, and its nonstop dialogue or argument with a Creator. Creatureship, in other words, is what I imagined myself drinking in from Wilson, and that requires enlivening the argument for and against our deaths. Somehow. And somehow, somewhere, I had to uncover that inherited poetic despair and face it—without heroin or speed, and without the madness of my college mentors? This is the moment of decision I keep coming back to, the moment in which I survived the Twentieth Century, as had the Blues-sourced composers in their fashion, from the Beatles *et. al.* to whatever postmodern poetry will stand up to the test of soul music.

As I discovered—almost reluctantly, fearing to lose my place in the poetry scene of the day—there's not a moment of inattention in the Hebrew Bible, except for human frailty. At least that's the way it got written and edited (as I came to drink it in)—with more fault to be found in the imprecision of the editing, perhaps. I'm sure that Barrie (bpNichol) and Frank (O'Hara) would have come up against that if they'd been allowed to live into old age. Actually, it's already there in *The Martyrology*, and in my last face-to-face with Barrie, circa 1971 in Toronto, he transferred this awareness to me, asking why I had written the cover of the putative last issue of *The Ant's Forefoot* (there were to be a few others once I'd landed back in New York) in Hebrew. I covered my inchoate reasoning with the usual '60s faux innocence: "I dunno. It felt like it would put the end of the mag in question, just as ancient Hebrew has come alive again in our lifetime."

6.

Just how my post-adolescent crisis, Israel's rebirth, *Blonde on Blonde*, and Harold Bloom's *The Anxiety of Influence* coincided, is something I need to come at from another direction: my encounter with "Higher Biblical Criticism." My generation's secret life is all there in the word "high"— if it wasn't getting high, then it was *not* getting high. Either way, the permutations of the word high included anxiety about its sources, all the way back to pagan mountaintop deities and "Lord Most High." The grandiosity inherent in "getting high" devolved into indifference to social responsibilities—in its extreme, it seemed fine to be a hermit in a cave, or an expat in Kyoto (the wonderful poets Whalen and Corman) or a Burroughs and Ginsberg traipsing through Tangier and Calcutta. But there was even more grandiosity to "not getting high," as if sobriety led to the sacred height of the scientific method. Although Freud had disproved that, my generation disapproved of Freud, entertaining a resistance to psychoanalysis as not scientific enough on the one hand, or not poetic enough on the other. It's funny to think of my poetic colleagues—stoned, inebriated, or stone-cold—as more scientific than thou, but that's what it amounted to, when highbrow paganism claimed the mantle of dispassionate rationality. Even if we were all plenty passionate, the farce is clear—we were, in fact, worshippers of "the god of consciousness." We self-consciously embraced farce itself as one end of the conscious spectrum, with quantum physics at the other end. So, if any form of "belief" wasn't farcical, than it had to be anchored in the physical drama of nature, where not only did everything have to die in order to feed some other form of matter or energy, but the lengths of indecision to which the quantum innards of an atom could go bordered on the ineffable (if not hilarious). Hence the necessity for consciousness to fix a vantage above all that; namely, to make itself a god. Meanwhile, awareness of this modern melodrama led the highest artists of our time to make of themselves self-deprecating characters, their naked honesty displacing the god. Yet we could not admit to this openly, for if so, both character and god would melt to the floor, like Dorothy's wicked witch in Oz. So we had to worship the god of consciousness at all cost.

Or you could melt to the floor. "What next?" becomes the question; what follows "the death of poetry," as several ModPo poets have denoted. With Stevens, we're on the cusp of metaphysics; with Ashbery, on the cusp of an artist's canvas; with Williams, on the cusp of turning into devoted nurses, *pace* Civil War Whitman. But I rather think of Dickinson, whose poems are prayer-like arguments to the god of consciousness: "Whatever, I'd rather be here, in this tight little space of neighborhood, house and room, than out plumbing the universe. Or rather, I have both, right in this room, right at the scene of writing." It was the scene of writing that was key to me for encountering Higher Biblical Criticism. I was reading Dickinson (who had just been unfolded in all her range by the publication of the 3-volume *Collected Poems* in the early '80s) at the same time I was coming to grips with biblical criticism—and its immense ignorance of the scene of writing. Or so it seemed to me—an ignorance rather than a willful avoidance.

The recent Nobel writer, Alice Munro, is among the *ne plus ultra* in post-Freudian depth of consciousness. Let's call it a "depth of field," in which memory and the present are under the microscope in one *mise-en-scene*—a 3D microscope, that is. Munro doesn't so much reproduce consciousness, as in Joyce or Ashbery, but rather the sense of ordinary living in it. "Ordinary," of course, can't be used anymore without the irony of Freud's phrase, "ordinary unhappiness," the goal for breaking through a neurosis. Where does that leave the soul? Is it no more than a literary metaphor? Not many modern writers have used it even as that, a metaphor for some ineffable state of being. Or even a quite describable state, as it was for Dante and Blake, and in more ironic ways, by the late Isaac Bashevis Singer. As his editor for a couple years in the '80s, I once asked Singer if the Holocaust crushed his belief in a soul. "No, no," he answered, "that was accomplished in my youth when I first read Dostoevsky." So it was modern consciousness that did it? "You shouldn't think Dostoevsky destroyed it, or ignored it like so many others. He continued an argument about it, after Kierkegaard, though the soul had not a chance of winning anymore."

Ever since a little crisis of soul on St. Mark's Place, in 1972—when it, not me, recognized the weathered Hebrew letters above a boarded-up Second Avenue synagogue ruin, as if it (not me) was in ancient Babylon—I've struggled to articulate that question to Singer, about how to remember the Holocaust. If your consciousness is totally alive, as it is with Alice Munro, perhaps you have no use for it, perhaps there's a corollary to it in everyone's memory. That's too chilling to consider. Let's say, rather, that somewhere in the human genome are trace memories of its species extinction, or the potential for it. Just as Freud named the death-drive, there must also be an extinction-drive, since all species eventually go extinct. And since the soul is that entity with a connection to us that has no death-drive—the usage of "soul-killing" a rude irony—then it also has no extinction-drive. That's how a poet Freud might have reasoned, but not any longer, not post-Holocaust after the murder of his sisters.

I would say, however, that the Holocaust reveals how the soul does have an extinction-drive. It was evident back there in ancient days, at the scene of writing in Jerusalem, when the making of a supernatural Covenant became literary in historical settings. Or in Aristotle's Athens, where it reigned philosophical. When the human species becomes extinct, the soul is also in fear of its existence. Anyway, a new poll shows that a third in the UK think Jews speak too much of the soul. Forgive me, not the soul—the poll said we speak too much of the Holocaust.

I suppose the souls of the extinct saber-toothed tiger or the mastodon are lost forever, as is that of Homo erectus—unless we have inherited at least a memory of it. Possibly the several elephant species alive today have inherited a memory of the mastodon, and even our house cat a trace of the saber-toothed tiger. But to ask it more modernly, when the plug is pulled from the brain of a Homo sapiens or a beloved, human-domesticated feline, where does the electricity go? Isn't it a kind of electricity that animates the brain, leaping through the synapses? Billions of organisms with brains die every day, with humans a small part of it, so that's a not insignificant amount of electricity lost. According to the laws of physics, no matter or energy is lost in the universe, it all transforms into something; and since the soul is immaterial, I'm not implying this electricity is it—yet there is a connection. Any individual brain is but a Homo sapiens representation, but if the species were to go extinct, if there were to be no more humans and human brains, I believe the human soul would be shocked, so to speak, by this electrical loss, shocked into somehow trying to prevent it. So that even today, when it doesn't yet seem we are on the brink of extinction (but who knows?) we may intuit the soul's anticipation and intervention, though unknowable to us.

In that sense, Alice Munro and Gertrude Stein, though neither was a visionary, do intuit our extinction and thereby alert us to the potential of a soul—or at least, in the warning of a Homo sapiens soul. Their intensity of confrontation with consciousness—an expansion of delight in ordinary unhappiness—is both funny and scary. When Munro was asked if she felt the Nobel recognition had come too late, being already in her eighties, she replied, "Not at all. I get to go out with a bang." That play upon T.S. Eliot's world-ending trope of going out "not with a bang but a whimper" is not all that simple. It's the "going out" that's soft-pedaled here, as if the dying itself is of little consequence. I'd say that's an intimation of the soul, which is somehow influencing that repression of fearing our own death and thereby facing us all with a stronger "return of the repressed" in the knowledge that we are missing something, that something immaterial is missing.

In a feeble attempt to compartmentalize this knowledge, some will distinguish consciousness from self-consciousness, with the former representing "soul". But that's still all materialist, as is the brain's "electrical" wiring. When the hand is over, it's over. For everyone—in or out. Does that mean life is a bad hand for everyone, winner or loser? Yet the game goes on, there are new hands, new stars form out of old ones throughout the universe. Life *is* a bad hand, everyone folds their cards. I never heard someone who said, "I had some great hands but I lost it all in the end," also say, "Nevertheless I was a winner!" Someone that naive can't play poker. There's a way around this, however, called superstition. There's superstition in religion, but even more of it in secular culture. Most ideas of fate are superstitious, it seems to me, as in "She died of a broken heart." Perhaps it was more likely to have been not enough mashed potatoes.

Good hands are not played by the superstitious, but their holders may very well believe in the supernatural. Let's look at that word "belief." The winner does or does not believe the loser has a better hand; he does, however, believe his chances are improved by believing that a poker god controls those chances. In that belief, the winner "works with" the god, who allows him to see the scene from above, and thus disembodied, the winner has an advantage over rivals who trust only their own knowledge and instincts. The losers have only fate on their side, and fate—as in knowing the end of the story while still at the beginning—is a narrow-minded writer. It's only the supernatural god who can create a drama out of everything and nothing; the winner is in sync with that, for every hand is such a drama.

Perhaps it's like that with life. If you don't have King David or the Kingdom of Heaven, you can have Shakespeare to enliven the daily domestic dramas, or at least poker. My dad was a chess nut, but I didn't understand why he disliked chess books and computer simulations. Now, I can understand that he had an inkling of the chess god, even though he always said chess was the king of games because it was based on knowledge and logic. But who made logic, after all; that is, who "created" the context for it, along with the Homo sapiens brain? It may be logical to answer, "chance," or the chances inherent in evolution, so where does that leave the logic of chess? I think my father understood that there was a chess god, and that you could "believe" in it at the same time that you know it is a belief. I'd call it "knowing belief." It allows you to align yourself with the supernatural, with the disembodied, but also to be aware that you are allowing yourself to be cast in this drama.

That's the thing that's so easily missed by my colleagues in the ModPo project. They reject "knowing belief," look down upon religious friends or Bible translators, many of whom (obviously not all) allow themselves entry into a cosmic drama that is larger than anything we have now, having been built up and renewed through the vicissitudes of millennia. I guess I was once such a "looking down at" ModPo writer, looking down at "believers" as gullible, as antithetically desiring the unknowable—but not aware of that disembodied point above from which one acquires such a view. Most six-year-olds have it, looking down upon their younger siblings who still believe in Santa or tooth fairies or Hallowe'en ghosts. I was dressing up for Halloween even at age twelve, for the game of it. Sadly though, I was "knowing," as I would be later, in sync with the "knowing" Pound of *The Cantos,* for whom the knowing Confucius had replaced the ancient gods. I was not, in other words, in possession of a "knowing belief." I would stumble into that later, along with discovering that the knowing Higher Biblical Criticism and its academic translators were often bereft of knowing belief.

Last week I was watching a YouTube interview from a few years ago with Philip Roth, following a link from a previous interview, also from some years ago, with Alice Munro—both had just won major literary awards, though not quite Nobels. You could see that once long ago they may have been uncomfortable with such interviews, but now they'd figured out ways to answer the inevitable questions satisfactorily and are unafraid to be occasionally humorous in response, especially Alice. Still, neither of them had much of interest to say, as if they did most of their thinking and acting out in their books and were otherwise spent of wisdom. "John Updike was the true master of my day" was the most passionate thing Roth had to offer, while Munro, when asked if, at 78, she had a sense of any wisdom acquired, said "No, not really. I'm the same person I was at 28, plus some experience."

Both writers displayed the self-deprecatory manner that has typified literary culture for at least half a century. Either one could have walked on to a Woody Allen film and fitted in without a day's rehearsal. Which is not to say they were not serious; on the contrary, they projected deep gravity about literature and writing and their own personal histories within those subjects—but seemed to have nothing to say about much else. I'm sure they had some opinions like all of us about politics or education or the future. Actually, I must take that back—about education or the future they probably had little to offer that you haven't heard on a dozen occasions from persons of lesser stature. The main drift is that it's for the best to stick to what you've learned on the learning curve of life, rather than to speculate on the unknown, much less the unknowable. Art is all, art is the answer, life is just a bowl of art anyways, a bowl or a planet in which we are a passing personality, dolled up intellectually for the trip.

There was a brief period at the last mid-century when that truism might have been turned inside out, so that it's the universe that could be considered ephemeral vis-a-vis the eternity a mind might conjure, however pessimistic, as in *Being and Nothingness,* or *Waiting for Godot.* A new realism, however, clunked all that on its head in the early '60s, be it Lenny Bruce or Godard, though it still trailed vapors of cosmic encounter with "meaning" (God is dead, *et. al.*). Soon enough, it boiled down to the artfully infinite sport of making art, and with subjectivity the pool to swim in, one could take down the tennis court of objective truth, pitted as it is with cracks and fissures from disuse. Now, consciousness floods over and encompasses every-thing, in a way that would probably have frightened Tolstoy and vexed Joyce and Woolf. What would be the point of the latter two being brought back to life today? What would they have to do they haven't already accomplished? When first alive, it seemed new pastures were being plowed, while today, no one needs anything more than doing it "my way." But that's not all bad, it's a huge weight off our backs. Now we can just sit back and enjoy the music, or the sound outside the music, as Cage once immersed himself in. Every generation will have its little rebellion and then go on to teach its little history that hasn't changed the world but certainly added style and some pizzazz to the culture.

I would say this is a bad hand. Poker-faced, you play it as so utterly real that even ISIS would fold. Yet there's always someone at the table who has never liked your poetry and will stay in to call. You show four ultra-real kings: Saul the mad; Zedkiyahu, of the empty eye-sockets; Ahasuerus, appointer of Haman; and Eichmann, king of the Holocaust universe. You win, because the Bible backs you up. Without it, you were still waiting for messianic, meaningful aces. They're in the cards all right, but they are a dream, nothing real—unless you have learned *Finnegans Wake* by heart.

7.

Daddy—my 88-year-old father-in-law—calls from Texas, asking Rhonda to tell him how to install the new phone/voice recorder he bought at Walmart. There's a snag: to satisfy daddy, the new digital recorder has to have the exact same phone answering message as on the old tape, which contains the sweet voice of Rhonda's mom, now five years deceased. In fact, this is the day of her yahrzeit. Daddy won't take no for an answer, after Rhonda explains the difficulty. She makes an attempt; I am listening with one ear, the other to the Tigers-Red Sox playoff. Aníbal Sánchez has a no-hitter going, Rhonda is quickly losing patience: "You bought the wrong kind of phone system to do that." And that is the wrong thing to say to daddy, because the Walmart lady told him it could be done. He seems to trust a stranger at Walmart more than his own daughter. At this thought, Rhonda loses it and throws the portable phone into my lap—fortunately an underhand toss. "Daddy?" I begin, though I would not know how to instruct him even without mother's answer message. But I feel the need to accomplish something else: I want to guilt daddy/Walmart for making Rhonda lose her patience (for which she herself will start to feel guilty in about an hour, since she might have been able to get the message transferred with some heroic internet patience).

If Rhonda's "no" to daddy is the first rebellion, the kind most children test out in adolescence, mine is the mature kind: I want to indict the culture, in the form of Walmart, for I otherwise have sympathy for daddy's desire. How could that woman have failed to notice daddy's age, his technophobia, and the complications of such a deeply sentimental quest to keep his departed wife's voice alive? I blame Walmart for hiring and/or mis-training its saleslady. So I want to get daddy to return the new phone system (the old one is still working, it's just short an extra handset) but to blame the lady for misleading him. Nothing rational will suffice, since it's already irrational enough that he trusted Walmart over his own daughter.

Flashing forward a bit, I'm in bed trying to fall asleep, thinking through for the umpteenth time what my rebellion against conventional Bible translation entails. It's the second, "mature" kind: it's the textual culture I can't help but indict for losing the ability to value the original scenes of writing, long ago in ancient Jerusalem—for just totally repressing it and instead offering the "text" as a product that can satisfy any and all demands of translation. No living wife to re-record a message? No problem. No living authors—no living Hebraic culture—to establish a context for the long Jewish historical presence in the land? No need. The people are dead and gone, unimportant to the textualists. What remains is the recorded message, and what's the difference if it's 5 years old or 3 thousand?

The Higher Biblical Criticism can be like that saleslady at Walmart, and it seems that academe shops there, in a manner of speaking. She tells us that we don't need to think about the Israelites; if you think, instead, like the rest of the world, you can copy Israel's message onto your own system, sans context. Characterizing the early anti-Semitic misunderstanding of these critics among Protestants, Robert Nicholson, writing on the critical website *Mosaic*, suggests that the writers of the Bible were seen as corrupt Walmart salespeople:

> "In the eyes of the higher critics, it was not God but the ancient Israelites themselves who had written their own 'deed' to the land of Canaan, 'prophesied' their own chosenness, and set out to actualize their self-serving prophecies to the detriment of everyone else."

"Self-serving," as opposed to serving God. In fact, in ancient cultures including Jewish and Greco-Roman, the divinity is historical; as old, if not older than the ancient Israelis themselves. Even the Gilgamesh epic writer takes his or her authority from the gods of the ever more ancient Sumerian Odes. Homer, Virgil, and the New Testament's Jewish writers all count on a long history of literary culture that engages divinity. To the prejudiced readers of the higher critics, however, the historical meaning that matters is not literary but grandiosely anthropological: they explain the fact that the message the Israelites received from God is an outdated system that the later religions of Christianity and Islam have upgraded. Israel, in this view, was a primitive society that was merely an answering machine for the divine. Israel's answer-message, then, can be copied, with the original discarded—and therefore the present incarnation of Israel can be chalked up to the same selfish motives, including the re-creating of Hebrew culture."

The anti-Jewish perspective of the higher criticism would go on to enjoy a long life in the established Protestant churches, enabling many liberal Christians to view the emergence of the state of Israel in 1948 as an act of selfishness committed by a demonstrably selfish people."

I have nothing against Walmart or Protestants, but we can see how this pov is still selling. To wit, Israel is a bad hand and it's wisecracked that Israelis ought to fold it and move to Texas. While that may sound too Walmartish for intellectuals, a version of that take in academe might be: Is Israel bluffing when it stands pat against most of the world? As if Judaism too is a bluff, with no messiah in the hole. And with those kinds of quasi-religious questions, I'm reminded again of poets & artists poker night on 1970s St. Mark's Place.

Nothing overtly religious at poker night, nor could you discern either selfish or Christian behavior: no one was either winning or losing "on purpose," and no one was allowing others to win out of a noble charity. What does stand out was the behavior of those who simply could not fold and stood pat to the bitter end, which led to a quick impoverishment. These players were often forced to go home "early," pockets empty, though thereby relieved of the obligation to play on until dawn like the rest of us. Being deprived of the social effervescence with which "Friday night poker" could fuel the rest of the week was a bummer. So you might extrapolate that those ancient Israelis depriving themselves of the society of the larger world, including Egypt and Rome, refusing to fold to them, were selfish (even with a bad hand). Actually, they had a diverse society of their own, and what's more, they had their own poets and artists—in particular, the poets who wrote most of the Bible, whether poetry or prose. These are the literary facts that the higher biblical criticism exposed—and then quickly covered up, attributing the winning Hebraic culture (in its ongoing survival) to a selfish desire to lord it over the rest of us.

The Jewish share of world population, at about 0.02 percent, is perhaps roughly equal to the number of potential poets (most of them yet to write or publish). Some of these in North America will never write a poem but become professionals who enable artistes. To describe the encouragement of populist art that could rise above the commercial mainstream, the term "mediocracy" was appropriated and long held dear by poetic sociologists in the '50s. My cousin Bernie Rosenberg was one of those sociologists, along with New School colleague Silverstein, who assumed he was helping poetry, along with hip adolescents, by diverting government funds that had been allocated for rehabilitating Juvenile Delinquents to the St. Mark's Poetry Project. In the early '70s, I was thus rehabilitated in the East Village, but did I consider myself above anything, let alone mainstream culture? Contrary-wise, I considered myself to the side of it, in the margins: I needed a mediocracy, because if there wasn't a commercial pop culture I couldn't be where I wanted to be, which was precisely in that margin. Nor would I have read the Bible and discovered how to engage it as a poet, because the Bible is marginal as well—not to politics and religion, but certainly to modern poetry. So I found the world of mediocracy a comfort, a world I could be anonymous in, since my poetry wasn't in it. The Bible that was written by "Anonymous" wasn't in it either—that is, the veritable text, the original text. The original writers in ancient Jerusalem, being lost, were deeply marginal. Could they underwrite a journey in search of their writing culture? I'd be starting with a bad hand: the scholars control the text. I held only two cards toward an inside straight, imagination and a poker face.

You could say it was the face of the juvenile delinquent rebelling against society. It was, in its unconscious sense, a species consciousness. All the way to back then, poetry is the first scene of writing, back to the oral campfire within a frigid cave, to when the poet seems as old as the world, making something out of nothing, even before language. Compare the faces of Holocaust survivors on Spielberg's video archive: when asked why they survived and others didn't, you don't want to hear the answer, or need to, since any dead one could have replaced them, it's the *species* talking, an ancient moment prior to civilization. Today, it would be the margin of society, which is perhaps why poetry must remain marginal for now—and a struggling life for the serious poet to survive on the margin today, but also a coup, to be able to.

If I'm a survivor, and I have felt like one since childhood, then of what? Not of Auschwitz, where cousins were dying the day I was born, but of its Edenic mirror: middle-class Detroit, where no bombs fell, and you had the right to not read Henry Ford's hate-filled free newspaper or to buy his cars. It was to be a survivor without knowing it, and therefore to arrive on the doorstep of golden age and have nothing to tell. To make a poem out of nothing—that was my teenage task. Teacher said use your experience, but I had none I could process. I hadn't seen a naked girl, I hadn't seen anyone die—yes I did, but I couldn't process it, I was numb inside. How can you grow and maybe die at the same time? So that's how it is for baby boomers: I still feel like I'm growing.

8.

A poem is a drama in which the principal character is the author. Even when the poem is "about" something else, whether the Trojan War or lilacs on a summer's day, it all comes down to the puppet-master behind the stage, a human weaving together unlikely mental events to form a play of the mind—one that is characteristic of that poet. You don't need a bio of the poet to enter the poem; it's the poet's way of looking and thinking, his/her stance toward words and the world, that is revealed in the poem itself. Sometimes the drama re-creates the conflict between innocence and experience, expectation and surprise, but it's a melodrama at best unless the resolution of discord is uncanny, as if we had seen a ghost—a vision that we sense and trust is uniquely the author's and made accessible to us. Of course there may be personae or characters within the poem, and unlike in a novel these character are historical—or made historical, as in the Bible. What about faeries in Spenser's *Faerie Queen*? Even so, characters of fantasy are historicized as if they came from an older myth.

In the larger sense of the Bible as a poem, the question of whether the characters are historical or mythic depends on the talent of the author to evoke a historical context that is uncanny, whether mythic in the Garden of Eden or set in Joseph's plausible Egypt. A decade ago, I wrote a historical biography of one biblical character, Abraham. Some critics claim that Abraham is a legend, yet even so, he is woven into a historical context by his writers that is more believable—that is, it can be tested against history—than a life of William Shakespeare. Abraham was not an author (though I argue that his home-schooled son, Isaac, wrote his father's story), yet Abraham is subject to a major author, namely the Creator—only a biblical poet, or several poets, could make this relationship as uncanny as the one between us, the readers, and the biblical poet.

During the same years I went in search of the lost authors of Abraham's life, Daniel Mendelsohn, in *The Lost*, was on the trail of relatives lost in the Holocaust. Daniel had people to interview; I had professionals to investigate: archaeologists, historians, scholars of many stripes. None of these was enough for either Daniel or myself. His six lost relatives became characters in his searching book; our glimpses of them were refracted back onto the author, Mendelsohn, so that we began to understand his losses as a writer: how meager was his own memory of their absence, in mere stories he was told, compared to the actual history they lived. Yet beyond the book, their lives and deaths are as if mythical, more real, more timeless, more unburied, than the characters he has made of them—they're as if brought back to life in the book but like the Holocaust itself, they remain larger than life, outside of history's boundaries. In a thousand years, when Mendelsohn and I go unremembered, the fate of the Jews in the Holocaust will be recounted. It's the same for Abraham, Sarah, the Creator, and their biblical writers: we understand the power of history when we feel the loss of it, the loss of the writers' ancestors' historical lives. It's hard to say how the writers expressed their loss without re-imagining their lives; on the other hand, Mendelsohn unfolds his life as a writer within his book, so that we see the complications of his sentences and chapters as reflections of how complicated it is to do justice to his lost family. But he blends his losses with his love of writing history as a truth-testing. It was the same that the biblical writers did for their ancestral family—except they went further, providing a cosmic theater in which their relatives and countrymen are creatures bound into an existential covenant with their Creator. What does He—and life itself—want from them? To feel the biblical writers working out the complications of the answer—the journey through human history—was answer enough for me. It was the impetus for the Bible getting written. Loss of those writers, for me as a writer, was the deepest loss; it forced me to go beyond asking how the Bible was written, in search of lost ancestors.

But the thing that's crucial about Mendelsohn's *The Lost: The Search for Six of Six Million*, is its variation on the argument that God abandoned the Jews during the Holocaust; or, He abandoned the world; or, in effect, He nullified His own existence. This post-existentialist argument is finally indifferent to God altogether, replacing Him and His biblical family with the author's personal family. At best, God is poker-faced.

Although Greek translator Mendelsohn has no use for Jewish poetry, his worldview is diametrically opposed to the major Jewish poet of the last century, Bialik, who, in his famous elegy for those slaughtered in the 1903-05 Kishinev pogroms, rages against the Jewish helplessness that Mendelsohn takes for granted as a condition for the Holocaust. A.M. Klein, who translated Bialik's poem into English twice—once in the '30s, once in the late '40s—turns his second translation, which channels the original author, into an interpretation of post-Holocaust ire against Jewish exile, Galut. It's the Galut of two thousand years that left Jewry in such a precarious position, and it also argues for Israel's rebirth; but this is not an argument Mendelsohn cares to make on behalf of his relatives, those lost and those who survived, including those he visits in Israel. To make that argument would require a more serious engagement with Judaism and Jewish history than interests him. Even before my return to those subjects, I admired Klein's second interpretive translation as an experiment that licensed my own with the Bible.

I have more to say about *The Lost* because it encapsulates the attitude of many North American peers to modern history. Mendelsohn makes prominent use of Genesis stories as instances of God's poker face toward genocide, yet he ignores the biblical prophets who evoke God's ultimate compassion. These prophetic poets of 2500 years ago are only the beginning of what is overlooked; Mendelsohn looks for little in Judaism (reference to Rashi's commentary notwithstanding) that rises above sociological background. It's enough to consider the Bible as family stories, he may think, anonymous tales that resemble those of his immediate relatives in their unflinching accounts of human cruelty and catastrophe—as when parallels are drawn between the Holocaust and the usual eschatological suspects in Genesis: the Flood, Sodom and Gomorrah, the sacrifice of Isaac.

So *The Lost*'s interest in family origins, even when attempting to give them biblical proportions, doesn't extend to the historical origins of the Bible, much less to the origins of species. It makes use of Friedman's fairly graceless Genesis translation, which gives Mendelsohn cues for naming Rashi "the preeminent" Jewish Bible commentator while ignoring Maimonides and a range of scholars from more recent centuries, starting with the creative kabbalistic midrash of Moshe de Leon, whose contribution to the *Zohar* in the 1200s came just two centuries after Rashi. Friedman also provides Mendelsohn with a biblical rationale for his book, in that Genesis is rendered "through the story of a single family." Yet Genesis is only the first of more or less forty books of the Hebrew Bible (some count just 24 by eliding into one the fragmentary books), and of the rest Mendelsohn states that the political and historical ramifications of the land of Israel (where the biblical writers breathed and died!) are irrelevant to him. Still, the several pages of direct exegesis of Genesis is more engaging than what's found in most North American Jewish writing of my generation, doubly unusual from a renowned scholar of Greek with only a smattering of Hebrew. The trouble is, he thinks it more than enough. He disposes of the Akedah, the passages about Abraham and young Isaac, by suggesting that a God willing to sacrifice his Covenant (as Abraham is willing to sacrifice his son)—and to blot out the seed of his chosen people the way he blotted out Sodom and Gomorrah, as well as the population of Earth prior to the Flood—was an unstable deity, like the poker face behind the Holocaust.

But that's an unfortunate misunderstanding, based on a conventional reading that overrides the purposeful exaggerations of the writers. When you look at the text from the writer's perspective, you see that he, or she in the case of J, blends mythic and historical—as a contemporary writer may mix high and low—introducing an element of uncanniness or ambiguity. Consider how a psychoanalyst maintains ambiguity about whether he believes the patient's narrative: the ancient Hebraic writer maintains a similar ambiguity toward a supernatural voice, such as the voice of the Creator. The biblical author could not have written such a strong drama otherwise; and the same for Homer—does he or doesn't he believe in the voice of Poseidon? It doesn't matter; he believes in the story, along with the myth-like origin of Homo sapiens. You can mundanely consider the supernatural gods in the *Odyssey* part of a willing suspension of disbelief, but that suspension is more acute in the Bible. In the case of the E writer of the Akedah, this author presents a test of the boundary between dream (or supernatural) and reality. And in the dream, there is no control, no defense for Abraham's anxiety; he has to walk through the irrational voice's wish toward the test of whether he can wake up and refuse the nightmare. E presents Abraham as sleep-walking, compelled by his anxious dream to follow its course; and just as Abraham is helpless and inarticulate, the writing style is hyper-real, presses forward without embellishment. E was a master of dream-voices, not a literalist like most literal interpretations of the Akedah that are imposed on the text. A reader deserves to know more about the historical situation of E writing in the northern Israeli capital of Samaria, a century after J in Jerusalem, but for now it's important to see what the poet does with dreams.

Abraham is saved—even more so than his son Isaac—as he is woken up from his nightmare by the literal thrashing of a ram caught in a thicket nearby. Abraham is awakened, that is, by and into the real. (There's literary evidence; I've given it in several chapters of my historical bio of Abraham, boiled down further in *An Educated Man*.) But what wasn't understood about the sacrificial scene until recent historical studies is that the issue of literal child sacrifice in the text is ahistorical; there had been no practice of child sacrifice in the region for many generations. Add to that a failure to historicize the author, E, and it's as if Freud had conceived or written *Interpretation of Dreams* without a dreamer. As one learns in analysis, there are certain questions that are obsessively asked, and the Jewish writer of this episode knew that there were certain questions in his culture at the time, and for all time, that would be asked by religious and secular alike. Is the drama true?—and does the writer believe in the Creator? The Jewish writer's story says, however, that it doesn't matter. The question why did E write it is similar to asking why Freud wrote *Interpretation of Dreams*. E knew that people's dreams were filled with the supernatural: ghosts of the dead, all kinds of irrational happenings—nearly everyone has been known to fly in dreams. The Akedah is all about Abraham's anxiety, as it would be if the leading character were a dreamer. The anxiety is that of hearing the voice of the Creator or the supernatural, symbolic of the anxiety or fear of death (Abraham's own death, not Isaac's). If it were a test, one either does not obey or one sacrifices—either way, the anxiety is not protracted. But this nightmare contains a deeper anxiety beneath the dream of being subject to an uncontrollable voice that represents life and death. The Akedah, as written by its ancient Jewish author, is a nightmare that is proven so when it's interrupted by reality—suddenly Abraham hears a very real ram in the thicket. Everyone from Augustine to Kierkegaard to Freud and Jung have mythologized the text for their religious or theoretical purposes, but in the process they have repressed authorship and with it, the powerful representation of the anxiety of death that can inhabit anyone's dreams.

The loss of the biblical writer E is a fundamental problem for a writer in the Judeo-Christian West. When one of our peers dies we still have others to represent the sense of being a writer in these times. The loss of the biblical writers, however, grew larger throughout my life, because they were as if lost without a trace, like Daniel Mendelsohn's relatives initially appeared to be. What is more, I feel the loss of the writers through Mendelsohn precisely because he has no feel for it, no driving curiosity as to how the biblical passages he quotes prominently in his book came to be. That's probably an unfair critique of Daniel; he has other fish to fry. But if he and I, and a few other of our colleagues were sitting around the poker table, it is as if I was raising the pot with my last chips on a nothing hand. Everyone knows I'm bluffing, that I'm desperate. Why are you doing it, they may want to ask, why throw your career as a poet away in order to become a rebellious translator, outside the game? I might answer: It's the only way I know how to write the lost Jewish writers at the origin of Western culture into our lives now; they're the great cosmic players we no longer know how to be. By giving them their lives back, we make it possible to absorb their influence.

Perhaps you can live species conscious and as a Jew in North America if you are conscious of exile. The best way for that is to emigrate to Israel and to fail at it, weighed down by personal baggage. That's how it was for me. Approaching my 70s, Rhonda and I think we will still find a way to get back there. Like the shadow history of world wars, it depends on the economy. If it improves enough to support half the amount of advance on royalties I used to get, we're on our way. As of now, my highly literary literary agent is scraping by in the genre of fantasy.

Yet a writer in exile within his own country is perhaps as American as it gets. Emily Dickinson, well situated in upper crust New England, exiled to her bedroom; Stein, Hemingway, Pound, Eliot, Plath in fashionable modernist exile; Hurston, Hughes, Baldwin, in racial shadow; Henry Roth, Hart Crane, Ted Berrigan, Foster Wallace, in mental exile. It's a matter of history, continental or personal; if you want it (history, that is) you're fighting for it, against the pasteurized European Union or tranquilized inner Beltway. I should have referred, perhaps, to fighting the faux stimulation of the Google highway, on which, like an American poet, you can put together any kind of mental wardrobe you wish: a Sophoclean undershirt, Homeric socks, Elizabethan codpiece, Baudelairean brassiere, Wordsworthian tie,

Whitmanian suspenders, Ginsbergian underpants, Stevensian suit. That would make you a postmodern exile, an exile from the future.

9.

At one point in Mark Cousins' potentially interesting documentary, *The Story of Film: An Odyssey*, writer and director Paul Schrader says "Sometimes today (2012) I miss the existentialist focus of my '70s films in contemporary work, but sometimes I also think it's old, just old." But there's a third possibility, missing in Schrader's interview within this documentary, and missing from the doc itself: restoring history. The doc is constantly harping on how the old was used in new ways, the new re-used in old ways, but it's always a progression, a moving on. By history, I mean taking Schrader's statement and applying it to his own film, *Chinatown* (1979). Rather than appreciating it new or old, let's use it as a lens on its making—what I'd call its scene of making (as in scene of writing). "1979 was a year of..." and the superlatives about movie-making flow. But in fact it was a year in the history of the world, not just movies. I want *Chinatown* to bring that back to me in a harmonics of visuals, dialogue, sound and music, costume, physical details, etc.—but also the deeper harmonics of the creatures who made the art, the geology that held it, the ecosystem that evolved its locale, the culture that translated it. Even the loss of that time contained within it the unfolding of the possibility of our own time and lives. So I want a vision of restoration over a vision of progress; you can restore creation, and possibly too a sense of your own having been created. "The poet is as old as the world," said Aristotle according to Grossman, "which is why institutions can't swallow him. He makes the world, he remakes it rebelliously."

A scene of making can be dangerous. Some of the great artists throughout history have been manic-depressive; their work has had access to it, to despair, transforming it into something that our "ordinary unhappiness" (Freud's phrase for normal) could appreciate. Such works are basic to our most emotional classical text, the Bible: a psalm; Jeremiah/ Isaiah; Jonah; Job—the Book of Job is where I went after translating psalms, wondering how long I could stay within the moment of losing my only reliable supporter at my father's death (later I learned my mother was the rock). It was a grief compounded by my having rejected him, which I would learn in analysis was my own childhood that I was rejecting for its having been wounded by a wounded veteran. In other words, no one to blame, as in the many forms of music I was immersed in, from classical (the despair in Schütz and Bach cantatas, eg. *Ich habe genug*) to classic

Blues, Jazz, and Rock 'n' roll. If you have artistic access to these genres you respond to both beat and offbeat, the ironies, because you have experienced uncontrollable despair, one way or another, where up is down, and vice versa. Songs of praise are songs of darkness; songs of loss and depression are songs of joy just for the gift of being able to keep breathing, keep singing. You need a poker face so that either pain or joy can play across it and you uncannily can't tell which. In the Blues, that face belonged to Blind Lemon Jefferson, Blind Willie McTell, Blind Boy Blake—no less than it did to our fundamental poet, the blind Homer. I had no trouble imagining the Joban poet was blind either.

Back in my own youth as a poet I was missing a third dimension. I had two dimensions, present and past, the latter mostly book-learned. But there was no future to speak of; instead, there was the Beatles' "When I get older... when I'm sixty-four." Time flows inexorably onward, you can't stop it and for that reason the future is abstract to the young: almost any ideal can change it. So it wasn't until almost forty, living in Jerusalem, that I thought I understood how the third dimension of the future grows out of the past, not the present. My post-graduate Delmore Schwartz poem, cited above, I now saw was eulogy writing, ostensibly for Schwartz but actually for myself, destined to be a fellow cadaver, in the future dimension where the need for connection and name-dropping drops away and you gaze astonished, instead, at the whole social stage-set. It's what futurist Ray Kurzweil tries to hyper-realize as "infinite virtual realities" in which we live on forever as avatars (thanks to having shucked our biology for virtual brain and organs). What astonishes, however, is that there isn't any need for eulogies, let alone memoirs.

Consider further the lead science news of the week: 40 billion potentially inhabitable (by creatures like us) planets in Milky Way alone. All the chatter (gone in 48 hours) was about what it might mean to us to find intelligent life out there, but what about what it would mean to the *other* planet? Knowledge of us, of Earth, would enrich them in some way, and thereby there'd be more meaning to our existence, as there was for Tarzan when Jane came along. I'm not being facetious; Tarzan was doing fine without Jane, just as we are (dystopia notwithstanding) as isolated intelligent life in the universe. But here's the further rub that science commentators are bringing up: chances of intelligent life on our terms, i.e. the infinitesimal blip in time of the past six thousand years, before which we didn't have even primitive writing, is unlikely to match up with same on planet X. Chances for communicating with intelligent life, therefore, are slim. They will be but a memory, or we will be.

Yet it's painful how feeble are our conceptions of intelligent life. It's a *relative* intelligence that we should consider, just as on Earth we are relatively more intelligent than a dolphin—perhaps. Even a cockroach has the intelligence to hide from a threat, to calculate the right time and place for food-gathering, to nest and to chill in whatever ways they do; and never mind that they've survived and evolved into hundreds of species during a hundred million years, doing just fine before there were New York City apartment walls to congregate behind, and no doubt they'll find a way onto our spaceships, sooner or later. Forget the spaceships for the time being; any kind of chemical code an advanced civilization might seed in their atmosphere, expressly for others seeking them out telescopically, will be enough to shake up our intelligence but good. Meanwhile, we can barely communicate with a dolphin past superficial pleasantries like "How's the water?" Do we know anything of the minds/nervous systems of the ten million plus species we share the planet with? Shouldn't we get prepared for planet X by learning to communicate with mice—not test them or train them or affect and interpret their behaviors but find out what's on their minds when they're not particularly fearful, hungry, or horny? Isn't that the way a relatively more intelligent species would approach us? Nor do we need to ask why we haven't seen *their* spaceships, when no doubt their telescopic powers render those unnecessary.

So it's not that we will have no more need for memory or history in either a virtual future or a planetary post-contact future (in that case, they will function as our data cloud, in terms of what they learn of us). Meanwhile, and since we can assume the future resembles this scenario (barring catastrophe), the human writer is freed up from recording the history of his/her time and thereby open again to Moses. "The human writer" in question, of course, is simply myself; I don't know of other poets and fictioneers who have come forward on this. But as I've said before, the primary image of the essential writer/thinker in civilization (*pace* blind Homer) is Moses writing for forty days alone on the mountain, since we still have a vestige of that writing in the Bible. And the primary image we have of the audience response—those dancing around the melted gold then and those consuming literature now—is indifference. Whoever witnessed the ancient scenes passed on their reports so convincingly to the following generations that even I can imagine what it was like to be at Mt. Sinai, and without need of religious faith. What's my proof? Same as the biblical writers in Jerusalem: faith in the writer's commitment to truth-testing, whether in the desert or in a palace archive. It's not a mystical faith, anymore than my faith in a mother's love; it's a rational faith, though of course it's not infallible, inasmuch as parents have been known to abandon children. In the same way, replication of DNA is occasionally faulty—and yet that's just the level of uncertainty we need as a species to have come into existence.

So maybe it's just a myth, like some say about the Holocaust. Maybe the surviving witnesses are inflexible team players. Maybe they're trying to move the goalposts. But if I'm a writer in ancient Jerusalem looking at historical source material, I'd see through that. Unless you want to say that the I too—like the Bible's writers—were part of a mass blinding, which would be a form of truth-testing in itself, in this case by hearing instead of seeing. Just the phrase truth-testing in itself, the possibility of such a phrase, blurs the line between myth and history, and makes uncertainty a necessary principle, in our developing opposable thumbs as well as quantum theory. Was it certain that Moses would go back for a second draft after smashing the tablets and that progress was inevitable? The best antidote to Moses's despair, I continue to think, is that what is new or progressive is what has been dug up from a buried past, the original scene of writing. To focus on it is shocking. It's a shock, with respect to the Bible, because it was writing intended to be itself an antidote to the weariness of exile. I doubt that educated readers in ancient Jerusalem were flabbergasted with how new each of the books of the Hebrew Bible was; instead of newness, they were like amazing antidotes to claims of progress, rooted in the past, revelatory.

One might think the New Testament breaks the mold, but even here its claims are merely of a new version to something much older, as if a "new" *Romeo and Juliet* (not merely a new production of the play) could make Shakespeare less relevant. Yet the new play could only hold its own by acknowledging Shakespeare—you can't pretend he didn't exist, anymore than you can pretend Michelangelo didn't paint the Sistine Chapel if you are painting a biblical scene. A new *Romeo and* Juliet, by bringing Shakespeare back to mind in ever clearer focus, risks a tin ear unless it re-echoes the original. This is what A.M. Klein does for Michelangelo and the Sistine Chapel in *The Second Scroll*, just five years after the Holocaust:"

> The whole ceiling is indeed in all its parts and divisions, its burdens and canticles, but a tremendous paean to the human form divine, a great psalter psalmodizing the beauty and vigour and worth of the races of mankind. It is the parable of the species that is pendent over me, and nowhere can I scan that ceiling but I must encounter my semblable...
>
> "In that altitude one temperature prevails—the temperature of the human body. One colour dominates this ceiling—the colour of the living skin; and behind the coagulation of the paint flows the one universal stream of everybody's blood....
>
> "In vain did Buonarotti seek to confine himself to the hermeneutics of his age; the Spirit intruded and lo! on that ceiling appeared the narrative of things to come, which came indeed, and behold above me the parable of my days.
>
> "Certainly I could not look upon those limbs, well fleshed and of the colour of health, each in its proper socket, each as of yore ordained, without recalling to mind another scattering of

limbs, other conglomerations of bodies the disjected members of which I had but recently beheld. For as I regarded the flights of athletes above me the tint subcutaneous of well-being faded, the flesh dwindled, the bones showed, and I saw again the *relictae* of the camps, entire cairns of cadavers, heaped and golgotha'd: a leg growing from its owners neck, an arm extended from another's shoulder, wrist by jawbone, ear on ankle: the human form divine crippled, jack-knifed, trussed, corded: reduced and broken down to its named bones, femur and tibia and clavicle and ulna and thorax and pelvis and cranium: the bundled ossuaries: all in their several social heapings heaped to be taken up by the mastodon bulldozer and scavangered into its sistine limepit....

"Lies on the ground the body of Adam anticipative. It has its due limbs, its due members, its quantum of blood in the veins. It resembles a man. Its length is extended and curved, its arm is fixed outright, its hand hippocratic in hue hangs limp. Awaits its completion, languid, a hemisphere; awaits; and encircled by spheres and cycles of potency, robed in the draped whirlwind, the future under His cloak and all possibles in His ambience trembling, with flight of power and might of majesty, with beauty, with splendour He brings to the earthen mould recumbent His finger's imminence— oh, benedictive touch!—life, and the glory of His countenance! And in his eyes is imaged God....He dared not transliterate it, Michelangelo, he dared not point the burden of his charge. But I read it plain and spell it out—summation and grand indictment— the unspeakable *nefas*—deicide."

It continues for several more pages, so that you're certain the poet Klein was literally standing there in the Vatican, in 1950. How else could that chapel become a bad hand? I tried to do the same for the biblical book of *Lamentations*, when I was provisionally commissioned by The Rabbinical Assembly in New York to contribute a poem for Yom HaShoah, Holocaust Memorial Day. Although *Lamentations* was already a bad hand 2,500 years ago, it wasn't much read in our day, outside of liturgy. My version was much longer than the poem my rabbinical sponsors envisioned, and it was rejected—strangely enough, by the excuse that it was too much "like a translation." Still, it was the same excuse I'd heard before from literary venues, i.e. "we're not publishing translations this year." Finally, I read it publicly in a joint reading with Eugene McCarthy, the antiwar presidential candidate, at NYC's Shakespeare Public Theatre. This was after Senator McCarthy's candidacy ended disconsolately, so I placated myself about how my *Lamentations* would not be out of place with his latest role in public life as a poet flogging a new book of poems. It made sense; it was the week of Yom HaShoah.

Nobody laughed or cried. It was the most deadpan audience ever, due, to be honest, to incomprehension at why the jauntily parodistic verse of McCarthy should be upstaged by loss—and thereby recalling McCarthy's electoral failing. Or, was it, i.e. *Lamentations*, itself a poker faced parody? It could have been, if only it wasn't so close to a translation. If I had been one of his "Get Clean for Gene" whisker-shaving hippie campaigners, I could have pulled off the biggest joke of the evening, poking self-deprecating Holocaust fun at McCarthy's retirement from politics. Instead, I was like a Jeremiah (putative though unlikely author of *Lamentations*) totally out of place, as was the original prophet inveighing at the ancient royal court. That was how I consoled myself for only a smattering of disinterested applause. What was I thinking? It might have been "appropriate" to have volunteered for a Holocaust-related event, but this was a bad hand. I thought I could at least play that hand congenially with Gene, when a group of us went out for drinks afterward; I knew that Gene graduated from Minnesota's unique St. John's University and would have read the Bible there as a "great book of Western civilization". He said: "I don't think we're ready for Jeremiah yet". It was sweet of him, yet the comment also suggested I didn't belong there, gin-and-tonic in hand. In fact, I was the losing poet that year when Harper, publisher for three previous volumes of my 'A Poet's Bible' series, rejected *Book of Lamentations*. There's no market for it, I was told; religious book-buyers have an interest in your prophets and psalms, and secular readers in Job, but no one is preoccupied with lamentation. Religious readers especially want their books to be good news, not bad news. So. No market for Lamentations.

[This excerpt taken from 3rd chapter; the indented lines are to be read antiphonally; the ellipses denote cuts from my original version]

>It is I who have seen
>>with just human eyes
>
>suffering beyond the power of men
>>to know is there
>
>a wrath so deep
>>we are struck dumb
>
>and we are sheep
>>seized by animal terror

defenseless before a world unleashed
  from anything human

we have seen its frenzy raised like an arm
  but we feel our shepherd's blow

He has led me into darkness
  a valley no light can reach

nothing to illumine the smallest step I take
  though I follow what he alone may teach

he has turned against me
  with the arm that pointed my way

it is I alone who felt his hand
  all sleepless night and day again

he reduced me to skin and bones
  my skin was paper for his heavy hand

I was under siege
  I was herded into ghettoes

...I have woken with my heart in pieces
  I have breakfasted on ashes

my life was pulled from my grasp
  my soul was in exile

I was a hollow shell
  I was a stranger to myself

peace was a dry husk, an empty word
  I was blown in the wind.

I forgot what goodness means
  shalom meant nothing to me

and I thought: my spirit is dead
  hope in God is beyond me

I was broken down, mumbling
    I was shattered by anxiety

the more I thought about my suffering—
    remembering the agony of my losses—

the more I tasted wormwood
    turning to poison within me

and now, still, I remember everything
    my soul staggers into exile:

Memory the weight on my back
    and deep in my breast every crushing detail

I cannot close my eyes before it
    I cannot rise from my bed

and yet I do each
    and I rouse my heart

that the memory itself so vividly lives
    awakens a deathless hope...

how good to find patience
    to let rejected hope return

and how good to learn
    to bear the burden young

to sit silent and alone
    when the weight falls on your shoulders

to feel the weight of your maker
    as all hope seems lost

to put your mouth to dust
    (perhaps living is still worthwhile)

How good to be desolate and alone
    because the Lord does not reject forever

after the intensity of anger
    mercy returns in a firm embrace

because his love lasts forever
    beyond anything we can know...

we were not tormented lightly
    yet nothing in him desired suffering

he didn't desire to make us earth's prisoners
    returning to the dust at our feet...

His own creation abandoning him
    is a horror

but men can say and do as they want
    they can act like gods: speak and it comes to pass

but they become heartless idols speaking
    they will pass into dust and silence

they couldn't have opened their eyes
    if the Lord did not desire it

and they strut in iron over us
    yet the Lord does not will it—

because the words for good and evil
    both came from him

We the living have a complaint
    ignorance

a strong man or woman remembers
    their weakness

instead of running from the past
    turn to face the source

open your heart on the rough path of knowing
    open your mind on the hard road of understanding

the solid ground supports
    firm trust

let us search our ways
    examine the difficulties within:

Where the will and faith turn bitter
    repent that loss, return to him

take your heart in your hands
    lift it high

sweetness flows from a broken heart
    to heaven…

the earth was a vast pen for us
    you were hidden beyond the clouds

our prayers were hollow echoes
    our hopes were crushed flowers

littering the ground like discolored pages
    ripped from prayer books

you had made us garbage
    in the world's eyes

human refuse
    reeking in a senseless world

Our misery only enraged them
    all our enemies gathered to jeer us

we were beaten as a whining dog
    our blood pounded in our ears

their mouths were opened wide
    pouring out hatred

the world in open chorus
    blind and shameless

we had fallen into a hole
    the world was a hunter's pit

death was our horizon
    terror as far as our eyes could see…

I was brought down for no reason
    like a bird with a stone

by people who hate me just for being
    again they bring me down, again

I am thrown into a pit
    a stone is rolled over me

I who sing to the sky
    am not to breathe

the nations of the world were like water
    flowing over my head

to whom could I turn
    I said to myself "I am gone"…

you saw their barbarous vengeance
    you saw their final solution

my life was a living death
    I was butchered for you

my death was the solution to all their problems
    all their imagination was brought to my dying

You heard their hatred crafted against me
    as shameless as daily prayers

holy alliances condemning me
    you saw the papers drawn up openly

their minds and their mouths fastened on me
    like bloodsuckers

behind my back or in their company
    I was spittle on their lips

in conference or on the street
    I am the scapegoat uniting them

I lighten their labors
    I am the guinea pig of their salvation...

For the hands they raise to slaughter us
    with your hand, Lord, strike them deeply within

let their pride be the poison they swallow
    their hearts are stones, their minds tombstones

etched there forever let all their words mock them
    with their bloody thoughts spilling into silent dust.

So—too close to the original? Or, in the mind of a contemporary poetry reader, not "original" enough? Still, even if less than one percent of new verse is seriously original, it's necessary to maintain a pose of originality, simply to be acceptable. But that was fifty years ago; now, you have to know (or at least pretend) how to make fun of originality itself, to exaggerate or ironize it. I should be deadpanning the Bible, or at least demystifying it. Yet there I was, making it sound like it could have been written as recently as our parents' generation, back in their day when genocide was too shocking to say or write anything about, original *or* unoriginal. Perhaps post-original would be the term I'd apply to resurrecting the biblical poets. Nothing new about resurrection; it's as old as Moses coming down the mountain with a second draft that may have been "close to" the first smashed one. Hopefully not too close, for then it might have been derided as unoriginal.

10.

While deadpan has been the face of choice for over a century among American poets, perhaps the greatest exemplars of it in my East Village youth went nameless, working behind restaurant counters. These Holocaust survivors could have taught us to plumb a deeper realm of history but no one was really looking at them. Yet they were there on the scene, and they helped make me conscious of absence: Although we were mostly born in the '40s, years of the worst carnage in human history, we thought

A Life in a Poem

nothing was missing, that there was a direct line between us and the prewar surrealists. Let me look back there again and reset the table.

Back in the '60s, when I was still an undergraduate, I was juggling two subjects at the outset of my literary career: one was *The Cantos* by Ezra Pound, of which I was under the influence; the second was the Holocaust, stimulated by the first major history none of my contemporaries were reading, Raul Hilberg's *The Destruction of the European Jews*. In both cases, I was given a reflection of myself as a survivor of catastrophe. And in both instances, it was taboo to talk about the whole story in America.

My aunts in Detroit, who had survived Auschwitz and coddled me in childhood, were encouraged by their American family to forget about the past and concentrate on new lives. No one wanted to hear their tales of matchless disaster; no one was sure their experiences, so unlike any the civilized world had known, could be believed.

On the other hand, I was just reading Pound's Bollingen Prize-winning *Pisan Cantos*, in which he found himself incarcerated by the U.S. Army as a war criminal. It was hard for me or most other poets to believe the charges (the transcripts of his anti-Semitic and anti-American lectures on Italian radio were not yet published) and we were all somewhat infected with anti-Americanism, then as now. Our collegiality with such American stalwarts as Whitman, Stein, and Stevens had been replaced by fashionable suspicion. We simply did not talk about the catastrophe of Pound's huge hatreds (and neither did he), as if the past was not worthy of our new lives as postwar intellectual dissenters.

As poets we somewhat resembled the naive stereotype of Holocaust survivors: we had drawn a line under the past, in good German fashion, and we were barely even conscious of our schizoid existence. After all, who cared? The academic poets of the age who might have, such as Lowell, Berryman, Plath, and Jarrell were all on the verge of suicide, or, like Charles Reznikoff, not yet equipped with the courage to write his late great epic poem, *Holocaust*. And since we were like Holocaust survivors ourselves, we were content to be underground—in fact, we were proudly underground writers, living in the bohemian impoverishment of New York's Lower East Side, just as it was being renamed the East Village. But the great irony of that day was that we were literally rubbing shoulders with actual survivors of the death camps, and we were quite cavalier about it, if not unconscious. Even today, it shocks me to recall the tattooed numbers on the arms of survivors who served my coffee and "challah bread" at local luncheon parlors as narrow as subway cars, like the B&H Dairy restaurant on Second Avenue.

Probably the most invisible and unfashionable of those down-to-earth emporiums was the L&G luncheonette, directly across the street from St. Mark's Church. It was there I felt most comfortable, even as most of my colleagues from the St. Mark's Poetry Project preferred the ersatz atmosphere of Veselka (not yet the semi-gentrified diner it is today), a faux-Ukrainian cafe on the other side of Second Avenue, or the likewise faux-Ukrainian Kiev a few blocks down—with their happily un-American fare, just as likely served by former Nazi camp guards as by Holocaust survivors. The Kiev was a lot cheaper than the Uptown Ratners that still held on next door, serving those purists who spilled out of the last surviving theater of Yiddish Broadway, perched precariously across the street.

L&G did not serve foreign food; it served "American" food. Its waiters and cashier were dressed American rather than affecting East European or Bohemian slackerdom. They did not slouch; they were stocky men, stout barrels in white short-sleeve shirts, even in winter. Still, they stood out from the East Village carnival like a Versace label. And labels are the point: the indelibly tattooed concentration camp number on their arms labeled these waiters and counter-men as angels from the dead—the true (and thus invisible) "angel-headed hipsters" that Ginsberg and Kerouac had been writing about.

"Forget what you can't do anything about"—this was the advice most often proffered to these men by well-meaning Americans. Forget that you are angels; what good are angels anyway? But in fact we self-empowered poets *could* do something about it, if we had wanted to. We could listen and internalize, which is what I found myself doing, greasy hamburger in hand (white horseradish under the bun, in place of pickle relish). We could learn to write as survivors ourselves—which we were, in point of fact: survivors of the catastrophe of Europe, where Pound and all our literary forebears had bet the house and lost. But instead of doing that, my colleagues and I were simply too full of resistance and wild oats. It was only decades later that I learned how thoroughly the L&G had worked on me.

Along with much of the East Village poetic community back in the sixties, I was a theorist of chance. From John Cage to Jackson Mac Low, "blind" chance was a player in our works. And chance was a godsend, enlivening our recent encounters with grim literary authority and the personal catastrophes of post-adolescence. Instead of analyzing this, we grandiosely tossed history out the window. That was our form of literary social activism: sweeping away the bourgeois intellectuals who had brooded too long on history, like Auden, still among the living then, and on St. Mark's Place, no less.

I recall one of the annual New Year's Day readings at St. Mark's Church in the early '70s, when I met some of my colleagues rarely seen at the L&G Luncheonette—Ron Padgett, Anne Waldman, Lewis Warsh—now filling the counter, ragged manuscripts in hand. The action on New Year's Day always surprised the counter-men, and I tried to explain this literary ritual to them. "It's a marathon, a nonstop twenty-four-hour theater of poets presenting a slice of their lives." The chasm of understanding, however, was too great. "From this you can make a living?" asked the counter-men. The fact that these Holocaust survivors could work at all, after the work-to-death ethic of the camps, was miraculous: to throw some things on the grill and watch, while you smoked a cigarette with no one to shoot you, was surreal poetry enough to them.

We young poets were the miracle-doubting ones, especially after Jimi Hendrix and Janis Joplin died in quick succession. Ron, Anne, Lewis and I could talk like working-class writers about "everyday life" and "necessity" but at the time we showed no serious interest in the authentic history of the survivors serving us. Our idea of history was rebelliously aesthetic: it had seemed to begin a month after *The New American Poetry* came on the market. Not that we discounted the European catastrophe; rather, we felt clueless before it, so that questioning how or why seemed a mug's game.

A retreat into human consciousness (and seeking to widen it, like a highway) looked like the best answer to the concealed bestiality in civilization and its dream of totalitarian social engineering. Meanwhile, the angels from the dead stirred the eggs and slung the hash, sneaking sympathetic glimpses at the faux cosmopolitans they served. This sympathy was based on the sense that we were losers too, although too young to know it; and like them, we still found bearable work to do, like writing manuscripts that few were going to buy, and taking surprising solace in a cigarette.

What were they thinking, the angelic counter-men, not about us but about the beatific cataclysm of their own lives? I never really asked nor do recollections of conversations with them help much. Some had wives, some had rooms, some "lived with their brother"—the most mundane of lives. One had a daughter about to enter college. "Which one?" I asked. "The one upstate, Cornell," he answered. "Wow, that will cost a mint!" I offered. He shrugged. "That's what she wants." He clearly hadn't yet faced the music nor had the daughter. Tuition crisis would be her prelude to facing the Holocaust since, unlike the typical poor who planned to start in community college, she was a dreamer up until the last minute, like her father. "I never thought they would come for us, even after I heard they were not making airplane parts at Auschwitz." Either his daughter would be forced to wake up and listen to that, or she would throw away the key to the family closet.

Practical matters were only a fraction of the thoughts of the counter-man with the unfashionable tattoo. He told me he hadn't thought about what might have been if there was no Holocaust because "Europe was a graveyard." In other words, he couldn't think pre-Holocaust, just as most of us today don't think post-Holocaust anymore. Instead, history begins with us, and with actively finding the key to the problem of America (the rest of the world was like the Kiev restaurant, open twenty-four hours for us to mentally slum in). We hardly guessed back then that we'd have to mature in thought; we assumed that *action* was what it took. We were social activists in art.

And not for me (not yet) the postmodern nostalgia of the Second Avenue Deli, shining across the Avenue from the L&G. That place was filled with older people from the suburbs reliving their childhoods. But then, one day in 1989, a decade after I'd moved away, my colleague Harold Bloom demanded that we trek over to the Deli and relive the glorious past. It was only after we were seated in a plump plastic-covered red-upholstered booth that I noticed how childlike the atmosphere was. "Here, taste my stuffed cabbage." "Just put the rolls in your pocket, Morris." "This kugel is not sweet enough. Waiter!"

And so on. Bloom barely glanced at the oversize menu; suddenly, as if he had memorized the whole thing, his pudgy forefinger darted down on an item while he was talking to me, not even looking. "Tell the waiter I'll have that," he said, as I looked down at the print.

"Stuffed kishka platter?"

"Yes, dear. My mama used to serve it."

Here was Bloom the child prodigy all over again. The deli was in fact filled with former child prodigies, but they had all grown out of the tiny kingdoms where the family had doted on them. Chastened by life, they were now content to shock their own children, who had driven them down to "Abe's place" (the owner). These suburban progeny of the professional class had rarely seen their hard-working parents assume such carefree exuberance. They got tipsy on Dr. Brown's celery beverage and falling down drunk on trying to stuff the oversized Reuben into their mouths. They half-talked, half-guffawed with their mouths full, squiggles of coleslaw dangling down, as they came close to resembling adult-sized toddlers stuffed into high chairs.

This does not describe Bloom, however, who remained a prodigy well into his senior years. Far from acting childish, he lectured our aged, limping waiter on his eternal hauteur, reminding him that Isaac Bashevis Singer had caricatured his Warsaw precursor quite well in *The Family Moskat*. Then Bloom turned to me in a somewhat lowered voice, complaining that "these fellows don't read."

Actually, I doubted that anyone around us was a reader—and now it was clear to me that that included Bloom himself, in the sense that he could not see or read himself. Not that he didn't try, but that his self-dramatizations approached the tragedy of the authentic prodigy, unable to grow older and thus overplaying a misguided idea of the grandfatherly sage. In place of adulthood for Bloom had come a ripe expansion of influence and wit, dazzling his students young and old with a Shakespearean play-within-a-play of seeming maturity. Nevertheless, it was an acting-out of his pet Nietzschean theory of historical disjunction that Bloom trafficked in: there is no development between youth and age, just catastrophe and a chutzpadik overcoming of it.

In other words, Bloom and the L&G counter-men had registered a similar sense of historical disaster but with a crucial distinction. The L&G men had survived and they knew and embodied it, their history tattooed on their arms. But Bloom was not an authentic survivor; he had instead appropriated the role of survivor for a personal theater of his own accomplishments—as indeed had a good portion of the '60s generation, in an endless acting-out of youth. The language of the faux-survivors was an irreverent English; the language of the Holocaust survivors was an angelic Yiddish.

They spoke this almost disembodied Yiddish among themselves and occasionally with me, who had learned it in childhood. They reminded me of my Yiddish-speaking uncles, except that the latter, who had evaded the Holocaust by arriving in America a few years before it, had retained the appearance of commercial success, in an unbroken continuity from their tradesmen forebears—successful enough to send their kids to college. And like them, I had pretty much lost my Yiddish. This didn't bother me at all in my L&G days of the early '70s, but I became acutely conscious of the loss in the '90s, when the L&G had been replaced by a Yemenite Israeli café.

I used to walk from Tribeca to that café at least once a week for the Israeli hummus-ful and Yemenite spinach egg brioche, addictions I had picked up in the vibrant cultural mélange of contemporary Israel. I had an urge to keep up my spoken Hebrew since I'd become an Israeli-American in the '80s. Now, like most Israelis, I had internalized the ideal of surviving. There was nothing nostalgic going on in the Yemenite café; it was as authentic as breathing. The waiters and the owners and the clientele were all on the same page, keeping their cultural lifeblood alive. There were no camels tethered to the curb on Ninth Street, and the L&G counter-men had become just as anachronistic in a matter of two decades—but like them these Israelis were living in a present that kept the past alive without one camel saddlebag of nostalgia. This was not a Yemenite site like Indian or Chinese or Ukrainian restaurants; almost invisible, it was more directly related to the hamburger purveyance of the L&G, though fewer Jews had been found there. It was a disguised outpost of those who had survived the ideological carnage of the twentieth century, sans tattoos but still amazed by their freedom.

One Sunday a trio of Israeli Arab men came in. They spoke in self-consciously loud Arabic, but soon the owner and waiters and a few regulars were talking back in their even more animated Judeo-Arabic. You can't help picking up some Arabic in Israel and I understood the Arabs were claiming older roots in Israel while the Israelis were contending that their Judaic customs maintained during almost two thousand years in Yemen were proof of deeper origins in the land. Nobody was upset; it was more like a game of one-upmanship, with the winner buying the loser a round of Maccabee beer. Actually, it seemed the Arabs had come precisely because they'd heard about these drinks on the house. It was nothing so benign back in the Middle East, of course, but it might be one day.

At least that's the myth of everyday life I was partial to, in my St. Mark's poetry youth. Yet I'd imbibed a deeper lesson from the L&G counter-men: only the angels are likely to survive. Better stick close to them in these outposts wherever they appear. And learn the language. Better yet, enough of myths, East Village or the '60s. Visit Israel and face the music. Language becomes the music of history there, disaster and survival, as it lets the air out of our myths.